U.S. Department of the Interior
Bureau of Land Management

BLM-Alaska Open File Report 61
BLM/AK/ST-97/002+3800+313
February 1997

Alaska State Office
222 W. Seventh Avenue, #13
Anchorage, Alaska 99513

I0434745

Prospecting and Mining Activity in the Rampart, Manley Hot Springs and Fort Gibbon Mining Districts of Alaska, 1894 to the Present Era

Rosalie E. L'Ecuyer

Glen Gulch, Manley Hot Springs District, 1902.

Author

Rosalie E. L'Ecuyer has a Bachelor of Arts degree in History and a Master of Arts in Government. In addition, after completing her Thesis Requirement with this report, the author received a Master of Arts in Professional Writing from the University of Alaska Fairbanks in May 1995.

Open File Reports

Open File Reports identify the results of inventories or other investigations that are made available to the public outside the formal BLM-Alaska technical publication series. These reports can include preliminary or incomplete data and are not published and distributed in quantity. The reports are available at BLM offices in Alaska, the USDI Resources Library in Anchorage, various libraries of the University of Alaska, and other selected locations.

Copies are also available for inspection at the USDI Natural Resources Library in Washington, D.C., and at the BLM Service Center Library in Denver.

Cover photo courtesy Herbert Heller Collection, University of Alaska Fairbanks, Accession Number 79-44-606N.

Prospecting and Mining Activity in the Rampart, Manley Hot Springs and Fort Gibbon Mining Districts of Alaska, 1894 to the Present Era

Rosalie E. L'Ecuyer

U. S. Department of the Interior
Bureau of Land Management
Northern District
Fairbanks, Alaska

Table of Contents

Maps

Appendices

List of Illustrations

All photographs listed below and included in the text are in collections held by the Alaska Archives and Manuscripts, Alaska and Polar Regions Department, Elmer E. Rasmuson Library, University of Alaska Fairbanks.

Preface

I chose to write my thesis on the contiguous mining districts of Rampart, Manley Hot Springs, and Fort Gibbon in Interior Alaska after I finished a shorter public history on the Ruby-Poorman mining districts. I recognized that the histories of the smaller mining districts of Alaska have, for the most part, been overlooked, even discounted, in the emphasis on the larger, more productive districts like Nome and Fairbanks. Yet Rampart, where formal location of claims began in April 1896, later than at Circle City but four months before George Washington Carmack's strike in the Klondike, became a jumping-off place for gold prospecting elsewhere in Alaska's Interior. Although many who reached Rampart in 1897 and 1898 left Alaska after only a year or two, several who called themselves Ramparters contributed to the rapid growth of Alaska at the turn of the twentieth century. Men like Lynn Smith, Wally Laboski, his brother Mike, and Joe Kaminski—all early residents of Rampart, later of Ruby and elsewhere in Alaska—made Alaska their permanent home.

During my research, I found myself comparing and contrasting the development of Rampart and Ruby. The first Rampart miners located single claims of twenty or less acres, only one claim per creek, and seldom sank a shaft deeper than fifteen feet. In 1897, Ramparters struggled to set up their town according to United States principles, longed for mail from Outside, and established patterns followed later in other mining towns of the Interior. Over the succeeding fourteen years, Alaska and Alaska mining changed very extensively. Ruby boomed into being in 1911 after the strike at Long Creek. Ruby miners joined several 160-acre associations, sometimes on the same creek, and dug shafts to eighty or more feet. Through the Organic Act of 1912, Alaska became a territory, and Ruby elected Dan Sutherland and Henry Roden—both former Rampart miners—as their district's first territorial senators. By then mail and freight delivery had improved, and the telegraph brought daily news.

The creek recorders in early Rampart kept the first recorders' books as the miners considered each creek a separate mining district. In late 1900, the then newly appointed U.S. commissioner and recorder, Andrew J. Balliet, consolidated the records at Rampart. About that same time, someone reorganized and copied the earlier creek records and made errors in dates and possibly also in names. For several years the Rampart office served as the primary, although not exclusive, recording office for much of the Interior. With the opening of the commissioner's office at Hot Springs, now Manley Hot Springs, the recording scope of the Rampart office was reduced, and records applicable to the Hot Springs district were copied and transferred there. The Fort Gibbon precinct office in the town of Tanana, so named to prevent any confusion with Fairbanks in the Tanana Valley or Hot Springs on the Tanana River, started under John Bathurst. Commissioner Phil Gallaher took over from Bathurst in January 1909, but he left to be commissioner in Ruby in August 1911. As a result of the continual modifications in mining areas and recording offices, mining district boundaries blurred or overlapped at times.

Supposedly, about 1,500 people resided in Rampart during the peak year 1898–1899. I could not verify that number, but I came across several thousand names from the multiple sources covering the almost one hundred years. I understand how important names of early miners are today to persons who want to trace their ancestry. Many present-day Alaskans descend from those Ramparters. In noting names from the three districts, I encountered some of the same research problems that I had met with Ruby, the biggest one being spelling. The spelling of personal and place names differed, sometimes even within the same location notice. Additionally, many records were handwritten in flourishing penmanship so that an "m" resembled an "n," or an "e" an "i." I did the best I could to determine the correct spelling, but I do not guarantee total accuracy. As I noted in the Ruby research, records often gave the first and middle initials of a person's name, man or woman, rather than the full first name; some only mentioned a last name. I did not always learn the first name. Since brothers, sisters, husbands, and wives were among the early mining population, two or more people, usually but not always related, might share the same last name.

I discovered almost as many place names as personal names. The miners located claims on almost every creek, right or left fork, limit, tributary, pup, bench, gravel bar, or gulch in the three districts.

From time to time through 1940, geologists from the U.S. Geological Survey visited the mining operations in the three districts and published their findings in the bulletin series. When mining declined in the Rampart and Fort Gibbon districts, the geologists paid very little attention to those districts but maintained an on-going interest in the Hot Springs district. I used considerable information from the U.S. Geological Survey annual and special bulletins and water supply reports, but researchers specifically concerned with the geological history of the area should consult the actual reports.

As I ended my research, I realized it could be extended because many threads may still be followed. Moreover, in selecting material for the thesis, I culled out much detail and many names. I acknowledge, therefore, that I have not included all available information, yet I have presented enough to set forth what I believe to be the first public history of the mining districts of Rampart, Manley Hot Springs, and Fort Gibbon. Others, or I myself, may amend or add to it with further research in the years ahead.

Rosalie E. L'Ecuyer
Fairbanks, Alaska
March 1995

Acknowledgements

I appreciate all the assistance, suggestions, materials, and support I received in researching and writing my thesis on the Rampart, Manley Hot Springs, and Fort Gibbon mining districts.

First, I thank my advisory committee from the University of Alaska Fairbanks—Michael Schuldiner, Ph.D., English Department, chair; Claus-M. Naske, Ph.D., History Department; and Mark Box, D.Phil., English Department. I acknowledge the help of many others: Howard L. Smith, Bureau of Land Management, Kobuk District Office, Fairbanks; Robert E. King, Bureau of Land Management, Alaska State Office, Anchorage; the staff of the Elmer E. Rasmuson Library, most especially Ron Inouye, Alaska Bibliography, and the staff of the Archives and Manuscripts, Alaska and Polar Regions Department, University of Alaska Fairbanks; Mark Badger, former station manager, KUAC, University of Alaska Fairbanks; Craig Gerlach, Department of Anthropology, University of Alaska Fairbanks; Erik Hansen, State of Alaska Department of Natural Resources, Division of Mining, Fairbanks; Jane Blevins and the staff of the District Recorder, Fairbanks; Sharon Young, Sandra Singer, and the staff of the State Recorder, Anchorage; Jill L. Schneider, Geological Survey, Anchorage; Lawrence E. Hibpshman, Acting State Archivist, Juneau; Harry A. Noah, former Commissioner, Department of Natural Resources, Juneau; the Forestry staff, Tanana Chiefs Conference, Inc., Fairbanks; Al "Bear" Ketzler, Jr., Tanana Chiefs Conference, Inc., Fairbanks; and Ardis Wiehl, Subregional Director, Yukon-Tanana subregion, Tanana Chiefs Conference, Inc., Fairbanks.

I also thank Michael Carey, *Anchorage Daily News*, Anchorage; Shirley Germaine, Catholic Archdiocese of Anchorage; Pat and Irene Ryan, retired mining engineers, Anchorage; Rev. Louis L. Renner, S.J., editor, *The Alaskan Shepherd*, Catholic Diocese of Fairbanks; the late Harry Havrilack, former miner and magistrate in Rampart; Bruce Savage, Savage Mining Company, Manley Hot Springs; Ed Salter, Salter & Associates, Manley Hot Springs; Stanley Dayo, miner, Manley Hot Springs; Earl H. Beistline, mining consultant, Fairbanks; Gloria Kelly, Kelly Mining, Manley Hot Springs; Don DeLima, DeLima Placers, Manley Hot Springs; Curt Madison, photographer, *Crisp Images*, Manley Hot Springs, and George Miscovich, former miner, Fairbanks.

Many descendants of the early Rampart and Hot Springs miners courteously gave of their time in sharing information with me. I, therefore, thank Ellen Wiehl, Executive Director, Baan O Yeel Kon Corporation, and the Athabascan people of Rampart whose ancestors welcomed and intermarried with the miners; George Sundborg, Seattle, and George Sundborg, Jr., Fairbanks, nephew and grandnephew of George Walter Sundborg; Effie Folger Kokrine, Fairbanks, granddaughter of John and Lucy Folger; Poldine Carlo, Fairbanks, former miner with her husband Bill Carlo and daughter-in-law of Carlo Jackett; Donetta Schaefer, Baker, Montana, granddaughter of Katie Wiehl Boucher and Horace Boucher; John S. Graham, III, Baltimore, Maryland, grandson of Herman Tofty; and Fran Kohler, Fairbanks, daughter of D. G. Hosler.

I could not have produced my work without the special support I received from Lael Morgan and Steve Lay, Epicenter Press, Fairbanks; Don Lee, Executive Director, Naomi Carroll, administrative assistant, and Richard Simmonds, volunteer visitor program, Denakkanaaga, Inc., Fairbanks; the MAPW writers' group—Carlene Bowne, Kathy Dubbs, Sharon McLeod Everette, Sharon Keasey, Sue Mitchell, Martha Springer, Dan Solie, and Barbara Townsend—all of Fairbanks; and finally, I thank my two sisters, Eleanor and Virginia L'Ecuyer, who have consistently supported me throughout my life.

Introduction

Abstract

This thesis on the Rampart, Manley Hot Springs, and Fort Gibbon mining districts of Alaska provides the first comprehensive public history of prospecting and mining activity in these three districts within the gold belt of Interior Alaska. Spanning almost one hundred years, the history begins in 1894 and extracts material from early recorders' books, old newspapers, correspondence of miners whose dreams drew them to the gold fields, and U.S. Geological Survey reports that analyzed Alaska's natural resources and mining economy. It surveys mining development from stampedes during the boom years of the turn of the twentieth century through periods of decline and on into the modern, mechanized, open-pit operations near the beginning of the twenty-first century. It concludes with an extensive annotated bibliography designed to assist other researchers in finding specialized, in-depth information about the three districts.

Until now, the history of the Rampart, Manley Hot Springs, and Fort Gibbon mining districts in Interior Alaska has been buried in archival files and recorders' books or told in pieces in disparate, unconnected articles, books, and U.S. Geological Survey reports. This public history draws together for the first time multiple sources to outline events and take note of some of the people who helped open up the Interior of Alaska to mining and settlement. It uncovers a part of Alaska's Gold Rush history almost unaccounted for due to the greater research emphasis on the more productive, larger, and more sensational mining camps of Nome and Fairbanks.

Location map of report area

The history proceeds chronologically from the initial strike at Rampart in 1894 to the present day. It features some individuals in relationship to their activities in a district at a particular period of time. Many of them contributed much to progress in Alaska. The history also tells the story of the creeks which were there before the miners arrived, gave up their auriferous rock to the relentless attack of miners' pick, hydraulic Giant, and bulldozer, and yet remain in place today, some still producing gold almost one hundred years after a prospector first discovered them.

Chapter 1—"Discovery Period, 1894–1899"—relates the frenzied early days of the Rampart district when James Langford and others followed John Minook's lead in seeking gold on Little Minook Creek and its tributaries. The miners carefully set their rules for each creek and operated in a parliamentary procedure, making motions and decisions by majority vote. In 1896, the Little Minook Creek claimholders specifically excluded Indians except John Minook from locating claims on their creek. After the news of the Klondike strike reached continental United States in July 1897, scores of people from every walk of life stampeded to the gold fields in Canada, hundreds, perhaps as many as 1,500, stopping off in Rampart on the Yukon River. A former governor of the state of Washington, college graduates, physicians, lawyers, journalists, and immigrants from Europe struggled to live in a remote subarctic wilderness, utterly different from any place they had ever known. There they staked claims on nearby creeks in every direction, rushing to beat their competitors to unlocated ground as word of another strike reached them. Each new arrival seemed driven by the personal goal of quick riches through the discovery of great amounts of gold. Few achieved that dream. Nevertheless, although not attracted to homesteading, several took time to plot standard blocks for the fast-growing city of Rampart and to establish a city governmental framework which rapidly changed from democratic miners' meetings, to a limited trusteeship, to a single military overseer, and finally to an elected

mayor. They also set up a hospital, which soon failed financially. Injury or death sometimes ended their adventure. Some tried to cheat their peers or steal for survival. Several left Alaska, dejected by their lack of success, their vision of wealth shattered. Mrs. C[lara] E. Wright, editor of Rampart's first newspaper, *The Rampart Whirlpool,* a short-lived monthly in 1899, aptly captured in the title the swirl of activity that swiftly caught up the Ramparters and moved them along. She reported the Eureka Creek strike of the six Boston boys, led by Elliot L. Gaetz of Nova Scotia, which opened up prospecting on the Tanana River side of the mountain divide, over the hill from Rampart, and led eventually to the development of the Manley Hot Springs district. Author Rex Beach, who as a young man, experienced that Rampart whirlpool from 1897 to 1899, captured some of the stress, greed, and discrimination of the Rampart camp in his novel *The Barrier.*

Chapter 2—"Federal Government Oversight, 1900–1905"—addresses the decision of the federal authorities to appoint a civil commissioner in Rampart in late 1900 to record claims according to U.S. mining law, to hold coroner's hearings, and to act as federal magistrate. Commissioner Andrew J. Balliet's first case resulted from Rampart's first murder. During the period, Judge James Wickersham of the Third Judicial District, Alaska, sometimes held his mobile court in Rampart. U.S. Geological Survey geologists examined the geology of the creeks and tributaries from Rampart to Eureka. In July 1903, a traveling subcommittee of U.S. senators, studying conditions in Alaska, listened to the complaints and recommendations of Rampart miners and to formal testimony by selected witnesses. Ramparters responded by initiating the senators into the Rampart camp of the Arctic Brotherhood. In this time frame, prospecting and mining expanded in the Eureka creek area, particularly along lucrative Glen Gulch. Lengthy litigations evolved over disputes in claim ownership as various claim holders, including Valeria Myers and Ella R. Garratt, took their opposing claimants to court. Hundreds of miners left Rampart for the golden sands in Nome and later for the lure of Pedro Creek in the Tanana Valley in the mining camp which came to be known as Fairbanks. The one operating coal mine on the Yukon River, the Pioneer mine, closed in bankruptcy concluded by a marshal's sale, its funds mismanaged by its owner Tom Drew. Some miners, like William B. Ballou, however, persevered in Rampart, and Ballou helped advance mining techniques by introducing a hydraulic plant on Ruby Creek.

Chapter 3—"Growth of the Hot Springs and Fort Gibbon Districts, 1906-1918"— focuses, in part, on the entrepreneurial activities of Frank G. Manley, whose birth name was Hillyard Bascom Knowles. Manley arrived from Fairbanks with vast amounts of cash, quickly purchased the majority of claims in the Eureka area, and leased the hot springs homestead of John F. Karshner, where he built a hotel. He constructed a road from the homestead eastward to Eureka, a distance of about twenty-five miles, and successfully mined his numerous claims for a few years. After his incarceration in Texas and the destruction of his hotel by fire, he turned his attention to other mining districts. Meanwhile, in late 1906, Michael J. Sullivan had discovered gold along Sullivan Creek, where a settlement called Sullivan City arose during the stampede to Sullivan country on the west side of the Manley Hot Springs district. Prospectors and business men, including Manley, banded together to form eight-member associations to file for 160-acre claims on all the creeks and gulches of the newly uncovered ground. Among the members was Ramparter Herman Tofty, who had once mined on Big Minook Creek. Gradually, both Sullivan City and its surrounding country became known as Tofty, a name that has continued in use even though Herman Tofty left Alaska in 1909. As the Sullivan /Tofty country developed, prospecting was also expanding on Moran, Grant, and Morelock creeks near the village of Tanana in the Fort Gibbon district. This district, though, had a checkered history and never grew to the extent of the Manley Hot Springs district. At the same time, two U.S. Geological Survey engineers recommended the construction of a hydroelectric power plant on

Troublesome Creek to assist mine operators in Rampart. The plant was never built. Instead, mining in Rampart declined. The city of Rampart, once bustling with hundreds of people coming and going, lost most of its population and almost resembled a deserted ghost town. The advent of World War I further slowed mining since labor became scarce and supplies, when available, costly.

Chapter 4—"Between the Two World Wars, 1919-1941"—shows that after World War I, mining had become a business, not always profitable. Several ventures lost money. One such company set up a dredge on American Creek, the only dredge in the district. Dredging operations failed initially but later succeeded under another firm's management. The Cleary Hill Mines of Fairbanks likewise succeeded in its mines in Tofty. Mining also continued on Little Minook Creek where claims had been located as far back as 1896 and in the Eureka area discovered by the "Boston boys" in 1899. Unfortunately, because of World War II, Congressional action closed down Alaska's non-essential gold mining industry in 1942, and mine operators turned their heavy equipment over to the U.S. military forces for use in constructing airstrips and the original Alaska highway.

Chapter 5—"Into the Present Era, 1946-1994"—discusses the slow post-war return of Alaska's gold-mining industry to normal operations. Mine operators had to replace their expensive, earth-moving equipment and had to finance resumption of their operations. Meanwhile, Geological Survey teams looked at gold mines in the three districts for sources of radioactive materials. They concluded that there were no radioactive materials in sufficient quantity for commercial exploitation as a byproduct of gold and tin production. As time went on, the mining business increased. Some years as many as twenty-one operators worked in the three districts; in other years, as few as thirteen. When Alaska achieved statehood, the drive for economic progress gave rise to the proposal for a gigantic, multibillion-dollar dam at Rampart Canyon, the whirlpool on the Yukon

River below Rampart, which was to provide low-cost electric power. The massive dam project would inundate 10,600 square miles from Rampart almost to the Canadian border, destroying all villages, forests, wildlife habitats, and subsurface mineral resources in its path. The entire Rampart mining district was scheduled to be under water. Opposed for several reasons, the proposal for a dam lost support and died. The gold-mining industry continued in Rampart.

Today's gold miners operate sophisticated machinery and comply with stringent governmental regulations regarding the protection of historic places and the restoration of mined land to its natural pre-mined condition and appearance. Amazingly, the creeks and gulches being mined now are among those discovered by James Langford in 1896, by the Boston boys in 1899, and by Michael J. Sullivan in 1906.

Appendices— The first two appendices following the text summarize the estimated production of the three districts from information gathered by U.S. Geological Survey personnel and list the persons the U.S.G.S. personnel thanked for assisting them in their studies. The next two appendices identify coal lands and lodes located within the three districts. Appendix 5 refers to photographs pertinent to the three districts available in collections in the Alaska Archives and Manuscripts, Alaska and Polar Regions Department, Elmer E. Rasmuson Library, University of Alaska Fairbanks. Appendix 6 locates relevant places, primarily creeks, in the three districts, generally connecting them with some note about their earliest history.

Endnotes—This public history of the Rampart, Manley Hot Springs, and Fort Gibbon mining districts concludes each chapter with a note section, providing endnotes on sources for the information cited in the chapter. At the end of the report, there is an extensive annotated bibliography of archival materials, recorders' record books, newspapers, and published works containing information about one or more of the three mining districts.

Public history, however, is never complete because history is a never-ending story of people, places, and events which can be examined and re-examined from different perspectives or with additional material. Therefore, this history too can be said to be ongoing as some day other researchers, with new approaches, will look again at the three mining districts. In particular, the history of the three districts and the impact of their people on Alaska history should never be forgotten or discounted.

Chapter 1. Discovery Period, 1894–1899

There are a few going out with a big sack of dust, but when one goes out with plenty, there are hundreds with nothing. A few are lucky, but the many live on expectations.
–Perry Judkins, Rampart, Alaska, September 11, 1898[1]

In the early 1890s few people sought gold along the creeks in the area of the Yukon River just below the lower ramparts in Interior Alaska. There nature revolved through its seasonal cycles unchallenged. The powerful river flowed westward, downstream from Canada, passing Circle City, Fort Yukon, and Fort Hamlin, rolling through the ramparts, angling a bit to the east, creating swirling eddies between the high walls of a narrow canyon on its way to Norton Sound and the Bering Sea, almost one thousand river miles away; the river froze up, broke up, and flowed again.[2] Birches and alders grew in abundance, sprouted leaves, and shed their greenery; some crashed to the ground, not downed by axe or whipsaw but by lightning strike, beaver teeth, or heavy snows. Caribou, bear, and moose drank from nearby streams and drifted slowly amid the brush and forest in search of food or mate. Geese and ducks flew south before the onslaught of winter cold and returned in the spring to nest under the midnight sun. Occasionally, small family groups of Athabascan Indians camped for a while to fish for salmon and smoke-dry their catch or to hunt wild game for meat and clothing. To them, dates and clocks did not matter. Time passed, and survival activities took place according to the schedule nature dictated. — Then the frenetic pace of stampedes for gold punctuated the tranquility of nature's annual course and accelerated use of nature's resources.

At first, events unrolled slowly. In the summer of 1894 or perhaps 1893, John Minook, an Alaskan of mixed Athabascan and Russian

heritage, found traces of gold in paying quantities along a stream that came to be known as Little Minook Creek. Assisted by some Indians, he sluiced about $1.50 worth of gold from gravel before a sudden rush of water carried away all but one of his sluice boxes.[3] During the fall of 1894, long-time prospectors Peter Johnson, James S. Langford, O[liver] C. Miller, Dave Dawson, Bill Hunter, P. B. Peterson, and others learned of Minook's discovery and began prospecting along the creek. Langford found pay during the winter of 1895–1896 on a spot which became Discovery, Little Minook Creek. He partnered with Peter Johnson to open the ground. Meanwhile, Bill Hunter prospected on Hunter Creek, where he staked his Discovery claim.[4]

On April 20, 1896, the miners passed formal by-laws for their district, which they called the Rampart mining district, comprising Little Minook and Hunter creeks and the tributaries, bars and benches of those creeks. In regulating themselves, the miners agreed to limit claims to 1,000 feet and number them one-up and one-down from Discovery. Attentive to one another's claims and water rights, they specified:

- that water should not be backed up on another claim;
- that drainage should be permitted where it was most convenient;
- that only muck and sand might be sluiced onto another claim;
- that the claimholder held all rights to all timber on the claim; and
- that no moss, brush, stumps, or other debris could be discarded into the creek.

In particular, they stated that no Indian except John Minook should hold or represent ground in the district. Representation or assessment, a term for the minimum work required to be done on a claim by the owner or his representative during a prescribed period to maintain ownership of the claim, initially had to be performed, apparently continuously, between June 15 and July 15 and finished by November 30. Subsequently, in 1898, the miners amended and defined representation as two holes to bedrock or one hole to bedrock with a ten-foot drift (tunnel) from the shaft, all annual requirements to be completed before January 1.[5]

James Langford formally filed his Discovery claim on April 29, 1896, in the creek record maintained by recorder M[anford] W. Sinclair. Charles Williams filed for No. 1 above on May 4; P. B. Peterson, No. 3 above on July 18; and Peter Johnson, Langford's partner, filed for No. 6 above on September 22.[6] According to *The Rampart Whirlpool*, the claim holders on Little Minook, except for Langford and Johnson, each working by himself on his claim, became dispirited trying to dig to bedrock. On No. 7 above, Charles Stephan raised a cabin, sank a shaft, and gave up, as did John Sally on No. 8 above and Billy McLean on No. 9. In April 1897, the trio decided to leave the creek. They walked to the cabin of James Langford and Peter Johnson on No. 6 above and discovered that the partners had nearly reached bedrock. After the three resumed their departure trek, Pete Johnson caught up with them at the mouth of the creek to disclose that Langford had just panned rich dirt. Reinvigorated by the news, the travelers returned to their individual claims. Stephan deepened his shaft by another foot and one-half and panned a $1.50 value. In the next seventeen days, Langford and Johnson extracted 122 ounces of coarse gold. As the warm summer arrived, they ceased their winter drifting.[7]

At first, whenever a claim holder on Little Minook wanted representation during the winter or another person to perform the representation for him, he called a miners' meeting to receive concurrence from the other claimholders. Agreement was always unanimous since other claimholders often desired the same permission. George Thomas, who held No. 15 above as of August 28, 1896, asked for winter representation on May 26, 1897. The miners present—Daniel L. Carolan, M. W. Sinclair, Ernest H. Chapman, C. Williams, P. B. Peterson, Peter

Johnson, James S. Langford, Preston Ireland, Louis Shequin, Thomas Evans, Charles Stephan, Robert Craven, and John Minook—agreed to the request. On June 22, John Minook requested and received similar agreement for his claim No. 19.[8]

As a result of the gradually heightened activity, a mining settlement of businesses and residences, initially named Minook City, began to emerge on the banks of the Yukon River. Even though the residents had come to prospect, not to homestead, they recognized that their small settlement needed rules, order, and defined citizen responsibilities. On June 6, 1897, therefore, the miners convened to decide on townsite plats. They elected M. W. Sinclair to chair their meeting and J. P. Bouscaren to act as secretary and town recorder. O. C. Miller proposed that every citizen be entitled to locate one lot, fifty feet by one hundred feet. The lot was to be cleared within thirty days and a cabin built on it within one year. The location had to be recorded at once. After the cabin was in place, a citizen could locate another lot and begin again fulfilling the clearing and cabin-raising requirements. The miners accepted Miller's motion. James Langford then moved, and the miners approved, that the town be named Rampart. The miners also agreed to set apart fifty feet of waterfront for Front Street and to lay out a parallel street one hundred feet back. Each lot holder was to clear the street the width of his lot. Holders of corner lots cleared both the front and side streets.[9]

Lot assignments to Rampart's first settlers began on June 7. Blocks had seven to nine lots each. Al Mayo, the store owner who had moved his family to Rampart from Old Station near the junction of the Tanana and the Yukon rivers, received lots 1 through 4 in block 2.[10] Originally from Maine, Mayo, according to his personal account, had been in the Union Army with General Sherman in Macon, Georgia. He arrived in Alaska in 1868, eventually became a trader connected with the Alaska Commercial Company, and married an Alaska Native by the name of Margaret.[11]

John Minook took lot 5, block 2, which, on

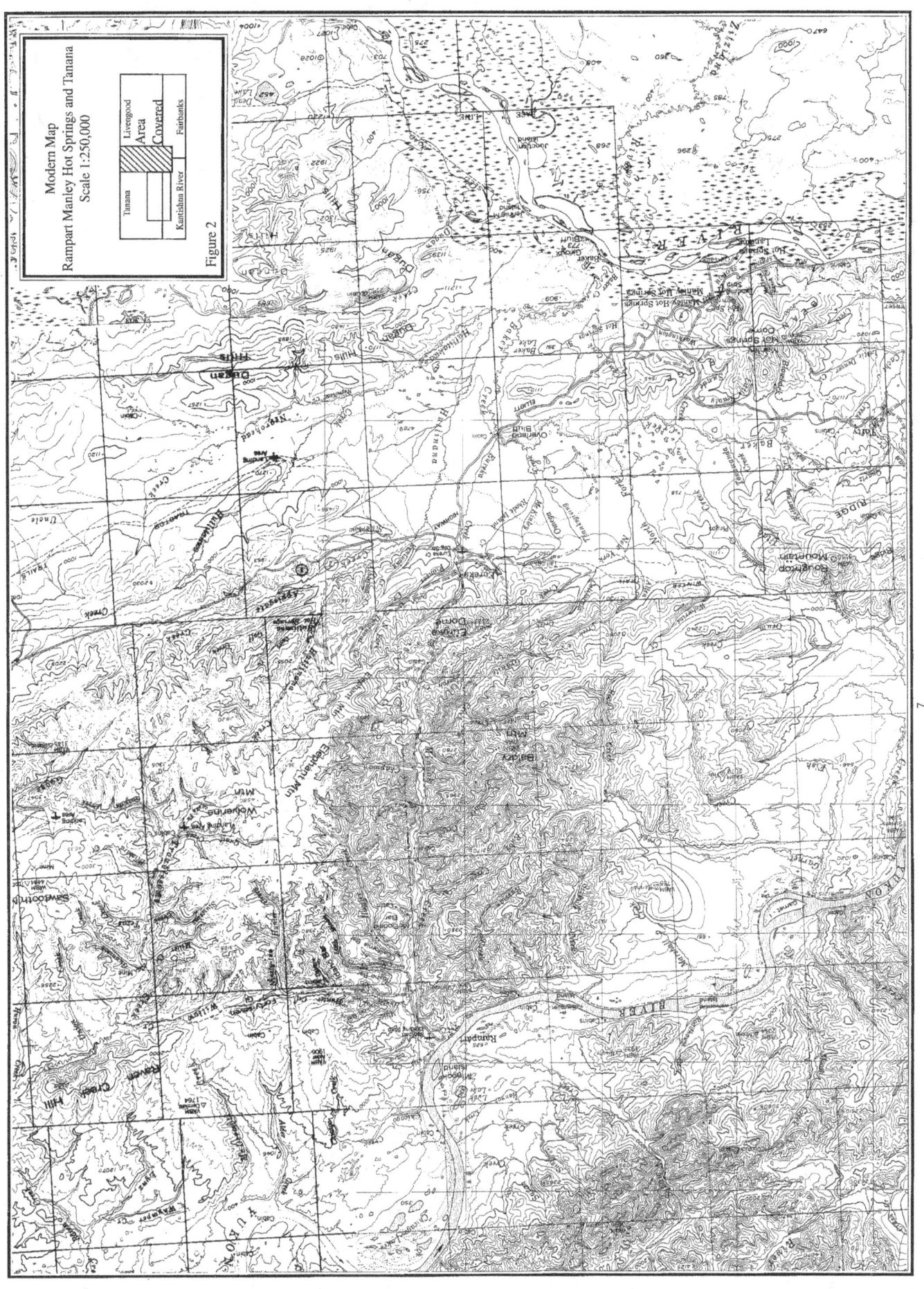

Modern Map
Rampart Manley Hot Springs and Tanana
Scale 1:250,000

Livengood
Area
Covered

Tanana

Kantishna River   Fairbanks

Figure 2

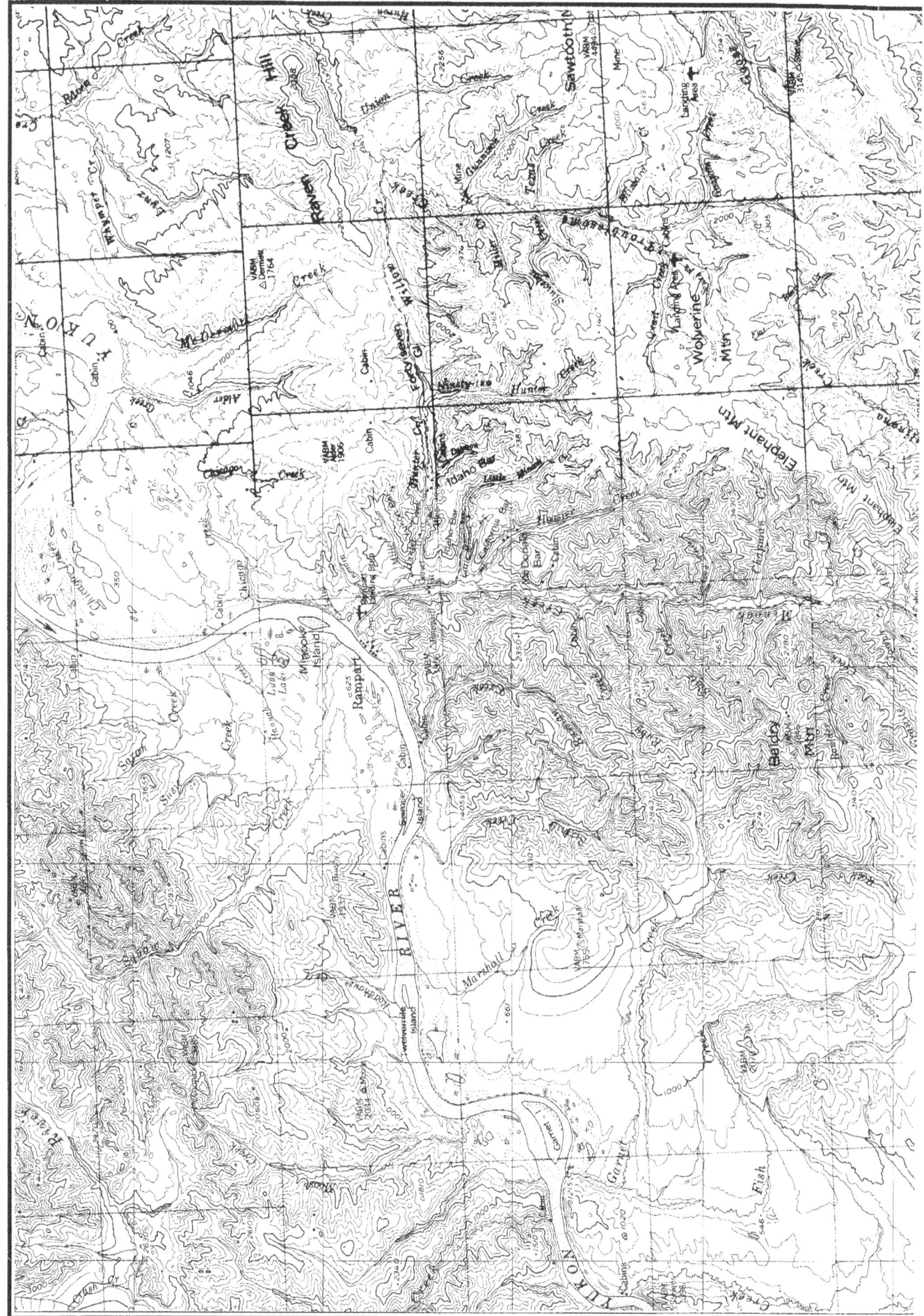

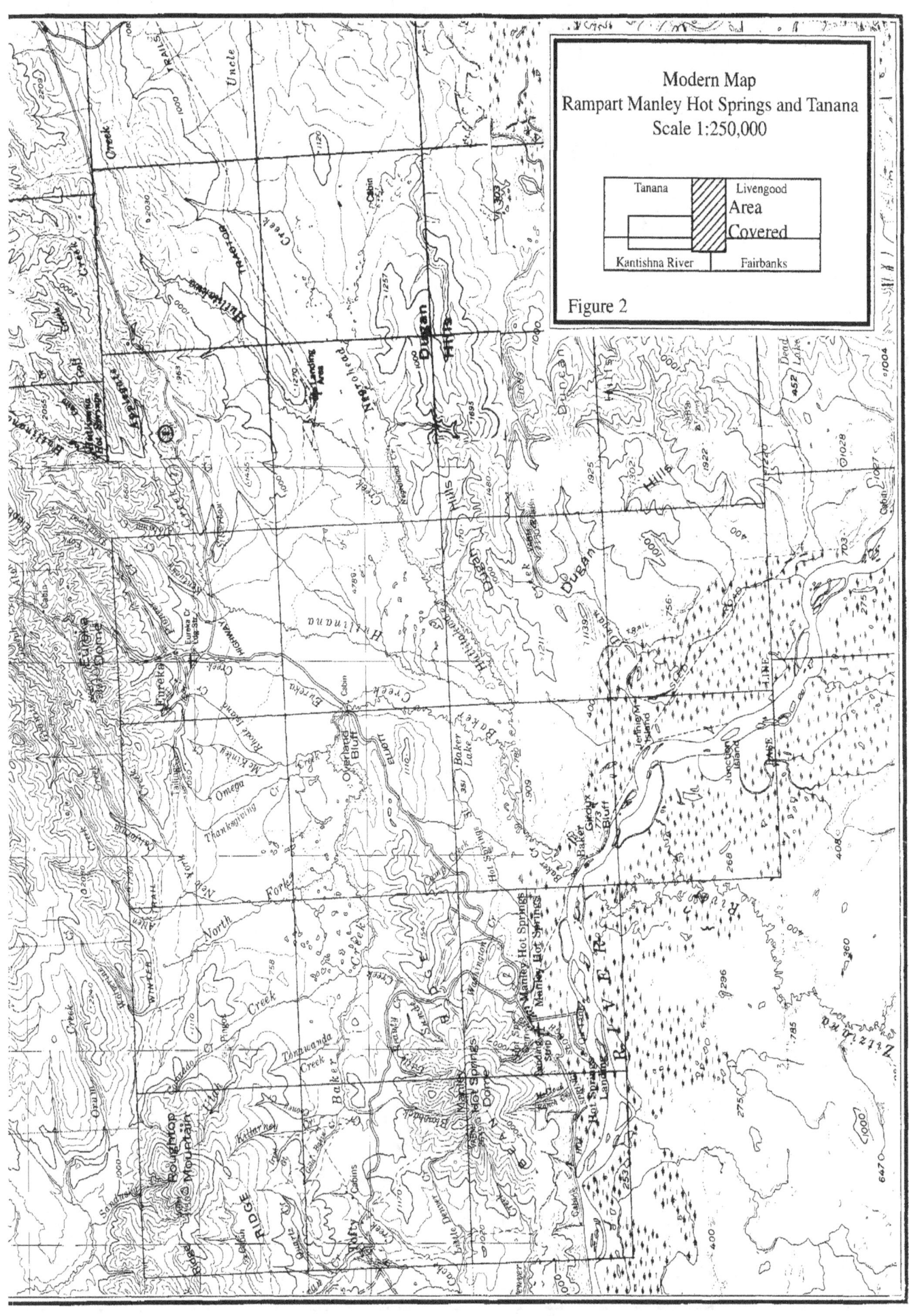

Modern Map
Rampart Manley Hot Springs and Tanana
Scale 1:250,000

Tanana		Livengood
		Area
		Covered
Kantishna River		Fairbanks

Figure 2

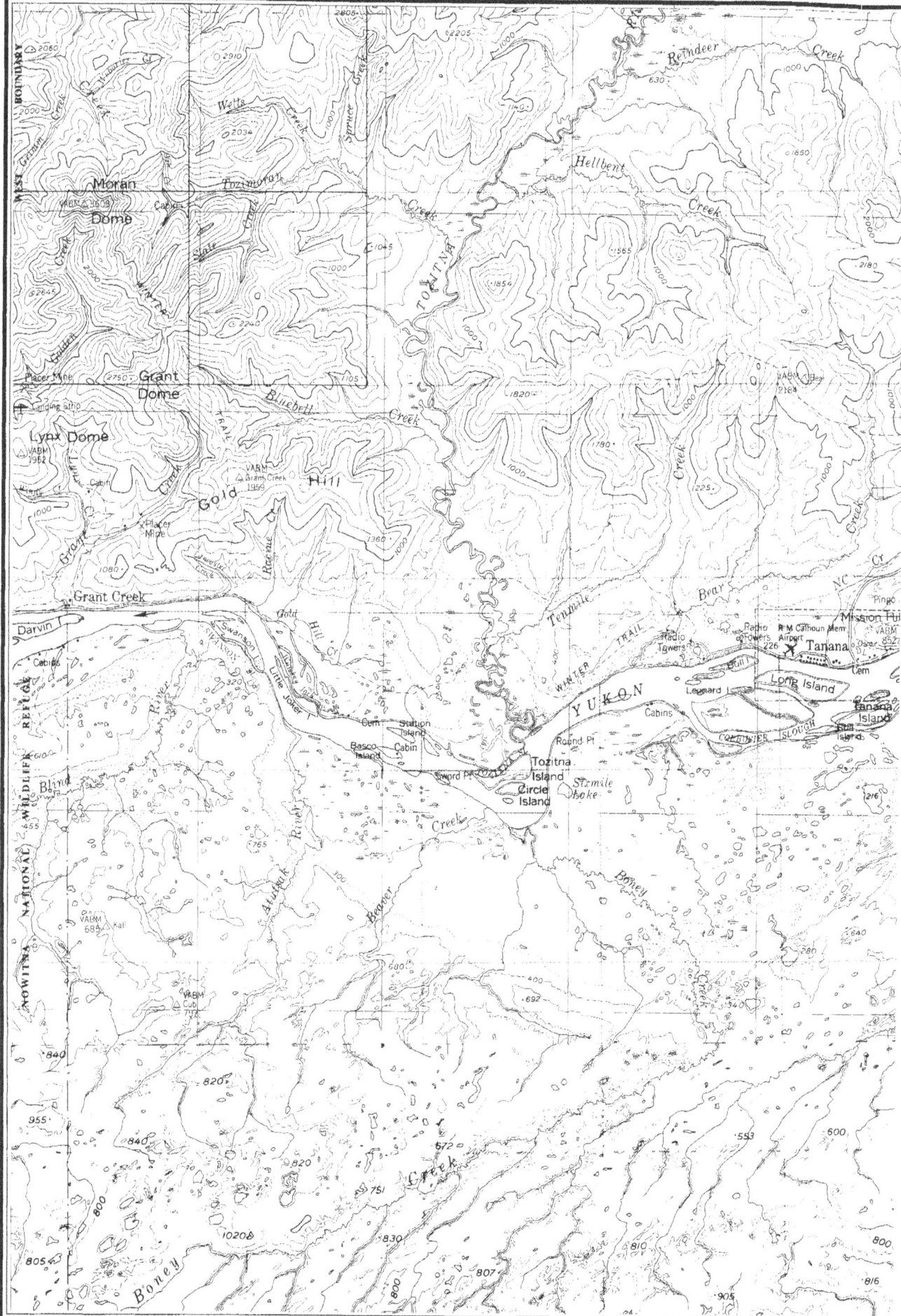

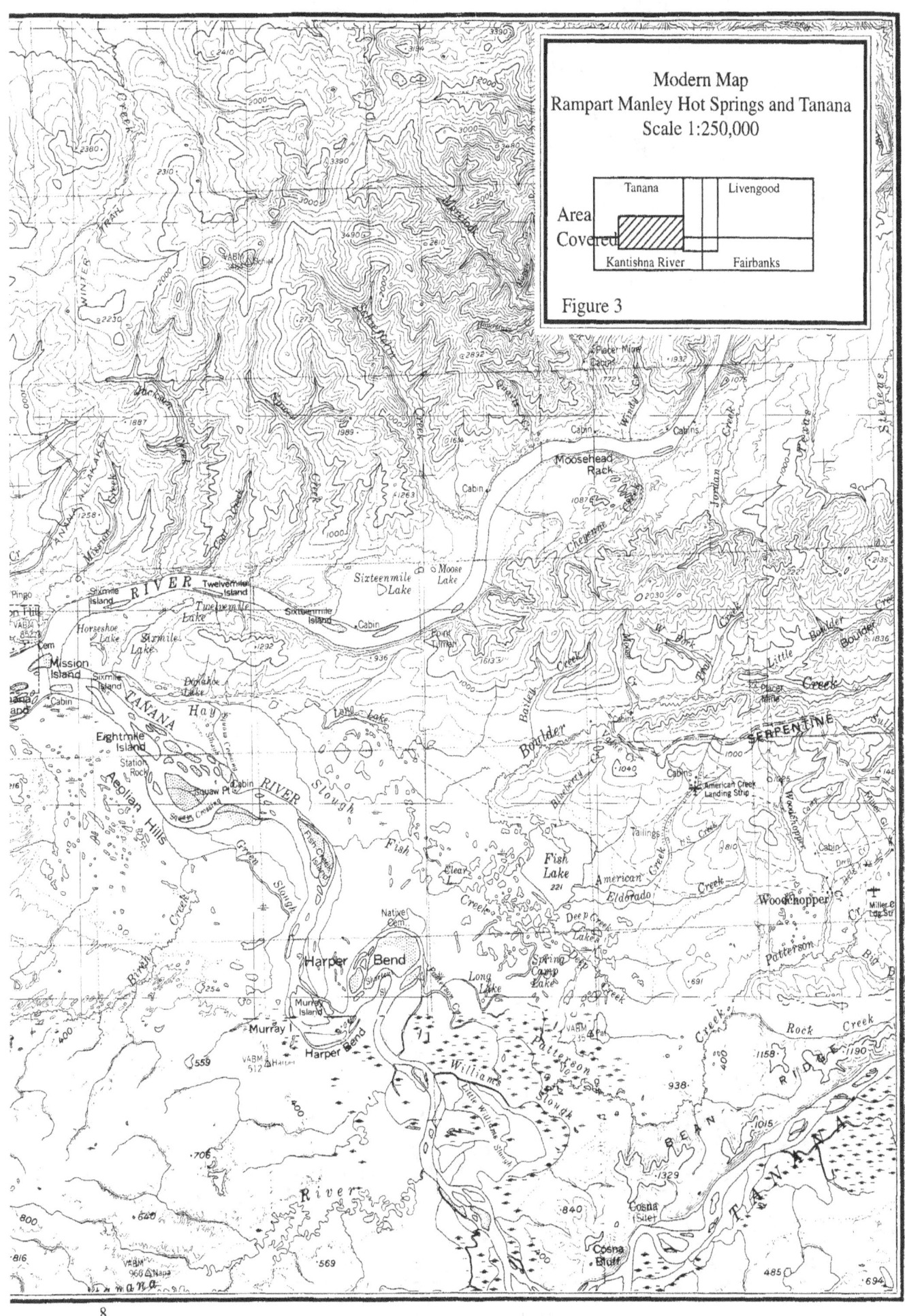

Modern Map
Rampart Manley Hot Springs and Tanana
Scale 1:250,000

Area
Covered

| Tanana | Livengood |
| Kantishna River | Fairbanks |

Figure 3

8

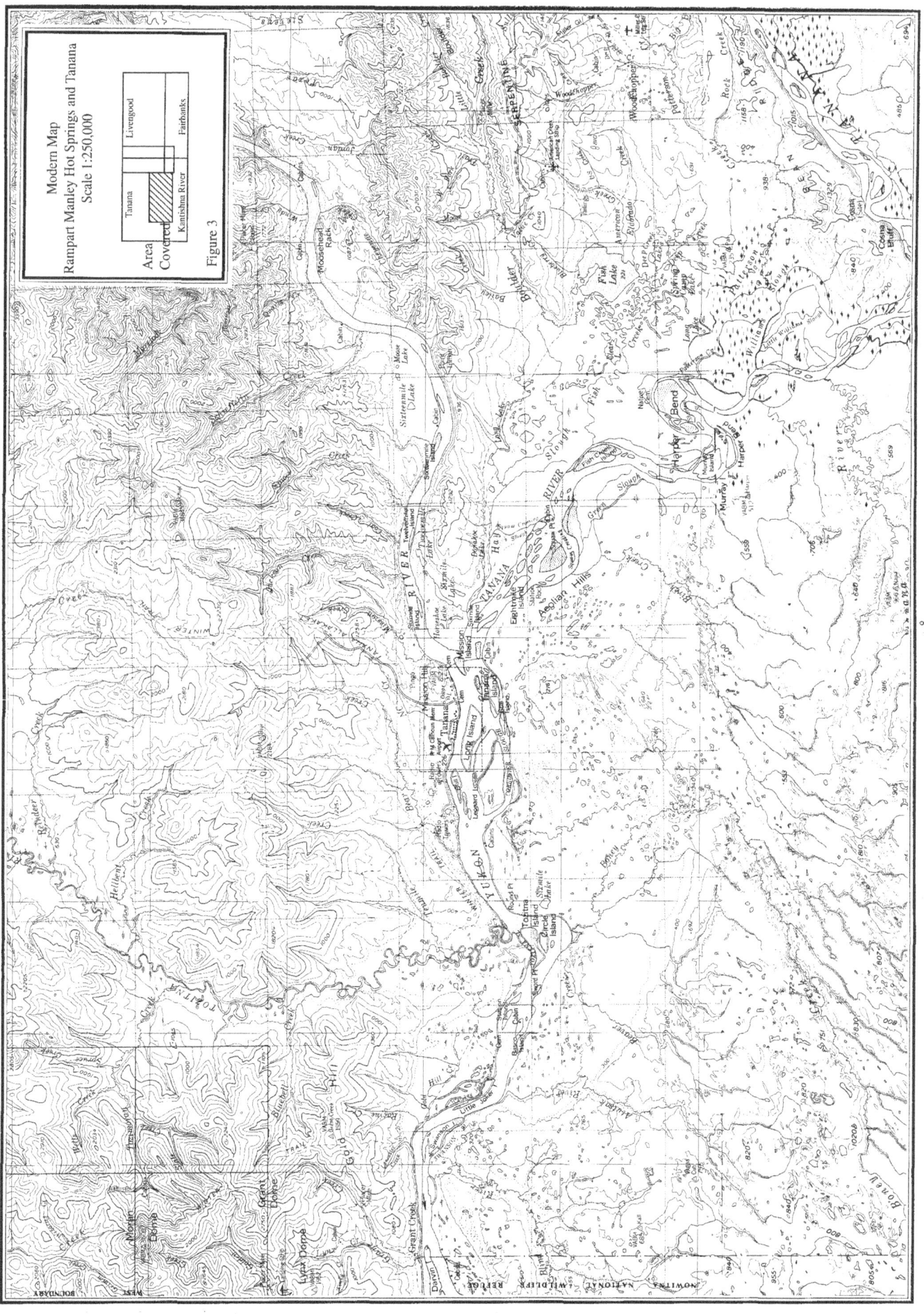

Modern Map
Rampart Manley Hot Springs and Tanana
Scale 1:250,000

Figure 3

June 19, he transferred to P[eter] T[rimble] Rowe, Episcopal Bishop of Alaska; as of August 31 he had lot 6, block 8. Tom Crawford held lot 6, block 2, and lot 3, block 3. James Langford located lot 9, block 2; his partner, Peter Johnson, lot 7, block 3. Some Indians also filed.[12]

When the news of the Canadian Klondike boom, ignited by George Washington Carmack's strike on August 17, 1896, reached the contiguous United States in July 1897, the historic stampede to the gold fields of the Klondike and the Yukon River began.[13] Men, and some women, came from New England, the South, the Midwest, the West Coast, and from Europe. Among them were college graduates, physicians, lawyers, writers, tradesmen, farmers, cooks, coal miners, and gamblers, all lured by the dream of golden riches. Many would-be

Klondikers, entering the Yukon River through St. Michael, stopped off at Rampart. Consequently, filing for town lots expanded rapidly, and the townspeople revised and re-revised the plat design to accommodate the increased population.

The port of Seattle bustled as passengers swarmed on board ships bound for the Klondike. The steamer *Portland* left Seattle for "mammon's shrine" at noon on Thursday, July 22, 1897. Passengers included General Edward M. Carr; Captain Andrew J. Balliet; John H. McGraw, governor of Washington State from 1892 to 1896; Mr. and Mrs. A. B. Llewelyn; H. F. Thumm; Charles H. Knapp; and Mr. and Mrs. Thomas Urquhart. The *Seattle Post-Intelligencer* commissioned passenger George Hyde Preston to go up the Yukon River to

Figure 4. Building boom in Rampart, 1897. Courtesy of the Vertical File, University of Alaska Fairbanks. Accession Number 64-92-719.

Dawson to provide the newspaper with "reliable" correspondence about "the great gold fields."[14]

A few weeks later, on August 11, the steamer *Eliza Anderson* departed Seattle with Oliver Tingley, Chris Keenan, W. S. [Scott] Harmon, and Charles I. Range aboard.[15] Passenger Thomas Wiedemann identified Keenan, Harry Lewis, and Pat Kerns as personal representatives of Montana mining magnate Marcus Daley, and the only experienced miners among the *Eliza Anderson*'s 116 passengers.[16]

Many people willingly gave up good jobs to seek the elusive gold. Seattle Mayor William D. Wood resigned his office to head the Seattle-Yukon Commercial Company. The company chartered the steamer *Humboldt*, which sailed on Wednesday, August 18, with Wood, Louis E. Boukofsky, J. C. Spicer, and many others on board.[17]

The steamer *Cleveland*, which carried 200 passengers northward to St. Michael, had left Seattle at noon on Thursday, August 5. Among the passengers were Captain Patrick M. Ray and Lt. Wilds P. Richardson, Eighth Infantry; E. T. Barnette; Adolph Bock; Ed Patterson; Frank M. Canton; and George P. MacGowan.[18] When the steamer reached St. Michael in mid-August, there appeared to be no immediate means to continue the journey by river steamer up the Yukon to Dawson. E. T. Barnette persuaded fifty-nine passengers from the *Cleveland* to join him in establishing the Yukon Miners Cooperative Association at $200 each. The cooperative purchased the *St. Michael* for $10,500 from the Jesuit Fathers of the Roman Catholic mission at Koserefski (Holy Cross).[19] The *St. Michael*, with a sixteen-man volunteer crew including purser George MacGowan, left St. Michael on August 29 and reached Rampart at 8 a.m., on Tuesday, September 14 (more likely September 7).[20] As the *St. Michael* approached the landing, Barnette directed that the American flag be raised for what he most likely intended as a triumphant entry. Suddenly, steam hissed and the boiler died. It took Barnette and his crew twenty hours to restore power.[21] MacGowan and others decided to get off. When their supplies were unloaded, some apparently grumbled that they did not receive their fair share.[22]

As newcomers poured off the river boats at Rampart, the miners already in place saw opportunities to sell or lease their cabins and their claims, or interest in their claims, for cash, promissory notes, or the completion of representation work. MacGowan, along with shipmates John C. Powell and George M[el] Reed, immediately bought a clean cabin twelve by fourteen feet for $650. Every chink in the rough logs was stuffed with moss to keep out the cold air. The three cabinmates stored 4,000 pounds of supplies in a cache ten feet above the ground. Inside the cabin they found three comfortable bunks in one corner. On the walls they hung up their weapons—Colt six shooter, Smith and Wesson, and Bowie knives.[23]

On September 8, 1897, Langford sold Discovery, Little Minook, to William H. Hubbard of Chicago for $5,000, $1,000 of which was in provisions. The next May, Hubbard sold one-half interest in Discovery for $1.00 to Michael Cudahy, Ernest A. Hammill, and Portus B. Weare, associates in the North American Transportation & Trading Company (NAT&T).[24]

On September 10, Ernest H. Chapman and M.W. Sinclair, who jointly owned No. 12 above, Little Minook, sold it for $4,000 to Charles O. Johnson and Duke F. Baxter. Johnson and Baxter immediately leased their claim to W. T. Bell, P. Hancock, and R. Aschenhagen. In July 1898, they announced their intent to apply for a patent on No. 12. Baxter also purchased the upper 500 feet of No. 2 below from J. W. Baker on September 4, 1897. On September 14, he arranged for R[ay] E. Norton, Thomas M. McCabe, and John G. Crowley to work his claim and erect a cabin. In June 1898, he sought agreement from the miners on Little Minook to lease the claim for winter representation. Forty miners, including R. E. Norton, R[ex] E. Beach, and J[oe] L. Muldowney, acquiesced.[25]

During the late summer of 1897, many of the new arrivals found the creeks within an eight-mile distance of Rampart almost filled with claimholders and struck out toward more distant creeks. Frank "Old" Gleason of Davenport,

Iowa, who was apparently president of the Yukon Miners Cooperative Association remnant in Rampart, tipped off MacGowan and his friends to good prospects. On Thursday, September 16, they went by boat upstream about twenty miles to a landing where they drew lots on their order of claims. Very early on Friday morning the group, each with a twenty-pound backpack, hiked inland through the woods to Alder Creek. Unused to exertion, they encountered great difficulties fording streams, climbing over fallen trees, and tripping over the underbrush. Water seeped into their boots, and they soon became uncomfortably wet. Although some begged for rest, the group plunged on until noon, aware others ahead of them were equally intent on staking claims. They finished locating their claims by 2 p.m., dried their clothing, snacked on tea and hardtack, and started their return trip. First in line, association treasurer Pat Boland led them into bog land where they walked in futile circles until they used MacGowan's compass to take the right course and found the river steamer by 11:30 p.m.

The stress and pain of their first prospecting stampede caused several to break down in tears. Their discontent increased when the steamer's captain decided not to return to Rampart. They built a raft to drift downstream to Rampart. When the cold mid-September night set in and winds, seemingly of hurricane force, raged, MacGowan lit a fire on the raft, and all shivered under their blankets until they reached their destination safely. Recovery came quickly, though, because three days later, on Sunday, September 19, Fred Gleason, Franklin, and MacGowan prospected near Rampart.[26]

Two days later, MacGowan, Reed, and Powell entered a legal partnership to share their claims on Dawson, Hoosier, Julia, and Alder creeks. Three days later, on September 24, they purchased side-by-side town lots.

MacGowan kept track of the daily weather and temperature. He also learned the laws of the mining camp where there were no locks on doors or caches. Anyone convicted by a jury of stealing would receive a public whipping, of 100 lashes, and would be released to float downriver on a raft to an uncertain end, probably death. If a miner was away from his cabin, any other miner had a right to enter that cabin, eat food from the shelves, and sleep there, but not to remove anything from the cabin.[27]

Meanwhile, at 8 p.m. on September 18, miners involved with Julia Creek crammed into the tent of F[rank] G. Kress. They elected N[ewton] P. R. Hatch chairman and recorder; they chose Garnet W. Coen secretary. At the suggestion of W. W. Painter, they set up a bylaws committee composed of George Reed, James Finney, and Coen. Agreeing with the committee's proposals, they named the district the Coen mining district and established the recording fee at $3.00 with an additional $3.00 for construction of the creek trail. If, within sixty days, a claim holder cut a satisfactory trail along his claim, he would be refunded the $3.00. Recorder Hatch would survey and number the claims within fifteen days. Claim holders had ten days after survey to record their claims. For representation, each claim holder was to perform twenty days work between January 1 and September 1. G. W. Coen and C. Sellinger jointly filed for Discovery, Julia Creek, on October 5, 1897. Coen also claimed No. 1 below. A preliminary list of claim holders, dated September 13, identified Sally Minook with No. 6 above, and Indian girl Susan with No. 7 above. When the time came to file, the two women either chose not to file or were not permitted to file. Several miners failed to do their representation work, and other miners re-located the claims on January 1, 1899. Frank Canton, who bought No. 13 above from J[ames] R. Austin, was one of the many who abandoned his claim on the creek. Edward Patterson filed for No. 14 above and deeded it to George M. Reed, who, in turn, deeded it to the Klondike Gold Mining and Manufacturing Company of Colorado, all three transactions taking place on September 18, 1897. Reed, who had entered into an agreement with the Colorado firm on July 26, 1897, transferred No. 24 above to the company, on September 18, 1898.[28]

Miners connected with Russian Creek mining

district organized on September 30, 1897, and elected Charles Bevans chairman and Fred B. Gleason secretary. They restricted claims to 500 feet and prohibited anyone from locating more than one claim on the creek and from locating a claim both on the creek and also on a tributary. Claims would be jumpable if not recorded within ten days after location. Representation required work of $300 value to be accomplished between January 1 and the next January 1. The recording fee was $2.50, and James Rosewall was chosen recorder. At length, Rosewall was unseated as unsatisfactory, and Walter Hall replaced him.[29]

Prospectors already in the Alaska Interior were attracted to the activity in Rampart. One of them, John Folger, moved to the camp in the summer of 1897. For a while, he had lot 0 (zero), block 2, next to Al Mayo's store. By September 2, he held lot 6, block 5; his wife, Lucy Folger, held lot 0, block A (revised block 2).[30] That fall Folger helped organize the Chapman Creek mining district. The district recording fee was $5.00 to cover the fee for the recorder to mark a trail. Claim holders had thirty days to record their claim. The representation period required twenty days work between January 1 and July 1. B[en] S[anford] Goodhue, Chapman Creek recorder, entered Folger's Discovery claim as of November 4, 1897, and at Folger's request, later amended the recording to grant one-half interest to Michael Doud. Ernest H. Chapman had filed for No. 1 above as of September 25. Goodhue claimed No. 4 above; David McMillan, No. 5 above; Louis E. Goepfert, No. 7 above; and R. E. Beach, No. 4 below, all on November 4.[31]

On November 6, 1897, miners crowded into Joe Wiehl's cabin to form the Big Minook Creek mining district. Present were Wiehl, Jack W. Baker, S[amuel] F. McDill, Carlo Jackett, Albert Hughes, Charles Hermanson, Joseph Anicich, and A. B. Williams. They elected Williams chairman and Hughes secretary and creek recorder. Joe Wiehl informed the group that he had prospected benches of Big Minook and in October had located Discovery bench claim. He recommended use of hydraulic mining tech-niques. The miners agreed on a $5.00 recording fee (later reduced to $2.50), a thirty-day period for recording locations, and representation of twenty days or $200 value within one year of location. They limited claims to twenty acres per U.S. mining law. Big Minook, the largest creek in the area, eventually had about 128 twenty-acre claims, many of which rapidly changed hands and were subdivided into partial interests. On December 20, 1897, W. A. Welch, agent for the Klondyke Gold Mining and Transportation Company, Inc., of West Virginia, negotiated with Wiehl, Anicich, Baker, Hermanson, Hughes, Jackett, McDill, and Williams, as well as with William M. Rank and Aaron Dahlgren. In return for their combined claims—Discovery, Nos. 1 through 5 above, and Nos. 1 through 4 below—the Klondyke com-pany was to give the miners 800,000 shares of stock, three positions on the board of directors, and the right to name the company's vice president. In addition, the company would outfit an expedition for the company's business in Alaska. The deal was to be completed in Seattle on or about July 15, 1898.[32] The agreement apparently fell through.[33]

The Big Minook negotiations were not the only offers in progress. Through much of late November and early December 1897, George MacGowan talked with John Sally about taking over Sally's claim, No. 8 above, Little Minook. At first, MacGowan sought a lease; later, in union with Mel Reed and John Powell, he offered $10,000, $1,000 in immediate cash. He succeeded in obtaining a fifteen-day option for $11,000. His desire for the claim increased when Sally uncovered a nugget worth $21.50. He sparked Governor McGraw's enthusiasm for the claim, and McGraw involved his partner, General Carr. Carr told MacGowan that if he (Carr) and McGraw purchased the claim, MacGowan could have three shares for $10,000. Carr also informed MacGowan that the two partners had connections to Addick of Baltimore and had $5 million at their disposal.[34] MacGowan, Powell, and Reed lost their option as time ran out. On December 6, Carr and McGraw offered Sally $11,000, $1,000 before

December 15, and the rest when Sally arrived at the law office of Preston, Carr, and Gilman in Seattle. The arrangement protected the rights of Charles Bevan, who, at the time, was leasing and working the claim. On December 14, Carr and Sally signed the proposal for $11,000 in gold coin. Bill Joyce and McGraw witnessed the signing. The transfer of No. 8 above to Carr became final on July 25, 1898. The claim was reputed to have been one of the richest, if not the richest, in the district for several years, and it was worked for decades.[35]

Meanwhile, not everyone who had started out that summer from Seattle reached Rampart or the Klondike before freeze-up. After an adventurous journey on the *Eliza Anderson* to St. Michael, Thomas Wiedermann and the other passengers transferred to the *W. K. Merwin* and its accompanying scow. They started up the Yukon River the morning of October 10 and soon met the stranded *Seattle No. 1*, the river steamer of William D. Wood's company. By October 15, the ice had solidified, locking the *Merwin*, the scow, and the Alaska Commercial's steamer *Alice* in for the winter near the Eskimo village of Annock, about twenty-five miles up from the village of Nunabislogarth (Nunapithlugak).[36]

Perry Judkins and his friend Robert Chamberlin arrived in St. Michael aboard the *Navarro*. As of October 2, twelve vessels were there, and more were expected.[37] At the time, the port had two towns—St. Michael, the Alaska Commercial site; and a short distance away Fort Get-There, the NAT&T site.[38]

Judkins and seventy-five others spent the winter on the *Thomas Dwyer* at Nunivak Creek (Nanvaranak Slough), not far from the *Alice* and the *Merwin*. At Norton Sound on October 7, 1897, they had formed a passengers' association, electing Captain W. B. Robertson permanent chairman. The association continually argued and negotiated with Captain Anderson of the *Dwyer* about services and supply allocations. When Captain Robertson died on February 24, 1898, the passengers disputed with Anderson over the auction of Robertson's effects. The auction went ahead as the associa-

tion decided. To amuse themselves the group held debates, played checkers, chess, and cards, and even held football and baseball games in the snow. A few built a cabin on the bar by the *Dwyer*. They called the cabin "Neversweat" because they had not yet sweated at mining.[39]

Exactly how many people resided in Rampart during the fall of 1897 cannot be determined precisely. Captain Patrick Ray inspected Rampart in early September and reported that it had a population of 350 as of September 7, including the prospectors in mining camps twelve miles away. He actually counted seventy tents, one store, and ten huts. He expressed concern that miners in the Klondike would starve since supplies intended for them had been off-loaded at Rampart and at Fort Yukon.[40]

Groups and individuals continued to straggle into Rampart. Novelist Rex Beach may have exaggerated when he described his entrance to Rampart in the late autumn as being one of "1,500 souls and twelve saloon keepers, all dumped out in the bank of the Yukon to shift for ourselves in a region unmapped and unexplored."[41]

In November, some miners arrived with news. They had traveled on the steamer *Bella* from Dawson to Circle City. With two dog teams, they proceeded on to Fort Yukon where they found 300 down-and-out miners, determined to obtain whatever supplies existed in whatever way possible. Captain Ray, who by then happened to be at Fort Yukon, intervened. He faced eighty armed men and required them to cut cords of wood, at $5 per cord, to pay for their supplies. Ray allowed anyone with money to purchase up to $700 worth of supplies. He stipulated that anyone penniless and unwilling to work would be limited to ten days of rations. He then asked Dawson and other departure points to not permit any more people to enter the approaches to Alaska.[42]

Still, small groups of people came. Mayor Wood and his party rode by sled from Tanana.[43] Eighteen-year-old George Walter Sundborg walked 150 miles, reaching Rampart shortly before Christmas. Sundborg, staked by Henry Wetmore and four others in return for a 50-50 share in whatever he located, had left San Francisco on August 9 aboard the steamer *National City*, which entered the port of St. Michael on August 23. There, at the captain's instigation, Sundborg shot and killed a hawk that had been perched on a block of the steamer's mast, eating a golden finch. Those who saw his action considered it a bad luck omen. That same day, an accident with the barge on the steamer broke the steamer's mast, so Sundborg was given the nickname "Hoodoo." Hoodoo Sundborg finally entered the Yukon on the *Mae West*, which met a series of misfortunes and delays because the river pilot lacked experience with the channels and sandbars. Freeze-up stopped the *Mae West* at the mouth of the Tozikaket River. Sundborg and other passengers built a one-room shack on a nearby island. Then he continued on, stopping one night in an Indian brush shack. During the trip, his socks became damp, and a rubber shoe froze to one foot. A Captain Holt rubbed Sundborg's foot in snow melted by salt. Sundborg lost four toenails and all the skin off his foot, but his foot was spared amputation. He spent his first night in Rampart in a small cabin with nineteen other men, one of whom snored loudly and most of whom were sick from eating sour caribou. At rest in his new home, Sundborg discovered he was covered with lice.[44]

The continuing flow of people in and out increased the exchange of town lots. Lots not cleared of trees were forfeited as were lots declared abandoned. W. A. Welch, the Klondyke company agent, located 160 acres for commercial purposes. He claimed all the land from the low water mark of the Big Minook River, to 2,640 feet up the Yukon, except for lots already held by John Minook and W. P. Pinkham. C. L. V. Teeter sold one-half interest in his 160 acres for milling and commercial uses to W. N. Marshall and O. S. Osborn. Marshall consented to apply and pay expenses for a patent to the land; Osborn agreed to underwrite the cost of the patent survey.[45]

The frenzied development of town lots brought about the construction of cabins on good weather days. MacGowan calculated that the three partners needed 180 logs for their three new cabins and 390 eight-feet poles for three roofs. He concluded that the most difficult part involved cutting and drying moss and inserting it between the chinks.[46] To make a roof watertight and frost-free, a builder laid the poles down as a board base, placed moss on top of the poles, topped the moss with birch bark, put sod on the birch bark, and spread gravel over the sod.[47] In summer, some residents raised a vegetable garden on the flat roofs, planting radishes, lettuce, onions, peas, and beans.

As the winter darkness deepened and the temperature plummeted, a philosophic, lonely miner who had been aboard the *St. Michael*, thought to be B. W. Moore, Jr., of Montgomery, West Virginia, summed up survival lessons. He wrote his sage advice to himself in his Miller Creek diary:

Don'ts for Alaska from Observation December 13, 1897
Don't go out without waterproof matchbox filled.
Don't try to go out even 300 yards with wet feet in cold weather. Stop and make a fire.
Don't take a long trip or leave the trail by yourself. Be with someone as much as possible.
Don't try to go too far without eating and always arrange to have something to eat.
Pine [W. G. Pinecoffin] says a man will die in seven hours and thirty-five minutes unless he eats.
Don't believe everything you hear.
Don't be too ready and willing to go in cahoot.
Don't try to cross a mountain in winter without snowshoes.
Don't for God's sake, let a hungry man pass your cabin.
Don't be stingy, selfish, or crabby.
Don't think for a minute you know where the gold is, for it's just where you find it.
Don't go out without a piece of candle in your pocket. You can always get a fire with a candle.[48]

Because his partner, C. A. Packard, was in Rampart, the writer Moore was spending the night alone in his cabin on No. 6 above, Miller Creek, in the Ireland mining district. He was eating beans, which he called strawberries, and reading *The Shadow of a Crime* by English author Hall Caine. Bill Joyce, who for a time held No. 24 above on Little Minook, had stopped in the previous morning and evaluated Moore's mining as not being either in or near the paystreak. Still, Moore was happy because he had gotten a nice little nugget that day.

A few days later, Moore worked out an agreement with Frank Canton to share claims. Moore gave Canton one-half of No. 15 above, Chapman Creek. Canton, who had been appointed federal marshal for the region but was not yet acting in that capacity, swapped one-half of his claim No. 1 on a pup (a tiny creek) off Little Minook Creek at No. 9. Moore regretted leaving his warm quarters on Miller Creek for a less cozy tent on a pup in the subzero cold of late December, but he acknowledged he had not come to Rampart for comfort. Earlier, he had refused an offer of a lease from McLain. Had he accepted, he estimated he would be making $25 a day.[49] McLain had just sold No. 9 above, Little Minook, for $10,000 to Philip Kaffenburg of Chicago and to Al Mayo, Archie Mitchell, and Frank Hawley, all of Rampart. In June 1898, Hawley purchased the shares of Kaffenburg and Mayo and sold No. 9 along with interests in Nos. 16, 27, and 28 above to the Rampart Gold Mining Company of West Virginia.[50]

Also in December 1897, some miners crossed the Yukon to Troublesome Creek. On December 14, J[ames] R. Austin, recorder for the creek, recorded his own Discovery claim that he subsequently transferred to W. P. Pinkham. F. G. Kress located No. 1, H.W. Cantwell, No. 2, and S. A. Mansfield, No. 3. Other claims ran along the right fork of the creek.[51] On December 27 nine miners, including O. C. Miller, N. P. R. Hatch, and Frank and Fred Gleason, formed the Minook Quartz Mining and Milling Company of Alaska. They issued stock certificates to themselves, but the company apparently soon failed.[52]

Learning to live in a mining camp brought about changes in personal lifestyles. Many men had never cooked before. Rex Beach remarked that not one in ten knew "how to toss a flapjack."[53] One day Mel Reed and John Powell were felling trees when a tree toppled onto their lunch bags. Later, they teased MacGowan, saying that their lunch biscuits, which he had baked, withstood the impact. Another time, a Mr. Holt of Boston, living in Pinkham's cabin, inquired of his friend, Tom, how to cook rice. Following Tom's explicit directions, Holt boiled a quart-and-a-half of rice in syrup in a two-quart pail. The rice swelled to such an extent that Holt needed several pans to contain it. After that, he reportedly chased Tom around town with a double-barrel shotgun.[54]

The miners often had little to do during long winter evenings. Rex Beach enjoyed listening to tales told by Bill Joyce, for whom he had worked for a while on Little Minook Creek at $5 a day plus board. Beach described Joyce as a former Texas Ranger, seventy years old, lean, and hawkfaced. After a ten-hour workday, Joyce loped twelve miles into Rampart three times a week to be with his lady friend. Other days, Joyce would amuse his workers in their tent with his accounts. Beach credited Joyce as the source for Beach's first story.[55]

Perhaps due to the inexperience of most miners, accidents happened frequently. A man named Schofield almost suffocated in a mine off Dawson Creek, but Blanchard, a Stanford man, used a windless to pull him out.[56] Frank Canton got hit in the eye while grinding an axe at Jim Langford's cabin on Little Minook. A few days later, he hurt his side. Chris Keenan saved C. A. Packard from death on Chapman Creek. A man named Allison lost his left eye on the same creek.[57] George Walter Sundborg, twenty feet down a shaft on Hunter Creek, watched his partner slowly lower three logs to him by windlass. The logs suddenly fell around him, but without hitting him.[58] Downstream on the ice-locked Nunivak Creek, Robert Chamberlin, Ed Allen, and F. A. Wert spent a whole night looking for Perry Judkins and [W. H.] Davis before finding them safe in an Indian dugout four miles from the *Dwyer*.[59]

The stress of prospecting, mining, and surviving in the harsh climate took its toll. Henry B. Tucker, a New Yorker and son of the owner of Troy Press, succumbed early. Like so many others, he had been aboard the *St. Michael*. He and John Powell ventured out prospecting. They kept on despite poor weather that inhibited travel. Tucker fell several times and finally collapsed, unable to proceed. Powell left him to go for help. When he returned with a rescue party, Tucker was dead. The group wrapped Tucker's body in a rubber blanket and buried it along the trail. Several months later, Tom Crawford and Mr. Welch transported the body to Rampart for a formal burial service, led by Mr. Hubbard of NAT&T. The coffin, enlarged to hold the misshapen, frozen body, was pulled on a sled to its final resting place, the first grave in the Rampart cemetery.[60]

Tragedies did not stop the men at Rampart, sometimes referring to themselves as the Ramparters, from their relentless search for gold. Miners and onlookers met at 3 p.m. on February 5, 1898, at the cabin at the mouth of Little Minook to organize the Montana Creek mining district. The creek, about seven miles east of Rampart, appeared to be a continuation of Little Minook Gulch, although split off from that gulch by Big Minook. The miners elected Sidney Cohen chairman, N. P. R. Hatch secretary, and Frank Canton recorder. Claims were restricted to 500 feet up and down the creek except for Canton's Discovery claim, which was allowed to be 1,000 feet. The representation period, twenty days of work for a value of $200, ran from January 1 to the next January 1.[61]

As days grew longer, the Ramparters intensified their prospecting, testing new creeks. On April 28, miners met in the cabin of Frank J. Franken and N. P. R. Hatch to organize still another mining district—Lenora Gulch, two-and-a-half miles above the mouth of Big Minook, and the second creek running into Big Minook from the north side. They elected George M. Reed chairman, John C. Powell secretary, and Frank J. Franken recorder. They agreed that any U.S. citizen over the age of twenty-one could stake a claim, but claims, except for Franken's Discovery claim, had to be limited to 500 feet. The representation period would be May 1 to May 1, later amended to January 1 to January 1, with assessment valued at twenty days of work or $200. Up to eight people could share interest in a claim, but each one with an interest had to do the required assessment. Reed filed for No. 3 above and immediately transferred ownership to the Klondike and Boston Gold Mining and Manufacturing Company of Colorado.[62] The age requirement on Lenora Gulch eliminated young George Walter Sundborg. An older man had actually jumped a townsite lot located by Sundborg, justifying his actions because Sundborg was under twenty-one. At a meeting called to review the case, the miners voted to give the lot back to Sundborg.[63]

About the same time, Hoosier Creek was being organized. James Langford apparently filed for the Discovery claim with the recorder, J. Walsh. According to creek rules, no man could locate more than one claim in the district.[64] The Miller Creek diarist jotted down that he joined the "wild rush" to Hoosier on the "31st" of April but decided not to locate a claim there.[65]

Evidently, some of the miners had been wondering where the ultimate source for the gold was. Charles I. Range sought that source. Range, who had traveled to Alaska on the *Eliza Anderson* and had been trapped by the Yukon River freeze-up, probably on the ice-bound *Merwin*, had reached Rampart by dog team in late March. He prospected eight miles from Rampart on a side gulch known as No. 9 Pup. The pup descended from a mountain divide between Little Minook valley and Hunter Creek at the upper end of Little Minook Creek claim No. 9 above and the lower end of No. 10 above. Ascending almost to the top of the gulch, Range found gold-bearing gravel that panned between seventy-five cents and $2.00. Range determined that the entire divide between Hunter and Little Minook creeks consisted of a gravel bed at least a mile wide. It was the bed of a prehistoric river, pictured by the editor of *The Rampart Whirl-*

pool, Mrs. [Clara] E. Wright, as "a river that was worthy of the great hairy mammoths that crashed through its streams and cooled their claws in its limpid waters . . . this old channel . . . must have been the grandfather or the great grandfather of the noble Yukon. . . ."[66]

Range called his Discovery claim Idaho Bar, and the name also was adopted for the entire bar. Mrs. Wright suggested that the old channel, considered the source of gold not only for Hunter and Little Minook creeks but possibly also for all the nearby creeks, be known as Range Channel.[67] Her proposal was not accepted.

The Miller diarist walked from 4 p.m. on May 2 to noon on May 3 to round up his friends so that all would locate claims on Idaho Bar as near as possible to the gold source.[68] Later, George MacGowan and Mel Reed took snowshoes to mount the high, almost vertical, side of the mountain to the old channel where the snow was so firm that they did not need their snowshoes. The exceptionally strong, cold wind at the summit, however, forced them to take shelter at times.[69]

The Idaho Bar miners convened on May 4 at the cabin of H. H. Honnen on No. 9 above, Little Minook. They selected H. A. Bigelow chairman, Edward Earle Keeley secretary, and John Burkman recorder for one year. They chose Range, John Folger, W. S. Harmon, P. B. Peterson, and W. A. Trinkle to draft the bylaws.

The enacted bylaws established the discovery date as May 2, 1898, and credited both Range and Harmon with the discovery. They set the limits of claims at 600 feet by 1,000 feet and specified that claims be identified by a name, not a number. The first representation period extended from May 1 to July 31, 1898; the second period from August 1, 1898 to December 31, 1899. Claims not represented by July 31 could be relocated by another prospector. Representation required a shaft twenty feet deep or an open ditch or cut twenty feet by six feet. Almost one hundred miners quickly filed their claims, named for people, places, planets, animals, or things. G. F. French and F. W. Graf jointly held two contiguous claims, the Clipper

and the Razor; Oliver Tingley shared the Florence T with George Hyde Preston; B. W. Moore, Jr. held the Virginia Girl; H. L. Beach, the Julia; L. E. Boukofsky, the Little Jack; Thomas Crawford, Old Crapps; Mel Reed, the Boston; and George MacGowan claimed the New Haven.[70]

Later, seven miners, including C. A. Packard, chairman, and B.W. Moore, Jr., secretary, formed the Virginia mining district for bench claims away from the creeks but near Idaho Bar. The district bordered on the Little Eldorado and Big Minook districts and the Red Stocking quartz mine. Each of the seven filed separately, and then eight met again to consolidate their claims into a single claim renamed the Portledge. They authorized Packard to dispose of the combined claim.[71]

On May 22, 1898, town recorder J. P. Bouscaren called to order a meeting to try Sidney Cohen on a charge of attempted murder of H. L. Beach. Beach complained that Cohen had tried to kill him with an axe. After hearing from witnesses Scott, Coffenburg (probably Kaffenburg), Hermanson, and Carlson, the miners voted thirty-five to fourteen to acquit Cohen of the charge against him.[72]

On June 5, Bouscaren chaired a meeting, called with little notice, to discuss fire safety. A. P. Ozouf proposed that unless all town property lots were cleared and the brush burned within three days, those uncleared lots would be available for relocation. O. C. Miller modified Ozouf's motion to exempt lots whose holders were collecting logs to construct a cabin and extended the limit to ten days. More than half of the Rampart residents petitioned in protest against the quickly convoked meeting. George Hyde Preston chaired another meeting on June 11 that voided the action of the earlier one, required Bouscaren to return the recording fees for all relocated lots, and permitted lot holders another thirty days to clear their lots. The meeting also established a committee to amend the townsite laws and develop a plan for governing Rampart. Named to the committee were M. W. Sinclair, George F. Howard, George MacGowan, Sam Hubbard, Jr., C. H. Knapp,

Figure 5. George Mel Reed and John C. Powell in mosquito gear during breakup in Rampart, 1898. Reed, Powell, and MacGowan built the cabin from logs they hauled one mile across the Yukon River. Courtesy of the George B. MacGowan Collection, University of Alaska Fairbanks. Accession Number 92-096-61.

Andrew Balliet, and Tom Urquhart.[73]

After breakup, steamers that had been ice-bound in sloughs downriver gradually resumed their interrupted journeys. Perry Judkins had left the *Dwyer* to take a carpentry job on the *Margaret*, an Alaska Commercial steamer. He rode on the *Margaret* to Rampart, arriving Saturday, June 18, at 6:30 a.m. His friend, Robert Chamberlin, followed on the *Dwyer*, reaching Rampart three days later.[74] The *W. K. Merwin*, with Thomas Wiedemann on board, had difficulty navigating through the whirling rapids below Rampart. When the steamer finally docked, Governor McGraw welcomed the passengers. Believing they had just come from Seattle, he asked them for news of the outside world. Wiedemann did not stay at Rampart, but

continued on to the Klondike, his destination.[75]

Back in Seattle, the Chamber of Commerce had decided to attract as much business as possible to make the Queen City, Seattle, the premier outfitter and departure point to Alaska and the Klondike. For months in late 1897 and early 1898, Erastus Brainerd, the energetic secretary for the chamber's Bureau of Information, bombarded cities, states, and Congress with his appeals and opinions. He promoted Alaska over the Klondike so the expected wealth from mining would remain in United States hands. Specifically, he urged American citizens to bypass the Canadian Klondike to develop the valuable Alaska gold fields at Birch Creek and Circle City, as well as the recent discovery on Minook Creek. He favored the

Figure 6. Unidentified Rampart miners sluicing winter tailings, 1898. Courtesy of the George B. MacGowan Collection, University of Alaska Fairbanks. Accession Number 92-096-35.

division of Alaska into two territories, with one containing the Yukon gold fields. He stressed that American citizens should outfit in an American city, Seattle, for the American gold fields in Alaska.[76] Brainerd adopted his own advice, spending the next year, from the summer of 1898 to the summer of 1899, in Rampart.

The property holders of Rampart assembled at 8 p.m. on August 6. They elected George Hyde Preston chairman, and Colin Beaton secretary. On behalf of the committee, Sam Hubbard read the report, which recommended trustees for the city. John H. McGraw proposed that the entire district and all nearby mines be considered the Rampart mining district. Those present accepted the committee's report, but the practice of naming each creek a separate mining

district continued. The meeting adjourned, only to reconvene immediately. McGraw suggested setting up an association. Thereupon, Beaton enrolled ninety-one members who elected five trustees: John H. McGraw, Sam Hubbard, George Hyde Preston, Andrew J. Balliet, and Harold Sturges.[77]

After that session, George MacGowan completed arrangements to leave Rampart for good, as had many others who had arrived a year before. Unwilling to continue to perform the hard work of prospecting and mining and no longer naively fantasizing about spending an anticipated fortune, MacGowan had already ended his partnership with Reed and Powell. He gradually sold off his town lots. His personal residence went to Phoebe Hoover, a schoolteacher from Pennsylvania. Just before departing on the *Thomas Power*, he appointed George M. Dunham, a fellow Delta Kappa Epsilon from Kenyon College, his attorney-in-fact to look after his claims.[78]

While people continued to arrive and depart during the summer travel season, those who stayed organized new mining districts. On August 31, 1898, seven miners formed the Garnet Creek district. They elected W. H. Davis chairman and recorder and B. W. Moore, Jr., secretary. They changed the creek name from Stephens to Garnet and acknowledged U.S. mining laws for assessment. They required the first assessment, a total of twenty days work building a cabin or sinking a shaft, to be completed by January 1, 1900. B. W. Moore, Jr. held the Discovery claim.[79] The next day, Perry Judkins, along with Ed Allen, Dave Filer, and Bob Chamberlin, stampeded to "Stevens" Creek.[80]

Trustee McGraw called the people together on September 7 to discuss the building and maintenance of a city hospital. Jules Prevost, the Episcopalian priest for the region, permitted the city to use mission land and donated $500 to the cause. In accepting Prevost's offer, the Rampart citizens agreed to construct the hospital and operate it until July 1, 1899, at which time the hospital would revert to the ownership and control of the Episcopal mission. The people appointed a committee of three for hospital management and another committee of three for fundraising.[81] About the same time, at the trustees' direction, Tom Crawford began selling at public auction town lots not cleared by the owners within the time prescribed.[82]

Among other new arrivals that summer and early fall were Volney Richmond; Lynn Smith; William (Will or Billy) B. Ballou; First. Lt. Edwin Bell, Eighth Infantry, U.S. Army; Wyatt and Josie Earp; H[enry] J. Roden; and Robert Hunter Fitzhugh.

Richmond, of Hoosick Falls, New York, traveled with friends Harlan Belden, a grocery clerk; Frank Stevens, a dry goods clerk; Dr. Bowen, and three others to Rampart via the White Pass trail, and west down the Yukon. Because of his age, Dr. Bowen did the cooking

and light camp duties while Richmond and Belden pulled the sled with their food supplies.[83]

Jeweler Lynn Smith, a Hoosier from New Castle, Indiana, also followed the Canadian route. He came with his good friend C[harles] J. Rozelle, nicknamed Jap, and short-time acquaintances J. H[arry] [Mace] Paget and a man named Anway. Prior to his trip, Smith had learned that Rampart was about a thousand miles from St. Michael and that John H. McGraw led it. He received a letter of recommendation to be given to McGraw and advice to pack a full set of jewelers tools to start a watch repair and cleaning business once there. Upon arrival, he immediately prospected on recently discovered Quail Creek with Paget and Belden while Jap, Richmond, and Dr. Bowen cleared lots. Richmond soon left to prospect on the Koyukuk River, surviving "Indian style"— without a tent and eating game.

In time, Smith noted that Paget was lazy and learned that Anway, also lazy, and Dr. Bowen were returning home. He quickly discovered that cleaning watches brought in more money than prospecting and regretted he had not brought a large supply of watches to sell. He felt discouraged that Rampart had fallen under the control of real estate men and speculators who were handling claims and town lots; that jobs were going only to men who had been in Rampart the previous winter; and that only three or four prospectors had found sizeable amounts of gold.

Yet Smith realized Rampart was still growing, and estimated a population of 2,500 by winter. Within a few months, 207 tents had been set up. Businesses had increased to eight large stores, including one owned by the company of Mayor Wood, one shoe store, three bakeries, and five saloons. The hospital was under construction, and each resident was requested to "volunteer" one day's work; wages were $10 per day. Smith attended the gala opening of the hospital but could not find a dancing partner comparable to his former Indiana girl friends. He liked the new health policy whereby for $1.00 per month residents received a certificate good for all hospital and physician services. Most of all, he had become attracted to "nice . . . old maid" Phoebe Hoover, who knitted, crocheted, and entertained him. In time, his admiration for her increased. He characterized her as the "greatest hustler [he had ever seen] wearing bloomers" because she brought to Rampart 144 pairs of wool socks that she had purchased elsewhere for 40 cents and sold in Rampart for $1.25, making a profit of $122.[84]

Newcomer William B. Ballou, with friend Sam Pease and former co-worker Julius Bode, waited on the West Coast for friends who were among a group of Bostonians sailing from Boston via the Strait of Magellan on the Chelsea Gold Mining Company's schooner *Julia E. Whalen*. The ship was sold after its arrival at San Francisco. The reunited Boston party did carpentry work on the steamer *Clara* for the California Northwest Trading and Mining Company in return for passage up the Yukon, ostensibly to Weare at the junction of the Yukon and Tanana rivers.

When the steamer reached Weare, Ballou and his two companions, along with part of the *Julia E. Whalen* group, including Frank Moses of Providence, Rhode Island, and his St. Bernard dog, Jack, decided to continue on to Rampart, leaving only some Chelsea Company Bostonians at Weare. By October 19, Ballou was building a lean-to of fir boughs and a cabin on Little Minook Junior Creek in minus-six-degree weather. Then he belatedly joined stampedes to Ruby and New Haven creeks, arriving at both too late to locate any ground.[85]

Lieutenant Bell, with a small detachment of soldiers, perhaps eight, started Camp Rampart. He paid Tom Urquhart and O. C. Miller $6,000 for a building to be used as a barracks.[86]

At St. Michael, Wyatt and Josie Earp boarded the *Governor Pingree* for Dawson. By the time the boat stopped at Rampart in September, ice was already forming on the Yukon and the *Pingree* crew began to hunt for a safe slough to winter in. Tex Rickard invited the Earps to stay in Rampart. In contrast to Lynn Smith, who viewed Rampart with a downhearted outlook, Josie Earp regarded the town as lively and optimistic.

The Earps rented an unfurnished log cabin near a creek from Rex Beach. They used packing crates for a table, spruce poles entwined together for a bed, and burlap sacks for rugs. When Wyatt went to work for Al Mayo, Josie decorated her temporary home with calico, draping the single window, curtaining off the bed, and covering the table. She became close friends with neighbors Mrs. [Mary] Llewelyn and Mary's sister, Agnes, and with Al Mayo's wife, whom she called Aggie.[87]

H. J. Roden apparently settled in Rampart about the same time. He located the Roden claim on Big Minook as of September 30.[88]

Mining engineer Robert Hunter Fitzhugh, known as Hunter, had already been "in country" for a year; first at Telegraph Creek, later at Lake Teslin. He had written his family in Lexington, Kentucky, in June, asking them to send future letters to him in Rampart. By October he and two partners were tramping through a mossy swamp nine miles from Rampart, backpacking 230 pounds of supplies, crosscut saws, picks, shovels, and bedding. His share was ninety-three pounds. Fitzhugh, old man Peterson, and Dr. J. H. Hudgin were intending to prospect on an unidentified creek twenty-five miles from Rampart, directly over the mountains. John Minook had told him about the creek, and Fitzhugh valued Minook's word, which was "as good as gold in this country."[89]

At Mike Hess Creek, low water levels and freeze-up trapped the twelve miners of the U.S. Mining, Development and Lumber Company of Cincinnati, who were headed to the Klondike in their flat-bottomed boat, the *Arctic Boy*. While water was still running during their enforced rest, they prospected through sluice boxes attached to the side of their boat.[90]

In late October, trustee McGraw convened another meeting of the Rampart citizens to announce the resignation of all the trustees. The people readily accepted their resignation and, after some deliberation, also concurred with the resignation of John Powell and Tom Crawford from the hospital committee. Charles Knapp, Mr. Osborne, and Mr. Warner were named to audit the books of both the hospital committee

Figure 7. Sluice attached to the Arctic Boy, *which wintered in Mike Hess Creek, 1898–1899. Courtesy of the Merritt N. Murphy Collection, University of Alaska Fairbanks. Accession Number 64-100-103.*

and the trustees. Harold Sturges moved to ask Lieutenant Bell to run town matters. The next day Sidney Cohen, Mr. Warner, and J. D. McDonald, designated trustees for the hospital, began a subscription drive for the hospital fund.[91]

Lieutenant Bell gradually assumed the lead role in governing the town, including continuing the series of public auctions of town lots. *The Rampart Whirlpool* expounded on Rampart's rapidly shifting forms of government, beginning with "pure democracy," adopting a "modified oligarchy," and then "came a Caesar who holds the power, powder, and peroxide. Rampart is the only city in the past 2,000 years that has reversed the usual order in arriving at stable government."[92]

Not all new residents adapted to Rampart. John Snell, from Sausalito, California, had brought in 1,500 eggs to start a restaurant business. Believing all the eggs had gone bad, he committed suicide. After his funeral, Ramparters ate the good eggs beneath the rotten layer.[93]

Less disastrous an ending happened when a newly arrived black man, William Dolly, was arrested for stealing. Lieutenant Bell saved him from a public lashing, sentenced him to eight months of hard labor, and put him to work on the woodpile under guard. Dolly was not adept at chopping wood, but he liked to entertain. When two doctors threw a community party,

22

they played the banjo while he danced and sang.[94]

Other new arrivals established new districts. On October 11, Perry Judkins and nine others assembled to form the district of Rock Creek, adjoining Garnet Creek at No. 10 below on the south side. Dave Filer was elected chairman; M. J. Ellithorpe, secretary; and Judkins, holder of the Discovery claim located in September, was elected recorder. The miners accepted the U.S. mining laws and agreed that assessment was one four-foot by six-foot shaft at least fifteen feet deep.[95]

The same day, Judkins, Robert Chamberlin, and six others organized the Mariposa Bar district, a five-mile-long bar that began at the fork of Garnet and Rock creeks at No. 10 below, Garnet. Judkins was elected chairman and Filer secretary and recorder. E[d]. C. Allen filed for the Discovery claim, also located in September.[96]

Still other miners, including Frank Stevens, the discoverer, and Nicklos Nelson, met on November 5 to set up Triple Creek, a tributary of Big Minook between Slate and Granite creeks. They restricted claims to 500 feet and designated assessment as one hole to bedrock within the times specified by U.S. mining laws. F. R. Howard was elected recorder.[97]

In yet another district, discoverer Harry "Mace" Paget had already organized Bear Creek, some twenty-five miles from Rampart, including all its pups except Langford and Little Bear. The bylaws stipulated that any Native could hold a claim. Jap Rozelle and Phoebe Hoover located claims on the south fork.[98] Lynn Smith reluctantly took over a claim from a Ramparter who could not pay Paget the $5.00 recording fee. He judged he had thrown his $5.00 away. Paget supposedly recorded 244 claims in all.[99]

Contiguous to Bear Creek district lay the Arroyo Grande district, which had similar rules. Recorder T. W. Davidson authorized his deputy, H. D. Fountain, to do the recording.[100]

Paget and Frank Trempe informed Lynn Smith of a quartz lode at Bear. According to Paget, a mining expert among his friends in the Sault

Ste. Marie crowd at Rampart had assayed the quartz and valued it at $256 a ton. Smith trekked to the creek only to find a warm spring at its head had flooded the area. He returned to Rampart where an expert named Miller sampled his quartz and rated it second-class marble. Bear Creek was barren. Paget had salted the creek.[101]

The Bear Creek miners tried and convicted Paget. He was held by Lieutenant Bell at the military garrison. While the offense merited incarceration in a prison, the miners did not want to go to Sitka for a formal trial, so they decreed Paget had to leave after breakup. Paget did not want his wife in California to learn of his arrest. Lynn Smith thought secrecy beyond Rampart was impossible since there were fifty or more reporters in Rampart. In Smith's opinion, someone would disclose Paget's situation. At Paget's request, Jap Rozelle visited him at the guard house. Paget asked that Rozelle and Lynn Smith appeal to Lieutenant Bell to release him without his meeting the posted $1,000 bail bond. He also told Smith that Lieutenant Bell had no case against him and, therefore, no right to confine him. For his part, Bell informed Smith that he had offered to accompany Paget to the quartz ledge and to observe Paget panning. Bell had promised that he would let Paget go if Paget uncovered gold. When Paget refused to make the trip, Bell locked him up, later saying, "The evidence was so convincing, I could do nothing else."[102] For exercise, Paget sawed wood. In time, Bell allowed Paget out to care for a man with scurvy on the condition that Paget report to Bell once a day.[103]

Surprisingly, miners continued to prospect Bear Creek but found nothing.[104] *The Rampart Whirlpool* editor compared Bear Creek to a seductive siren at the base of the "mammoth lode" in interior Alaska:

As the mythical gold of Bear Creek,
So is the gold that we spend
On a prize fight or a wrestling match
Or the dog that we buy from a friend.[105]

The Ramparters celebrated holidays as best they could. Josie Earp hosted Thanksgiving dinner for Tex Rickard, Mr. and Mrs. Tom

"Eckert" (Urquhart), General Carr, Erastus Brainerd, and Governor McGraw. McGraw stayed home to nurse a severely sprained ankle, but the others dined on ptarmigan, vegetables, fruits, doughnuts, pie, and cake. Josie and [Jennie] Urquhart packed a basket to take to McGraw. After starting out and losing their way in a blizzard, they cowered and cried together in underbrush until rescued by their husbands, Wyatt and Tom, a long two hours later.[106]

At Christmas time, "Captain Burke" (Lieutenant Bell) gave a party at Mrs. Llewellyn's restaurant. He requested assistance from the women to make it a festive occasion. They succeeded in transforming canned food, served on an oilcloth tablecloth, into a tasty dinner. Artistic "Mrs. Morse" (Jane W. Bruner) created placecards by drawing tiny snow scenes on red wallpaper, touched with gilt paint. In early January 1899, Lieutenant Bell arrested Mrs. Bruner for applying her gilt paint to change small stones into gold nuggets and black sand into gold dust. She was sentenced to leave Rampart after breakup.[107] She located claims as she waited.[108]

Through fall 1898 and spring 1899, many Ramparters left camp for short periods of time to prospect on the Koyukuk River, at least 150 miles away via the Dall or Tanana rivers. Hubbard of NAT&T grubstaked John Minook and his partner, Dan Carolan, to prospect on the Koyukuk.[109] John Folger had discovered Tramway Bar the previous February.[110] In September, Folger invited Frank Moses and eight others to take a ten-day trip to Tramway. Moses brought along his St. Bernard, Jack. Each man carried a fifty-pound pack of provisions—rice, bacon, hardtack, and tea—and two blankets. Each also had a tool—either a shovel, gold pan, rifle, snowshoes, or pots and pans. The dog Jack, who had never toted a pack, at first balked at fifty pounds of rice on his back. Moses beat him into submission, an act Moses regretted and Jack forgave, loyally and unconditionally accepting the load. As their provisions dwindled and snowfall hindered their progress, four men returned to Rampart. The other six and Jack continued on, losing their way. Their supplies gave out. They found little wood for fire; the cold deepened; they shot at but missed a caribou; they spotted no more game. They were out of food—except for the dog Jack.[111]

Hearing nothing about the missing men, dubbed the Folger party, Ramparters concluded that they were dead. Everyone in Rampart was surprised and delighted when the group returned on New Year's Day—until someone inquired about Jack. The rest of the story gradually unfolded. Their meal of Jack had only temporarily revived the group. On the verge of collapse from starvation and without hope, the group had straggled into Arctic City. Restored to health there, they had come back to Rampart without further incident by a mail trail along the Tanana River.[112]

The near-death experience of the Folger party did not stop others from heading off to the Koyukuk. Before leaving for the Koyukuk, Charles Range and Scott Harmon sold to Erastus Brainerd their individual Idaho Bar claims and their joint Eliza Anderson claim on a fork off Peterson's Pup.[113]

George Walter Sundborg accompanied Fred Holms, a long-time miner, into the Koyukuk. En route, they encountered nine of twelve members of a Boston party. The nine asked Sundborg and Holms to look out for the other three, who had gone ahead with few supplies. Later, on a tree in the foothills of the Endicott Mountains, the two found a message, "Hurry up; we're almost out of grub." Two days later, Sundborg, traveling on snowshoes, saw a small tent with wolverine tracks around it. Entering the tent, he discovered a dead man, along with a diary. The diary disclosed that the man had lived there five or six days; his wood was gone and he had become too weak to cut more. His last meal consisted of a boiled rawhide lace from his boot. A mile from the tent, Sundborg and Holms came upon the remains of a second man, partly frozen in the ice, the exposed part eaten by wolverines. Half a mile from there, they located the skeleton of a third man, almost totally devoured. They thawed a hole and buried all three bodies in it. Through a military officer at Fort Hamlin, they turned over $360 in

Figure 8. Coal bunkers at the Pioneer coal mine, 1899. Courtesy of the Merritt N. Murphy Collection, University of Alaska Fairbanks. Accession Number 64-100-84.

gold coin found at the scene to the remaining nine men, by then back in Boston.[114]

Still the residents searched for gold. Jumping and relocating claims were acceptable practices if a claim had been abandoned or if the assessment had not been completed within the required period. Often relocators were referred to as "lead pencil miners" since they posted their names on location notices at the claim in place of the earlier location notice. Lead pencil was the common writing implement. Ink, a valuable commodity, froze in winter.

On February 7, 1899, Russian Creek miners met to decide on disputed claims Nos. 50 and 52. At issue was whether the claimholder had performed the required assessment before January 1, 1899. Walcott was elected chairman;

J. C. Powell, secretary. First, Alex Anderson testified about his relocating No. 50 on January 19. Next, D. P. Nestor told how he staked No. 52 on January 2 because he saw no evidence of assessment. Michael Izzo supported Nestor's assertion. R. E. Beach, the previous owner of both claims, said he had begun holes on both claims on Christmas Day. When he hurt his ankle and found himself unable to continue working on the claims, he had returned to Rampart and had then gone to Little Minook Creek to do light work. He had come back to Russian Creek on January 23 to take up the assessment work. He submitted letters from Lieutenant Bell and C. H. Knapp, deputy recorder for the creek, stating that Beach had appeared before them on January 3 to tell them

Figure 9. Unidentified workers in the shaft house, Pioneer coal mine, 1899. Courtesy of the Merritt N. Murphy Collection, University of Alaska Fairbanks. Accession Number 64-100-38.

that he had been hurt and would finish the assessment later. C. C. Cunningham added that Beach had asked him in early December and again on January 3 to work on Russian Creek for him (Beach). Both J. D. McDonald and J. G. Crowley testified that they had seen Beach with a sprained ankle. Other testimony regarding Beach's intent to do assessment followed. George Dunham moved that claims 50 and 52 be returned to Beach. The motion lost. Perhaps unsympathetic to Beach's excuse because Beach had waited until one week before the deadline to begin his assessment work, the miners voted to give claim 50 to Anderson and 52 to Nestor. Beach protested the decision.[115]

Although the miners quarreled, they also liked to joke. On Valentine's Day, 1899, thirty-seven men, including Valentine Schmitt, filed a single claim for Colony Pup, a tiny creek on the north side of claim No. 1 on Pup No. 1 of Little Minook.[116] The joke soured. At a February 16 meeting of Little Minook claim holders at Louis Shequin's cabin, J. A. Monaghan, one of the Colony Pup group, spoke up. Not considering Monaghan a claim holder, John McGraw challenged his right to speak. General Carr then proposed that the Colony Pup claim holders be barred from voting. A committee was appointed to decide. The committee deliberated a few minutes in the brisk cold outside the cabin and reported back that Colony Pup holders could not vote.[117]

Meanwhile, lack of food and the ailments of winter took their toll on the Ramparters. The

Figure 10. *Unidentified miners at Weare (Tanana), November 1899. Courtesy of the C. S. Farnsworth Collection, University of Alaska Fairbanks. Accession Number 72-175-61.*

hospital became so crowded with patients sick from scurvy or frozen with loss of limbs that others needing hospitalization were refused entry.[118] Consequently, Lieutenant Bell set up a free hospital, staffed by an Army doctor with Bear Creek prisoner Harry Paget as cook.[119] By April, there were only seven patients convalescing there.[120]

Since its opening, the city hospital, while well used, had not raised sufficient funds to cover costs, most likely because by late winter all residents and business owners were struggling financially, having little for themselves and less for donations, and because the monthly $1.00 hospital certificates did not bring in enough revenue to meet expenses. Creditors gradually slapped liens on the hospital for unpaid debts— H. K. Harrison, a lien for $296 labor fees; J. D. McDonald, $344 labor foreman fees; Edward R. Gregg, M.D., and Frederick W. Jerauld, M.D., $255 for professional services and medical supplies; the Pennsylvania Klondike Drilling and Mining Company, $135, for lumber; John Johnson, $80 for carpentry; and nurse Annie

Figure 11. Freighter Sam Heeter in front of the Rex Beach cabin in Rampart, 29 June 1909. Courtesy of the Francis Pope Collection, University of Alaska Fairbanks. Accession Number 66-15-643N.

Beattie, $503.15, salary.[121] Bankrupt, the hospital shut down.[122]

According to *The Rampart Whirlpool*, a self-appointed committee that suspected embezzlement audited the books and, apparently to the committee's surprise, determined that all funds had been spent appropriately. If the committee had waited a few months longer, the *Whirlpool* article continued, the summer season would have brought more funding sources, thereby making the hospital debt-free. With the hospital's premature closure, its creditors would probably receive only a small percentage of the amount owed them.[123]

By the time the city hospital stopped services, word had swiftly spread that six "Boston boys" associated with the Chelsea Gold Mining Company's *Julia E. Whelan* group, who had disembarked at Weare, had hit pay dirt at Eureka Creek on the Tanana River side of the mountain divide, about twenty-five miles below Rampart.[124] *The Rampart Whirlpool* gushed that the discovery would "throw in the shade any

previous discovery in Alaska and assure, without question, the reputation of Rampart City as a most successful mining camp."[125]

The newspaper report identified the Boston boys as Elliot L. Gaetz, carpenter; W. S. Ramsey, clerk; Angus Hebb, carpenter; J. W. Moore, joiner; H[erbert] A. Russell, cigar maker; and J[ohn] Walsh, hostler. The fall before, they had poled dories up the Tanana River, only to lose many supplies when some of their boats overturned. After freeze-up, they pulled their remaining supplies by sled up Baker Creek to Hootlanana Creek and on to Eureka. By Christmas, they had erected a cabin. Then two fell ill with scurvy and another suffered broken ribs; a fourth cooked meals for all.[126]

Confined to the cabin without writing materials, John Walsh penned on birch bark a Christmas message to his friends in Boston, a poem which read in part,

> *No brimming bowl bedecked our board–*
> *No fancy dish was there;*

Few things and scant we could afford
To each, but a meted share.
Beans at morning, night and noon,
Not the Hub beans baked and brown,
But frozen in air on icy spoon,
And icewater washed them down.

Fresh dog was scarce and the price
was high;
And the bear was in the cave;
And these you know are the choice
supply,
That this glacier region gave.
Then naught had we that make known
the feast,
Of things so sweet and rare,
Some stony bread that knew not yeast,
Just staple Klondyke fare.[127]

Gaetz (a native of Nova Scotia not of Boston) and Ramsey continued the outdoor work on their cabin and on prospect holes. For months they prospected unsuccessfully until two Frenchmen passing by instructed them on how to crosscut and where to begin.[128]

With the news of the Eureka Creek strike, another stampede erupted. Rex Beach was working for John Crowley on Little Minook Creek when they heard about the strike. Crowley told friends on No. 9 above while Beach rushed on ahead with a sixty-pound pack of provisions for one week, blankets, and cooking gear. He dashed down Little Minook, then up to the headwaters of Big Minook where overflow slowed his stride. After an hour's rest at midnight, he pushed on to the divide, taking a tea break at 6 a.m. By noon he had neared the valley of the Tanana. He soon learned that the Boston boys had already claimed most of the ground. Worn out by the rapid pace he had set for himself, he proceeded to a creek several miles away.[129]

Without sleeping, Perry Judkins, Robert Chamberlin, Dave Filer, and Ed Allen sped up Garnet Creek to the divide of the Tanana and Minook and descended into Boulder Creek. As the word spread, others hurried over the divide. Stampeders staked more than three hundred

claims in three days, not only on Eureka but also on New York, Chicago, Omega, Pioneer, and other creeks.[130] Within days, the claims had been recorded in separate creek district records. The six Boston boys had located claims in almost every creek district. For instance, Elliot Gaetz held Discovery, Eureka; Herbert Russell, Discovery, New York.[131]

On April 14, Perry Judkins and his friends formed the district for Omega Creek, the first creek east of California Creek, running into Baker Creek. The district included all tributaries except Chicago Creek. Each claim holder was to make a trail through his claim by October 1, 1899, or pay $2.50 for someone else to do it.[132]

At a meeting held on April 15 on claim No. 1, California Creek, miners set out rules for Allan Creek (named for Peter Allan), which ran along the southeastern slope of the Tanana divide, west of California and emptied into Baker Creek. Charles A. Rice was elected chairman and recorder; Bernard Vogt, secretary. Each claim was limited to 500 feet. Assessment required twenty days of work, ten days of which might be for constructing a cabin. The assessment period followed the calendar year, January 1 to December 31. Peter Allan located No. 3 above; artistic Jane Bruner, No. 13 below; Thomas J. Murphy, No. 15 below, which he transferred to the Cleveland and Alaska Gold Mining and Milling Company on June 23.[133]

By April 26, there was a big stampede to Wolverine Creek. Perry Judkins staked No. 8 above.[134] On May 12, claim holders for Montana Bar, between Alameda and Kentucky creeks, selected names for their claims. Jay Whipple served as recorder.[135]

The miners hired Hunter Fitzhugh at $15 a day to survey a trail from Rampart to the Eureka-Baker area, which he calculated to be 26.9 miles away. To do the work, he used a standard four-inch compass, measured with a three-eighth-inch rope. He moved through the dense stands of alder and spruce with snowshoes, and camped out for three nights with no stove. He also drew a comprehensive map of the route.[136]

Needing money, Perry Judkins undertook a job at the end of May 1899, with Tom Drew at the Pioneer coal mine on the Yukon about thirty miles above Rampart across from Mike Hess Creek. He worked for board and $7 for a ten-hour day, summer rate; $5, an eight-hour day, winter rate. His first tentmate was [J. J.] Kirkbride. The mine had a seventy-five-foot shaft and a 150-foot drift into the hill. Two coal bunkers held 160 tons of coal, eighty tons each. In early August, the workers put a lien on the mine for unpaid wages. Judkins continued at the mine, which produced 3.5 tons of coal in a two-week period. Steamers, including the revenue cutter *Nunivak*, stopped to take on coal through the summer months.[137]

As people moved in and out by steamer on the Yukon during the summer travel season, speculation surfaced over a strike at Cape Nome. Hunter Fitzhugh did not believe in its possibilities. From "discouraging" information, he considered Nome the most desolate area in the world, with "not a stick of timber as big as a broomstick."[138] Perry Judkins held a similar opinion. Although he knew hundreds were staking claims, he compared Cape Nome to Rampart, each with a few good claims, and noted that there had been a big rush to Nome all summer. To him, Nome was either the "biggest find ever or no good at all." Judkins concluded, "Alaska is famous for having the most and biggest liars on earth."[139] Lynn Smith, however, commented that everyone was at Cape Nome where rockers on the ocean beach produced $8 to $30 a day. He thought Jap Rozelle was in Nome, but, instead, Rozelle had gone on to Seattle, since Nome was apparently "not so good" as reported. At the same time, Smith traveled to Indiana and informed his family that Nome was very rich.[140]

Among others leaving Rampart—some to Nome, some to outside Alaska—were Josie and Wyatt Earp, Erastus Brainerd, Phoebe Hoover, the Urquharts, former Governor McGraw (supposedly with an estimated $75,000) and Ballou's friends, Pease and Bode.[141] Brainerd and McGraw retained their claims.

On the other hand, more soldiers came. After he completed his 1897 inspection of the mining camps on the American Yukon, Captain Ray had recommended that a small military presence of sixty men be established in Alaska to control lawlessness in the camps. In particular, he proposed that there be a military post on the north bank of the Yukon below the mouth of the Tanana River about eighty miles below Rampart near Weare, a NAT&T outpost where, in 1897, Ray had found spruce logs in place for a cabin foundation and a population of zero. Ray had set aside land for a military reservation, ten miles square. He requested six Canadian horses and one hundred reindeer for the post. He viewed reindeer as being more useful in winter than horses or dogs.[142]

The War Department concurred. On May 10, 1899, the Department designated that part of Alaska lying north of the sixty-first parallel of north latitude as the District of North Alaska and appointed the promoted Major Ray district commander. Ray, quickly raised to colonel, established Fort Egbert in Eagle.[143] In the late summer of 1899, Captain Charles S. Farnsworth, commander of Company E, Seventh Infantry, arrived in Weare to begin the new post of Fort Gibbon, named in honor of Brig. Gen. John Gibbon. By October, Captain Farnsworth had not yet encountered anyone who had mined gold successfully. He acknowledged that there was gold in the ground, but estimated that only one in five thousand found gold in paying quantities.[144]

A small, remote detachment from Farnsworth's company under First Lt. Benjamin J. Tillman replaced Lieutenant Bell in Rampart.[145] Bell received orders assigning him to Manila, Philippines.[146] Tillman did not assume Bell's authority in Rampart. Instead, Rampart reverted to civilian administration. Dr. Clarence E. Danforth was elected its first mayor on September 2, 1899. Others elected were C. H. Knapp, judge; Crawford, recorder; Walbridge, treasurer; and three trustees.[147]

By this time, Hunter Fitzhugh regularly attended Episcopalian church services. On at least one occasion there was a congregation of four—Jules Prevost; E. J. Knapp, who was in charge of the mission; Fitzhugh; and a small Indian boy. During the week, Fitzhugh worked No. 12 above, Hoosier, with George Hyde Preston, gold fields correspondent for the *Seattle Post-Intelligencer*. Even though he did not care for the articles Preston wrote, Fitzhugh admitted that they were published and that Preston received money for them. Their cabin library held works by Shakespeare, Browning, Longfellow, Scott, and Pepys. Other miners borrowed their books.[148]

Rex Beach became one of the many who left Rampart in 1899, apparently never to return.[149] Nevertheless, memories of his Rampart days stimulated his fertile imagination. His second book, *The Barrier*, a popular seller adapted for at least three film versions, recounts life, authentic and fictive, in Flambeau (Rampart in disguise).[150]

As its title intimates, the novel highlights barriers to interracial, cross-cultural romance and to women, especially Native women. The setting somewhat duplicates "mud hen" Rampart as Beach experienced it, with food shortages and starvation, even affecting "others who had wandered in from the Koyukuk . . . the taste of dog meat still fresh in their mouths" (an indirect reference to the end of poor Jackdog).[151]

At the beginning of the novel, Flambeau is a tiny Alaska settlement on the Yukon with one store, about one hundred men, mostly unsuccessful prospectors, and a small military garrison with the American flag on its pole.[152] The store owner is an Al Mayo-like figure named John Gale, the name of a real Ramparter. Gale has a Native wife, Alluna, and a beautiful elder daughter, Necia, who had recently returned from an unidentified mission school downriver, presumably the Roman Catholic mission school at Koserefski.[153] Gale readily extends credit to the residents as Beach once owed Mayo on account.[154]

The romantic hero, Lt. Meade Burrell, similar to Lt. Edwin Bell, descends, notwithstanding his Union first name, from a Confederate family in Kentucky, a family heritage resembling that of Hunter Fitzhugh. Burrell intervenes to save from public whipping a black man convicted by the miners of stealing a crate of hams.[155] The selfless protagonist, Napoleon, or 'Poleon, Doret, parallels the character 'Poleon Compeau, created by Canadian journalist Dave King.[156] Shakespeare George lends books to Necia, probably an allusion to George Hyde Preston and his cabin library. Character Father Barnum, directly associated with Rev. Francis Barnum, S. J., aboard the mission boat, eventually rescues Necia and 'Poleon from a tiny boat. Necia rushes along a short cut via Black Bear Creek, a take-off of Paget's Bear Creek, to beat a stampede to Lee's Creek, discovered by "No Creek" Lee, a one-eyed prospector like Allison. Lee's Creek bylaws expressly exclude women from locating claims, perhaps a reminder that Sally Minook and Susan did not locate on Julia Creek and that Little Minook Creek bylaws barred Indians except for John Minook. Burrell steps in and locates a claim as Necia's attorney-in-fact. After the stampede, Flambeau expands rapidly, with tents and cabins sprouting up almost overnight.

Josie Earp guessed that Beach patterned the brawling villain Ben Stark after Wyatt Earp.[157] Stark may have been a composite of Earp, Tex Rickard, other gamblers like Frank L. Werner and J. F. Barneyberg, or even Bill Dougherty.[158] Beach never identified his models, yet obviously, he wrote from his knowledge, acquaintanceships, and experience.

The Barrier fittingly summed up life in a mining camp on the Yukon River in Interior Alaska as the nineteenth century drew to a close.

End Notes Chapter 1. Discovery Period, 1894–1899.

Short Titles

The following shortened forms referring to depositories and series are used extensively through the chapter endnotes.

Archives, UAF	Alaska Archives and Manuscripts, Alaska and Polar Regions Department, Elmer E. Rasmuson Library, University of Alaska Fairbanks.
District Recorder, Fairbanks	State of Alaska Department of Natural Resources, Office of the Commissioner, District Recorder, Fairbanks, Alaska.
Division of Mining, Fairbanks	State of Alaska Department of Natural Resources, Division of Mining, Fairbanks, Alaska.
(folder)	A copy of a creek record, dated between 1896 and 1900, at the office of the District Recorder, Fairbanks. The original is retained at the office of the State Recorder, Anchorage, Alaska.
Fort Gibbon	Fort Gibbon recording district records at the office of the District Recorder, Fairbanks, Alaska.
Manley	Manley Hot Springs recording district records at the office of the District Recorder, Fairbanks, Alaska.
Rampart	Rampart recording district records at the office of the District Recorder, Fairbanks, Alaska.
U.S.G.S.	U.S. Geological Survey.

1. Perry Judkins to Alice Weston, 11 September 1898, Perry Judkins Collection, box 1, folder 1, Archives, UAF. Judkins, a native of Maine, became a miner in and around Mariposa County, California, where he met Alice Margarette Weston. He went to Alaska in 1897 to acquire gold to finance their marriage. His letters to Alice form the backbone of the collection. He left Rampart, Alaska, in mid-1901, without any fortune, his finances about the same as when he started his Alaska venture. He and Alice married on Christmas Day, 1901, and settled in Mt. Bullion, California.

2. The miners of the period estimated Rampart to be one thousand miles from St. Michael, based on the Yukon River course as it was then. A 1994 computer program used by the Forestry Department, Tanana Chiefs Conference, analyzed data on the river course as it is today and computed the distance as 895 river miles.

3. *The Rampart Whirlpool,* 1, no. 1, presumably dated 15 January 1899, Perry Judkins Collection, box 1, folder 18. The story of Minook Creek appears in *The Whirlpool.* Although all miners of the discovery period credited John Minook with the original discovery, they provided no information pinpointing the actual date of his discovery. At the time, gold averaged $16 an ounce, so a prospecting pan valued at $1.50 indicated the ground had good potential. *The Whirlpool* stated the discovery occurred "some years ago." Also, Mim Dixon,

"History–Rampart, Alaska," in *Baan O Yeel Kon Corporation Shareholder Handbook* (Fairbanks: Baan O Yeel Kon Corporation, 1980), (cited with permission), 3. Dixon places the discovery "about 1894," which fits well with the arrival of Langford and others in the fall of 1894. The year 1893, given in currently accepted historical datelines, evidently is an approximation reached many years after the fact. The spelling of Minook in correspondence and records varies considerably, as Manook, Mynook, and Munook as well as Minook. The miners honored John Minook by naming (Big) Minook, Little Minook, and Little Minook Junior creeks and Minook City after him.

4. *The Rampart Whirlpool* [15 January 1899]. The article also lists Joe Macguire, [M. W.] Sinclair, Al Cochran, Ike Long, and "others." The location records for Hunter Creek are not available. The miners usually designated the point or claim on which gold was first discovered on a creek as Discovery.

5. Rampart, Bylaws of Rampart Mining District: Little Minook and Hunter Creek Bylaws (folder), District Recorder, Fairbanks, 1. The bylaws appear to have been copied to incorporate the 1898 amendments. During the early years in and around Rampart without a U.S. commissioner in the region, the miners followed the organization pattern used at Little Minook Creek in April 1896. They conducted meetings according to parliamentary procedures with motions, seconds, and

voting on the motions, which either carried or lost. They often elected a chairman, secretary, and creek recorder at the meeting and set their own rules in formal articles and bylaws, creek by creek, for claim size and assessment, rules which sometimes were stricter than or at variance with the prevailing U.S. mining laws. The normal numbering system for claims started with Discovery. Claims to the left or downstream of Discovery were below Discovery, No. 1 below being directly adjacent to Discovery; claims to the right or upstream of Discovery were above Discovery, No. 1 above being directly adjacent to Discovery. Claims on small tributaries of discovered creeks were often numbered No. 1, No. 2, and so forth from the junction of the tributary with the creek without another Discovery claim or the above and below designations.

6. Rampart, Little Minook Creek (folder), vol. 2, District Recorder, Fairbanks, 1, 4, 9, 19. The records in this book were copied from an earlier book. There are three associated folders. The first folder, vol. 2, contains locations of claims on Little Minook Creek. The second folder, probably book 3, concentrates on claims on its tributaries; the third, also designated vol. 2, appears to be an index of the other two.

7. *The Rampart Whirlpool* [15 January 1899]. Also, Rampart, Little Minook Creek (folder), 2: 21, 23, 28. *The Whirlpool* article refers to "Stevens" on No. 7, but the creek record cites Charles Stephan. The creek record reveals John Sally filed for No. 8 on 29 July 1896, and William S. McLain (elsewhere McLane) for No. 9 on 28 July 1896.

8. Rampart, Little Minook Creek (folder), 2: 44, 60.

9. Rampart, Minook Creek (townsite) (folder), vol. 1, District Recorder, Fairbanks, 1.

10. Ibid., 2.10.

11. Robert Hunter Fitzhugh, letter to his family in the form of a diary, 24 December 1899, Robert Hunter Fitzhugh Collection, box 1, folder 22, Archives, UAF. Mayo told Hunter Fitzhugh about his experience in Georgia in "1863." The Mayo family genealogy (cited with permission) lists Al Mayo as born in Brownville, Maine, 18 July 1846. About 1874, he married Margaret (whose Indian name was Neehunilthnoh).

12. Rampart, Minook Creek (townsite) (folder), 1: 2, 4, 12. Liege had lot 8, block 6; Moses, lot 2, block 7; Henry, lot 4, block 7; Joe, lot 5, block 7; and Lines, lot 6, block 7. Many of the Indians had not yet adopted the white practice of having last names. The record lists at least twenty-six individuals receiving lots in June 1897; many more received lots during the remainder of 1897.

13. James Albert Johnson, *Carmack of the Klondike*

(Fairbanks: Epicenter Press, 1990), 79.

14. "To Seek Fortune: Pilgrims Start Today for Mammon's Shrine," *The Seattle Post-Intelligencer*, 22 July 1897. At least twenty people on the published passenger list went to Rampart, not to the Klondike.

15. Ibid., 11 August 1897. W. E. Harmon appears elsewhere as W. S. Harmon and once as Scott Harmon.

16. Thomas Wiedemann (The Klondike Kid), *Cheechako into Sourdough* (Portland, OR: Binfords & Mort, 1942), 13.

17. *The Seattle Post-Intelligencer,* 31 July, 15 and 19 August 1897.

18. Ibid., 5 August 1897.

19. Terrence Cole, *Crooked Past: The History of a Frontier Mining Camp: Fairbanks, Alaska,* (Fairbanks: University of Alaska Press, 1991), 7.

20. George P. MacGowan's diary, 73, George P. MacGowan Collection, box 1, folder 1, and incomplete manuscript, 203–05, ibid, box 1, folder 2, Archives, UAF. George MacGowan kept a dairy during his year-long stay in Rampart. MacGowan was born in San Francisco in 1863. His father, an immigrant from Scotland, served in the U.S. Army, so the family moved from post to post. During his youth, MacGowan spent time in New Haven, Connecticut, his mother's home town, and later attended Middlebury College in Vermont, where he was in the Delta Kappa Epsilon (DKE) fraternity. In Alaska, he considered New York City his home but was glad whenever he met fellow DKE fraternity brothers in Rampart. The collection lists the association members who paid $200 each. They were fully reimbursed after the sale of the *St. Michael* for $12,000. Also, *Seattle Post Intelligencer*, 5 August 1897, and Rampart, Minook Creek (townsite) (folder), 1: 16. Many names match names on the *Cleveland* passenger list of 5 August 1897, and names on the townsite list as of 8 September 1897. The 8 September enrollment suggests an arrival date of 7 September, not 14 September.

21. Cole, 9.

22. MacGowan's diary, 75, George P. MacGowan Collection.

23. Ibid., 73, 75. Rampart, Minook Creek (townsite) (folder), 1: 65. The real estate transaction for lot 2, block 6, from D. F. Baxter to MacGowan, Powell, and Reed took place on 14 September 1897.

24. Rampart, Little Minook Creek (folder), 2: 1–3, 143. NAT&T operated river steamers on the Yukon and a chain of stores or trading posts in settlements along the river. A $1.00 sale made the transaction legal. There may have been other, unspecified considerations that Hubbard, who represented NAT&T in Ram-

part for about a year, received from NAT&T.

25. Ibid., 35–36, 96–99, 139, 141.

26. MacGowan's diary, 75-81, 85, George P. MacGowan Collection. Frank Gleason, his wife, and adult son, Fred, came on the *St. Michael.*

27. MacGowan's diary, 83, 85, George P. MacGowan Collection. The partnership, actually signed on 8 October 1897, extended until 31 December 1898. Rampart, Minook Creek (townsite) (folder), 1: 20. Reed bought lot 1, Powell, 2, and MacGowan, 3 in block D–A.

28. Rampart, Julia Creek (folder), District Recorder, Fairbanks, no pagination. After the minutes of the 18 September 1897 meeting, the entries are mostly by claim number.

29. Rampart, Russian Creek (folder), District Recorder, Fairbanks, entries of 30 September 1897 and 11 May 1898. Because of dissatisfaction with recorder Rosewall, the Russian Creek miners met again on 11 May 1898 with Dr. Sidebottom, chairman, and Fred Gleason, secretary. They elected Hall the new recorder and began reconstructing the records.

30. Rampart, Minook Creek (townsite) (folder), 1: 4, 5, 10, 14.

31. Rampart, Chapman Creek (folder) District Recorder, Fairbanks, 1, 2, 5–6, 8, 32. The P. E. (sic) Beach claim was next to John Crowley's claim No. 3 below. Rex Beach and Crowley often held adjoining claims.

32. Rampart, Big Minook Creek (four folders with consecutive pagination), District Recorder, Fairbanks. Bylaws and Wiehl's Discovery claim filed for hydraulic mining, 1: 1–2, 10; claim No. 128, 3: 191; Klondyke company offer, 4: 306–07. Rampart, Minook Creek (townsite) (folder), 1: 12, 29. The Klondyke company held lot 8, block 10, as of 11 December 1897.

33. Rampart, Big Minook Creek, 2: 119. On 23 August 1899, Joe Wiehl sold one-half of his Discovery claim to William Smith in return for Smith doing assessment work and prospecting on the claim.

34. MacGowan's diary, 123, 127, 129, 137, 139, 143, 217, 219, George P. MacGowan Collection. MacGowan did not identify the firm of Addick of Baltimore, but the tenor of his entry indicated that the company or bank was most likely a large financial institution, well known at that time.

35. Rampart, Little Minook Creek (folder), 2: 23–27. The last two transactions suggest Carr alone purchased the claim, but McGraw seems to have been co-owner. Newspapers and some collections, including MacGowan's, indicate a common, prevailing assumption that the claim belonged to both Carr and McGraw and that it was a rich one.

36. Wiedemann, 63, 71, 72, 75, 80. Rampart, Minook Creek (townsite) (folder), 1: 20. Scott Harmon somehow reached Rampart ahead of the others on the *Eliza Anderson.* He held lot 7, block D–A, as of 26 September 1897. Rev. [Francis] Barnum, S.J., "The Yukon Delta Region," 1897, in *Alaska-Yukon Magazine,* January 1908, 422. Barnum uses the spelling Nunapithlugak.

37. Judkins to Alice, 2 October [1897], Perry Judkins Collection, box 1, folder 1.

38. Ibid. Also, Lynn Smith to Mother, 2 August 1902, Herbert Heller Collection, box 1, folder 5, Archives, UAF. Lynn Smith sometimes used NAT&T letterhead with the Fort Get-There address.

39. Judkins to Alice, 23 July 1898, Perry Judkins Collection, box 1, folder 5; Robert Chamberlin's diary, entries of 24 February–1 March 1898, ibid., box 1, folder 6; steamer *Navarro* passenger association, entries of 7, 15–18 October and 2 November 1897, ibid., folder 12. There is no Nunivak Creek (also reported as Nunivak Slough, Nunivak Bar), but the location corresponds to Nanvaranak Slough. See Donald S. Orth, *Dictionary of Alaska Place Names,* Geological Survey Professional Paper 567 (Washington: U.S. Government Printing Office, 1967), 673.

40. R. A. Alger, Letter from the Secretary of War: Alaska Gold Fields, 13 December 1897, 55th Cong., 2d sess., S. Doc. 14, Wickersham Collection 7769A, Archives, UAF. The letter responds to a Senate resolution of 9 December 1897. It contains the report of Captain P. H. Ray and Lt. W. P. Richardson, Eighth U.S. Infantry, "Relative to the Condition of Affairs in the Alaska Gold Fields."

41. Rex Beach, *Personal Exposures* (New York: Harper & Bros., Publishers, 1940), 46. *Personal Exposures* is Beach's autobiography and contains many reminiscences from his life in Alaska. Also Rampart, Minook Creek (townsite) (folder), 1: 22. R. E. Beach had lot 20, block K as of 8 October 1897.

42. MacGowan's diary, 131, George P. MacGowan Collection.

43. Ibid., 141.

44. George Sundborg, *Our Family: Described from What I Have Been Able to Find Out about It* (Washington, D. C.: privately published, 1970), (cited with permission), 97–100. Rampart, Minook Creek (townsite) (folder), 1: 16, 26. An E. L. Holt held lot 7, block F as of 8 September 1897 and an F. P. Holt held lot 8, block M2, on 2 December 1897.

45. Rampart, Minook Creek (townsite) (folder), 1: 94, 100, and Rampart, Big Minook Creek 1: 30.

46. MacGowan's diary, 111, George P. MacGowan Collection.

47. Judkins to Alice, 11 September 1898, Perry Judkins Collection, box 1, folder 1.

48. Rampart, Miller Creek (folder), District Recorder, Fairbanks, entry of 13 December 1897, no pagination. The writer is not readily identifiable, but he appears to be B. W. Moore, Jr., who is not listed as a passenger on the *St. Michael*, but W. G. Pinecoffin had two shares, one of which may have been Moore's.

49. Ibid., entries of 13, 17, 18, and 22 December 1897 and 1 February 1898. Rampart, Julia Creek (folder). The Julia Creek record refers to Miller Creek as being in the Ireland mining district, probably named for Preston Ireland. Rampart, Chapman Creek (folder). B. W. Moore, Jr., held No. 15 above. Also, MacGowan's diary, 101, George P. MacGowan Collection. MacGowan wrote that Canton had been appointed the marshal for the district. He thought that Canton was a good man for the job. Further, Rampart, Little Minook Creek (folder), 2: 70–73. Joyce filed for No. 24 above on 12 August 1897 and sold one-half interest in it to E. M. Carr on 12 September 1897. He sold the other half to Carr on 26 July 1898. Rampart, Little Minook Creek (folder), 3: 15. Canton's claim No. 1, located on 24 November 1897, was on the right hand fork of Peterson's Pup.

50. Rampart, Little Minook Creek (folder), 2: 28–30, 133, 136. Like No. 8 above, No. 9 above had a reputation for being a rich claim.

51. Rampart, Troublesome Creek (folder), District Recorder, Fairbanks, no pagination.

52. Rampart, Julia Creek (folder). The other five miners were T. S. Urquhart, Peter Johnson, F[rank] J. Franken, A. J. Beecher, and G. W. Thompson.

53. Beach, *Personal Exposures*, 46.

54. MacGowan's diary, 95, 109–11. George P. MacGowan Collection.

55. Beach, *Personal Exposures*, 37–38.

56. MacGowan's diary, 159, George P. MacGowan Collection.

57. Rampart, Miller Creek (folder), entries of 6, 10, and 19 January and 10 February 1898.

58. Sundborg, 100.

59. Chamberlin's diary, entry of 3 January 1898, Perry Judkins Collection, box 1, folder 6.

60. Cole, 10. Also, MacGowan's diary, 73, 183–87, 191, George P. MacGowan Collection. The second burial took place on 15 March 1898. MacGowan took photographs of the gravesite for Tucker's family.

61. Rampart, Montana Creek (folder), District Recorder, Fairbanks, no pagination. Present at the organizing meeting were John Burkman, A. McKinzie, F. J. Franken, F. M. Canton, Sidney Cohen, N. P. R. Hatch, John Minook and his son, and "numerous outsiders."

Most of the first claims were abandoned and relocated in 1900 by other miners. At a meeting at W. G. Thronson's cabin on Big Minook Creek on 24 March 1900, the creek miners decided that U.S. mining laws would govern the district, and they elected John Niven recorder, replacing John Bock, who had replaced Canton.

62. Rampart, Lenora Gulch (folder), District Recorder, Fairbanks, no pagination. The bylaws were passed on 28 April 1898. The requirement that all co-owners fulfill representation changed a prevalent practice of only one representation, regardless of how many people owned a share in a claim. On 17 August, George MacGowan moved to change the representation period. In Deed #2, 15 May 1898, Reed gave his claim to the Colorado company, presumably the same firm he had dealt with before, with a slightly changed name.

63. Sundborg, 100.

64. Rampart, Gunnison Creek and Tributaries (folder), District Recorder, Fairbanks, no pagination. Undated Hoosier Creek bylaws are at the back of the folder. There is no separate Hoosier Creek record.

65. Rampart, Miller Creek (folder), entry of 6 July 1898.

66. *The Rampart Whirlpool* [15 January 1899]. The editor was Mrs. C. E. Wright, sole owner and publisher. Her designation, Range Channel, was never accepted. Also, Rampart, Idaho Bar (folder), [vol. 2], District Recorder, Fairbanks, 22. The editor was probably Clara E. Wright who located the Doris claim on Idaho Bar on 27 September 1898.

67. *The Rampart Whirlpool* [15 January 1899].

68. Rampart, Miller Creek (folder), entry of 6 July 1898.

69. MacGowan's diary, 203–07, George P. MacGowan Collection.

70. Rampart, Idaho Bar (folder), [vol. 1], a copy prepared for Erastus Brainerd, District Recorder, Fairbanks, double pagination, (printed numbers used for reference), 19–23, 46, 53, 81, 83, 98, 113, 115–16, 146.

71. Rampart, Miller Creek (folder), entries of 15 and 30 August 1898. The other miners were J. L. Holland, Sunrise; J. J. Daily, Daily claim; E. Bartlett, Sunset; Charles M. Robinson, the Josephine; and later N. Degginger with W. G. Pinecoffin, and Leonard N. Moore had the Garnett; Packard held the Bessie. Also, Rampart, Idaho Bar (folder), [2]: 62, 88. S. S. Fertig relocated the Portledge on 5 March 1900 and immediately sold it to G. S. Stevenson. At that time, the Portledge was in the Idaho Bar district.

72. Rampart, Minook Creek (townsite) (folder), 1: 183, 26, 31. In some other entries, H. L. Beach ap-

pears closely associated with R. E. Beach such that H. L. may be R. E. This entry by Ed Patterson, secretary of the meeting, did not give the details of the actual incident or the testimony or first names of the witnesses. Philip Kaffenburg (sometimes seen as Kaffenburgh) held lot 1, block M2, as of 24 November 1897; Isaac and Walter Kaffenburg held lots 10 and 11, block Q.

73. Rampart, Minook Creek (townsite) (folder), 1: 184–186. Also, MacGowan's diary, 229, George P. MacGowan Collection. MacGowan made a brief note about being on the committee.

74. Judkins to Alice, 23 July 1898, Perry Judkins Collection, box 1, folder 5; Judkins's journal, entries of 18 and 21 June 1898, ibid., box 1, folder 7.

75. Wiedermann, 163.

76. Erastus Brainerd, *Alaska and the Klondyke*, Archives, UAF, microfilm. See also Rampart, Journal 1898–1901, District Recorder, Fairbanks, 84. Brainerd purchased lot 2, block 9 for $800 from Henry F. Thumm on 13 September 1898.

77. Rampart, Minook Creek (townsite) (folder), 1: 139–40. The text of the Hubbard report is not given.

78. MacGowan's diary, 145, 151, 195, 257, 259, 261, George P. MacGowan Collection. MacGowan left on 23 August 1898 and apparently never returned. Also, Rampart, Journal, 16–17, 52, 53, 62, 121. MacGowan conducted several real estate transactions. For a 49 percent commission, Dunham from Cleveland was to represent MacGowan's claims, specifically, No. 23, Dawson Creek; No. 15 above, Rampart Creek; No. 7 below, Chicago Creek; No. 27 above, Alder Creek; one-fourth interest in No. 4, left-hand pup, Alder Creek; No. 5, Hi'yu Creek; and No. 7 above, Lenora Creek. There is no indication that any of those claims was ever productive. Powell and Reed remained in Rampart for a few more years; their names appear in several records of the period. Phoebe Hoover bought many lots during fall 1898, according to several entries in the Journal.

79. Rampart, Garnet Creek (folder), District Recorder, Fairbanks, 8–11, 32, 80. The other miners were A. B. Austin, William Pike, Jacob Kroeker, J. L. Holland, and George Milfs. J. H. Green relocated Discovery on 3 January 1900. Chamberlin, who located No. 10 below, later became deputy recorder. The record also contains an insert with a few relocations on Rock Creek.

80. Judkins's journal, entry of 1 September 1898, Perry Judkins Collection, box 1, folder 7.

81. Rampart, Minook Creek (townsite) (folder), 141. The management committee consisted of Tom Crawford, John Powell, and one other; the fundraisers were Harold Sturges, Sidney Cohen, and a man named Williams.

82. Rampart, Journal, 80. Many public auctions of confiscated lots were held during the fall of 1898 and the spring of 1899.

83. Kitchener, L. D., *Flag over the North: The Story of the Northern Commercial Company* (Seattle: Superior Publishing Co., 1954), 9. Through contacts made at Rampart, Richmond became an employee of the Alaska Commercial Company and, ultimately, long-time president of the Northern Commercial Company. Frank Stevens remained, for the rest of his life, an active member initially of Rampart and later, of the Hot Springs community. His name appears frequently in the mining records of both districts.

84. Smith to Folks, various letters, 12 May–2 December 1898, Herbert Heller Collection, box 1, folder 1; George Hazzard to Smith, 25 January 1898, ibid.; Smith to Folks, 11 January 1899, ibid., box 1, folder 2. The hospital opened on 6 October 1898. The letters of Heller's uncle, R. Lynn Smith, mostly to his family in New Castle, Indiana, span almost thirty-five years [1898–1933] and reveal much about mining and other activities in Interior Alaska, especially in Rampart, Hot Springs, Ruby, and Fairbanks. Also, Judkins to Alice, 11 September and 3 November 1898, Perry Judkins Collection, box 1, folder 1. Judkins commented that there were about 500 log cabins in town as of September 1898 and 1,000 log cabins by early November. According to *The Rampart Whirlpool* [15 January 1899], Rampart was a community of 1,500 people, including graduates of Harvard, Yale, Princeton, Michigan, and Cornell. By then, Smith wrote that one hundred cabins were vacant. Also, Rampart, Idaho Bar (folder), [2]: 5. For $200, D. M. Burnside transferred his Idaho Bar claim, Florence B, on 1 August 1898, to Harlow (sic) O. Belden, Charles J. Rozelle, A. Lyons Smith (Lynn Smith), and Volney Richmond.

85. William B. Ballou to Dear Ones, 16 May 1898, William B. Ballou Collection, box 1, folder 45, Archives, UAF; Ballou to Folks, 3 July 1898, ibid., box 1, folder 54; Ballou to Folks, 14 July 1898, box 1, folder 55; Ballou to Folks, 19 August 1898, ibid., box 1, folder 58; Ballou to Walt, 22 August 1898, ibid., box 1, folder 59; Ballou to Folks, 7 December 1898, ibid., box 1, folder 63; *Deerfield Valley Times*, 11 May 1900, ibid., box 2, folder 181. Ballou, originally from Wilmington, Vermont, had worked for the Boston and Maine Railroad at Winter Hill, the B & M station in Somerville, Massachusetts, across the Charles River from Boston. He and Pease chose to cross from Boston to the West Coast by railroad through Canada rather than take the *Julia Whelan*. They joined Bode in San Francisco. Once Ballou reached Rampart, he estimated the camp's popu-

lation to be over 1,000. His silent, financial partner, who grubstaked some of his ventures, was Frank A. Cutting of Boston. Rampart, Journal, 58. Max Marbet sold lot 4, block P, to Pease and Ballou for $50 on 18 August 1898.

86. Ibid., 98–99. The building was on lot 8, block 5. The purchase price seems exceptionally high at a time when lots with cabins often went for less than $300 and uncleared lots at public auction, for under $25. Also Rampart, Minook Creek (townsite) (folder), 1: 138, 188. Miller purchased one-half of lot 8, block 5 from Bouscaren for $200. Miller had been involved in a dispute with those who relocated on his millsite, which might have had a building large enough to become a barracks. The millsite, however, was at another location.

87. Josephine Sarah Marcus Earp, *I Married Wyatt Earp: The Recollections of Josephine Sarah Marcus Earp*, ed. Glenn G. Boyer (Tucson: the University of Arizona Press, 1976), 163–170. Josie Earp states that Rex Beach said he purchased the cabin from its builder, a U.S. deputy marshal who had gone to Circle City. Also, William R. Hunt, *Distant Justice: Policing the Alaska Frontier* (Norman: University of Oklahoma Press, 1987), 78. Frank Canton, at one time a U.S. deputy marshal for Circle, said he sold his cabin in Rampart to Rex Beach. Rampart, Minook Creek (townsite) (folder), 1: 16, 101. Canton held lot 8, block E, but sold two-thirds interest in it to F. G. Kress and W. W. Painter. Ibid., 22, 26. The Beach real estate transactions are hard to follow. Beach held lot 20, block K, and later, lot 6, block B2. Rampart, Journal, 61, 72, 93, 193. At a meeting on 21 August 1898, chaired by John McGraw, Beach contested for lot 4, block 6. His receipt showed he located the lot at 12:30 a.m. on 7 June. His opponent's receipt was for 11 a.m., 7 June. The unanimous decision gave the lot to Beach. On 3 September, Beach appointed Colin Beaton to sell his lot 4, block 6, and lot 4, block M. Beaton sold the downriver one-half of lot 4, block 6, to David Brown and H. B. Kench on 17 September. N. S. Beach sold one-half lot 6, block B2, to Perry Welch and Thomas Geoghegan on 15 June 1899. There are many extant pictures of a cabin in Rampart said to have belonged to Rex Beach. The cabin was used as a residence for many decades but, eventually, was torn down. The site of the former cabin was not near a creek, so it can only be speculated, but not proven, that it was the cabin originally built by Canton, bought by Beach, and rented to the Earps. Rampart, Journal, 41–42. The journal contains entries on Mary F. Llewelyn and Agnes Ketcheson. Also, MacGowan's dairy, 115, George P. MacGowan Collection. Mrs Llewelyn had sewn a white canvas parka for MacGowan in October 1897.

88. Rampart, Big Minook Creek (folder), 1: 36.

89. Joanne Hook, "He Never Returned: Robert Hunter Fitzhugh in Alaska," *The Alaska Journal* 15.2 (Spring 1985): 34, 36. Also, Robert Hunter Fitzhugh to Father, 5 October 1898, Robert Hunter Fitzhugh Collection, box 1, folder 15, Archives, UAF. During the Civil War, Hunter Fitzhugh's father was on General Robert E. Lee's staff. Fitzhugh was born in Virginia in 1869; his family later moved to Kentucky.

90. Explanatory notes, Merritt N. Murphy Photo Collection, Archives, UAF.

91. Rampart, Minook Creek (townsite) (folder), 1: 141–43. The meetings took place on 29 and 30 October 1898. There is no available record of Bell actually taking over the town, but his name appears in several records, including records of the public auctions, indicating his authoritative role and complete public acceptance of that role.

92. *The Rampart Whirlpool*, [15 January 1899].

93. Smith to family (no salutation), 28 October 1898, Herbert Heller Collection, box 1, folder 1, and Smith to Sister, 10 December 1898, ibid. Snell's first suicide attempt was unsuccessful. The second time, he cut an artery and hanged himself on the crossleg in his cabin. Also *The Rampart Whirlpool*, [15 January 1899]. According to *The Whirlpool*, Snell cut his elbow, strung himself by a wire, and jumped off a box. The article refers to 18,000 eggs; there was a "rowdy sale" for the good eggs.

94. Earp, 179. Variations of this story appear in different accounts. Judkins to Alice, 3 November 1898, Perry Judkins Collection, box 1, folder 1; Judkins's journal, entry of 19 February 1899, ibid., box 1, folder 8. Beach, *Personal Exposures*, 48. Smith to Folks, 9 October 1898, Herbert Heller Collection, box 1, folder 1. Ballou to Folks, 7 December 1898, William B. Ballou Collection, box 1, folder 63. Ballou stated that the man was about to be publicly whipped, but the soldiers prevented the whipping. Judkins wrote that the sentence was one year, eight months; Lynn Smith, eight months; Beach, eight months on the woodpile for stealing a ham. Earp refers to the man as being from a river steamer, stealing a supply of canned milk. A crew member of the *W. K. Merwin*, named Martin, was caught stealing in February 1899. The canned milk may have been his offense. Also, *Alaska Forum*, Rampart, Alaska, 9 May 1901, M/F 36. In 1901, Dolly, almost frozen to death, was brought into Fort Gibbon from the Andreafsky area; he survived.

95. Rampart, *Rock Creek* (folder), District Recorder, Fairbanks, 2–4, 6, 9. Others at the 11 October 1898 meeting were W. H. Davis, Jacob Kroeker, H. L.

Liebrandt, Joseph Silva, William Pike, George Milfs, and H. B. Porter. Robert Chamberlin became deputy recorder. On 2 January 1900, Hunter Fitzhugh relocated Pike's claim, No. 6 above. Some other Rock Creek relocations are in the Garnet Creek record book for which Chamberlin was also deputy recorder. Also, mining claims, 11 October 1898, Perry Judkins Collection, box 1, folder 13, and Judkins to Alice, 3 November 1898, ibid., box 1, folder 1.

96. Rampart, Mariposa Bar and Omega Creek (folder), District Recorder, Fairbanks, no pagination. Others at the meeting were Rock Creek organizers Kroeker, Silva, Liebrandt, Ellithorpe, plus C. M. Wilson. Also, Judkins to Alice, 3 November 1898, Perry Judkins Collection, box 1, folder 1. Judkins named the bar for his sweetheart's home in Mariposa County, CA.

97. Rampart, Triple Creek (folder), District Recorder, Fairbanks, 1–2, 6. Others at the meeting were F. A. Sennett, E. A. Norman, and John Ellingston.

98. Rampart, Record of Beare (sic) Creek (folder), District Recorder, Fairbanks, 12–13. The $5.00 recording fee was above the usual $2.50 fee, but not unique. The recording book simply listed claim number, name of holder, and date of record, again a rare but not unique procedure. Only a few names are readily identifiable as Ramparters. Gulches within the district were Hobson's, Choice, New Burgh, Sampson, and Dewey.

99. Smith to Folks, 9 October and 2 December 1898, Herbert Heller Collection, box 1, folder 1; Smith to Mrs. John Tower and Edna, 14 October 1898, ibid. Smith refers to his holding claim No. 23 above, Little Bear Creek, but Little Bear was outside the district. Rampart, Beare Creek (folder). The claims listed in the Beare Creek record total 111.

100. Rampart, Arroyo Grande (folder), District Recorder, Fairbanks, no pagination. Associated gulches were Plumenden, McKinley, Lewis, and Alice. Paget held claim No. 8, Arroyo. Again, only a few names are readily identifiable as Ramparters.

101. Smith to Sister, 10 December 1898, Herbert Heller Collection, box 1, folder 1; C. J. Rozelle to Smith's family, 31 December 1898, ibid.; Smith to family (no salutation), 1 January 1899, ibid., box 1, folder 2. In late December 1898 at Quail Creek, worn out by a trip to Bear and Quail creeks, Lynn Smith fell very seriously ill with dysentery and symptoms of typhoid fever. C. J. (Jap) Rozelle nursed him and informed his family. Smith was not hospitalized, although earlier, other typhoid fever patients had been hospitalized.

102. Smith to Folks, 1 and 11 January 1899, ibid., box 1, folder 2. Paget insisted to Smith that he had never refused to go with Bell to Bear Creek. Richardson, (possibly Wilds P.), from Circle City was to come to Rampart to look into the matter. Also Judkins's journal, entry of 28 December 1898, Perry Judkins Collection, box 1, folder 7. Also, Rampart, Journal, 172. Before leaving Rampart, Paget sold lot 10, block E below, for $25 to A. J. Johnston on 5 May 1899.

103. Smith to family (no salutation), 2 March 1899, Herbert Heller Collection, box 1, folder 2.

104. Smith to Brother Arthur, 4 February 1899, ibid.

105. *The Rampart Whirlpool,* [15 January 1899].

106. Earp, 176. Earp identified the Urquharts as "Eckerts."

107. Earp, 178. Earp identified Bell as "Captain Burke" and Bruner as "Mrs. Morse." Also, Judkins's journal, entry of 8 January 1899, Perry Judkins Collection, box 1, folder 8. Also, Rampart, Journal, 125, 126, 129, 130. Mrs. Bruner bought lots at public auctions in December 1898.

108. Rampart, Big Minook Creek (folder), 3: 276; 4: 335. Bruner relocated No. 53 above, Big Minook, on 12 March 1899, and sold ten acres of the upper one-half of it to Ella Crosson on 7 April. Also Rampart, Rampart Creek (folder), District Recorder, Fairbanks, 6. Bruner located No. 5, left hand fork, Rampart Creek, on 16 February 1899. Also, Rampart, Slate Creek (folder), (continuation), District Recorder, Fairbanks, no pagination. Bruner located No. 35 above, Slate, on 3 April 1899.

109. Smith to Folks, 9 October 1898, Herbert Heller Collection, box 1, folder 1; Smith to Mrs. Tower and Edna, 14 October 1898, ibid.

110. Rampart, Minook Creek (townsite) (folder), 1: 180, 108-09. Folger located his twenty-acre Discovery placer claim on Tramway Bar on 23 February 1898 (also given as 24 February 1894). He described the site as being on the right bank of the Middle Fork of the Koyukuk River about 110 miles from Arctic City and one mile below the mouth of Chapman Creek. He also claimed 5,000 miners inches of water rights for it.

111. *Deerfield Valley Times,* 11 May 1900, William B. Ballou Collection, box 2, folder 181, and manuscript of story, ibid. box 2, folder 179. Ballou's story, "Jack: A Dog's Fortune in Alaska" appeared in installments in the *Deerfield Valley Times,* Wilmington, VT, beginning on Friday, 11 May 1900. Ballou refers to Folger as "Foraker." The distance to the Koyukuk River varied, depending on the route taken and the destination point on the Koyukuk.

112. *The Rampart Whirlpool,* [15 January 1899]. The newspaper identified the others in the Folger party as Jack Walsh, Jack Mallon, Isidore Vidal, and Herman Jacobi of San Francisco.

113. Rampart, Idaho Bar (folder), [2]: 44–47, 80, also loose inserts after 50. Range of Dayton, Washington,

sold Discovery, Idaho Bar, to Brainerd for $1.00 on 16 February 1899. Harmon of Burke, Idaho, sold his Yukon claim, Idaho Bar, to Brainerd also for $1.00 on the same day. Also, Rampart, Little Minook Creek, 3: 13–14. Range and Harmon jointly sold their Eliza Anderson claim No. 1 on Range's Pup, on the left hand fork of the left hand fork of Peterson's Pup. They apparently never returned to Rampart. Brainerd also bought the Margaret claim on Idaho Bar from Ben Sanford Goodhue on 1 February 1899. Brainerd apparently supported a change to the Idaho Bar bylaws allowing a holder of contiguous claims to do the assessment required for all the holder's claims on one claim. On 8 May 1899, Brainerd was elected recorder for Idaho Bar for one year; he appointed Charles H. Knapp to act as deputy recorder for him. Also, Judkins's journal, entry of 17 February 1899, Perry Judkins Collection, box 1, folder 8. Judkins commented that lots of people were going to the Koyukuk and that Range had sold his Idaho Bar claim to Brainerd for $12,000.

114. Sundborg, 101. Also, Ballou to Dear Ones, 10 June 1899, William B. Ballou Collection, box 1, folder 64B. Ballou referred to a party frozen on a sled on the Dall River on the way to the Koyukuk and to a party of three eaten by wolves, identifying one as a man named Hardy from Providence, RI. Additionally, Fitzhugh to Father, 18 May 1899, Robert Hunter Fitzhugh Collection, box 1, folder 17; Judkins's journal, entry of 30 April 1899, Perry Judkins Collection, box 1, folder 8. Fitzhugh and Judkins alluded to the story.

115. Rampart, Russian Creek (folder), entry of 7 February 1899. Also, Rampart, Chapman Creek (folder), 44–45. A similar dispute over assessment arose on Chapman Creek where miners decided in favor of the relocator, giving No. 3 below to C. C. Wise. Moreover, Rampart, Rampart Creek (folder), final pages. On 10 January 1899, a dispute on Rampart Creek led to the realization that the district record book was missing. The claim holders completely reorganized with new bylaws and re-recordings of claims.

116. Rampart, Little Minook Creek (folder), 2: 137.

117. Rampart, Little Minook Creek (folder), 3: 104–05.

118. Judkins's journal, entry of 20 February 1899, Perry Judkins Collection, box 1, folder 8.

119. Ballou to Dear Ones, 10 June 1899, William B. Ballou Collection, box 1, folder 64B.

120. Smith to Folks, 30 April 1899, Herbert Heller Collection, box 1, folder 2. *The Rampart Whirlpool*, April 1899, William B. Ballou Collection, box 2, folder 182. The newspaper identified the patients as Albert Whitke, Rock Springs, WY; John McInnis, New Bedford, MA; Nick Hoffman, Lexington, KY; George C. Hugh, Valley Grove, CO; Tom Lawler, CA; Felix Busse, ND; and Martin King, Philadelphia, PA.

121. Rampart, Journal, 116, 163, 165, 170, 174, 204.

122. Smith to Folks, 1 May 1899, Herbert Heller Collection, box 1, folder 2.

123. *The Rampart Whirlpool*, April 1899. *The Whirlpool* did not identify the members of the self-appointed committee.

124. Ballou to Dear Ones, 10 June 1899, William B. Ballou Collection, box 1, folder 64B.

125. *The Rampart Whirlpool*, April 1899.

126. Ibid.

127. Ibid.

128. Ibid., *Hot Springs Post*, [Manley] Hot Springs, Alaska, 6 and 20 March 1909, M/F 964. Elliot Gaetz died in Seattle at the age of thirty-six and was buried in his birth place of Muscodubait, (Musquodoboit), Nova Scotia. *Yukon Valley News*, Tanana, Alaska, 3 December 1910, M/F 1002. Boston boy Angus Hebb married widow Gaetz in the fall of 1910.

129. Beach, *Personal Exposures*, 59–61.

130. Judkins's journal, entries of 11–16 April 1899, Perry Judkins Collection, box 1, folder 8.

131. Manley, Locations, vol. 1, 1 May 1899–10 November 1909, District Recorder, Fairbanks, 2, 4, 23, 25, 40, 47, 50, 57, 70, 79–80, 141, 176–77. The book, compiled in 1909, contains copies of records from the original creek records for Eureka, Pioneer, Boston, Florida, Rhode Island, and New York creeks, Excelsior Bar, and selected entries from the Rampart district book, 1901–1902. The original cited creek records are not available. Gaetz's Discovery on Eureka is dated 21 March 1899; Gaetz was recorder for Eureka. On Boston Creek, Gaetz held No. 1; Walsh, No. 2; Moore, No. 3; Ramsey, No. 4; Russell, No. 5; and Hebb, No. 10. Perry Judkins held No. 18 below, Eureka, 16 April 1899; Robert Chamberlin, right fork, Rhode Island, 15 April, fraction off No. 20 below, Eureka, 18 April, and No. 27 above, Pioneer, 15 April; R. E. Beach, No. 16, right fork, Pioneer, and a fraction between Nos. 5 and 6, Eureka, 8 April; J. G. Crowley, No. 17, right fork, Pioneer, 8 April. Other miners included Herman Tofty, No. 21 below, Eureka, 8 April; Dan A. Sutherland, No. 1, Roovers Gulch, 9 April, and No. 7 below, Florida, 18 May; and H. J. Roden, No. 5 above, Eureka, 5 April. Sutherland and Roden were later elected senators to the first territorial legislature which convened in March 1913.

132. Rampart, Mariposa Bar and Omega Creek (folder). At the meeting were J. E. Jones, chairman, No. 1 above; J. O. Carter, secretary, No. 4; Chamberlin,

deputy recorder, No. 8; Judkins, No. 9; G. J. Milfs, No. 6; Joe Silva, No. 7; W. H. Davis, No. 2; Herman Ey, No. 5; and E. C. Allen, recorder, No. 3. Later Omega claims are in Manley, Locations, vol. 1.

133. Rampart, Allan Creek (folder), District Recorder, Fairbanks, 10–12, 28–29, 48–49, 174–75, 188. On 10 April, Bruner appointed recorder Rice to locate claims for her.

134. Judkins's journal, entries of 26 April and 20 May 1899, Perry Judkins Collection, box 1, folder 8. Frank Nagel was recorder for the Wolverine Creek district.

135. Rampart, Montana Bar (folder), District Recorder, Fairbanks, no pagination (about four pages in all; all entries are dated 12 May 1899). Montana Bar differs from Montana Creek.

136. Fitzhugh to Father, 18 May 1899, Robert Hunter Fitzhugh Collection, box 1, folder 17. The map is not available. After completing the work, Fitzhugh said he would do no more engineering jobs for less than $20 a day.

137. Judkins's journal, various entries of 31 May–December 31, 1899, Perry Judkins Collection, box 1, folder 8; Judkins to Alice, 4 and 27 August 1899, ibid., box 1, folder 2.

138. Fitzhugh to Mother, 12 July 1899, Robert Hunter Fitzhugh Collection, box 1, folder 20.

139. Judkins to Alice, 27 August 1899, Perry Judkins Collection, box 1, folder 2, and Judkins' journal, entry of 9 July 1899, ibid., box 1, folder 8.

140. Smith to Folks, 10 and 18 August and 7 September 1899, Herbert Heller Collection, box 1, folder 2, Smith to Father, 30 August 1899, ibid., and Rozelle to Robert Smith, 6 September 1899, ibid.

141. Earp, 184–85. Rampart, Journal, 228. Hoover appointed Tom Crawford her agent to sell her lots. Smith to Folks, 20 June 1899, Herbert Heller Collection, box 1, folder 2. Fitzhugh to Father, 18 May 1899, Robert Hunter Fitzhugh Collection, box 1, folder 17. McGraw reportedly cleaned up $60,000 in two weeks with the clean-up being only one-sixth completed. Ballou to Mother, 31 August 1899, William B. Ballou Collection, box 1, folder 68. Also, Alaska Forum, Rampart, Alaska, 7 March 1901, M/F 36. Tom Urquhart and Wyatt Earp left Nome for Seattle in the fall of 1900.

142. Alger.

143. Military history of Fort Gibbon, [Maj. Gen.] C[harles] S. Farnsworth Collection, box 1, folder 1, Archives, UAF.

144. Farnsworth to Daniel Galey, 14 October 1899, ibid., box 1, folder 3; Farnsworth to Young, 15 February 1900, ibid., box 1, folder 4. Farnsworth reported that Lt. J. S. Herron, Eighth Cavalry, Dr. Carter, two enlisted men, and two packers, all with the [Capt. E. F.] Glenn expedition, had found refuge at Fort Gibbon, arriving half-starved and half-clothed on 12 December 1899. They had lost all their horses, food, and equipment and had spent two months with the Kuskokwim Indians.

145. Military history of Fort Gibbon, ibid., box 1, folder 1. Brig. Gen. John Gibbon had died 1 February 1896, after fifty years of active duty. Also, Smith to Folks, 2 August 1899, Herbert Heller Collection, box 1, folder 2. Lynn Smith wrote that the soldiers were there; 220 had gotten off at Tanana.

146. Fitzhugh to Mother, 12 July 1899, Robert Hunter Fitzhugh Collection, box 1, folder 20.

147. Judkins's journal, entry of 2 September 1899, Perry Judkins Collection, box 1, folder 8. Dr. Hudgin, an associate of Hunter Fitzhugh, was one of the trustees.

148. Fitzhugh to Mother, 12 November 1899, Robert Hunter Fitzhugh Collection, box 1, folder 21.

149. Beach, Personal Exposures, 62. Beach lived in Nome and later visited Alaska, but he apparently never stopped in Rampart. He took a trip to Katmai before the 1912 volcanic eruption with former Ramparter Ray Norton, who quit his job as a newspaperman in California to join Beach.

150. Rex Beach, The Barrier (New York: A. L. Burt Company in arrangement with Harper Brothers, 1908). Also, Beach, Personal Exposures, 43–45. Beach discussed movie rights for The Barrier.

151. Beach, Personal Exposures, 58, and The Barrier, 2.

152. The Rampart Whirlpool, April 1899. Lt. Bell's garrison raised a silk American flag during ceremonies in April 1899.

153. Rampart, Journal, 100, 190. John A. Gale purchased lot 3, block 12, at public auction on 24 September 1898 and sold it to L. E. Gregg on 6 June 1899 for $15.

154. Beach, Personal Exposures, 50. At the end of his first winter in Rampart, Beach was "mildly in debt" to Mayo.

155. Beach, The Barrier, 146–51.

156. Dave King, "De Cole Deck on 'Poleon Compeau," 1899, in Alaska–Yukon Magazine, June 1907, 328, 335–36.

157. Earp, 173.

158. MacGowan's diary, 231, George P. MacGowan Collection. MacGowan rated gamblers Werner and Barneyb(e)rg "devishly pleasant and obliging fellows." Rampart, Minook Creek (townsite) (folder), 1: 127. Barneyberg bought and sold a town lot. Frank L. Werner was a witness. Also, Beach, Personal Exposures, 97–

102. Beach described the changeable, volatile, double-sided nature of Dougherty, possibly the prototype for Beach's short story "Laughing Bill Hyde." Although Dougherty was in Rampart in 1898 or 1899, his name does not appear in Rampart records.

Chapter 2. Federal Government Oversight, 1900–1905

I think that within such a reasonable length of time as it takes a commonwealth to grow, this region will be as densely populated as the northern part of the United States—that is, the Dakotas and Montana—and will be as good and valuable a country from a mining standpoint, and possibly from an agricultural standpoint.
–Judge James Wickersham, Rampart, Alaska, July 22, 1903[1]

By the time the new year of 1900 began, patterns of activity had formed. Many creek bylaws set assessment periods according to the calendar year. Therefore, if assessment work had not been performed on a claim as of December 31, the holder's right to the claim lapsed and the claim became available for relocation. Cagey, speculative, or practical prospectors who had been in Rampart since 1897 or 1898 and wanted to expand their holdings on fully staked creeks watched as other prospectors left Rampart without doing assessments on their claims. They often celebrated New Year's Day by staking forfeited claims, scrambling stampede-style to reach a creek ahead of anyone else. Some staked for themselves; some staked with intent to sell to the anticipated new arrivals in the summer.

Consequently, many relocations occurred in January 1900. For example, Charles P. Towle relocated No. 119 above, Big Minook, on January 5. Frank Stevens, acting for Charles B. Allen, located the Allen claim on No. 16 above, Big Minook, on January 15. Others, like W. L. McDonald, registered for certification of completed assessment to protect their claims from relocation.[2]

Controversies over claims increased. On behalf of Emma H. Jordan, Charles I. Jordan staked a claim on January 23, contiguous to No. 22 above, Little Minook Junior. Jordan reported in his location record that he had acted according to U.S. and local laws except where he was

prevented by John Bock, who, for reasons unknown, threatened Jordan. Valeria Myers, once co-owner of No. 22 with Bock, later protested other actions by Bock. She asserted that Bock's claim No. 23 was originally No. 22 and sought to prevent Bock from selling any part of No. 23, by then known as No. 24. She further asserted that during the mining season 1899–1900, Bock had unlawfully taken gold from the original No. 22.[3] Myers' struggles in court over No. 22 and then No. 24, as both plaintiff and defendant, lasted for more than a year. When working on No. 22, William Ballou refused to obey orders from Lt. Benjamin Tillman to stop work until the case was settled. At one point, according to Ballou, the opposing counsel admitted that he had no case.[4]

Meanwhile, Ballou wondered whether the Smithsonian Institution would tell him the value of old horns and bones of extinct animals he had unearthed. The horns resembled buffalo horns, four inches in diameter and twenty inches long. Two ivory mastodon tusks measured six inches in diameter and six feet long.[5]

At Fort Gibbon, Captain Farnsworth complained about the slow progess in construction of the barracks. The contractors did not seem to care whether or not they carried out their contracts. In disgust, Farnsworth wrote, "Our civilian employees are the most incompetent lot of men ever turned loose on a community, and it seems to be now evident that they only came here to spend the winter in idleness and then go hunting gold when warm weather comes."[6] At another time, he added:

Our mechanics are just learning their trades and are independent and impudent to the post commander. . . . They have an idea that they can all go out at any time and dig gold and make a good living. . . . big surprise in store for them next summer when they will be given a chance to try their luck outside.[7]

Farnsworth's aggravation remained high because most of the fort's clothing and its commissary supplies had been lost in a ship-wreck. His troops had to patch their uniforms with blanket pieces.[8]

Through the winter months, a gigantic, continuous stampede of prospectors and others headed to the new mining field at Cape Nome. In frigid cold, prospectors from Rampart, Dawson, and elsewhere dashed off to Nome. According to William Ballou, the rush to Nome over the ice would become a "matter of history" some day. He estimated that over 5,000 people had passed by Rampart en route to Nome, additional hundreds leaving from Rampart. One day, twenty-nine teams departed before 10 a.m. Freighter Sam Heeter left with five men and the only two horses in Rampart. One horse fell ill along the way and had to be killed. Indians coming after the Heeter party butchered the dead horse and sold a quarter to Heeter, who apparently thought the meat was from a freshly killed moose.[9]

Hunter Fitzhugh saw as many as twenty groups a day passing through Rampart from Dawson, mostly going by dog sled. Two men traveled with footwear and an axe, but without blankets, food, or stove. According to Fitzhugh, they expected to rely along the way on wood-cutters, prospectors, and "merciful Providence." Another man rode a bike with its tires wrapped in canvas. He had pedaled 800 miles in eleven days, apparently without problems.[10]

Similarly, thirty miles above Rampart at the Pioneer coal mine, Perry Judkins expressed exasperation with the incessant stream of stampeders, as two to eight men stopped at the mine each day. The transients could not be turned away, but they caused difficulties. One night, eight men arrived with twenty dogs, necessitating cooking five separate meals over one stove. The last dog was fed supper at breakfast time. As a result the mine renovated a cabin for passersby. Judkins was aware some Ramparters going to Nome were selling good claims at half their value. His friend, Bob Chamberlin, contracted "Nome fever." He left

Rampart for Nome, eventually prospecting at Port Clarence.[11]

Captain Farnsworth had also noticed many men going to Nome. He expected that everyone around Weare would leave after breakup. He had not heard of any gold discoveries in his area and assumed that not many men were prospect-ing close by.[12]

At the end of May, Lynn Smith, away from Rampart for ten months, prepared to return. A smallpox outbreak threatened to detain the steamer *Ohio* in Seattle, but the ship finally received clearance to proceed. Aboard the *Ohio*, Smith met about twenty Ramparters going back to Alaska, including the artistic Mrs. Jane Bruner, the gilt-paint lady, and Harry Paget, the Bear Creek recorder. When the ship approached Norton Sound, intending to land at Nome, it was quarantined offshore. Smith witnessed Natives being removed to St. Michael from Egg Island, where, Smith supposed, their ancestors probably camped for hundreds of years. Government officials were conducting the transfer so they could use the island as a quarantine station. Dr. Frederick Jerauld, a former Ramparter on board, authorized the *Ohio* to dock at Nome. Smith, unimpressed by what he saw in the gold camp, speculated that Nome would be "depopulated" sooner than Dawson had been. Disenchanted Ramparters at Nome were already on their way back to Rampart.[13] Over at Rampart, Fitzhugh had a comparable viewpoint. He noticed the returning Ramparters and believed the Cape Nome gold bubble had burst. He also thought the smallpox epidemic had ended.[14]

At the Alaska Commercial Company in St. Michael, Lynn Smith found two other former Ramparters employed there—Volney Richmond and Frank Moses.[15] Through Herman Wobber, the manager of the A. C. store in Rampart, Richmond had obtained the position at the A.C. store in St. Michael the previous March.[16] Smith informed his sister Polly that Richmond had been "awfully good" to him.[17] When Smith reached Rampart, he learned that many Indians had died in the smallpox epidemic. Also, the government was installing telegraph wires across Alaska. Rampart would be connected by wire to the outside world by March 1901.[18]

The smallpox quarantine apparently slowed down the mail to Fort Gibbon. The mail was fumigated at St. Michael, and all newspapers and magazines were burned. Letters were forwarded to their destination.

On August 8, Captain Farnsworth received General Order No. 19, signed by Capt. W[ilds] P. Richardson, assigning Farnsworth, his company, and its detachments to Fort Egbert. First Lt. W[illiam] C. Rogers, Company One, Seventh Infantry, at Egbert, was to deactivate the post at Circle City, assume command of the men there, and then relieve Lieutenant Tillman at the Rampart station.[19]

In mid-July, Farnsworth had directed Sergeant Lucas to board the steamer *Argo* and to set up a log camp on the Tolovana River. Then, Lucas and his crew were to continue nineteen miles up Hay Creek, a tributary of the Tolovana, to a hay meadow near the site of an old Indian village, to cut 1,500 pounds of hay before the rainy season started. Each man was required to have a head net and pair of gloves for protection against the mosquitos. After Farnsworth took over Fort Egbert, he was informed that the *Argo*, with its hay cargo, rested high and dry on a sand bar in the Tanana River, eight miles from Fort Gibbon, and might be wintered-in there. The town of Weare itself had boomed, and now had three saloons, an Alaska Commercial store, and cabins. Lots were selling at premium prices.[20]

Meanwhile, Perry Judkins quit the Pioneer coal mine at the end of July, a year after he began work there. He returned to mining on Big Minook since others had been successful on claims around his.[21] He and several other miners, including B. W. Moore, Jr., placed liens on the coal mine for unpaid wages.[22] By November, the coal mine had shut down, facing foreclosure. Judkins hoped that the Alaska Commercial Company, the coal mine's chief creditor, would get the mine so the workers would be paid.[23]

The end came gradually to the coal mine. A 1900 Act of Congress extended coal land laws to Alaska. Holders of coal claims on unsurveyed lands were permitted to have their claims surveyed as nearby townships were surveyed. The *Alaska Forum* postulated that Tom Drew could hold his mine so long as he operated or watched over it. The claim and the mortgage to Alaska Commercial had been recorded in Rampart books, but neither, as the *Forum* analyzed the situation, appeared to be legal since title to coal lands in Alaska would not be obtainable for several years.[24]

Routine winter work on the claims was underway in the Rampart district when tragedy struck in early November. Hunter Fitzhugh, by then sharing a cabin on Slate Creek with [F. E.] Drake, went out on the evening of November 4 to hunt ptarmigan and failed to return home. During the night, Drake looked for him without success. A large search party soon found the body, buried under a snowslide on a mountain side.[25] The body was taken to St. Andrew's Hospital, the Episcopal hospital that rose from the defunct city hospital.[26] For the funeral on Sunday, November 11, Lynn Smith, his new lady interest, Ella Garratt, and other women wound evergreen boughs into wreaths. Smith sang during the service.[27]

In his last letter, Fitzhugh had informed his mother that he and a Mormon from Utah had whipsawed 600 feet of lumber for his cabin's floor, door, and windows. He repeated a Yukon story, writing, "When one of us who has not been so good as he should be dies, the devil puts him to whipsawing. If he is faithful and doesn't complain under the trial, he is simply burned through eternity like an ordinary goat."[28]

Another tragedy followed soon after Fitzhugh's accidental death. Dan Carolan, partner and son-in-law of John Minook, walked into the NAT&T store on Monday afternoon, December 17, and calmly shot clerk "NAT Joe" Muldowney four times with a .44 caliber revolver. Witness Tom Crawford raced out of the store to get help. Carolan immediately turned himself over to the soldiers at the garrison.[29]

Lynn Smith stayed with the unconscious Muldowney, who died two days later. Bishop P. T. Rowe presided at the funeral.[30] Carolan did not divulge why he had murdered Muldowney although there were persistent rumors that Muldowney had made advances toward Carolan's wife, Lucy Minook Carolan, and may have raped her.[31]

Lawyer Andrew J. Balliet, who had just been appointed Rampart's first federal commissioner, convened a coroner's jury. The jury officially determined that Muldowney had died by gunshots inflicted by Carolon. At the preliminary hearing on the case, Commissioner Balliet fined J. L. Green, Carolan's defense attorney, $25 for contempt of court because he objected to Green's tactics. [32]

Lt. William Rogers, who had arrived in Rampart a few days earlier, reported to Farnsworth about the alleged rape of Carolan's wife. Rogers was glad to turn Carolan over to Balliet. He revealed that the "damned soldiers" had prevented a potential lynching.[33] At a trial in Eagle in late July 1901, the jury convicted Carolan of murder in the first degree and imprisoned him for life on McNeil Island near Tacoma, Washington. Friends of Carolan solicited funds for an appeal, based on "extenuating circumstances" that came out at the trial, presumably more about the alleged rape. In April 1905, Ramparters learned of a report that Carolan, whom they considered a quiet, industrious man, would be pardoned because he had committed his crime in the heat of passion over the alleged assault by Muldowney on Carolan's wife.[34] Carolan did not return to Rampart.

Like its predecessor, the city hospital, St. Andrew's Hospital encountered monetary difficulties. In late December 1900 after Muldowney's funeral, Bishop Rowe complained that the hospital had provided $150 in services in agreement with the Rampart city council but the council paid only $24 of the bill. The bishop asserted that since the hospital had no funding and could not carry on alone, the hospital would have to turn away non-paying patients unless the city met its obligation.[35]

Andrew Balliet's multiple duties as U.S. commissioner made him the official recorder for the entire Rampart district from Troublesome Creek to Eureka and Baker creeks. Accordingly,

he ordered that all creek record books be submitted to him at once.[36] The large books he established and maintained became the only official records from December 1900 on. The practice of Rampart miners' organizing individual creek districts, creek by creek, beginning with the Little Minook Creek bylaws and location records in April 1896, ended with the opening of Balliet's office, the repository for all records.

The new year, 1901, precipitated the annual exodus to the creeks to relocate claims on which no assessment work had been performed. The *Alaska Forum* counted about seventy-five people who, with their hatchets, departed Rampart on the last day of the year. Lieutenant Rogers and an army physician, Dr. Tweedie, participated in the rush to Hunter Creek.[37]

The *Forum* also pointed out the possible conflicts between U.S. mining laws and more restrictive creek laws. Since the U.S. laws allowed twenty-acre claims (1,320 feet long), a formal court decision would most likely stand by the U.S. laws and overrule creek laws restricting claims to 500 feet. Accordingly, if a miner chose to stake a twenty-acre claim on a restricted creek, the federal court would agree with him if the size of his claim was disputed.[38]

By late January, Rampart had been a city for almost five years although its population had decreased from the high period of 1897–1899. The *Forum* interviewed several businessmen about a proposal to incorporate the city. Some like A. Baker, Dr. Hudgin, and I. Kaffenburg favored the proposal outright; A. Liebes, H. Wobber, and E. D. Wiggin hesitated, concerned about potential costs; J. Nelson, J. L. Green, and H. Haven agreed because half of the income collected for annual licensing of businesses such as saloons would be retained for a town school.[39]

Miners on the creeks had little interest in incorporation. Like many, William Ballou shifted from claim to claim, sometimes working for himself, sometimes working for others. He was partnering with Andrew Balliet on Balliet's claim No. 15, Hoosier Creek, when Balliet became commissioner. He supervised teams on

Nos. 21, 22, and 25 above, Little Minook Junior, while spending time alone on Hoosier. After the Hoosier claim flooded, he returned to the McGraw-Carr claim, No. 8 above, Little Minook Creek, where he had been the previous fall. He also sometimes substituted in the recording office when Balliet was away.[40]

In the meantime, Perry Judkins was working on Idaho Bar under Jack Crowley who watched over the claims of Erastus Brainerd. When attorney J. L. Green and city treasurer H. W. Walbridge visited the bar one day, the *Forum* assumed that the two men were obtaining statements from Judkins in the Pioneer coal mine case, statements to be forwarded to the court of Judge James Wickersham in Eagle.[41]

The *Forum* recounted the history of the coal mine, originally the Black Diamond mine, located in 1895 jointly by O. C. Miller, Jules Prevost, and Al Mayo. In 1897, Miller dropped out, and Tom Drew relocated the mine as the Pioneer. J. P. Bouscaren purchased Miller's improvements and became an equal partner with Drew until Tom Crawford bought out Bouscaren on Drew's behalf. Over a three-year period, Crawford extended to Drew credit of several thousand in cash, supplies, and equipment; he received from Drew only $400 in reimbursement. The Alaska Commercial Company loaned Drew $5,000, which Drew divided, part for back wages and the rest for himself. According to the *Forum*, Drew continually appropriated income from coal sales to provide him with a comfortable lifestyle from Dawson to St. Michael and, thereby, built up debts, apparently totaling over $25,000. Nevertheless, Drew rejected an offer of $50,000 for the mine.[42]

Judge Wickersham held a special session of court in Rampart on March 4, the first court session at Rampart.[43] The recently promoted Capt. William Rogers thought that the judge had handled satisfactorily, at least from an outsider's viewpoint, two "prickly cases," undoubtedly the Valeria Myers and Pioneer coal mine cases.[44] William Ballou reacted differently. In his opinion, the court brought in too much law. He corresponded about the situation, reflecting, "The lawyers are the only people that are

making any money. . . . Two years ago we got along very well without any law, but now, almost everyone seems to have a grievance and is going to law about it."[45]

Judge Wickersham also commented on the session during which *Forum* editor James B. Wingate served as deputy clerk. In *Allen v. Myers*, the largest of the lawsuits of Valeria Myers, Wickersham wrote that the court had no jurisdiction in the case as it was presented. He finally dismissed the case so that the parties could prepare new suits. He enjoined against removal of gold until the case could be tried on its own merits.[46]

Perry Judkins felt disheartened that the judge did not appoint a receiver for the coal mine. Like Ballou, Judkins also believed that the lawyers would get most of the money.[47] A few days after the March court session, Marshal Godfrey Gmehle served Tom Drew with papers regarding the unpaid wages for Judkins and his co-workers.[48] The case, however, was not resolved for many months. In August, Ramparters finally learned that the coal mine would be sold to the highest bidder at a marshal's sale on September 3 in Eagle.[49] The new marshal, [George] Dreibelbis, then went to the mine to place an attachment on it.[50] Sold as scheduled, the mine never re-opened.

During his March stay in Rampart, Wickersham visited the claims of John McGraw and Erastus Brainerd, Seattle friends who had recovered enough gold "to get back on their financial feet." He also saw mammoth tusks and the horns of an extinct Alaska buffalo, most likely from Ballou's specimens. Nevertheless, Wickersham evaluated Rampart as not at all comparable to the Klondike.[51]

By late March, Judkins and the others had quit working at Idaho Bar, fearing they would not be paid.[52] They awaited "capitalist" Erastus Brainerd, who arrived via the steamer *Hamilton* on June 18. Brainerd carried along a small testing stamp mill. Within a week, he had arranged to ship forty sacks of gravel to Seattle for testing so he could decide whether or not to set up a plant costing $250,000.[53]

Judkins did not wait for his overdue pay. He

left Rampart for good on June 3 aboard the steamer *Aurum*, owned by Ramparters. Near Andreafsky, the *Aurum* took the wrong channel. Priests on the *St. Joseph*, the mission boat owned by the Jesuit Fathers at Holy Cross (formerly Koserefski), redirected the *Aurum*, saving it from a trip 200 miles out of its way. Commissioner Balliet, agent for Erastus Brainerd, sent Judkins, by then in Teller City, his last paycheck. Balliet carefully deducted twelve cents, the charge for the postal money order.[54]

In early July, Oliver Lorencen struck heavy pay dirt on No. 1 above, Glen Gulch, considered a tributary of both Rhode Island and Baker creeks on the Tanana side, thirty miles from Rampart. James W. Dillon, who shared Discovery, Glen Gulch, with his Eagle Mining Company partners William P. Beardsley and John (Jack) Belsea, rocked out $72 within a few hours. The gold channel connected with Kentucky Creek. Charles B. Allen on No. 1 below, Glen Gulch, turned down an offer of $25,000 for his claim. Meanwhile, Perry Bigelow jumped Lorencen's claim, and a foraging bear ripped Lorencen's tent above his bunk as he lay in it.[55]

The Glen Gulch pay streak extended to a bench claim located by [George R.] Shirley, 1,500 feet west of the gulch.[56] In addition to the bar between Glen Gulch and Gold Run, Shirley was involved in a claim on What Cheer Bar, a bar between Pioneer and Eureka creeks. Voluminous staking occurred on the Tanana side of the divide as far east as Elephant Gulch on the Hootlanana.[57] Although prospecting continued for forty miles, an insufficient supply of water for sluicing hindered the work.[58] During this period, a few miners joined forces to obtain more acreage per claim. E. T. Townsend, M. E. Koonce, and others located the seventy-acre Massachusetts mine on Pioneer Creek and the 160-acre Pennsylvania mine on a bench of Pioneer Creek Gulch.[59]

In an offshoot of Bigelow's attempt to take over Lorencen's claim, H. J. Roden filed suit against Bigelow to force him to fulfill a contract with Roden and his partner, M. S. Gill. Roden and Gill had consented to crosscut the claim in return for the upper half of No. 1. Because the claim was returned to Lorencen, Roden charged Bigelow with fraud.[60] Lorencen subsequently sold No. 1 above, Glen Gulch, to O. A. Diver for $100 and $4,000 when Diver reached bedrock.[61] Roden, who retained interest in the area, insisted on the need to improve the trail from Rampart to Glen Gulch. In an apparent reference to the trail to Eureka surveyed by Hunter Fitzhugh in 1899, Roden stressed he did not want another thirty-mile trail through a swamp.[62]

Jack Belsea staked No. 4 above, Glen Gulch, for Ella R. Garratt.[63] Garratt sold the north one-half of No. 4 to [Henry F.] Thumm. Belsea then stated he had a half-interest in the claim, but Garratt had a paper testifying to the transfer of Belsea's interest to her, a paper Belsea branded a forgery. Eagle Mining partner James Dillon hired legal counsel for Belsea, thus initiating a lengthy, intense court battle rivaling in complexity the numerous Valeria Myers' cases and involving even more people.[64] A man named Osborne jumped the claim on behalf of Belsea. The teams holding leases on both halves of the claim continued working.[65]

Garratt married J. [Fred] Struthers in St. Michael, but the case continued.[66] Lynn Smith, at first dismayed by Garratt's marriage, was consoled because Garratt, the girl who looked at men "dove-like," had given her "honey bug" (Smith) a lease (lay) on the lower half of No. 4.[67] Nevertheless, the new Mrs. Struthers filed suit against Belsea, Frank Stevens, Diver, honey bug Lynn Smith, and others for $22,000 in damages.[68] Her mother, previously friendly with Lynn Smith, considered him a "traitor," an appellation Smith did not care for.[69] Still he continued with his lay, happy since partner Wally Laboski had already found a $12 nugget.[70]

The controversial case simmered and sputtered for months. After the team of Lynn Smith, Gus Conradt, and Wally Laboski had finished their winter gravel dumps, Frank Hiatt, a friend and partner of George Walter Sundborg and supporter of Garratt, bicycled to Nome to

Figure 12. The so-called $3,000 ditching gang, Glen Gulch, 21 May 1902. *Courtesy of the Herbert Heller Collection, University of Alaska Fairbanks. Accession Number 79-44-606N.*

contact Judge Wickersham, then in Nome, about an injunction Garratt wanted. Lynn Smith hoped Hiatt's crankshaft would break along the way. The dumps could not be cleaned until the judge took action, and the lay men did not know how much gold was in their dumps or how much their share would be after normal and court expenses were deducted. Smith worried about the outcome as he foresaw court costs eating up profits.[71]

Hiatt reached Nome in fourteen days, having switched to a dog sled at Unalakleet. He returned on April 15 with papers and instructions appointing Marshal George Dreibelbis receiver and authorizing him to hire men to wash up the dumps.[72]

In August, Smith went to the Wickersham court in Eagle on the side of Belsea's Eagle Mining Company. Garratt won. The lay men also won, getting 55 percent with court expenses divided among all, laymen and principals. Smith received $800 with another $1,800 from the dump. John Belsea appealed. His Eagle Mining Company partner James Dillon, who had fallen gravely ill of Bright's disease, died in Eagle. Lynn Smith characterized the trial as a

"great carnival of perjurors on both sides." In his estimation, he had remained neutral, his testimony hurting both sides.[73]

Meanwhile, summertime brought a substantial change at the army garrison. Captain Rogers was transferred to the Twenty-seventh Infantry, Plattsburgh Barracks, New York. Lt. H. M. Dickman was named to replace him. Then, the army decided to deactivate the station, sending the detachment to Fort Gibbon on the government steamer *General Jefferson Davis*.[74] A frustrated Lynn Smith noted that the army broke up, destroyed, condemned, or freighted away supplies and materials which could have been very useful to Ramparters.[75]

On the other hand, William Ballou had a surprise encounter with army personnel. On the way back to Rampart after being gone a few months, he met in a Dawson dance hall Lt. Benjamin Tillman, whom Rogers had replaced. Tillman was rapidly spending his $500 quarterly pay from Fort Egbert in one evening by drinking and dancing the night away. Canadian Mounties who copied Tillman's spree were in bed by 2 a.m.[76]

Activities along the Tanana side of the divide

Figure 13. Unidentified miners, Glen Gulch, 21 May 1902. Courtesy of the Herbert Heller Collection, University of Alaska Fairbanks. Accession Number 79-44-605N.

expanded in fall 1901. Among the numerous claims filed, P. A. Conroy located No. 4 above, Silver Bow Creek; Tom Antonson, No. 1 above, Thanksgiving Creek; and F. E. Drake, No. 6 above, Anaconda Creek.[77]

To celebrate Christmas, miners in Glen Gulch prepared to attend a party for the Indians, hosted by Riley, manager of the Belt & Hendricks Store at Deakyme, the trading post off Baker Creek, eighteen miles south of Glen Gulch.[78] About twenty-one "fools," including Lynn Smith, hiked to the Indian potlatch at Deakyme where Native children, very lightly and only partially clothed, ran barefoot in snow at temperatures of 30 below.[79]

William Ballou returned to work on No. 8 above, Little Minook, unhappy that he had not spent the summer in Glen Gulch. As he and his partners—Frank and Tommy McGraw and Billy McLean—worked their drift, they came across pieces of loose, coarse gold and stored the pieces in their mouths, swallowing the dirt. They, thereby, acquired some gold immediately

while piling up their winter dump of gravel for springtime sluicing. Ballou usually accumulated twenty to thirty dollars, once forty dollars, worth of gold in his cheek by day's end.[80]

That winter, Frank McGraw purchased McLean's interest. Ballou became chief engineer in charge of firing the boiler. The boiler thawed the dirt and ran the engine for the hoist, saw, and pump. As part of his daily duties, Ballou thawed ice from the creek for the boiler, sawed wood for the fires, oiled machinery, sharpened pick axes, and repaired the pipe lines. He described some of his cabin mates at length. Mike Laboski, an Austrian then twenty-five years old, had spent five years in the coal mines of Pennsylvania. Meyers, a German immigrant, amused the group with his stories. Bergstrom, from Sweden, was both blacksmith and minister. Dick Parker, probably a Californian, took part in local prize fights. Downing, a cow puncher from Oregon, had a quiet personality with a dry, sarcastic wit. English, a hunter, came from Idaho. [Sam] Heeter, a Yankee, had lived in Cape Colony, South Africa, and, therefore, rooted for the British to be defeated in the Boer War.[81]

In early April 1902 Ballou, Lynn Smith, and George Langford walked to Glen Gulch, Gold Run, Rhode Island Creek, and up to Mike Hess Creek, a round-trip distance of 110 miles, sometimes making thirty miles a day. Ballou saw dumps at Glen Gulch estimated to be worth $400,000. Claims on Rhode Island Creek were selling for $3,000 to $5,000.[82]

With the approach of summer, Ballou sat in as receiver for the absent owners of No. 9 above, Little Minook. Soon thereafter, he observed surveyors for the Alaskan Central Railway, a railroad planned to stretch from Rampart to Valdez. Skeptical of the outcome, he did not expect to be around to watch the first train arrive in Rampart.[83] Lynn Smith, too, had little faith in the projected railroad. Because former Governor McGraw and the "Seattle capitalists" backed the project, Smith thought that failure was almost certain. Later in Eagle, Smith met Hubbard (presumably Sam) who was there on behalf of the railroad across Valdez. Hubbard urged Smith to investigate quartz mining in the Interior.[84]

At the request of an agent of the Northern Commercial Company, successor to the Alaska Commercial Company, Ballou traveled upstream to Fort Hamlin. There he inventoried the stock at the N. C. store, shipped it off, and closed down the trading post. The store had been a place for trappers, particularly Natives, to sell or trade their furs. The influx of miners increased the area population, driving the game away to other habitats. Since the fur trade had decreased, the need for the store ceased.[85]

During the summer, geologists from the U. S. Geological Survey studied the region. Arthur J. Collier visited Glenn Creek (Glen Gulch). In his report, he noted the softness of the trail from Rampart to Glen Gulch, a softness that impeded travel in warm weather. He explained that eight miles south of Rampart, there was a series of siliceous slates, quartzites, and schists that crossed the divide to Glen Gulch. He found the only productive placers on Glen Gulch to be the

four or five claims at the head of the creek. Bedrock was a graphitic schist that the miners called "slate." The bedrock had white quartz stringers. At the outcrop decomposed stringers and bedrock could be shoveled out like fine gravel. A waxy clay called "gumbo," probably decomposed rock, sometimes appeared above the bedrock. Collier learned from a representative of the Eagle Mining Company that the gulch had produced an estimated $150,000 before August 1, 1902.[86]

Collier also examined Gold Run, one mile west of and parallel to the gulch. The bedrock there was composed of angular "blocky schist" similar to schist on Glen Gulch. An uncompleted wash-up from one Gold Run dump had produced $1,000.[87]

On Rhode Island Creek, Collier found graphitic schists along with pebbles and boulders of igneous rocks, some green, suggesting alteration. Along the bench between Glen Gulch and Gold Run, the bedrock was covered by clay that carried some gold. The gold spread downhill several thousand feet. A two-mile ditch brought in water from Rhode Island Creek.[88]

Collier believed the lowland of Baker Flats might have been the bed of an extinct lake and Glen Gulch was part extinct beach and part peneplain, or nearly level plain. Since uncovered gold pieces were not water worn, they had not been moved far from their origin. Collier hypothesized that mineralization had occurred in the bedrock north of Baker Flats. Through wave and stream action, the gold from the mineralization concentrated along the edge of the extinct lake. Consequently, gold from the extinct beach formed the creek and bench placers discovered in 1902.[89]

Collier also looked at coal resources along the Yukon. The Rampart series of rocks had a greenish color with considerable volcanic material, probably from the Devonian period. The coal itself, generally lignite from the Kenai series, derived from the Cretaceous or Tertiary age.[90]

Collier spent some time at the closed Drew (Pioneer) mine, which he rated the most important point for coal mining on the Yukon. At the mine, almost-vertical sandstones had beds probably 5,000 feet thick. The coal seams were interspersed with beds of fire-clay and fine-grained sandstones. The exploited coal bed was the sixth from the bottom. About 1,200 tons of coal had been produced, most of it sold to steamers at $15 a short ton. The use was not entirely satisfactory, perhaps because the coal miners had not separated out enough dirt from the coal, perhaps because the firemen aboard the steamers were inexperienced, or perhaps because the steamers had grates unsuitable for the grade of coal. Collier referred to an unsuccessful test of the Pioneer coal conducted earlier, probably in 1899, on the revenue cutter *Nunivak*. According to H. N. Wood, assistant engineer, U.S. Revenue-Cutter Service, the Pioneer coal:

> used mixed with Comox coal in the proportion of two parts of Yukon to one part Comox, moderate steaming could be done. Used with wood, it served fairly well, about 400 pounds being used with one cord of wood. Used to maintain low-banked fires when the engine was stopped, it seemed to be fully as good as Comox coal. If, however, a fire was wanted to furnish steam for running a ten-kilowatt dynamo, the Yukon coal was inferior, due chiefly to the waste caused by the sifting of the coal through the grates when the fires were disturbed with fresh coal or fire tools.[91]

Wood suggested that with:

> some experimenting to determine the best kinds of grates, amount of grate surface, and draft most suitable, and the proper way to handle the coal in the furnace, results could be obtained. . . . 1,200 to 1,500 pounds Comox coal equal 2,000 to 2,500 pounds of Yukon coal, equal $1\frac{1}{4}$ to $1\frac{1}{2}$ cords of spruce wood.[92]

Geologist Collier mentioned other coal resources near Rampart. He thought the coal beds on Minook Creek might be younger than the beds at the Pioneer mine although at both locations coal-bearing sandstones rested unconformably on rocks belonging to the Rampart series. The Minook Creek lignite beds had been on fire from time to time. The coal was a glossy lignite that dried up into small cubical grains. The works at former coal mines at Minook Creek and on the left bank of the Yukon, two miles below Rampart, had caved in.[93]

As Collier carried out his study, the final issue of the *Rampart Miner* reported in August a new gold discovery in the Slough of Superstition, soon named Hot Springs Slough, fifteen miles from Baker Station on the Tanana River. Discoverers Mike Laboski, Jim Dalton, and J. F. [Dad] Karshner had told the *Miner* that there were no signs of human life ever being there. Indians were said to be afraid to enter the area although some had camps five miles away. The slough led to creeks being prospected for the first time—Boulder, Hot Springs (for the hot springs on it), Spring, Hunker, Idaho, Washington, and Terre Haute. The quartz ledges had minerals of unknown types.[94]

About the same time, [John C.] Fluga, [D. L.] Fancher, and [Charles] Beach hit pay dirt on the lower Hootlanana where about one hundred miners were raising cabins. Reportedly, an offer of $30,000 for Discovery, presumably Beach's, had been rejected.[95]

In September, while acting as recorder in place of Andrew J. Balliet who had left Rampart, Ballou showed the public record of a claim to a prospective buyer. The owner and seller of the claim, angry and drunk, pushed a .44 caliber Colt under Ballou's nose, threatening, "You, son of a bitch, I'll shoot you." Thinking the man "impolite," Ballou shoved the gun aside. Another man assisted Ballou in wresting the gun away. During the ensuing fight, Ballou hit the jaw of the seller, picked him up by the pants and collar, "inviting" him outside without fully opening the door. Door and man landed on the sidewalk. Ballou wrapped up the episode with a few kicks from his heavy trail shoes. The next day, the seller left town on a boat.[96]

News of a strike in yet another new gold field arrived in early October 1902. The telegraph operator at the Chena River station telegraphed to the operator at Deakyme that there had been a strike twenty miles up the Chena, about two hundred miles south of Rampart in the Tanana Valley. A prospector had entered a trading post at the mouth of the Chena with a poke of gold dust.[97] Many Ramparters, including Gus Conradt, Lynn Smith's partner on No. 4 above, Glen Gulch, joined the stampede south to the Chena strike, which soon developed into two competing camps, one named Chena and the other, Fairbanks.[98]

Lynn Smith chose not to go with Conradt. He may have regretted his decision. In 1903, he was at his home in Rampart on New Year's Day, the day the Indians traditionally celebrated by going cabin to cabin in a ritual combining "trick or treat" with a blanket toss. Even though the miners shared their food, they might still be tossed. Following his custom, Smith presented to his Indian callers lard, crackers, and dried fruit. In return, the Indians tossed him so high that he could see the flag on the top of the NAT&T store and during the final of many tosses, he sailed through the blanket, landing on the hard, icy ground—to the Indians' amusement, but not to his.[99]

During the winter of 1902–1903, Ramparters began to travel back and forth between Rampart and Chena, often via Deakyme. G. H. Hensley in Chena wrote to Rampart that there was good pay in Gold Stream and Pedro Creek.[100] William Ballou had difficulty retaining workers for No. 9 above, Little Minook, as men joined the stampede. He heard encouraging reports about Chena and wondered if the exodus would depopulate Rampart. Balancing his own personal accounts for almost five years, Ballou realized he had only broken even. In his winter doldrums, he admitted that he was "beginning to hate this desolate waste of a country" because he "was not so ambitious" as he had been.[101]

After its energetic beginning, the new camp did not fare well. Due to a lack of supplies, costs for existing supplies at Chena soared— flour, $40 for a fifty-pound sack; axes, $10 each; bacon, $1 a pound. Lynn Smith turned down an offer to manage the Belt & Hendricks store at Deakyme, a supplier for the Chena

district. The manager's salary equaled the salary Smith was then getting at the NAT&T store in Rampart, but the managerial responsibilities were far heavier. He did not want more work for the same money.[102]

By late February 1903, word came that there was "no gold" in Chena.[103] William Ballou cancelled a planned trip to Chena when he found out the whole Chena country had already been staked by "Circle City boys." Unsuccessful Ramparters were returning, reporting no food available. They considered it too expensive to transport food from Rampart by dog team. Ballou recognized that news of the Chena River strike was spreading from Seattle to Boston, promoted by the backers of the Alaskan Central Railway. Nevertheless, Ballou cogently foresaw that there would be many strikes in the valley of the Tanana that some day would be a very prosperous region of Alaska.[104]

At the same time, Ballou complained about the slowess of mail service to Rampart. A change in postal contracts had increased the weight pull on dogs to 400 pounds, thereby decreasing the speed at which mail couriers' dog teams could travel.[105]

Interest in Rampart claims continued. Erastus Brainerd, from his residence in Seattle, applied for patents on three Idaho Bar claims. Andrew Balliet, by then also in Seattle, assisted Brainerd in the application process.[106] In addition, two of the original creek record books for Hunter Creek disappeared from Commissioner J. L. Green's office during a period of litigation over some claims on Hunter. Not long before, Volume 2 of the general records had mysteriously disappeared, reappearing a month later.[107]

In July the Rampart Gold Mines Company brought hydraulic machinery for its claim on Big Minook.[108] The same month Ella R. Garratt Struthers of St. Michael accepted $2,500 from John Belsea to transfer to Belsea the lower one-half of No. 4 above, Glen Gulch, closing out two years of litigation.[109]

Also in July, Rampart hosted four U.S. senators, their staff, and accompanying news reporters for hearings of the Senate Subcommittee of the Committee on Territories. Knowing he would be testifying before the senators, Judge Wickersham set a court session at Rampart to hear petitions on the incorporation of Fairbanks and Rampart. Wickersham had just completed a trip through Kantishna. En route to Rampart, hiking from Deakyme, he stopped off at Glen Gulch for a meal with his Eagle Mining friends, William Beardsley and Jack Belsea, and stayed overnight with Frank Stevens. On reaching Rampart, he had his first shave in two months and his first bath in probably equally as long a time. The barber pitched into the Yukon River Wickersham's disreputable, smelly clothes, with, to Wickersham's dismay, a $100 gold watch attached. Then Wickersham filed with the commissioner his Discovery claim on the Chitsiak along with a map of the Kantishna region. Prospectors used his map to locate rich claims he had overlooked.[110]

On the morning of Monday, July 20, the government steamer *Jeff Davis* arrived at Rampart; Senator Dillingham, Vermont, chairman of the subcommittee; Senator Nelson, Minnesota; Senator Patterson, Colorado; Senator Burnham, New Hampshire; and their entourage disembarked. Dr. Wilcox of the surgeon general's staff, who roamed through Rampart, became excited at seeing the horns of an extinct Alaska buffalo.[111] Senators Dillingham, Burnham, and Nelson stayed with William Ballou for three days. The miners complained to the senators about taxation without representation, lack of roads, and poor mail service. They wanted a 2,000-mile stage service in winter, mailboats in summer, and a railroad from the coast. They favored government subsidies to businesses in the form of land grants and millions of dollars.[112]

The subcommittee journeyed from Dawson along the Yukon through Alaska from Eagle to St. Michael and Nome to investigate natural resources—mining, agriculture, fisheries, and lumber; government—territorial and local government, the federal court, and a delegate to Congress; development of services—lighthouses, roads, and mail; and the condition of the people—Natives, homesteaders, and the insane. The information collected compared less

favorable conditions in Alaska to more favorable conditions in Canada.[113]

Five persons participated in the officially recorded testimony in Rampart—Abraham Spring, Fairbanks, and D. A. McKenzie, Coldfoot, on July 20; Judge Wickersham, Eagle, and E. J. Knapp, Rampart, on July 22; and M. V. Hendricks, Chena, on July 23. Abe Spring talked about the absence of local mining laws and the greed of first miners in opening up a new area. The first miners staked as many claims as they could because existing laws seldom restricted them. Spring requested a small, compact pamphlet of clearly stated U.S. mining laws so that each miner would know his rights and obligations as well as penalties if he failed to comply. At the same time, Spring advocated that Congress not weigh down miners with too many restrictions and too many laws. He opposed the power of attorney, believing the individual should stake claims in person, not through an appointed delegate, but he did recommend the legalization of 160-acre claims.[114]

Spring also addressed his concern for improved roads and trails, leading to placer mines. As an example of a poor trail, he cited the almost impassable, thirty-mile trail from Rampart to Glen Gulch. He referenced the hydraulic mining plant, probably the one owned by the Rampart Gold Mines Company, which lay useless on the bank of the Yukon that summer mining season since it could not be freighted to the creek claim until the trail hardened after freeze-up. Spring emphasized trail-building because he realized the construction of wagon roads would be many years in the future.[115]

D. A. McKenzie, who had traveled one thousand miles in twenty days to reach Rampart, also advocated roads, particularly a road from the mouth of the Orinzic River to Coldfoot. He thought that U.S. mining laws should be amended to restrict a locator to one claim per creek and its tributaries.[116]

At the senators' request, Judge Wickersham testified from the standpoint of his extensive travels on court business from Eagle to Valdez, Unalaska, Nome, and points in-between. He asserted that Alaska was "primarily a mining country. . . . There is hardly a stream running into the Tanana or Yukon in this area which does not carry gold, some of them in paying quantities, though most of them have been very little prospected."[117]

Wickersham regarded the U.S. mining code as too liberal in the context of the miners' staking claims through power of attorney. Otherwise, he considered the well-established code good. He explained the issue of the high rates for transporting supplies from St. Michael upstream on the Yukon and over to the camps on the creeks. He suggested that there be a branch road from the crossing of the Tanana, north along the Tanana valley to Fairbanks and thence up to Rampart, paid through a tax on the miners which he believed the miners would accept.[118]

E. J. Knapp, the Episcopal lay missionary at Rampart, described to the senators the condition of the Indians around Rampart. In Knapp's judgment, the Indians' living conditions were reasonably adequate, but their state of health was not. He called, therefore, for the strict enforcement of the law forbidding the sale of whiskey to Indians and an increase in the severity of penalties assessed on a convicted seller. He argued against the idea of reservations, noting that the Indians around Rampart had specifically said they did not want to live on reservations. He stressed to the senators that the Indians complained about the activities of white men in the Indian hunting grounds, explaining:

On returning from their winter hunting trip this past season, the Indians report the presence of increasing numbers of white men—trappers, prospectors, and miners—in remote regions among the hills at the headwaters of the tributaries of the Yukon, where they are accustomed to go to hunt. They say that large tracts of country are being burned over through fires started by white men and are being ruined for hunting purposes. The Indians themselves are . . . careful in lighting and extinguishing fires in the woods, and especially careful during a dry season. They appreciate the impor-

tance to themselves of keeping the country from being burned over, for forest fires drive away the game. . . . It is no uncommon occurrence for white men during the summer season to start forest fires to obtain relief from the mosquitoes. In the immediate neighborhood of a mining gulch, a forest fire is, in a way, a distinct advantage to the miner. . . . [The charred wood is] more useful for carrying on mining operations.[119]

In the final recorded testimony at Rampart, M. V. Hendricks, NAT&T representative at Chena, spoke about the routes south from the Tanana to the Kenai and from the Tanana to Valdez. He considered the Valdez trail the better of the two to open up and develop the Interior for mining, and he recommended that Fairbanks be the Interior's core city.[120]

To celebrate the conclusion of the hearings, Ramparters in the Arctic Brotherhood, Camp No. 15, initiated the senators and their staff at a smoker in their lodge. Through the senators, they invited President Teddy Roosevelt to join their camp.[121] When the senatorial party reboarded the steamer *Jeff Davis,* Rampart camp members, in white parkas for the send-off ceremony, gathered along the bank of the Yukon and let out their "malemute howl."[122]

After completing their hearings in Alaska, the senators of the subcommittee submitted their findings and recommendations to the full Senate. They rated the extensive Yukon district, 80,000 to 100,000 square miles, as the third in gold production after the Seward Peninsula and Juneau. They commented on the absence of public wagon roads, elaborated on the distance and problems of freighting goods into the Interior, and singled out the federal government's inaction as the reason for the slow development of the Yukon district. According to the subcommittee,

The inaction of our government is manifest. It has done nothing to relieve this condition. It has neither built roads nor provided other means of transportation, and the hardy and adventurous citizens who have sought wealth hidden

Figure 14. Rampart Camp No. 15, Arctic Brotherhood, send-off for the senatorial party, 23 July 1903. Courtesy of the Herbert Heller Collection, University of Alaska Fairbanks. Accession Number 79-44-620.

in the valley of the Yukon, the Koyukuk, and Seward Peninsula have done so amidst difficulties that can only be understood by those who have made a study of the situation.

The action of the Dominion government [Canada] has been in marked contrast to the inaction of the United States. . . .[123]

Consequently, the subcommittee advocated a system of wagon roads, beginning with a road from Valdez to Eagle. The committee questioned the practice of staking claims by power of attorney, the lack of assessment work before such power-of-attorney staking, and relocation of a claim by the original owner to avoid assessment work on the original claim. The subcommittee concluded that abuse of the system, not the system itself, was at fault. The members recommended four changes to U.S.

mining laws:

1. Proof of performance of some assessment work on a staked claim before the claim could be recorded;
2. Extension of the length of assessment on a claim per calendar year to at least thirty days, not including days of travel to and from the claim;
3. Filing of affidavits of assessment work by the claimant and two witnesses with the commissioner by the last day of the year; and
4. Restriction of each person to staking, locating, or holding—except by purchase—only one claim on the same creek.[124]

A week after the senators left, Gen. Frederick Funston, commander, Department of the Columbia, the army designation for the Northwest command in the Columbia River region, including Alaska, reached Rampart, probably to inspect the telegraph office. During the period, Judge Wickersham heard presentations requesting permission for a vote to incorporate Rampart, Fairbanks, and Chena.[125]

With the approach of the date for residents to vote on incorporation of Rampart, opposition to incorporation increased. Sam Heeter thought the only ones who would benefit from incorporation would be the office holders.[126] Lynn Smith suggested that if incorporation was approved, John Minook, the founder of mining in Rampart, be nominated to the council. Smith's proposal raised a "shindy," a noisy disturbance.[127] Incorporation failed.

During this period, William Ballou had become interested in Ruby Creek. For $375, he purchased from Wally Laboski No. 5 above, Ruby, and a one-half-interest in the Bear Valley bench claim on What Cheer Bar.[128] He actually

acquired by purchase or lease fifteen claims on Ruby Creek. He left Rampart in September to raise $15,000 for a hydraulic plant to develop the claims and to charter the Ruby Gold Mining Company in Portland, Maine.[129]

When he was outside, William Ballou accomplished perhaps more than he had originally planned. He married long-time acquaintance Dollie Crosier of Springfield, Massachusetts, in March 1904.[130] In mid-April, he incorporated the Ruby Gold Mining Company under Maine laws, deeding to it No. 5 above, Ruby Creek, one-half interest in Bear Valley bench claim, and one-half interest in both No. 5 above and No. 8 above, Hoosier Creek. Young Spencer Cutting, son of Ballou's silent financial partner, Bostonian Frank A. Cutting, witnessed the transaction and prepared to join Ballou and Dollie at Ruby Creek.[131]

When the Ballous reached San Francisco,

Figure 15. *John Minook and his family, Rampart, circa 1900. Minook's daughter, Lucy Minook Carolan, is the second woman from the left. Courtesy of the Vertical File, University of Alaska Fairbanks. Accession Number 897-2N.*

Ballou was determined to learn more about hydraulic mining. At that time, California considered hydraulic mining detrimental to agriculture since the heavy streams of water against the hills caused mudslides, and so California law restricted hydraulic mining to those few miners who held a special permit and operated under instructions that miners considered "impossible" to follow. Those miners who hydraulicked illegally and secretly functioned like operators of whiskey stills in Kentucky. For Ballou to observe illegal hydraulicking in Nevada City, California, he had to give letters of recommendation from a Charlie Harris and, apparently, had to buy drinks for the mining community. He was watched for two days and then escorted to a mine a mile from the hotel at Nevada City. The old miner there, who had arrived from Maine in the 1850s, welcomed Ballou once he was convinced that Ballou was not a spy for the state of California. His hydraulicking operation was the only one Ballou saw. While there, Ballou became attracted to quartz mining. Ballou's hydraulicking outfit weighed fifty tons and cost $56.50 per ton to ship to Alaska on the *St. Paul*.[132]

Like Ballou, other miners were making advances in mining methods. M. S. Gill, planning on working a claim on Shirley Bar, intended to use a four-inch centifugal pump to force dirt into boxes with a small nozzle.[133] J. W. Moore sold his share in a hydraulic plant on lower Hoosier to A. H. Monroe.[134] In Seattle, John Stanley, general manager of the A. F. Schmitz Alaska Dredging and Mining Company, supervised shipment of a dredging plant to Big Minook.[135] L. M. Davis, president and general manager, Rampart Hydraulic Mining Company of Arizona, was scheduled to bring to Rampart in July the "biggest hydraulic outfit ever on the Yukon."[136]

Interest in Chena and Fairbanks continued. Courier Emil Fursteneau arrived in Rampart in mid-May, predicting Chena was going to be the great city on the Tanana.[137] Lynn Smith spent time at Chena in February 1904, before he visited his home in Indiana. On his way out, he found out that Bill Faulkner had sold an interest in What Cheer Bar for $10,000. With hindsight, Smith regretted that he had refused an earlier opportunity to buy into What Cheer for only $1,500.[138] Frank Hiatt reported that food supplies had always been available in Chena and Fairbanks for those with the money to pay for them.[139] The belief that provisioners received all the profit from the miners' work was undoubtedly widespread. Rampart miners probably related to the plaintive "Pay: The Koyukuk Miner's Lament," which advised:

Listen to the windlass
All the livelong day.
How the creaking of its crank
Sings the song of "Pay."

We who delve in this land
Simply have a lay.
Ours to do the digging
The store takes all our "Pay."

All the world's a windlass
Turning day by day.
Labor gets the waste dirt.
The FEW take all the "Pay." J. H. J [140]

Newcomers still arrived in Rampart, although in lesser numbers than in earlier years. Joe Wiehl, Discovery, Big Minook, returned with his brother, S. B. Wiehl, nephew, J[ohn] H. Wiehl, and nieces Katie and Lizzie Wiehl. The two women were to run the Florence Restaurant, presumably in Al Mayo's Florence Hotel.[141] Mayo's unusual sense of humor showed in one of his weekly advertisements:

IF
If you want a good Cigar,
If you want a good Drink,
If you want a good Bed,
If—If you want to get Robbed,
Go to Florence Hotel.[142]

On July 7, the Rampart miners protested because the large stores had reduced the price of gold dust and demanded cash, not credit, for supplies. The next evening, they established the Miners Protective Association of Rampart, electing M. W. Sinclair president, William Ballou secretary, and newly arrived Spencer Cutting treasurer. The association members pledged to do business with independent merchants who had not reduced gold prices. The members voted that:

> We condemn the action of the two commercial companies of this camp in depreciating the price of gold dust from $16 per ounce to $15.50. The change from the credit system to the present cash basis is antagonistic to the best interests of the miner who is compelled by conditions of climate to work the winter mining season and await his spring wash-up for funds. . . [143]

In September 1904, U.S.G.S. geologists L. M. Prindle and Frank Hess made a comprehensive assessment of the Rampart district. They estimated the gold production for 1903–1904 to have been $235,000 and all production since 1896 to have been over $1,000,000.[144]

The geologists pointed out the height of the region, extending from the summit of Wolverine Mountain 4,640 feet above sea level, to 400 feet above sea level on the Yukon. They mentioned that the area north of the divide between the Yukon and the Tanana was rough with steep-sided ridges and deep, narrow canyons. In contrast, the area south of the divide had long, sloping ridges and open valleys leading into Baker Flats. On a clear day, someone standing on the ridge above Baker valley could see Mount McKinley and Mount Foraker in the distance. Minook Creek, about twenty-five miles long, flowed beneath a bench that was an old floor. The bench and the "high bench" resulted from processes of stream development still at work.[145]

Prindle and Hess noted that on the Tanana River side of the divide the streams of economic importance were only a few miles long. They mentioned the government's agricultural experiment stations at Rampart and at Hot Springs.[146]

According to the geologists, the oldest rocks of the area were garnetiferous mica-quartz schists and marble. They appeared near Ruby Creek and on Minook Creek. Earlier, geologist J. E. Spurr had identified large areas of shales, cherts, limestones, tuffs, conglomerates, and diabases as the Rampart series formation from the Devonian period. The most extensive mass of igneous material occurred in the lower valleys of Little Minook and Hunter creeks.[147]

The geologists focused on Little Minook Creek, stating that mining only took place in the creek's lower three miles. The creek had produced about $475,000 since 1896, but no gold in quantity had been found above the point where Little Minook received drainage from the high bench gravels. Since so much of the ground had been "gophered" by past mining methods, it had become expensive to mine the remaining good ground.[148]

In the opinion of the geologists, Hunter Creek resembled Little Minook. The depth to bedrock was about forty feet. The gold was finer than that of Little Minook; some of it was rough. The geologists thought that the miners might erroneously take for stream deposits soft, decomposed tuffs and loosely consolidated shales and sandstones with plant remains. They, therefore, recommended that miners carefully compare newly exposed bedrock to the material already worked to determine the nature of the new undeveloped ground. They also noticed the hydraulicking being done on Hunter and the process of fractional ground sluicing there, whereby a ground-sluiced section was allowed to thaw for a week or so while another section was ground sluiced.[149]

Prindle and Hess studied other creeks as well. They realized that much of the two-mile-long Little Minook Junior Creek had been worked out and that a hydraulic plant was being installed on Hoosier Creek. No work, however, was in progress on Florida Creek. The pair wrote at length about the gravels on the high bars—Idaho Bar, McDonald Bar—situated 500 to 700 feet above the creeks. The gravels included quartzite, quartzite breccia, vein quartz, chert, and decomposed fragments of softer rocks. The geologists suggested that those gravels were probably the source of much of the gold in the stream gravels, pointing out that the concentration of the gold on the high gravels and a similar concentration of gold in narrow valleys below illustrated the process of reconcentration.[150]

The geologists saw the preparation for hydraulicking on Ruby Creek where some silver nuggets had been found. Silver had also been uncovered on Slate Creek where the bedrock was dark, shaly limestone; green and purple shale; and chert. The geologists knew of plans to hydraulick Big Minook in 1905. They went over to Quail Creek, a tributary of Troublesome Creek, and noted evidence of some sluicing. The bedrock on Quail consisted mainly of black and gray slaty shales with quartz seams. Gravels held shale quartzites, vein quartz, coarse conglomerate, and igneous material.[151]

To the south across the divide, the geologists considered Pioneer, Eureka, Rhode Island, Omega, and Thanksgiving creeks, Glen Gulch, and Gold Run to be of economic importance. They found no work was being done on the Hutlina (Hootlanana). They considered that What Cheer Bar, 2,000 feet back of Pioneer Creek and 250 feet above the creek, showed examples of "earth creep." Most of the well-worn gold there appeared in the lower portion of the gravels. Seattle Bar, according to the geologists, resembled What Cheer. The geologists presumed that the Pioneer Creek of long ago occupied parts of what was by 1904 a bench and that the old creek concentrated a pay streak in the bench gravels.[152]

In contrast to Pioneer Creek, the geologists observed that Eureka Creek, about one and one-half miles northwest of Pioneer until it turned to join Pioneer at Baker Flats, had less well-developed gravels and considerable clay. Some of its gold was rough. In their study, the geologists learned that Glen Gulch had produced about $275,000 since 1901—$35,000 in the summer of 1904—and that Shirley bench had also produced much gold, characterized as well rounded and "shotty." Gold Run shared the "shotty" characteristics. Omega Creek had both smooth and rough gold; nuggets from Omega contained quartz. Thanksgiving Creek likewise had smooth and rough gold and nuggets with quartz.[153]

Prindle and Hess concluded that the cost of production often reached close to 50 percent of the cost of the output. They recognized that the expense of installing a hydraulic plant in the Rampart district far exceeded expenses for installing a comparable plant in the continental United States. They recommended, therefore, that mine operators exercise caution and study in planning hydraulicking and equal care in managing the operation.[154]

After the geologists left and the summer mining season ended, the editor of the *Alaska Forum*, James B. Wingate, initiated a long muckraking attack against Marshal George Dreibelbis, Commissioner J. Lindley Green, and Judge Wickersham. Dreibelbis had transferred to Fairbanks, but the *Forum* denounced him for apparently entrapping individuals who sold whiskey to Indians, for charging the government $1.00 per meal per prisoner, and for supposedly receiving graft during his receivership of Garratt's No. 4 above, Glen Gulch.[155]

In addition, the *Forum* targeted Commissioner Green. In July 1903, a secret federal grand jury had investigated a complaint of incompetency against Green and had exonerated him. The *Forum* remained unhappy and unconvinced about the jury's decision.[156]

The *Forum* considered Judge Wickersham unqualified for reappointment to the court. As an example of Wickersham's being unfit for office, the *Forum* referred to the judge's order to a jury in July 1903 to find defendant Jack Mennis "not guilty" of a charge of stealing $1,445 in gold dust from Wickersham's friends at the Eagle Mining Compay, Glen Gulch. Mennis was freed, and, the *Forum* intimated, retrieved his cache of stolen gold dust.[157]

The *Forum* also reported apparent irregularities regarding the fee deposited by John Minook for his application for U.S. citizenship. Minook, possibly to confirm publicly his right to hold claims in the same manner as any other U.S. citizen twenty-one years or older, had applied to Wickersham's court for final citizenship in August 1903, presumably during the session in Rampart. Judge Wickersham had questioned Minook and his witnesses about Minook's character. Wickersham then referred to the provisions of the treaty between the U.S. and

Russia at the 1867 purchase of Alaska. Wickersham doubted the court's power to grant Minook's request. The judge directed Minook to deposit $10 with the court for final citizenship papers, promising the money would be returned if the court could not issue citizenship papers. In July 1904, John Minook received a written notice from Judge Wickersham, determining that, in Wickersham's judgment, "the applicant is a citizen of the United States by virtue of the third article of the treaty with Russia ceding Alaska to the United States."[158] Wickersham's court, therefore, could not issue citizenship papers to John Minook since he was already a citizen at the time of his application, and the court could not make him any more a citizen than he already was. The court, the *Forum* pointed out, did not refund the $10 deposit to Minook. Apparently, there was no record of the deposit. Tongue-in-cheek, the *Forum* suggested that the missing $10 might have been invested so that, at some future date, heirs of John Minook would collect the $10 together with its accumulated interest.[159]

At one point Wickersham apparently retaliated. According to a *Forum* editorial, Wickersham had called Rampart "a shoestring town." His "henchmen" reportedly stated that he would never again hold court at Rampart since the miners had rejected incorporation.[160]

During the fall 1904, Wickersham's friends, the partnership of the Eagle Mining Company, had more problems. The company dug a ditch to bring water down from the head of Boston Creek, up Eureka Creek, and over to No. 3 above, Glen Gulch. However, the ditch builder used the wrong end of the tripod in measuring, so that the finished ditch was four feet lower at the head than at the end. As a result, the water destined for the claim flowed in the reverse direction, toward Boston Creek.[161]

By that time, some miners had turned their attention to a new district, the Toolavana (Tolovana), halfway between Rampart and Fairbanks, sixty-five miles to either place. Sixteen creeks had been staked, and sixty claims had been recorded in Fairbanks, some on the north fork, Nortakakat, some on the south fork,

Chataneeka. Bill Cheeseman, George Gillis, and J. Gullich thought that Minecaga on the Tolivana would be an ideal spot for a townsite.[162] Spencer Cutting assayed stream tin in the district at 20 to 30 percent pure tin.[163]

In late 1904, the government opened a segregated school, one session for white children, one session for the Indian children from the village.[164] In another development during the period, wolves bothered Rampart and the camps in numbers and to an extent never previously experienced. Wolves ate one dog and severely harmed another at the roadhouse at No. 104, Big Minook; they also killed several dogs at the Indian village above Rampart.[165]

News of new camps continued to draw prospectors from their old field to the latest one. In January 1905, some miners in the Tanana area were stampeding to the Tozikaket, seventy-five miles from the river's mouth.[166] Freighter Walter Sundborg on the way from Fairbanks to Rampart met mushers from Nome headed to the new camp.[167]

As some prospectors left, others stayed on. During June 1905, M. S. Gill purchased the claims of the Eagle Mining Company on Glen Gulch for $45,000. Beardsley and Belsea disposed of the claims so that they could concentrate their attention on their more recent holdings on Esther (Ester) Creek near Fairbanks. Gill reportedly extracted $36,000 worth of gold from his newly acquired claim, 2 above, Glen Gulch.[168]

After a year in existence, the Miners Protective Association of Rampart reported that the members, all miners, had expended $20,000 bringing in their own outfits, presumably thereby, avoiding local merchants. The members held elections for a new slate of officers. They chose George W. Ledger president, Louis Iverson vice president, and S. R. Hudson treasurer; they re-elected William Ballou secretary.[169]

In September 1905, Wally Laboski and others joined a rush to a strike on the Novikaket. John Minook, returning from the region, considered the strike better than the Klondike, so good, in fact, that he decided to remain at home to catch fish.[170]

The unusual presence of a caribou herd attracted considerable attention. That fall of 1905, caribou came within eight miles of Rampart, precipitating a stampede of hunters toward the herd. According to John Minook, Indian hunters killed over ninety caribou and distributed five to each family. White hunters killed nearly sixty.[171] William Ballou failed to kill any, returning unsuccessful from his hunt in Troublesome River country.[172]

By the end of 1905, miners were turning their attention away from Rampart. Some stayed in Rampart, but others drifted away, spreading across the Interior, many crossing the divide into the valley of Baker Flats, some continuing down to Fairbanks, and some proceeding on to Kantishna.

End Notes Chapter 2. Federal Government Oversight, 1900–1905.

Short Titles

The following shortened forms referring to depositories and series are used extensively through the chapter endnotes.

Archives, UAF	Alaska Archives and Manuscripts, Alaska and Polar Regions Department, Elmer E. Rasmuson Library, University of Alaska Fairbanks.
District Recorder, Fairbanks	State of Alaska Department of Natural Resources, Office of the Commissioner, District Recorder, Fairbanks, Alaska.
Division of Mining, Fairbanks	State of Alaska Department of Natural Resources, Division of Mining, Fairbanks, Alaska.
(folder)	A copy of a creek record, dated between 1896 and 1900, at the office of the District Recorder, Fairbanks. The original is retained at the office of the State Recorder, Anchorage, Alaska.
Fort Gibbon	Fort Gibbon recording district records at the office of the District Recorder, Fairbanks, Alaska.
Manley	Manley Hot Springs recording district records at the office of the District Recorder, Fairbanks, Alaska.
Rampart	Rampart recording district records at the office of the District Recorder, Fairbanks, Alaska.
U.S.G.S.	U.S. Geological Survey.

1. U.S. Senate, *Conditions in Alaska: Hearings before Subcommittee of Committee on Territories Appointed to Investigate Conditions in Alaska*, 58th Cong., 2d sess., S. Rept. 282, pt. 2 (Washington: Government Printing Office, 1904), 120.

2. Rampart, Big Minook Creek (folder), 2: 128–30.

3. Rampart, Little Minook Junior Creek (folder), District Recorder, Fairbanks, 73–74, 93, 120, 135. As other records show, Myers bought and sold many claims during the period.

4. Ballou to Walt, 26 February 1900, William B. Ballou Collection, box 1, folder 80, and legal paper filed 15 December 1900, ibid., box 2, folder 184. There are many comments on aspects of the Myers's cases scattered through the Ballou correspondence and records, 1900-1901.

5. Ballou to Walt, 26 February 1900, ibid., box 1, folder 80.

6. Farnsworth to Lt. Rogers, 30 January 1900, C. S. Farnsworth Collection, box 1, folder 4.

7. Farnsworth to Young, 15 February 1900, ibid., box 1, folder 4.

8. Ibid.

9. Ballou to Mother, 12 April 1900, William B. Ballou Collection, box 1, folder 82, and Ballou to Walt, 22 June 1900, ibid., box 1, folder 84. Ballou himself spent a few days in Nome in mid-June 1900 on his way out for the summer. During his short stay, there were at least three shootings—"one dead man for breakfast every morning."

10. Fitzhugh to Mother, 2 March 1900, Robert Hunter Fitzhugh Collection, box 1, folder 24. The bicyclist had taken his bike up the Inland Passage by steamer and by railroad to Lake Bennett. He was "doing first rate."

11. Judkins to Alice, 15 February and 11 March 1900, and 6 January 1901, Perry Judkins Collection, box 1, folder 3. By late December, Chamberlin was urging Judkins to join him.

12. Farnsworth to Col. P. H. Ray, 21 February 1900, C. S. Farnsworth Collection, box 1, folder 4.

13. Smith to Folks, 30 May and 16 June 1900, Herbert Heller Collection, box 1, folder 3. Smith did not reveal the destination of Bruner and Paget, but most *Ohio* passengers were on their way to Nome.

14. Fitzhugh to Mother, 1 August 1900, Robert Hunter Fitzhugh Collection, box 1, folder 27.

15. Smith to Folks, (no date) July 1900, Herbert Heller Collection, box 1, folder 3, and Smith to Mary, 23 July 1900, ibid.

16. Kitchener, 108, 153. Mayo had sold his interest

in the store in 1899. He operated a sawmill at Mike Hess Creek and the Florence Hotel. Also, minutes of the passenger association, steamer *Navarro*, 7 October 1897, Perry Judkins Collection, box 1, folder 12. Wobber had been secretary of the *Dwyer's* passenger association and had wintered at Nunivak Slough in 1897-early 1898.

17. Smith to Polly, 7 September 1900, Herbert Heller Collection, box 1, folder 3.

18. Smith to Mother, 18 September 1900, ibid., box 1, folder 3.

19. Richardson to Farnsworth, General Order No. 19, 30 July 1900, C. S. Farnsworth Collection, box 1, folder 5, and Farnsworth to Will, 14 August 1900, ibid., box 1, folder 5.

20. Farnsworth to Sgt. Joseph Lucas, order of 12 July 1900, ibid., box 1, folder 5; Dr. Weirick to Farnsworth, 11 September 1900, ibid., box 1, folder 5.

21. Judkins to Alice, (date unclear, probably August 1900), Perry Judkins Collection, box 1, folder 3.

22. Rampart, Journal, 271–75, 278–79, 281. Other workers attaching liens for wages were John Spencer, William Smith, William Smouse, and Mike Dwyer.

23. Judkins to Alice, 6 November 1900, Perry Judkins Collection, box 1, folder 3.

24. *Alaska Forum*, 1 November 1900. The *Forum* started weekly publication on 27 September 1900. *The Rampart Whirlpool* apparently ceased publication in 1899.

25. Ibid., 8 November and 15 November 1900.

26. Clipping from *The Morning Herald*, Lexington, KY, 13 January 1901, Robert Hunter Fitzhugh Collection, box 1, folder 29.

27. Smith to Folks, 15 November 1900, Herbert Heller Collection, box 1, folder 3. Smith, a singer, frequently led the singing at church services and other celebrations.

28. Fitzhugh to Mother, 29 October 1900, Robert Hunter Fitzhugh Collection, box 1, folder 28, and clippings, December 1900-January 1901, ibid., box 1, folder 29. Folder 29 contains newspaper clippings about Fitzhugh's death and letters from Episcopal missionary, Edward J. Knapp, who presided at the funeral, and from former partner George Hyde Preston.

29. *Alaska Forum*, 20 December 1900. Also, *Seattle Post Intelligencer*, 5 August 1897. Muldowney had been a passenger on the *Cleveland* with George MacGowan and E. T. Barnette. His name appears in some location records, more often as a witness than as a locator.

30. Smith to Folks, 18 December and 24 December 1900, Herbert Heller Collection, box 1, folder 3.

31. *Alaska Forum*, 20 December 1900.

32. Ibid., 20 December and 28 December 1900. Muldowney, age 27, was from Poughkeepsie, NY.

33. Rogers to Farnsworth, 2 January [1901], C. S. Farnsworth Collection, box 1, folder 4.

34. *Alaska Forum*, 1 August and 15 August 1901, and 29 April 1905. Also, Hunt, 161–64. The Hunt book presents the Carolan case based on information from the court records of the July 1901 trial in Eagle. The defense had insisted that Muldowney had raped Lucy Carolan.

35. *Alaska Forum*, 3 January 1901.

36. Ibid., 20 December 1900 and 3 January 1901. C. H. Knapp, elected judge in September 1899, occasionally signed himself as U. S. commissioner, but he never held the position officially. Balliet started the Rampart recording district, initiating new books and gathering in all the earlier records, both creek and townsite. Even the town of Peavy on the Koyukuk River intended to respond to Balliet's request. Since the Peavy office was to close on 1 June 1901, the registrar there planned to send Peavy's records to Balliet by that date.

37. Ibid., 3 January 1901. Hatchet miners resembled lead pencil miners. The terminology referred to the hatchet-mark applied by locators and relocators in blazing trees at the boundaries of claims.

38. Ibid., 10 January 1901.

39. Ibid., 31 January 1901.

40. Ballou to Walt, 12 October 1900, William B. Ballou Collection, box 1, folder 90; Ballou to Mother, 22 November 1900, ibid., box 1, folder 91; Ballou to Mother, 15 December 1900, ibid., box 1, folder 92; Ballou to Mother, 9 January 1901, ibid., box 2, folder 93; Ballou to Mother, 17 February 1901, ibid., box 2, folder 95; Ballou to Mother, 21 April 1901, ibid., box 2, folder 99. In the fall of 1900, Ballou worked for a time on the McGraw-Carr claim, No. 8 above, Little Minook, with Frank and Tommy McGraw. A small capital letter B, possibly for Ballou, appears over Balliet's signature in some of the recorder books of the period.

41. *Alaska Forum*, 28 December 1900, and 10 January and 17 January 1901. Crowley saw to the development and assessment work on the Brainerd claims. He reported to the *Forum* on temperature inversion. The high Idaho Bar, 1,000 feet above the Yukon, was warmer by twenty-five degrees than the temperature down at the camp. Judkins, Smouse, Dwyer—all with liens against the coal mine—worked for Crowley on Discovery with Atwood, Thisby, and four others.

42. Ibid., 17 January 1901. Extracts of coal mine locations are in Appendix 3. Also, Rampart, Journal, 216–

19. The mortgage indenture between Drew and A. C. was transacted in Dawson on 4 August 1899.

43. *Alaska Forum*, 14 February and 7 March 1901. The 7 March issue includes an item of casual interest, reporting that in the fall of 1900, there had been an unsolved (never solved) robbery of $20,000 in gold dust from the A. C. shipping warehouse.

44. Rogers to Farnsworth, 10 March 1901, C. S. Farnsworth Collection, box 1, folder 7, and Farnsworth to Rogers, 18 February 1901, ibid., box 1, folder 7. Farnsworth congratulated Rogers on his promotion. Also, Ballou to Mother, 17 February 1901, William B. Ballou Collection, box 2, folder 95, and Ballou to Walt, 11 March 1901, ibid., box 2, folder 96. The other prickly case related to No. 24, Little Minook Junior, one of the Myers's cases. Ballou was on a $2,000 bond for Allen and "the Montana boys" who worked No. 24. When the case went against them, the opposing counsel tried to attach the bond. Judge Wickersham ruled against the attachment.

45. Ballou to Mother, 14 March 1901, ibid., box 2, folder 97.

46. Hon. James Wickersham, *Old Yukon: Tales–Trails–and Trials* (Washington, D. C.: Washington Law Book Co., 1938), 70–71.

47. Judkins to Alice, 10 March 1901, Perry Judkins Collection, box 1, folder 3.

48. *Alaska Forum*, 14 March 1901.

49. Ibid., 22 August 1901. The notification referred to a court judgment of 7 November 1900 in favor of A. C. and against Drew.

50. Ibid., 5 October 1901. The article did not identify the buyer. It also did not disclose whether the workers, Judkins and others, received their back wages. Dreibelbis replaced Gmehle. Also, Smith to Mother, 3 August 1901, Herbert Heller Collection, box 1, folder 4. Smith refused to take the deputy marshal position which paid only $2,000 a year.

51. Wickersham, 71.

52. Judkins to Alice, 29 March 1901, Perry Judkins Collection, box 1, folder 3. Judkins was owed about $50.

53. *Alaska Forum*, 13 June, 20 June, 25 July, and 21 December 1901. During his stay, Brainerd obtained seven claims on Idaho Bar. Outgoing passengers on the *Hamilton* were Frank and Tom McGraw, M. N. Kimball, W. B. Ballou, and Skagway Kate (Hattie LaVear). Rampart, Journal, 146, 147, 163, 169, 226. LaVear had purchased and sold town lots, 1898–1899. She returned from Tanana in December 1901 to build a saloon and dance hall which [R.] Stoddard was to manage for her since law prohibited women from running a saloon. Also, Rampart, Big Minook Creek (folder), 2: 156–57. LaVear had a one-half interest in No. 102, Big Minook, as of 6 June 1900.

54. Judkins to Alice, 26 June 1901, Perry Judkins Collection, box 1, folder 3, and receipt from Andrew J. Balliet, 2 July 1901, ibid., box 1, folder 17. By the end of 1901, Judkins had returned to California to marry his patient sweetheart. He apparently never went back to Rampart. Also, Manley, Locations, vol. 3, 28 August 1904–7 September 1912, District Recorder, Fairbanks, 1–2, entry 283. On 24 February 1906, Nicklos Nelson, acting as agent for Perry Judkins, located for Judkins the Dandy Bar claim, parallel to No. 1 below, Thanksgiving Creek.

55. *Alaska Forum*, 18 July, 25 July, 15 August, and 22 August 1901. Dillon took out $100 a day. Also, Rampart, Locations and Affidavits, 1901, District Recorder, Fairbanks, 69, 79, 101, 117, 118, 120. Bigelow filed his claim to No. 1 above before Lorencen filed his but had to rescind the claim in favor of Lorencen. Lorencen also held No. 1 below, Kentucky; Beardsley, Discovery, Glen Gulch; Dillon, No. 2 above, Glen; and Belsea, No. 3 above, Glen. Also, Manley, Deeds, 25 April 1901–6 May 1908, vol. 1, District Recorder, Fairbanks, 63–65. On 1 July 1901, Dillon, Beardsley, and Belsea signed a memorandum of agreement setting up the three-way even share in several Eagle Mining claims.

56. *Alaska Forum*, 8 August 1901.

57. Manley, Locations, 1: 286–87, 332–33, 359–60. Many claims were recorded during 1901 for the lucrative Glen Gulch, What Cheer Bar, and Eureka Creek areas. Every piece of ground—creek, bench, and bar—was staked. Also, Rampart District, Mining Locations and Declaratory Statements, vol. 1, 1901–1902, District Recorder, Fairbanks, 25–26, 94–95. Some of the location records from this book were copied into the Manley book in 1909.

58. *Alaska Forum*, 8 August 1901.

59. Rampart, Mining Locations, 1: 142–43. The practice of forming associations for 160-acre claims gradually gathered momentum after 1901.

60. *Alaska Forum*, 28 September 1901. With this issue, the *Forum* switched to publication on Saturdays.

61. Ibid., 23 November 1901. There were two men named Diver, O. A. and F. E., presumably brothers. Manley, Deeds, 1: 66–67. The transfer from Lorencen to Diver took place on 16 November 1901.

62. *The Rampart Miner*, Rampart, Alaska, 17 September 1901, M/F 142. The *Miner* competed with the *Forum* for a short while. Also, Manley, Locations, 1: 298–99. Roden located No. 3 below, Glen Gulch, on 8 July 1901.

63. Rampart, Locations and Affidavits, 1901, 103–04.

64. *Alaska Forum*, 22 August and 12 September 1901. Also, Manley, Deeds, 1: 15–16. The sale took place on 19 August 1901. Smith to Elizabeth, 24 September 1901, Herbert Heller Collection, box 1, folder 4. Smith wrote that Garratt received $1,700 cash for the sale.

65. *Alaska Forum*, 19 September and 5 October 1901. The very complicated leasing arrangements split the two half-claims into many pieces. At least three lay teams—Gill and Roden, Gaetz, Hebb, and Spyres, Moulton and Wood—worked the upper (Thumm) half; three teams—Wally Laboski, August (Gus) Conradt, and Lynn Smith, Meston and Severson, Stevens and Diver—the lower (Garratt) half. Also, Manley, Deeds, 1: 38–39. George Thisby may have been involved with Thumm's upper half.

66. *Alaska Forum*, 28 September 1901.

67. Smith to Art and Harry, 31 August 1901, Herbert Heller Collection, box 1, folder 4, and Smith to Elizabeth, 24 September 1901, ibid. Smith wrote that Roden "bilked" Garratt out of a half interest and that Roden valued No. 4 above as the "best" claim on the gulch. Also, Sundborg, 102–03. According to the Sundborg account, Sundborg knew the Garratts for a long time. Mr. and Mrs. Garratt, Ella's parents, had run a hotel in Calistoga, CA, and had come to Alaska with Sundborg on the *National City*. As Sundborg witnessed the dispute over No. 4 above, he indicated Gill and Roden paid $10,000 for a half-interest on the Garratt claim. They found it very rich but filled in their prospecting hole, declaring the claim no good. Henry Thumm, who may have been silently in with Gill and Roden, bought one-half interest for $10,000. (Smith said $1,700.) Garratt gave lays to Frank Hiatt, Sundborg, and others. Sundborg said the lays produced between $75,000 and $100,000 each.

68. *Alaska Forum*, 30 November 1901. Also, Manley, Deeds, 1: 71.

69. Smith to Polly, 13 January [1902], Herbert Heller Collection, box 1, folder 4.

70. Smith to Folks, 10 November 1901, ibid.

71. Smith to Mother, 14 March and 20 March 1902, ibid., box 1, folder 5, and Smith to Folks, 4 May 1902, ibid. Lynn Smith stated the marshal was the receiver in the case and a good friend. He gave numerous details about the situation.

72. *Alaska Forum*, 19 April 1902. Also, Smith to Mother, 24 July 1902, Herbert Heller Collection, box 1, folder 5. Wickersham was to hear the case in Rampart on 21 July, but he did not arrive. Mrs. Struthers come to Rampart for the expected trial.

73. Smith to Mother, 16 August and 23 August 1902, ibid. The Garratt name was generally used for the case.

74. *Alaska Forum*, 6 June, 27 June, and 1 August 1901. Also, Ballou to Mother, 13 February 1903, William B. Ballou Collection, box 2, folder 130. In 1903, Ballou received a letter from Rogers, by then in Manila.

75. Smith to Mother, 27 July 1901, Herbert Heller Collection, box 1, folder 4.

76. Ballou to Walt, 18 September 1901, Dawson, Yukon Territory, William B. Ballou Collection, box 2, folder 104.

77. Rampart, Mining Locations and Declaratory Statements, 1: 275–76.

78. *Alaska Forum*, 28 December 1901. The spelling of Deakyme varied. It probably originated as DeaKyne. Rampart, Big Minook Creek (folders), 2: 97 and 4: 356. A Capt. E. H. DeaKyne held claim No. 12 below, Big Minook, in 1898 and 1899.

79. Smith to Mother, 22 October 1901, Herbert Heller Collection, box 1, folder 4, and Smith to Polly, 6 January [1902], ibid. On 29 December 1901, the temperature was 30 below in Glen Gulch and 68 below in Rampart. Deakyme was considered within easy reach. With no divides to cross, the Glen Gulch miners could walk the eighteen miles and back in the same day. Also, *Alaska Forum*, 1 February 1902. Because of difficulties in landing freight at Deakyme, the Belt & Hendricks store was to be moved five miles to the mouth of Baker Creek on the Tanana opposite the site of the N. C. store at Baker Station. For a while, the new location apparently was called both Deakyme and Baker Station.

80. Ballou to Mother, 19 October 1901, William B. Ballou Collection, box 2, folder 107, and Ballou to Walt, 10 December 1901, ibid., box 2, folder 109.

81. Ballou to Mother, 29 January 1902, ibid., box 2, folder 111, and Ballou to Walt, 21 February 1901, ibid., box 2, folder 112. Mike Laboski was the brother of Wally Laboski, partner of Lynn Smith on No. 4 above, Glen Gulch. Also, *Alaska Forum*, 19 September 1901. Rampart received correspondence from Shamokin, PA, asking the whereabouts of Mike and Wally Laboski, presumed dead.

82. Ballou to Mother, 15 April 1902, William B. Ballou Collection, box 2, folder 115. Lynn Smith did not refer to the trip in his correspondence.

83. Ballou to Mother, 27 May 1902, ibid., box 2, folder 117, and Ballou to Mother, 15 June 1902, ibid., box 2, folder 119.

84. Smith to Mother, 25 June and 16 August 1902, Herbert Heller Collection, box 1, folder 5. Also, *The Rampart Miner*, 19 August 1902. The railroad was to reach Rampart in two years.

85. Ballou to Mother, 11 July 1902, William B. Ballou Collection, box 2, folder 121.

86. Arthur J. Collier, "The Glenn Creek Gold Mining District, Alaska," in *Contributions to Economic Geology,* edited by S. F. Emmons and C. W. Hayes, U.S.G.S. Bulletin 213 (Washington: Government Printing Office, 1903), 49–52. Collier described the Rampart-Glenn Creek trail, probably the one Roden expressed concern about, as following Big Minook Creek twenty-five miles to its head, across a divide 1,700 feet above the Yukon, and down into Glen Gulch, which was 800 feet above the Yukon. In the summer, it took two days to walk the thirty miles of trail.

87. Ibid., 53.

88. Ibid., 54–55.

89. Ibid., 56.

90. Arthur J. Collier, *Coal Resources of the Yukon,* U.S.G.S. Bulletin 218 (Washington: Government Printing Office, 1903), 16, 19. An earlier version of Collier's coal report appeared as an article in Bulletin 213.

91. Ibid., 37–41. The bulletin contains a picture of the Drew mine, a geologic sketch, and analytic charts.

92. Ibid., 41. Comox coal sold for $15 a long ton at St. Michael; wood cost $6 to $10 per cord.

93. Ibid., 42.

94. *The Rampart Miner,* 19 August 1902 (final issue). Also, Rampart, Mining Locations and Declaratory Statements, 1: 440–42, 568–69. Karshner located Discovery, Spring Creek, and Discovery, Hot Springs Creek, both on 10 August 1902; Dalton located No. 9 above, Washington Creek, and No. 1 above, Idaho Creek, both on 11 August 1902.

95. *Alaska Forum,* 4 October 1902. Also, Rampart, Mining Locations and Declaratory Statements, 1: 353–54, 518–19, 532–33. There were two Discovery claims on the Hootlanana — John Murray's Discovery, Upper Hootlanana, located 17 May 1902; Charles Beach's Lower Discovery, located 21 July 1902. Fancher located No. 1 above, Lower Discovery, on 21 July 1902.

96. Ballou to Walt, 22 September 1902, William B. Ballou Collection, box 2, folder 125, and Ballou to Mother, 3 November 1902, ibid., box 2, folder 126. Attorney J. Lindley Green was appointed U. S. commissioner in place of Balliet, relieving Ballou of responsibilities as the substitute recorder. Balliet apparently did not return to Rampart, but as a lawyer and notary public in Seattle, he sometimes had legal transactions involving Rampart. Also, Rampart, Mining Locations and Declaratory Statements, 1: 520. Green became recorder on or about 15 October 1902.

97. *Alaska Forum,* 4 October 1902. The short news item does not identify the prospector (Felix Pedro) or the trader (E. T. Barnette).

98. Smith to Mother, 30 December 1902, Herbert Heller Collection, box 1, folder 5.

99. Smith to Mother, 5 January 1903, ibid., box 1, folder 6, and C. J. Rozelle to Smith's family, 3 January 1899, ibid., box 1, folder 1; and also Farnsworth to mother-in-law, Mother Bosard, 25 December 1899, C. S. Farnsworth Collection, box 1, folder 3. The annual practice, held some time between Christmas and New Year's at Rampart and Fort Gibbon, was mentioned earlier, but there was no other mention of someone falling through the blanket. Also, Smith to Mother, 27 December 1903, Herbert Heller Collection, box 1, folder 6. Smith was tossed again on 26 December 1903.

100. *Alaska Forum,* 7 February and 14 February 1903. Chena was often spelled Chenoa.

101. Ballou to Mother, 13 February 1903, William B. Ballou Collection, box 2, folder 130, and Ballou to Walt, also 13 February 1903, ibid., box 2, folder 131.

102. Smith to Folks, 6 March 1903, Herbert Heller Collection, box 1, folder 6. Also, *Alaska Foruum,* 11 June 1904. Belt & Hendricks closed its trading post at Baker Station (Deakyme) in June 1904.

103. Ibid., 28 February 1903.

104. Ballou to Mother, 14 March 1903, William B. Ballou Collection, box 2, folder 132. Also, Smith to Mother, 19 June 1903, Herbert Heller Collection, box 1, folder 6. Smith mentioned that all the people coming back were broke.

105. Ballou to Mother, 13 February 1903, William B. Ballou Collection, box 2, folder 130.

106. *Alaska Forum,* 14 February 1903 and 28 May 1904. Balliet assisted Brainerd with the application process which took over a year. Brainerd, resident at 1114 Fifth Avenue, Seattle, filed Mineral Application No. 37 on 11 April 1904 for Discovery (also known as the Idaho Bar claim), Yukon, and Margaret, all on Idaho Bar.

107. *Alaska Forum,* 7 March 1903. The Hunter Creek records are still not available. Hunter Creek, vol. 3, which disappeared, is, however, referenced in existing records. It contained locations recorded in 1897.

108. Ibid., 18 July 1903.

109. Manley, Deeds, 1: 183–84.

110. Wickersham, 166, 216, 269, 310–12, 319–20. Also, Rampart, Fee Book, vol. 3. 1902–1908, District Recorder, Fairbanks, 14 July 1903. The location records and map for Wickersham's claims, filed in |Locations|, vol. 2, are not readily available, but the fee book has entries for Wickersham's payment of recorder fees for three Chitsiak claims for himself, his wife, and his son—Discovery, No. 4 above, and No. 5 above.

111. Wickersham, 413, 415.

112. Ballou to Mother, 25 July 1903, William B.

Ballou Collection, box 2, folder 139. Besides the formal testimony, there may have been many impromptu conversations between the Ramparters and the senators.

113. U.S. Senate, S. Rept. 282, pt. 2. The paragraph summarizes the topics covered through the report.

114. Ibid., 95–98. Each testimony covered many topics.

115. Ibid., 99–100.

116. Ibid., 107–08, 110, 112.

117. Ibid., 119.

118. Ibid., 121, 123.

119. Ibid., 130–32.

120. Ibid., 133–34.

121. Ballou to Mother, 25 July 1903, William B. Ballou Collection, box 2, folder 139. Also, Smith to Mother, 24 July 1903, Herbert Heller Collection, box 1, folder 6. Lynn Smith, too, entertained the senatorial party and attended the initiation ceremony.

122. Wickersham, 415.

123. U.S. Senate, *Conditions in Alaska: Report of the Subcommittee of Committee on Territories Appointed to Investigate Conditions in Alaska*, 58th Cong., 2d sess., S. Rept. 282, pt. 1 (Washington: Government Printing Office, 1904), 6–7, 9–10.

124. Ibid., 11, 19–20.

125. Wickersham, 415–17. Although the army detachment had left the Rampart garrison, apparently two men maintained the government telegraph line in Rampart. Wickersham's court session at Rampart ended on 12 August 1903.

126. *Alaska Forum*, 17 October 1903.

127. Ibid., 7 November 1903.

128. Manley, Deeds, 1: 180, 185–86. The transaction took place on 22 July 1903. On 20 June, Laboski had sold one-half interest in the Bear Valley bench to J. Kaminski for $500.

129. Ballou to Walt, 16 September 1903, aboard the steamer *Sarah*, William B. Ballou Collection, box 2, folder 140, and Ballou to Walt, 17 November 1903, Boston, MA, ibid., box 2, folder 143.

130. Ballou to Mother, 16 April 1904, Boston, MA, ibid., box 2, folder 144.

131. Manley, Deeds, 1: 233-34.

132. Ballou to Walt, 17 May 1904, San Francisco, CA, William B. Ballou Collection, box 2, folder 145. Ballou referred to purchasing "a first class saloon to square" with the mining community of Nevada City. Also, *Alaska Forum*, 18 June and 2 July 1904. Cutting arrived in Rampart on the *Sarah* in mid-June; the Ballous reached Rampart several days later on the *Susie*. The hydraulic plant had reached St. Michael by early July.

133. Ibid., 9 April and 4 June 1904. Gill had to stop his operation on Shirley Bar because of a lack of water.

134. Ibid., 7 May 1904.

135. Ibid., 21 May 1904.

136. Ibid., 11 June and 9 July 1904. Davis was apparently expected on Hunter Creek where hydraulicking operations were at capacity.

137. Ibid., 21 May 1904.

138. Smith to Mother, 29 June, 15 July, and 27 September 1904, Herbert Heller Collection, box 1, folder 7, and Smith to Herbert Heller, 10 February 1904, ibid. Smith returned to Rampart in July and was back in Chena in September. *Alaska Forum*, 28 May 1904. Faulkner sold to A. H. Lane of Lane and Olson. He was leaving to obtain medical care. Manley, Deeds, 1: 196-97. On 2 September 1903, Lynn Smith had purchased the Wedge claim on What Cheer Bar for $50 from John Crowley. Smith's claim adjoined the claims of Faulkner and Mike Laboski. Apparently, the Wedge claim was not so successful as Faulkner's claim.

139. *Alaska Forum*, 16 April 1904.

140. Ibid., J. H. J. was not identified.

141. Ibid., 18 June 1904 and 7 October 1905. In late September 1905, S. F. (or S. B.) Wiehl, by then a deckhand on the *Jeff Davis* was drowned in the Tanana River near its mouth when waves inundated the small boat he was in while he was working to assist in moving the grounded government steamer. His body was apparently never found. Also Al Mayo family genealogy (cited with permission). John Wiehl married Florence Mayo.

142. *Alaska Forum*, 25 June 1904.

143. *Alaska Forum*, 9 July and 2 July 1904. NAT&T had recently announced its new policy of gold dust at $15.50 and no credit.

144. L. M. Prindle and F. L. Hess, "Rampart Placer Region," in *Report on Progress of Investigations of Mineral Resources in Alaska in 1904*, edited by Alfred H. Brooks et al., U.S.G.S. Bulletin 259 (Washington: Government Printing Office, 1905), 106; Brooks, 15, 17, 25. Brooks made some introductory remarks about Rampart being the most westerly of the camps in the broad belt of metamorphosed rock stretching from Dawson.

145. Prindle and Hess, 106–08.

146. Ibid., 108–09.

147. Ibid., 109–11.

148. Ibid., 111–12. In their discussion of the drainage from the high bench gravels, the geologists, in effect, supported the conclusions of the miners in 1898 who attributed the gold in Little Minook to Range

Channel, the high bed of the prehistoric Yukon near the gravels of Idaho Bar.

149. Ibid., 112.

150. Ibid., 112–14.

151. Ibid., 114–15.

152. Ibid., 115–17.

153. Ibid., 117–19.

154. Ibid., 119. Also, see L. M. Prindle and Frank L. Hess, *The Rampart Gold Placer Region, Alaska,* U.S.G.S. Bulletin 280 (Washington: Government Printing Office, 1906). This report stated that the town of Rampart had a population of about 200 in summer 1904; the entire locality had a population of about 300. And see Frank L. Hess, "Placers of the Rampart Region," in *The Fairbanks and Rampart Quadrangles, Yukon-Tanana Region, Alaska,* edited by L. M. Prindle, U.S.G.S. Bulletin 337 (Washington: Government Printing Office, 1908), 64–98. The Hess report expands upon the first Prindle and Hess report with features of history, photographs of specimens, and production graphs. The report raised the production figures to $1,112,00 since 1896, $232,900 for 1904. It also mentioned the apparent course of an old channel (presumably Range Channel) either toward or from the northeast and stated miners were going to Hutlina Creek (Hootlanana) for winter work.

155. *Alaska Forum,* 22 October 1904. Wingate had been deputy clerk during Wickersham's session in Rampart in March 1901.

156. Ibid., 24 December 1904.

157. Ibid., 3 December 1904. A charge for the same crime against Harry Richmond (also known as Harry Little) was dropped although he was held in jail as a witness against Mennis. Some time after the trial, Harry Richmond was charged with sandbagging and robbing a man in Circle City. At the time, it was a somewhat common practice to knock someone unconscious with a sandbag during a robbery attempt.

158. Ibid., 10 December 1904.

159. Ibid., 10 December 1904 and 23 September 1905. In September 1905, Wingate again raised the question about John Minook's $10 deposit.

160. Ibid., 29 October 1904.

161. Ibid., 24 December 1904.

162. Ibid., 15 October 1904.

163. Ibid., 31 December 1904.

164. Ballou to Mother and P.S. from Dollie, 7 October 1904, William B. Ballou Collection, box 2, Folder 150, and Dollie to mother-in-law, Mother, 6 January 1905, ibid., box 2, folder 151. There were fifty children, presumably not all school age, in the Indian village. The children learned more easily than their teacher anticipated they would. They were particularly adept at music.

165. *Alaska Forum,* 24 December 1904.

166. Ibid., 14 January 1905.

167. Ibid., 4 February 1905. It is not clear whether or not the new camp was on the Tanana.

168. Ibid., 17 June, 5 August, and 9 September 1905. Also Smith to Herbert, 17 August 1905, Herbert Heller Collection, box 1, folder 8, and Smith to Mother, (no date) September 1905, ibid. Lynn Smith mentioned that his old friends, Beardsley of Canton, Ohio, and Belsea of Alliance, Ohio, owned Nos. 2 and 3, Esther Creek. Ella Garratt had also moved to Chena.

169. *Alaska Forum,* 21 October and 11 November 1905.

170. Ibid., 16 September 1905.

171. Ibid., 11 November and 25 November 1905.

172. Ballou to Walt, Mother, and Family, 13 January 1906, William B. Ballou Collection, box 2, folder 157.

Chapter 3. Growth of the Hot Springs and Fort Gibbon Districts, 1906–1918

The mining business is a life study and then you can learn things.
–William B. Ballou, Rampart, March 10, 1906[1]

In the beginning of 1906, Ballou and his wife remained in Rampart while others continued to move away. Ballou had done so well financially with his Ruby Creek hydraulicking plant in summer 1905 that Spencer Cutting was trying to raise $250,000 in London for a second plant 16 miles long.[2]

In January, the Rampart miners opposed a resolution adopted by Alaskan miners adopted in Seattle the previous November that supported a $25 annual license fee in lieu of $100 annual assessment work. The Ramparters preferred continuation of the required assessment since they believed the license alternative was against the best interests of miners.[3] Presumably, they wanted claims worked and fortfeited if not worked, whereas licensing would relieve the licensee of the work requirement. Ironically, Lynn Smith, who was then spending more time in Chena than in Rampart, lost all his claims in Rampart because he failed to perform representation work on them.[4]

The Rampart Gold Mines Company, which had expended considerable funds in trying unsuccessfully to establish a hydraulic operation on Big Minook, merged with the Hoosier Hydraulic Company and moved to Hoosier Creek. There the work apparently succeeded because conditions were more favorable to hydraulicking.[5] Over on the Tanana River side of the divide, M. S. Gill bought the hydraulic plant and leases on Rhode Island Creek from A. H. Monroe and the Gold Bug Mining Company.[6]

Roads remained a matter of concern to the miners. When a bridge over Little Minook gave away, John Stanley, manager of the A. F. Schmitz company, which leased Discovery and

No. 1 above Little Minook from Charles B. Allen, reopened the old 1897 trail between Hunter and Little Minook. Major Wilds P. Richardson, head of the Alaska Road Commission, promised a $20,000 wagon road from Rampart to Eureka via Little Minook Creek. Expectations heightened over a projected road from Chena to Rampart, designed to provide access to a large, unprospected area between the Tanana and Yukon rivers.[7] A new government mail trail directly cross-country from Rampart to the village of Tanana reduced the trip from 220 miles by river to 80 miles.[8]

The safety of gold shipments was a concern to banks. A mystery robbery on July 11 aroused excitement, curiosity and headlines in Interior Alaska when a box containing $78,000 in gold bricks, consigned by the Washington-Alaska Bank in Fairbanks to the Washington Trust Company in Seattle, vanished from the docked steamer *Ida May* at Fort Gibbon. The Northern Commercial Company established a reward of $5,000 for information leading to the recovery of the box and arrest of the thieves.[9] Lynn Smith investigated for the Alaska-Pacific Express Company, which had insured the shipment and had accepted full responsibility for its delivery.[10] W. C. Rodman, N.C. agent at Fort Gibbon, soon found the box in a nearby swamp. Although the box appeared to be safely sealed, when opened it held only $9,000 plus bags of buckshot and weighed less than it had at point of shipment. Volney Richmond, by then the N. C. agent in Fairbanks, tracked the box which had been put aboard the steamer *Tanana* at Fairbanks and then transferred to the Ida May at Chena. Seven days after the robbery the first arrest was made in Fairbanks and other arrests in Fairbanks and Fort Gibbon quickly followed. Commissioner E. M. Carr of Fairbanks, former Ramparter and holder of claim No. 8 above Little Minook, presided over the arraignment of George

Raphael, who confessed to purchasing the buckshot and implicated Robert Miller, night watchman aboard the *Tanana*. Miller and his accomplices had switched the gold for the buckshot on the *Tanana*, made certain the tampered box was turned over to the *Ida May* as scheduled, and then returned with the stolen gold on the *Tanana* to Fairbanks. Meanwhile, "Hard Rock Charley" Tague and his friend McDonald had seized the opportunity to remove the box secretly from the *Ida May* to a hiding place in the swamp. The second unexpected, and unconnected robbery, interrupted Miller's plan to have the buckshot-filled box arrive in Seattle before the substitution was discovered. Miller eventually turned over most of the stolen gold to authorities. Judge Wickersham sentenced Miller to two years at McNeil Island with 120 days per year deducted for good behavior provided Miller cooperate in recovering about $19,000 still missing.[11] Although the final outcome is unclear, presumably Miller cooperated.

While the investigation was proceeding, the *Alaska Forum* warned the men of Rampart that they were threatened with a "menace to their commercial existence" because Frank G. Manley, "the mining magnate of Fairbanks," had set up a trading post at Baker Creek (Hot Springs).[12] Manley, whose birth name was Hillyard Bascom Knowles, had also begun to absorb the claims on the Tanana side of the divide, occasionally referred to as Baker Creek country.[13] He was known to have successful mining claims in Fairbanks and connections to Fairbanks banks, yet the large amount of cash he liberally distributed for claims in the Eureka area must have astounded and delighted its recipients.

Through Ben F. Baker, former manager of the NAT&T store in Rampart, Manley acquired the What Cheer Bar Company for $80,000 on July 23, 1906.[14] Four days later, Frank Stevens transferred to Manley a two-thirds interest in claims on Gold Run Swail, Gold Run Creek, and Shirley and Excelsior bars along with the upper 600 feet of the well-known No. 4, Glen Gulch.[15] The same day, James Lawrence turned

claims on Gold Run Creek and Excelsior Bar over to Manley.[16] In early August, through Baker, Manley picked up the Boothby Creek claims of J. Willis Boothby for $15,000.[17] For $10,500, Otto F. Kroehle gave over to Manley claims on Gold Run Swail, Gold Run Creek, Shirley and Excelsior bars, and the lower 600 feet of No. 4 above, Glen Gulch.[18] For $42,000, M. S. Gill turned over to Manley shares of claims on Glen Gulch, Eureka, Rhode Island, and Gold Run creeks, and Shirley and Excelsior bars.[19] E. T. Townsend followed with more Rhode Island Creek claims.[20] Manley joined with Jerome A. Chute to assume claims on Thanksgiving, Chicago, and Omega creeks, paying $25,000 to the partnership of A. O. Anderson and C. H. Olson, lesser amounts to others.[21]

According to the *Alaska Forum*, D.F. Karshner received $30,000, $20,000 of it in cash, from Manley for a lease to his Hot Springs property.[22] In late October, several individuals, including J. M. Hall, Smith Hall, and Rose Sellander, transferred to Manley their interest in the saline spring on the Karshner homestead.[23]

Manley acted swiftly to develop access to his far-flung claims, building a road twenty-four miles from Hot Springs to the small settlement of Eureka and planning construction of a ditch from the Hootlanana fifteen miles to Thanksgiving Creek.[24] He brought in a churn drill, the first such drill in the region, for prospecting.[25]

William Ballou, whose Ruby Gold Mining stock had tumbled as a result of "another" poor season, wryly reported to his brother, "Last summer, a fellow named Manley struck camp with all kinds of money and has been buying ground left and right to $250,000. I tried to work our [hydraulic] plant off on him for $15,000, but he wouldn't stand for it."[26]

By this time, the practice of establishing 160-acre claims of eight equal shares had become very popular. Manley, or H. B. Knowles, held one-eighth ownership in such claims. Occasionally, Sam Bonnifield of Fairbanks partnered with him.[27]

As Manley purchased most claims on the creeks opened up by the discoveries of the

Boston boys, Oliver Lorencen, George R. Shirley, and others in the vicinity of Baker Creek, trapper and prospector Michael Joseph Sullivan quietly prospected a new area not far from the town of Hot Springs. Sullivan and some friends had been working in the region off and on since 1903. In 1905, his friend Clint DuMire renamed a creek known as Zach tich da la na, Sullivan Creek.[28] On November 21, 1906, Sullivan located Discovery, Sullivan Creek; on November 22, Discovery, Innisfail Creek; and on December 14, Discovery, Killarney Creek. He waited until February 21, 1907, to record his claims, the first claims recorded for the area which came to be known as Sullivan country.[29]

During the summer of 1907, Sullivan country developed at stampede pace. Matthew Harter discovered Harter Creek, a tributary of Cache Creek, in turn, a tributary of Sullivan Creek.[30] George Kemper discovered Patterson Creek.[31] Many 160-acre claims sprang up on Sullivan Creek, Cache Creek, Tofty Gulch, Easy Money Gulch (renamed Quartz Creek), Houklee Gulch, Miller Gulch, Woodchopper Creek, Deep Creek, and others. Michael J. Sullivan, Herman Tofty, Sam Houklee, and Patrick (Paddy) Maloney were involved in some groups; Wally and Mike Laboski, in others; Charles VanDyke, Al Dalton, and Rod McKenzie, in still others.[32] Sullivan City grew up at Discovery, Sullivan Creek. Within a short time, its name changed to Tofty.[33] Similarly, Sullivan country evolved into the Tofty area. Some years later, Michael Sullivan, presumably in jest, supposedly threatened to groundsluice the town of Tofty unless he received ground rent for use of his Discovery site.[34]

Although the mining focus had shifted away from Rampart, mining continued there. William Ballou applied for the position of commissioner for Rampart and received it, effective March 1, 1907. To prepare for his post, he had to brush up on the civil and criminal code. He liked the fact that Rampart had a spacious "skookum house" (jail) which was often full. In the office of commissioner, he served as judge of a precinct comparable in geographic area to the size of New England. He acted as recorder, town clerk, coroner, notary public, and magistrate for civil marriages. His salary, anticipated to be about $3,000 a year, came from collected fees.[35]

Ballou apparently served satisfactorily. After he was in office five months, *The Hot Springs Echo and Tanana Citizen* praised him:

> *Judge Ballou, the present commissioner, is a man of more than ordinary ability, and after a residence within the bounds of this precinct of many years, has the confidence and respect of all who know him. In the conduct of his office he is head and shoulders above any commissioner we have known and met in Alaska. . . . We will quote his first charge to the jury in the first civil case tried before him. . . . 'Gentlemen,' said he, 'I am no lawyer. You have heard the evidence. The case is yours.'*[36]

In the fall of 1907, Ballou's niece Edna Marcy accepted an appointment to teach at the Indian school in Rampart. She received $90 per month for nine months, boarded with the commissioner, then mining on Hunter Creek, and helped Dollie with their young son, William Hosea.[37]

As other commissioners had learned, their multiple duties usually prevented them from paying attention to their own mining claims and their fee income frequently failed to meet their ordinary living expenses. John Bathurst, commissioner at Tanana, had tried to resign in 1906, saying there was a "problem making a living." He belittled the job, succinctly advising would-be successors, "There is considerable less than nothing in it, which should be a matter of consideration to aspirants."[38] Nevertheless, Bathurst continued in office until Phil Gallaher replaced him on January 1, 1909.[39] Ballou resigned after one year. Rampart had no commissioner for a year, and with the position vacant, a petty crime spree broke out in Rampart. In one week alone, four cabins were broken into, and Sam Heeter's chicken coop was robbed of eight chickens. At length, the federal government appointed Dr. J. H. Hudgin commissioner on April 7, 1909.[40]

Much later, Archdeacon Hudson Stuck,

annoyed by Commissioner Hudgin's decision to dismiss an assault case that Stuck had insisted be prosecuted, referred to Hudgin as a good man, but an old, retired physician who knew nothing about the law. Stuck recognized that unsalaried magistrates in Alaska had to survive on insufficient fees. As a consequence, in his estimation, "capable" men would not accept appointment to a commissioner's office.[41]

Water for mining operations had always been a concern to the miners in the Rampart district. Too much water from thawing, break-up, excessive run-off, or underground streams flooded prospect holes; too little water during the hot, arid months of June and July reduced the miners' capability for sluicing and hydraulicking. If the drought was severe enough to dry up some creeks, operations ceased. U.S. Geological Survey engineer C. C. Covert and assistant engineer C. E. Ellsworth examined the Alaska Interior from Fairbanks to Circle from a water-supply viewpoint during three successive summers, 1907–1909. They likened Rampart's water supply to that of Fairbanks, believing that the topography did not favor water supply by gravity feed. In their opinion, unless a storage system for water could be set up, miners would have to rely on pumping. The engineers reported on various ditches, including those constructed by Frank G. Manley to carry water to the bench gravels on Thanksgiving and Pioneer creeks. Similarly, they discussed a ditch that Jerome Chute had built for Eureka Creek, as well as other ditches constructed by Sullivan Creek miners for operations near Tofty Gulch. They recognized that the region needed an increase in available water and considered the potential use of streams to generate hydroelectric power to the camps.[42] They predicted an increased demand for hydroelectric power and regarded its development as the solution to the water-supply problems, a solution that would eliminate the need for ditches. They concluded that Troublesome Creek, a forty-mile stream which entered Mike Hess Creek ten miles from the Yukon, appeared to be the only creek near the Rampart mines with sufficient run-off and gradation to be developed to provide hydroelec-

tric power. Aware of the natural formation in winter of "winter glaciers" connected with streams that were dammed or clogged, they proposed the establishment of winter glaciers by artificial means as sources for additional water. While accepting the miners' need for timber for fuel, they regretted the loss of timber in watershed areas and advocated the conservation of the forest as a natural way to retain water and distribute it gradually.[43]

Engineer Ellsworth, in his 1909 trip, realized that less expensive mining methods than hydraulicking had to be devised to penetrate down to the deep ground. The deep ground, thought to be rich, could not be reached by open-cut operations, which used the existing water supply, nor by the construction of drifts, which were subject to sudden flooding by underground channels, termed "live water."[44]

Covert and Ellsworth also took note of the work done by the Alaska Road Commission such as a six-mile long road up Minook valley, improvements in Frank Manley's road, by then thirty miles from Hot Springs to the Baker Creek area, and a road between Hot Springs and Patterson Creek, all of which facilitated the transport of supplies to the mines.[45]

Meanwhile, Lynn Smith had turned his attention to the Sullivan Creek region. In August 1907, he and Latham Jones went from Esther Creek to Hot Springs. From the Springs, he hiked fifteen miles in eight hours through mud knee-high to reach the new site but arrived too late to locate new ground. He concluded the strike was good but not exciting. By late fall, however, he was prospecting on Cooney Creek, about eleven miles from Hot Springs. He travelled to Rampart to record three claims. Although every one still at Rampart welcomed him, he could only remain one day. He thought Rampart appeared unnatural and deserted with shacks fallen down, a state of decay typical of dying mining camps.[46]

By early 1908, Lynn Smith had finished a cabin on Cooney where he had dug thirteen holes to bedrock. He believed the ground was not rich enough to justify incurring heavy expenses in machinery and labor; operations

74

Figure 16. *Hydraulicking on Hunter Creek, circa 1908. Courtesy of the William B. Ballou Collection, University of Alaska Fairbanks. Accession Number 72-47-5.*

could be profitable only if the operator managed expenses prudently. Unsuccessful, in May 1908 he grumbled that he had not made a dollar since the previous July, although he had never worked so hard. About six weeks later, he again returned to Rampart to sell his wood supply there. Once more, he saw an almost dead camp with only a few old friends living in it. Lack of rain for two months had caused the closure of all mining operations.[47]

In mid-1908 Peter Jepsen, Charles Fornander, H. W. Winde, and Ben F. Baker formed a partnership and bought interests in the Dakota Association, Sullivan Creek, and other claims near Tofty.[48] In June 1909, Fornander turned over to Jepsen his interest in the Dakota and in the Junction, also on Sullivan Creek, and in the Coeur d'Alene Association on Woodchopper Creek, along with boilers, hoists, pumps, fittings, cabins, and sluice boxes.[49] Fornander

Figure 17. Shoveling in on What Cheer Bar, 1909. Courtesy of the Falcon Joslin Collection, University of Alaska Fairbanks. Accession Number 79-307N.

left the Sullivan region. He re-appeared as a co-discoverer of Long Creek in the Ruby district, recording claims there in the spring of 1911.[50]

The rapid division and re-division of one-eighth interests in 160-acre claims created a confused situation in which many owners held minute shares in a single claim. For example, on July 21, 1908, Joe Eglar of Fairbanks paid E. H. Herbert $5,000 for Herbert's interests in ten claims, ranging from the whole of No. 22 below, Big Boulder Creek, to 1/256 interest in the Independence Association, Tofty Gulch.[51] Likewise, on August 10, 1908, Joe Kaminski transfered to M. S. Gill 3/64 interest in the Independence Association and small shares in fifteen other claims in the Sullivan region.[52] Such multiple ownerships in an association greatly reduced profits per share, if any, and sometimes created a void in responsibility for development of the association.

The Hot Springs mining district had problems. In one particular instance, U.S. Commissioner V. L. Bevington placed gold dust valued at about $3,000 and some nugget jewelry into the custody of deputy marshal and former road overseer for Hot Springs George B. Gibson for safe transit to Fairbanks. As soon as Gibson arrived in Fairbanks, he sold the gold dust and mailed the money to relatives, a part in one packet to Los Angeles and the bulk in two separate packets to Nova Scotia. When Gibson was arrested, he had very little money in his possession. Fortunately for the owners of the gold dust, Nova Scotian officials confiscated the two packets and mailed them back to Hot Springs. A contrite Gibson pleaded guilty to a charge of embezzlement and was sentenced to five years at McNeil Island.[53]

In December 1908, George W. Ledger, president of the Rampart Miners Association, visited Sullivan Creek to encourage miners there to form a branch of the association. He stressed that it existed to obtain better mining laws for Alaska, better roads, and a square deal for miners in all legislation. The miners apparently decided to set up their own organization. Four months later, Ledger presided at a meeting of the Sullivan Creek Miners Association in Tofty. The Sullivan miners wished to petition the new road overseer, Jack Price, to use road

Figure 18. Lower end of Eureka Creek near the settlement of Eureka, 1909. Courtesy of the Falcon Joslin Collection, University of Alaska Fairbanks. According to Joslin, the hillside held three paystreaks, Shirley Bar, Green bench, and Alice bench. Water was ditched from Rhode Island Creek to Shirley Bar, thence to Glen Gulch, and joined with water from the Boston ditch to work Alice bench. When Joslin took the photograph, Frank G. Manley owned almost all the claims in the Eureka area. Accession Number 79-41-286N.

tax funds to work along the slough road.[54] They succeeded. In early May, Price's workers started the Hot Springs–Bryan City "boulevard" from the south end of the slough bridge to the Tanana River, a distance of one and one-half miles at a cost of $2,000.[55]

As prospectors drifted westward through the Alaska Interior, some concentrated on the area near the town of Tanana where there had been prospecting off and on for almost three decades, seemingly without success. A well-known miners' story, probably embellished as it was re-told, spoke of the spring 1883 expedition of Edward Schieffelin, renowned miner from Tombstone, Arizona. Beginning at Al Mayo's trading post at Old Station, then known as Fort Adams and located not far from the junction of the Tanana and Yukon rivers, Schieffelin and his team were said to have prospected in spots as far up the Yukon as Fort Yukon and eighty miles along the Tanana. Test panning was said to have

yielded values of $10 to $15 per a day, averaging $10 per day per man. Nevertheless, Schieffelin foresaw that because of the long winters and short summers, he would not profit much from mining in Alaska, so he gave up consideration of gold mining along the Yukon.[56] In 1890, though, someone tried to develop a lode mine, possibly the first lode mine in the Alaska Interior, near Gold Hill, then only a spot in the wilderness.[57] During the early days at Fort Gibbon, Capt. Charles S. Farnsworth had been acquainted with prospectors near the post, although he saw none who succeeded. In June 1904, Jack Miles prospected Morelock Creek for John Stanley, manager of the A. F. Schmitz company. Although there was discussion of working Morelock with hydraulic or dredging equipment, nothing apparently materialized.[58]

By 1907, however, activity had increased markedly in the vicinity of Gold Hill (or nearby Gold Mountain) in the Fort Gibbon district. As a

Figure 19. Cabin at the entrance to Sullivan Creek, circa 1910. Courtesy of the Wilson F. Erskine Collection, University of Alaska Fairbanks. The cabin was located at the Sullivan Creek bridge where the government winter trail crossed the creek, thirteen and one-half miles from Hot Springs. Accession Number 70-28-86N.

result, the Gold Hill region, on the north side of the Yukon River, about fifteen miles from it, and twenty-five to thirty-five miles below the mouth of the Tanana River, attracted more prospectors.[59] The region extended westward from the valley of the Tozitna River to the mountains north of the U.S. military telegraph station at the Birches and to the headwater drainage of the Melozitna River, an area of about 600 square miles.[60]

The pace of filing new claims accelerated. John Carey located a twenty-acre claim, No. 7 below, Mason Creek. William Moran located Discovery, Golden Creek, and Discovery, Moran Creek. J. J. O'Brien located Discovery, Grant Creek. As in the Hot Springs district, 160-acre claims spread along Mason, Grant, Slate, and other creeks, quickly taking up available ground. Some shareholders such as Charles Coulombe, Joseph Dehu, and James Farley had apparently not been in Rampart. Others like

James Langford, Sam Heeter, Milton P. Fleischman, Joe Kaminski, and Wally Laboski were well-known Ramparters.[61] George H. Tiffany, NAT&T agent and postmaster at Tanana, had begun his NAT&T career in Rampart as a co-worker of Lynn Smith and had married his wife, Louise, there.[62] In April 1908, John Minook, along with Andrew, Louise, and Eliza Minook, and M. S. Gill, located a 100-acre claim on Dome Creek where the Langford family later filed an eighty-acre claim. Clarence Berry, a major winner in the Klondike stakes of 1898, H. F. Berry, and their associates held claims on Mission, Lynx, and Jackson creeks.[63]

Geologist A[lfred] G[eddes] Maddren quickly inspected the Gold Hill area in late June and early July, 1908. At the time, a scarcity of water combined with excessive dryness had reduced activity sharply. Maddren considered the 160-acre claims restrictive of progress because independent individuals, on whose initiative mining advances depended, ceased to prospect due to the lack of available ground. He observed, from a geologic perspective, that a mountain divide, stretching east to west, naturally separated the region into a northern and southern section. On one side, Grant, Illinois, and Mason creeks flowed southward into the Yukon; on the other, Moran, Eureka, Hudson, Langford, and Tiffany creeks flowed northward into the Melozitna. The mountains of the region, Maddren indicated, were formed from metamorphic rocks of the type termed Birch Creek schist, most rocks being quartzite schists and micaceous quartz schists. During his trip he saw the abandoned, caved-in tunnel of the old lode mine.[64]

Maddren also learned that about twenty prospecting holes had been dug during the winter of 1907–1908; the miners used the old method of wood fires for thawing frozen ground. Reportedly, $700 worth of gold had been extracted in 1908 from a claim on Mason Creek near the mouth of Last Chance Creek. Grant Creek gold consisted of small nuggets, one worth $17, and medium-fine gold. In contrast, gold near the head of Mason Creek resembled birdshot pellets.[65]

In 1909, a small group of Tanana miners who had been working for three years on a quartz ledge called Scroggie reportedly retaliated against an unidentified ex-policeman from Fairbanks who had jumped their claim. Since the miners had no money to pay legal fees, they took their own out-of-court action. They gathered ropes, switches of green birch, axes, and a parka and then requested the claim jumper to go. When he refused, the miners tied him up, threw the parka over his head, and switched him until he wept. Next, they put a rope around his neck, handed him an axe, and forced him, with a few kicks, to cut down his location notices. After suffering that persuasion, the claim jumper voluntarily left the area. Although there were several witnesses to the incident, no one identified any of the miners involved in the retribution—vigilante justice without attribution.[66]

As new mining camps arose, a camp newspa-

per often began publication soon thereafter. Tanana had a succession of papers. The newspaper *Tanana Leader* poked fun at the multiple names for the town of Tanana. Its first issue, published at "We-gib-tan-are-bon-ana" (for Weare, Gibbon, and Tanana) supported the name Gibbon to distinguish clearly that the town was not associated with Fairbanks in the Tanana Valley.[67] Because of its geographic location, some considered Tanana the "Hub of Alaska." Almost all commerce done in the Interior by water transportation passed through the port of Tanana; passengers waited at Tanana for steamers along the Tanana to Fairbanks or down the Yukon to St. Michael.[68]

Charles S. Farnsworth, by then a major in the Sixteenth Infantry, was reassigned to Fort Gibbon in August 1910. He immediately noticed the differences from his first tour of duty there. By 1910, the town of Tanana had grown to a population of 200. The stores had high prices but were better than he thought they would be. As before, though, he complained about the inefficiency of the civilian workforce. He attributed its poor quality to low wages. The government offered only $2 to $5 per day, but prevailing wages in the area were $5 for laborers and $8 to $10 for mechanics.[69]

Major Farnsworth dryly summarized the consequences of a new Congressional game law for Alaska. The legal wording prohibited hunting when game was most plentiful and permitted the hunting of ducks and geese between November and March, a five-month period, as Farnsworth pointed out, "when ice was three to ten feet thick and no man, living or dead, ever saw a duck or goose in this section of Alaska during these months."[70] As a result, hunters violated the law. Game wardens and U.S. marshals only charged those violaters they did not like. The Indians were allowed subsistence hunting but were forbidden to continue their earlier business practice of selling or trading the meat.[71] In early Rampart days, the Indians frequently supplied game in the fall to the restaurants and miners in exchange for money or goods.

In the meantime, fortunes in the Sullivan

region fluctuated. Mining experienced an upswing in late January 1909, when John J. Cooney and Gus Benson made what was considered a new strike on Liberty bench, Sullivan Creek.[72] A few weeks later, the team of McFadden and Barker reported a rich streak on their Belmont claim on Cache Creek near the government road and the camp of Tofty.[73] Within days, Richard C. Morris and R.W. Jones obtained good results on the Homeward Bound fraction on Harter Creek. Their fraction claim was situated one and one-half miles from Tofty toward Hot Springs; their shaft was located only twenty feet from the government road and just 100 yards from the Belmont. The success of his neighbors aroused Ed[win] Richards, who owned the most claims on Cache and Harter creeks, to order a big boiler for his operations.[74]

During this period, the U.S. Geological Survey geologists regularly reviewed the activity, or lack thereof, in the Rampart, Hot Springs, and Gold Hill (Fort Gibbon) districts. In 1909, geologist Alfred H. Brooks reported that there were instances of stream tin in Sullivan Creek and that there was productive mining on Mason and Grant creeks in Gold Hill, a district where placer gold had not been carefully prospected before.[75]

A significant Sullivan region partnership formed in early 1910 when Sylvester Howell of Fairbanks transferred several interests on Sullivan, Cooney, Camp, Rock, and Cache creeks to Mrs. Jennie Cleveland, then of Dome, Alaska.[76] Subsequently, Cleveland and Howell operated together from Tofty.

Tofty miner Adolph Bock also increased his acquisitions. He received interests from G. A. Olson, specifically No. 1 below, Patterson Creek, which Olson had obtained from Matthew Harter.[77]

Also in 1910, Geological Survey engineers C. E. Ellsworth and G. L. Parker stated that the overall production, $325,000, in the Hot Springs district equaled that of 1909. Although there had been increases from the mines on Sullivan and Cache creeks, production from the Baker creek mines had been reduced. In the Tofty area, the producers were weighing the practicality of

producing tin from the available stream tin as a byproduct of gold mining. Most of the mining used open-cut methods dependent on water. Lack of water resulted in the closure of many operations for much of the season.[78] Ellsworth and Parker also noted a decrease in output in Rampart which they attributed principally to the presumption that rich pay streaks had been completely mined.[79]

Throughout 1910, Lynn Smith continued to work in the Tofty area, with interests on Cache, Cooney, and Killarney creeks. He occasionally took breaks in Hot Springs, Tanana, and even Seattle. He purchased a horse which enabled him to drive a wagon or sleigh to the creeks, a preferable alternative to his usual, and still primary, mode of transportation, walking. In the spring, he commented that people were stampeding from Rampart, Hot Springs, and Tanana to the new strike on the Iditarod; two of those who were broke on leaving for the new strike returned with $12,500 each. By the fall, when many people in Hot Springs and Fairbanks were "quartz crazy," Smith and a man named McInnis located three quartz claims. Assayed samples from the largest claim indicated a value of $8.50 per ton; the second, $6.00 per ton; and the third, $4.00 per ton. Optimistic about a future in quartz mining, Smith wrote, "People had been killed for less values in quartz."[80]

As of February 15, 1911, Lynn Smith had concluded that quartz mining in the Hot Springs district was not economically practical. He opened a store in Tofty with Fred Howard, a hotel owner in Kemperville on the Tanana River at the mouth of Hot Springs Slough.[81] They later added a third partner by the name of Curtis. Smith retained his share in a quartz ledge, and his hopes revived when another sample assayed at $15 per ton and still another at $134.64 per ton.[82]

Geologist Henry M. Eakin provided an in-depth geologic reconnaissance of the Rampart, Hot Springs, and Gold Hill regions in 1911. By that time, the town of Tanana was the largest settlement in the area, surpassing Rampart, Hot Springs, Tofty, Eureka, and others. Eakin observed that perhaps as much as four-fifths of the timbered areas had been burned over since 1901, thereby diminishing the amount of timber available to the miners for fuel and lumber. Wages for miners remained the same as they had been for several years: $5 per day plus board, which averaged an additional $1.50 for a total cost to the operator of $6.50 per worker per day. Little of value had been produced from the Gold Hill area. Prospecting holes as deep as 135 feet had been dug there, but they were soon flooded by underground streams.[83]

Eakin suggested that some of the gold in the Hot Springs region may have been connected to the distribution of carbonaceous beds and to the presence of hematite deposits. He commented on the "peculiar" type of gold-bearing bench deposits on What Cheer Bar and on the shallow gravels, worked by open-cut methods on Quartz Creek and Tofty Gulch. He realized that the cost of mining varied with the type of equipment used. Cost estimates for operations ranged upward from a low of thirty-five cents a square foot of bedrock ($2.50 a yard for gravel).[84]

Both Eakin and geologist Frank L. Hess reported the occurrences of cassiterite, the oxide of tin, on Sullivan Creek. Although the value of gravels with tin appeared to be between $10 and $20 a yard, most of the owners regarded tin as a "nuisance" because the cumbersome, time-consuming method of separating tin ore from other materials drew activity away from the prime operation, the recovery of gold.[85] Sullivan Creek miner Joe Eglar, however, took the time to complete the bothersome chore and netted $209 from a shipment of 1,200 pounds of ore containing 55 percent tin.[86]

The next year, 1912, engineer C. E. Ellsworth, with R.W. Davenport, examined the Tofty area and noticed ten to fifteen outfits mining on American Creek, a stream five miles long which emptied into Fish Lake. There, on the Wild Goose Association claim, the contents of three pans of gravel yielded gold value at $100. Unfortunately, no water was available for ground sluicing. The U.S.G.S. party saw that open cut-mining was in progress in Tofty Gulch, that some mining was proceeding on Miller and Cache creeks, and that there was prospecting on

Cooney Creek where considerable amounts of tin had been found.[87]

In Rampart, Ellsworth and Davenport found only open-cut mining methods in use. On Quail Creek, splash dams removed the overburden and concentrated the gold into sufficient quantities for recovery in sluice boxes.[88] Water problems continued. Little Minook Creek, the largest producer of gold in the Rampart district, had insufficient water for sluicing during the better part of every mining season. Because Little Minook was relatively short, splash dams set up on the creek did not have enough length of flow to be effective. Ellsworth and Davenport, therefore, repeated Ellsworth's earlier conclusion that Troublesome Creek was the most likely stream capable of being developed as a source for hydroelectric power for the Rampart mines.[89]

Meanwhile, Lynn Smith's aspirations diminished in 1912, coincident with a major natural disturbance in Alaska. On June 12, Tofty experienced the far-reaching effects of the volcanic eruption of Mount Katmai on the Alaska Peninsula several hundreds of miles south of Tofty. The eruption, one of the world's greatest, created the Valley of Ten Thousand Smokes. Tofty people heard noise and felt shaking. For two days, the air was smoky and ashen. Smith's mood matched the atmospheric conditions. In July, Smith found Tofty "dull"; in August, he surmised that Tofty was in its "last days." He decided to dispose of all his shares in the Hot Springs district, his claims on the creek and store in Tofty. He switched his residence to Ruby and, eventually, to Fairbanks.[90]

By 1913, after his return from incarceration in Texas and the destruction of his hotel by fire, Frank G. Manley had lost interest in mining at Hot Springs. Matt Ries sold the Pioneer ditch and Manley's lumber on Glen Gulch to the partnership of Frank and Graham. Whatever remained of Manley's mining machinery was transported to Manley's claims in the Iditarod district.[91] When the first session of the territorial legislature in Juneau debated an eight-hour bill for labor shifts in mining operations, Manley and Tom Aitken were among the operators who personally spoke to the assembled legislators in opposition to the proposal.[92] Although the mine laborers sought an eight-hour day, mine operators, desiring the maximum output at least expense during the short summer mining season, wanted an option for ten-hour, possibly twelve, shifts. The eight-hour shift became law in 1915.

On July 30, 1913, changes in federal law limited the size of claims to forty acres, thereby eliminating future 160-acre association claims. Claim holders had to perform at least $100 worth of development work and $100 worth of assessment work annually for every twenty acres and had to file an affidavit attesting to the work each year with their district's recorder.[93]

Operations in Hot Springs remained unchanged. On Houklee Gulch, Adolph Bock found pay in bedrock 120 feet deep.[94] While mining the Houklee pay, he also intended to drill on Woodchopper Creek, predicting the rise of a town at Woodchopper by spring 1914.[95] Territorial Mine Inspector William Maloney toured the Hot Springs district in January 1915, a month when very little work was in progress. He saw that ground at Woodchopper Creek was being prepared for summer operations.[96]

By then, the settlement of Rampart had declined almost to a ghost town. Archdeacon Hudson Stuck viewed the long rows of vacant cabins and stores with boarded up windows and thought they gave the town a melancholy appearance. The Indians had deserted their village a mile above Rampart, and some had joined the twenty-five to thirty white people, the Ballou family included, still residing in the town.[97] The vital, bustling Rampart of the late 1890s, which accommodated a steady flow of incoming and outgoing people, had disappeared forever.

According to Stuck, Hot Springs was also suffering, in particular because many trees had been cut down, giving the region a naked look. On the other hand, the port of Tanana was still thriving, principally as a result of the summer steamer trade and the year-round presence of the military garrison at Fort Gibbon.[98]

In August 1915, U.S.G.S. geologist Gerald A.

Waring studied another source of water supply useful to the people for relaxed bathing and agriculture, namely, the mineral hot springs of subarctic Interior Alaska. The Hutlinana (Hootlanana) Hot Springs was situated about eight and one-half miles east of the post office at the settlement of Eureka. Its temperature was 114^0F. Potatoes and other vegetables grew satisfactorily in a nearby garden. To reach the springs, miners had to go down a steep, one-thousand-foot trail and back up to return home. Baker Hot Springs, known as the Karshner homestead and leased for ten years by Frank G. Manley, also had a temperature of 114^0F. Its water nurtured potatoes, cabbages, and other vegetables. The temperature of the Little Melozitna Hot Springs on Hot Springs Creek in the Fort Gibbon district was only 99 1/2^{0}F. Miners could get to it by walking twenty-seven miles north and inland from the Hub Roadhouse on the Yukon. In contrast, the temperature of the Melozitna Hot Springs, which was about sixteen miles from Kokrines, a trading post one hundred miles below Tanana, registered 131^0F. People traveled there in the winter but seldom in summer when the trail was at its worst. Geologist Waring predicted that the nearby creek, which at the time he saw it was already undercutting the bank of the hot springs, would eventually destroy the bank and release the springs at water level. Another Kokrines area springs was Horner Hot Springs, three-quarters of a mile from the Yukon, where F. G. Horner had a cabin and garden. Its temperature stood at 117^0F.[99]

By the summer of 1917, the United States was at war in Europe. In the Hot Springs district, mining continued its downward spiral. According to U.S.G.S. geologist Theodore Chapin, most rich ground had been depleted. The firm of Cleveland and Howell, which had a large crew on Woodchopper Creek in 1915 and 1916, had stopped its operations there, although the firm worked for a short time on Big Boulder Creek. A further wartime complication was the high expense of food and mining supplies. Consequently, the operators concentrated on mining the richest ground still available. A few small operators re-processed old tailings, the discards of earlier clean-ups, by using improved methods to find gold missed during the original processing by less refined methods.[100]

Although the Sullivan Creek miners initally considered that the recovery of tin interfered with their production of gold, most had begun recovering cassiterite. By 1917, miners were netting twelve to thirteen cents per pound for the ore. They had found a relatively simple way of adjusting the height of sluice boxes to separate the lighter cassiterite from the heavier gold. Some cassiterite consisted of grains as fine as beach sand; other, of small rocks several inches to a foot in diameter. The miners, however, encountered considerable difficulty in separating unwanted pyrite and hematite concentrates from the cassiterite and failed to extract part of the cassiterite intertwined with other concentrates.[101]

As World War I dragged on, mining activity declined further in the three districts. The excitement of the early discovery days had long since passed. A gradual exodus of people had been underway for several years. The war drew young men into military service, creating a labor shortage in many places. The war also put a finish to many operations, as operators chose not to continue, not to cope with shortages and high expenses. More and more, miners left Alaska, some never to return. The Ballou family of Rampart, William B., Dollie, and son William Hosea, joined these who departed to resume their life in the contiguous United States.[102] Those who stayed looked hopefully to a full resumption of gold mining after the war ended.

End Notes Chapter 3. Growth of the Hot Springs and Fort Gibbon Districts, 1906–1918.

Short Titles

The following shortened forms referring to depositories and series are used extensively through the chapter endnotes.

Archives, UAF	Alaska Archives and Manuscripts, Alaska and Polar Regions Department, Elmer E. Rasmuson Library, University of Alaska Fairbanks.
District Recorder, Fairbanks	State of Alaska Department of Natural Resources, Office of the Commissioner, District Recorder, Fairbanks, Alaska.
Division of Mining, Fairbanks	State of Alaska Department of Natural Resources, Division of Mining, Fairbanks, Alaska.
(folder)	A copy of a creek record, dated between 1896 and 1900, at the office of the District Recorder, Fairbanks. The original is retained at the office of the State Recorder, Anchorage, Alaska.
Fort Gibbon	Fort Gibbon recording district records at the office of the District Recorder, Fairbanks, Alaska.
Manley	Manley Hot Springs recording district records at the office of the District Recorder, Fairbanks, Alaska.
Rampart	Rampart recording district records at the office of the District Recorder, Fairbanks, Alaska.
U.S.G.S.	U.S. Geological Survey.

1. Ballou to Father and Mother, 10 March 1906, William B. Ballou Collection, box 2, folder 158. Ballou was not discouraged by his two-year experience with hydraulicking. He learned from it. He had put in a dam at the lower end of his workings to catch water. An automatic gate was to free the dammed-up water to flush off the tailings from the sluice boxes. Ballou was trying to eliminate use of the hydraulic elevator so that he could use the water set aside for the elevator to operate another hydraulic plant.

2. Ballou to Walt, Mother, and Family, 13 January 1906, ibid., box 2, folder 157. Ballou may have been somewhat sarcastic in his comments. His hydraulicking venture had not been successful.

3. *Yukon Press,* Tanana and Fort Gibbon, 13 January 1906, M/F 1008.

4. Smith to Mother, 16 February and 16 July 1906, Herbert Heller Collection, box 1, folder 9. By July, Smith was working on Discovery and No. 1 below, Esther Creek, for L[atham] A. Jones and George McQuarrie. Formerly of Rampart, both had been "broke" the year before.

5. *Alaska Forum*, 13 January and 7 July 1906. Also, Ballou to Walt, Mother, and Family, 13 January 1906, William B. Ballou Collection, box 2, folder 157. Ballou wrote that the operators of the Big Minook plant, which

cost $60,000, had given up and leased to Hoosier Creek operators. He admitted that the hydraulic business of the district was not good, although he was confident about his next plant.

6. *Alaska Forum*, 7 July 1906.

7. Ibid., 2 June, 23 June, 30 June, and 4 August 1906. A party from the Road Commission, specifically, surveyor Brown, Al Bartlett, Dan Courtney, and Paul Ziegler, surveyed for the Chena-Rampart road in early August.

8. Smith to Polly, 15 October 1906, Herbert Heller Collection, box 1, folder 9.

9. *Alaska Forum*, 14 July 1906. Also, Kitchener, 312.

10. Smith to Mother, 26 July 1906, Herbert Heller Collection, box 1, folder 9.

11. *Alaska Forum*, 4 August 1906. Also, *Fairbanks Daily Times*, 12 July, 17 July, 19 July, 23 July, 25 July, 28 July, 8 August, 4 September, and 6 September 1906, M/F 88. Those arrested included Robert Miller, George Raphael, Al P. Kelso of the Floradora, his younger brother H. E. Kelso, Charles Tague, Tague's friend McDonald, and later Fred McCarron. Reporting of the story apparently died out after Miller's trial. Also *Fairbanks Evening News*, 17 July and 8 August 1906. The 8 August text is physically tattered and burned and, consequently, difficult to read.

12. *Alaska Forum*, 14 July 1906.

13. Manley's will, 17 December 1909, Tanana Valley Gold Dredging Company Collection, Legal Section, box 9, Manley Papers, Archives, UAF. The will, which was made at San Angelo, Tom Green County, Texas, gave Manley's true name as Hillyard Bascom Knowles. Also, Cora Chase Charlton, "Was He Justified?" *Alaska-Yukon Magazine*, April 1909, 47–51. Coincidentally, Charlton's fiction story about two characters named Hillyard and Bascom was published in 1909. Charlton undoubtedly knew Manley as she spent time both in Hot Springs and Fairbanks.

14. Manley, Deeds, 1: 309–314. From David Scott, James Dalton, James R. Green, A. H. Lane, and L. H. Hall, Baker took over the North Star, Triumph, Horseshoe, Success, Last Chance, Johnny Wise, May E, and Laverne as well as one-half interest in the Dunkle, Huckleberry, and Eureka and associated water rights, all of which Baker deeded to Manley. Also, *Alaska Forum*, 21 July 1906.

15. Manley, Deeds. 1: 321–22.

16. Ibid., 1: 324–25.

17. Ibid., 1: 330–33. Also, *Alaska Forum*, 4 August 1906.

18. Manley, Deeds, 1: 345–46.

19. Ibid., 1: 346–48. Also, *Alaska Forum*, 28 July 1906.

20. Manley, Deeds, 1: 362–66.

21. Ibid., 1: 384–92. Manley and Chute bought claims from Robert Meston for $2,500; from George Washington Jones, for $1.00; from E. B. Power, for $1,200; and Nicklos Nelson, for $5,000. Nelson's claims included the Dandy bench, located earlier in 1906 for Perry Judkins. Also, *Hot Springs Post*, 1 October 1908. Nelson, a native of Finland, died in 1908.

22. *Alaska Forum*, 14 July 1906. A town developed around Karshner's homestead with its natural hot spring. The town was known variously as Karshner Hot Springs, Baker, Baker Hot Springs, Hot Springs, and ultimately Manley Hot Springs. The first Baker or Baker Station (Deakyme) closed. Also, Manley, Leases, vol. 1, 7 October 1907–6 May 1958, 72–74. Dad Karshner leased his 320-acre homestead to Manley on 25 September 1906 for ten years. Manley had an option to extend the lease an additional twenty years. L[ucien] S. Robe surveyed the homestead on 16 July 1906. Also, Smith to Mother, 26 August 1907, Herbert Heller Collection, box 1, folder 10. Lynn Smith witnessed Karshner's staking of his homestead in 1902. Additionally, Manley, Mortgages, vol. 1, 27 July 1903–25 November 1959 and 11 July 1964–25 May 1968, 172–73, 189–90, 198–99. Patent No. 498680 for the

homestead was granted to Cordelia M. Karshner, Dad's widow, on 12 November 1915.

23. Manley, Deeds, 1: 376–83. A. L. Dalton, A.V. Thorns, and Ben Baker also relinquished their interest in the saline springs.

24. *Alaska Forum*, 28 July and 4 August 1906. The *Forum* editor retired, and the *Forum* ceased publication on 4 August 1906.

25. Alfred H. Brooks et al., *Report on Progress of Investigations of Mineral Resources of Alaska in 1906*, U.S.G.S. Bulletin 314 (Washington: Government Printing Office, 1907), 14, 37–38. Brooks traveled with a Road Commission survey party from Fairbanks to Rampart. He reported on Manley's road to Glen Gulch, the Hootlanana ditch, and the churn drill. Brooks referred to the survey party as headed by engineer J. L. McPherson. McPherson's name did not appear in the *Alaska Forumm*'s eport of the survey party.

26. Ballou to Walt, 27 November 1906, William B. Ballou Collection, box 2, folder 160. No longer optimistic, Ballou intended to give up Ruby Creek to work a claim on Hunter Creek.

27. Manley, Locations, 3: 10–12, 27, entries No. 323, 327, and 374. Sunnyside Association 2, between Rhode Island and Omega creeks, was located on 27 August 1906 by J. Ronan, Charles Courtright, W. P. Edgar, J. L. Stanley, H. B. Knowles, G. T. Edgar, R. E. Edgar, and William Stanley. Sunnyside 6, also located on 27 August, involved F. G. Manley, A. V. Thorns, J. L. McComes, William Faulkner, S. A. Bonnifield, D. N. Freeman, L[ucien] S. Robe, and M. S. Gill. The Nevada Association, between New York and Allan creeks, was located on 21 August by Roy V. Nye, W. B. Knowles, H. C. Knowles, William Brelle, S. A. Bonnifield, E. S. Knowles, B. H. Knowles, and Fred Brelle. Also, Smith to Mother, 26 August 1907, Herbert Heller Collection, box 1, folder 10. In August 1907, Lynn Smith indicated that in ten days with twelve workers Manley's company cleaned up $68,000 from just one set of sluice boxes. Additionally, Manley, Leases, 1: 23–35. Many, if not all, of Frank Manley's extensive holdings were itemized in his lease to Thomas P. Aitken on 5 May 1909. Aitken operated the lease with his partner H. T. Curry.

28. *Hot Springs Echo*, 4 July and 18 July 1908, M/F 677.

29. Manley, Locations, 3: 63. Discovery, Sullivan Creek, later became known as Upper Discovery.

30. Ibid., 3: 97.

31. Ibid., 3: 103. Also, *Hot Springs Echo and Tanana Citizen*, 27 July 1907, M/F 677. Matthew Harter, George Kemper, and Charles P. Snyder were errone-

ously credited with the initial development of Sullivan country apparently because of their activity on the benches of Sullivan Creek, sixteen miles from Hot Springs, near to the survey line of the then new government road.

32. Manley, Locations, 3: 88–106.

33. Manley, Deeds, vol. 2, 8 May 1908–29 February 1912, 93, 174, 223–24. The designation Sullivan City was in use at least from July 1907 through mid-fall 1908 and sporadically, thereafter, through 1910. By October 1908, the designation Tofty appeared. In January 1909, there was a reference to the joint designation "town of Sullivan or Tofty on Sullivan Creek." About 1914, the Tofty settlement was moved about one and one-half miles closer to the town of Hot Springs, probably closer to the Kemper-Snyder, Lower Discovery claim. Also, the *Hot Springs Echo* and the *Hot Springs Post* carried advertisments and articles about the same businesses, businesses sometimes associated with Sullivan City and sometimes with Tofty, even within the same issue. According to the *Post*, other new towns very near Hot Springs were Kemperville and Bryan City. Also, according to the *Hot Springs Post* issue of 26 December 1908, Jack Hayes comprised one-third of the population of Bryan City.

34. *Hot Springs Echo*, 20 April 1913.

35. Ballou to Walt, 27 January 1907, William B. Ballou Collection, box 2, folder 161.

36. *Hot Springs Echo and Tanana Citizen*, 3 August 1907. At the time, the miners of Hot Springs were pressuring for the appointment of a commissioner for the Hot Springs district. V. L. Bevington was apppointed commissioner for Hot Springs in 1908.

37. Ballou to Walt, 15 August 1907, William B. Ballou Collection, box 2, folder 162, Ballou to Walt, 26 September 1908, ibid., folder 163. Edna began her second year of teaching on 1 September 1908. Photographs she took in Rampart are part of the Ballou collection. Also, Sundborg, 107. Edna was bridesmaid for Lulu Bode at Lulu's marriage to George Walter Sundborg in Rampart on 21 July 1908. Ballou to Walt, 1 October 1909, William B. Ballou Collection, box 2, folder 164, and Ballou to Walt, 19 June 1910, ibid., folder 165. The next year (1909–1910) Edna and her cousin, Millie, also a niece of William Ballou, taught at Tanana.

38. *Yukon Press*, 24 March 1906. In contrast to its praise for Ballou, the *Hot Springs Echo and Tanana Citizen* frequently criticized Bathurst and sought his dismissal.

39. *Hot Springs Post*, 2 January 1909.

40. Ibid., 27 March and 17 April 1909. Judge Bevington, commissioner of Hot Springs resigned, ef-

fective June 1, 1910. Smith to Mother, 16 April 1910, Herbert Heller Collection, box 1, folder 12. Bevington offered Lynn Smith the commissioner's job. Smith refused. He thought that the position would pay $1,000 to $1,500 per year. He acknowledged that he did not feel confident about his ability to handle the job; in addition, he knew he had to pay attention to his claims. Ballou to Walt, 19 June 1910, William B. Ballou Collection, box 2, folder 165. Ballou also declined to replace Bevington. He "couldn't afford the honor." He estimated the annual income to be $800 to $1,000.

41. Hudson Stuck, D.D., F.R.G.S., *Voyages on the Yukon and its Tributaries: A Narrative of Summer Travel in the Interior of Alaska* (New York: Charles Scribner's Sons, 1917), 117.

42. C. C. Covert and C. E. Ellsworth, "Water Supply of the Yukon-Tanana Region," in *Mineral Resources of Alaska: Report on Progress of Investigations in 1908*, ed. Alfred H. Brooks, et al., U.S.G.S. Bulletin 379 (Washington: Government Printing Office, 1909), 226-228. Also, Manley, Annual Labor, vol. 1, 21 August 1908–28 December 1918, District Recorder, Fairbanks, 25–28, 30–33. The construction work on several ditches in 1907 was counted toward the requirement for annual assessment. Work on the Boston Ditch from Boston Creek to Glen Gulch, performed by the crew of A. V. Thorns for Frank G. Manley, was valued at $8,700; work on the What Cheer Bar Ditch, four miles along Pioneer Creek, at $6,500; work on the Thanksgiving Ditch from California Creek, $24,000.

43. C. C. Covert and C. E. Ellsworth, *Water-Supply Investigations in the Yukon-Tanana Region, Alaska, 1907 and 1908: Fairbanks, Circle, and Rampart Districts*, U.S.G.S. Water-Supply Paper 228 (Washington: Government Printing Office, 1909), 63, 69, 99, 103–04. Also, C. E. Ellsworth, "Water Supply of the Yukon-Tanana Region, 1909," in *Mineral Resources of Alaska: Report on Progress of Investigations in 1909*, ed. Alfred H. Brooks, et. al., U.S.G.S. Bulletin 442 (Washington: Government Printing Office, 1910), 275.

44. C. E. Ellsworth, "Placer Mining in the Yukon-Tanana Region," in *Mineral Resources of Alaska: Report on Progress of Investigations in 1909*, ed. Alfred H. Brooks, et al., U.S.G.S. Bulletin 442 (Washington: Government Printing Office, 1910), 240.

45. Covert and Ellsworth, Water-Supply Paper 228, 60–61.

46. Smith to Mother, 26 August and 30 November 1907, Herbert Heller Collection, box 1, folder 10.

47. Smith to Mother, 11 January [1908] and 17 March [1908], Herbert Heller Collection, box 1, folder 10, and Smith to Mother, 18 May and 5 July 1908, and 16 January 1909, ibid., box 1, folder 11. Also, *Hot Springs*

Post, 8 October 1908. The *Post* reported that Lynn Smith, Jim Orr, and Dan Brown had left Monday, [5 October], to prospect on Cooney Creek during the winter. Additionally, Manley, Leases, 1: 9–10, 13–15. Lynn Smith held a one-sixteenth share in the Dakota Association, Sullivan Creek, which other miners leased. Smith considered Dakota very rich and expected $5,000 for his share of the output within two years.

48. Manley, Deeds, 2: 7–9, 35–38, 44–45, 175–76.

49. Ibid., 2: 267–68.

50. Rosalie E. L'Ecuyer, *Ruby-Porman Mining District, Ruby Quadrangle, Alaska*, BLM-Alaska Open File Report 49 (Anchorage: Bureau of Land Management, U. S. Department of the Interior, 1993), 2–3.

51. Manley, Deeds, 2: 52–53, 323–24. On 15 September 1909, Eglar purchased Herman Tofty's interests in the Independence Association for $8,000.

52. Ibid., 2: 74–76.

53. *Hot Springs Post*, 12 December 1908, 2 January and 16 January 1909.

54. Ibid., 26 December 1908. The same issue reported that J. Fred Struthers, husband of Ella Garratt, had left his prospecting at the lower end of the Midnight Sun Association, Sullivan Creek, to be with his wife at Chena for the holidays. Also, ibid., 24 April 1909. The meeting took place on Sunday, 17 April 1909.

55. Ibid., 8 May 1909.

56. Kitchener, 276.

57. A[lfred] G[eddes] Maddren, "Placers of the Gold Hill District," in *Mineral Resources of Alaska: Report of Investigations in 1908*, ed. Alfred H. Brooks, et al., U.S.G.S. Bulletin 379 (Washington: Government Printing Office, 1909), 236.

58. *Alaska Forum*, 18 June 1904.

59. Alfred H. Brooks, et al., *Mineral Resources of Alaska: Report on Progress of Investigations in 1907*, U.S.G.S. Bulletin 345 (Washington: Government Printing Office, 1908), 46.

60. Maddren, 234.

61. Fort Gibbon, Mining Locations, 1907–1908, District Recorder, Fairbanks, 1, 11, 15, 46, 47, 60–63, 66, 75, 95–96, 160.

62. Smith to Mother, 4 February 1902, Herbert Heller Collection, box 1, folder 5, and Smith to Folks, 6 March 1903, ibid., folder 6. Lynn Smith had a strong, continuing friendship with the Tiffanys and frequently visted them in Tanana. Their pictures are in the Heller collection.

63. Fort Gibbon, Mining Locations, 1907–1908, 80, 128–41, 235.

64. Maddren, 235–37.

65. A. G. Maddren, *The Innoko Gold-Placer District, Alaska, with Accounts of the Central Kuskokwim Valley and the Ruby Creek and Gold Hill Placers*, U.S.G.S. Bulletin 410 (Washington: Government Printing Office, 1910), 83.

66. *Hot Springs Post*, 6 March 1909.

67. Ibid., 13 March 1909. The *Post* quoted the *Leader*.

68. Ibid., 8 April 1909.

69. Farnsworth to Capt. W. S. McBroom, 22 September 1910, C. S. Farnsworth Collection, box 1, folder 11; Farnsworth to Col. Cornelius Gardener, 18 November 1910, ibid., folder 12.

70. Farnsworth to F. H. Cook, 7 April 1911, ibid., box 1, folder 15.

71. Farnsworth to Walter Fox, 28 May 1911, ibid.; Farnsworth to Brig. Gen. Marion P. Maus, 30 May 1911, ibid. Farnsworth was ordered to Washington, D.C. He left Fort Gibbon about 4 June 1911 and was stationed at Harrisburg, PA. He never returned to Alaska, although he maintained his interest in the territory the rest of his life.

72. *Hot Springs Post*, 30 January 1909. Also, Manley, Deeds, 2: 470–71. Cooney transferred Liberty bench and other interests to John Renza on 1 September 1911.

73. *Hot Springs Post*, 20 February 1909.

74. Ibid., 27 February 1909. Also, Manley, Deeds, 2: 310–11. Richards purchased interests in fifteen claims, ten of them on Cache Creek, from Alex Gragen for $1,500 on 26 August 1909.

75. Alfred Brooks, et al., *Mineral Resources of Alaska: Report on Progress of Investigations in 1909*, U.S.G.S. Bulletin 442 (Washington: Government Printing Office, 1910), 39, 44–45.

76. Manley, Deeds, 2: 369–71. Cleveland and Howell were heavily involved in leases, quit claims, purchases, and assessments of claims in the Hot Springs district for many years.

77. Ibid., 2: 423–24, 428–29. Also, Manley, Leases, 1: 173–76, 200–02, 225. In 1915, Bock leased the lower end of Lorraine Association on Woodchopper Creek from the partnership of Bock, Fred Wagner, and Martin Danielson. Bock and Danielson leased several claims on Deep Creek to Alec Larson in 1916. In 1917, Cleveland and Howell gave up their leases on Woodchopper Creek to Bock and Danielson.

78. C. E. Ellsworth and G. L. Parker, "Placer Mining in the Yukon-Tanana Region," in *Mineral Resources of Alaska: Report on Progress of Investigations in 1910*, ed. Alfred H. Brooks, et al., U.S.G.S. Bulletin 480 (Washington: Government Printing Office, 1911), 166.

79. Ibid., 167.

80. Smith to Folks or Mother, 16 March, 10 April, 30 April, 12 June, 3 July, 10 August, and 26 November 1910, Herbert Heller Collection, box 1, folder 12.

81. Smith to Clarence, 15 February 1911, ibid., box 1, folder 13. Smith gave his address as 562 Tin Can Alley, Sullivan Creek.

82. Smith to Mother, 16 August and 19 November 1911, Herbert Heller Collection, box 1, folder 13.

83. Henry M. Eakin, "The Rampart and Hot Springs Regions," in *Mineral Resources of Alaska: Report on Progress of Investigations in 1911,* ed. Alfred H. Brooks, et al., U.S.G.S. Bulletin 520 (Washington: Government Printing Office, 1912), 272–73, 276. Eakin expanded his report in Bulletin 535.

84. Ibid., 277, 278–79, 281, 284.

85. Ibid., 285–86.

86. Frank L. Hess, "Tin Resources of Alaska," in *Mineral Resources of Alaska: Report on Progress of Investigations in 1911,* ed. Alfred H. Brooks, et al., U.S.G.S. Bulletin 520 (Washington: Government Printing Office, 1912), 92.

87. C. E. Ellsworth and R. W. Davenport, "Placer Mining in the Yukon-Tanana Region," in *Mineral Resources of Alaska: Report on the Progress of Investigations in 1912,* ed. Alfred H. Brooks, et al., U.S G.S. Bulletin 542 (Washington: Government Printing Office, 1913), 220–21.

88. Ibid., 221.

89. C. E. Ellsworth and R. W. Davenport, *Surface Water Supply of the Yukon-Tanana Region, Alaska,* U.S. G. S. Water-Supply Paper 342 (Washington: Government Printing Office, 1915), 218, 229.

90. Smith to Folks, 22 June, 2 July, 18 August, 15 September, and 21 September 1912, Herbert Heller Collection, box 1, folder 14. Also, *Fairbanks Daily News-Miner,* 8 March, 10 March, and 13 March 1933. At the time of Lynn Smith's death in Seattle on 10 March 1933, he was serving his second term as U.S. marshal, Fourth Division, Alaska, stationed in Fairbanks. Coincidentally, his close friend since 1898, Frank Stevens, had died in Manley Hot Springs on 4 March 1933.

91. *Hot Springs Echo,* 23 February 1913.

92. Ibid., 30 March 1913.

93. L'Ecuyer, 8. The information was derived from *The Ruby Record-Citizen,* 2 August 1913.

94. *Hot Springs Echo,* 16 March 1913.

95. Ibid., 4 May 1913.

96. Wiliam Maloney, *Report of the Territorial Mine Inspector to the Governor of Alaska for the Year 1915* (Juneau: [Territorial Mine Inspector], 1916), 17. Maloney listed six operators, namely, A. Bock, J. McKinzie, William Albright, R.C. Koebsch, John Jacobs, and S. Howell.

97. Stuck, 134.

98. Ibid., 270.

99. Gerald A. Waring, *Mineral Springs of Alaska,* U.S.G.S. Water-Supply Paper 418 (Washington: Government Printing Office, 1917), 64–69. Also, L. M. Prindle, "Occurrences of Gold in the Yukon-Tanana Region," Bulletin 345, 184. Earlier, geologist Prindle had considered the hot springs a factor in the mineralization of the region.

100. Theodore Chapin, "Mining in the Hot Springs District," in *Mineral Resources of Alaska: Report on Progress of Investigations in 1917,* ed. G[eorge] C. Martin, U.S.G.S. Bulletin 692 (Washington: Government Printing Office, 1919), 331.

101. Ibid., 332–33.

102. Ballou to Walt, 21 February 1915, William B. Ballou Collection, box 2, folder 169. Ballou had mentioned that the school in Rampart had been stopped because of lack of funding. He worried about his son's education. After that, his collection of letters petered out either because he seldom wrote or because his letters of that period were not saved. Zipf to Ballou, 21 May 1930, Herbert Heller Collection, box 2, folder 22. Ballou never returned; he resided in Seattle in 1930.

Chapter 4. Between the Two World Wars, 1919-1941

The principal mineral industry in the Rampart and Hot Springs districts has been and still is the exploitation of gold placers. Stream tin is also recovered as a byproduct in the working of some of the placers, and other metallic minerals that are found in the placer concentrates show that other metals besides gold are present in the country rock, though not necessarily in commercial quantities.

—Geologist J. B. Mertie, Jr., report for the year 1931[1]

By the time of World War I, gold mining had become a business. The era of hectic stampedes with prospectors hastening hither and thither to stake ground at new discoveries had died out about 1912 when Alaska became a territory. Some one-man operators still painstakingly dug drift tunnels with pick and shovel, but the trend toward a few large operations with advanced equipment, as exemplified in 1907 by the multiple holdings of Frank G. Manley, gradually increased. In a sense, the mining industry had come of age; the adventure and romance of the Gold Rush period had subsided. Many Gold Rush pioneers remained in mining, yet relatively few new people were attracted into the field.

Mining and prospecting had continued during the war, but manpower shortages and high expenses had caused mine operators throughout Alaska to curtail their efforts. The general pace of recovery in the years immediately after the armistice remained slow. In the Rampart district, activity on Little Minook Creek, the chief producer in Rampart, and on some other creeks proceeded as usual; prospecting within the Gold Hill region in the Fort Gibbon district, however, had halted.

In the Hot Springs district, development was steady and routine, albeit not necessarily profitable. In November 1918, Mike Murray leased his Tanana Association claim on American Creek to Harry Riley and Frank Sawdy.[2] A year later, Frank Stevens, acting as agent for Frank G. Manley, leased to A. H. Lane the Boston Ditch, which provided water from Boston Creek to Excelsior Bar.[3] By 1920, a partnership of four men operated the only plant on Woodchopper Creek, considered to be almost worked out. Prospecting in Gold Basin and on claims near Tofty, also thought to be almost worked out, had uncertain futures.[4] The suppositions proved unfounded as operations in the Woodchopper, Gold Basin, and Tofty areas continued for several more years.

By 1922, Ed Ness discovered that in working his claim on American Creek with a steam scraper, he barely broke even—"not much profit" after paying wages ($6.00 a day) and board ($3.50 a day) for a crew of six plus a cook and expending over $17,000 on equipment.[5] Similarly, J. R. Frank, who had taken over in 1912 about sixty claims formerly operated by Manley along Pioneer, Doric, and Seattle Junior creeks, Skookum Gulch, and What Cheer Bar, produced about $25,000 in 1922, but with expenses, he averaged only between seven and twenty cents per cubic yard of gravel, a factor resulting in little profit.[6] The same year, the firm of Cleveland and Howell on Sullivan Creek plunged to at least $60,000 in debt.[7]

In the Rampart district in 1922, the Rampart Gold Mining Company of Des Moines, Iowa, intended to set up a dredge on [Big] Minook Creek.[8] Although the company performed annual assessment work on its claims for a number of years, the dredge never materialized.[9]

By contrast, the American Creek Dredging Company, under Charles Lewis, president and general manager, pursued plans to dredge American Creek in the Hot Springs district. In June 1926, August Conradt of Fairbanks, former Ramparter and partner of Lynn Smith on Glen Gluch, reported to the U.S. Bureau of Mines that the company had been capitalized for $300,000 and it intended to prospect ground on American Creek and tributaries Colorado and

New York creeks, activity that was expected to yield gold at a rate of 90 to 95 cents per cubic yard. The company had contracted for a flume dredge from the Yuba Manufacturing Company—Yuba No. 70—for a cost of from $80,000 to $83,000 when fully erected.[10] Because the company did not raise enough money from the sale of its stock to purchase the dredge, its board of directors authorized the sale of bonds payable in three years at 10 percent annual interest rate and entered into a mortgage agreement with the First National Bank of Fairbanks in November 1926.[11] In 1927, Luther C. Hess of Fairbanks became company president; Lewis left but soon returned as manager; Conradt became vice president.[12]

The dredge was the first and only dredge in the Hot Springs district, which at the time was normally worked by hydraulicking or drifting. It began operations toward the end of the 1927 summer mining season. As a consequence of its late start and difficulties with frozen ground, the dredge initially accomplished little.[13] The next year, management indecision over the optimum plan for dredge operations interfered with actual operations.[14] The territorial mining department evaluated the project as having started out wrong. To the department, the company's problems stemmed from commencing operations before the ground had been adequately prepared for dredging, encountering financial trouble, changing for a period from Lewis's management, and selecting the incorrect type of dredge. The department hypothesized that results would have been improved if the dredge had a screen and stacker. The department predicted that dredge operations, which depended on a good water supply for preparing ground, would fail if not properly managed.[15]

The dredge had an uneven pattern of operations—idle some summer seasons, active for part or for entire other summers, first failing, then rising to success. The dredge did operate in 1930.[16] Then the dredging company ran into more financial difficulty. In March 1931, Fairbanks businessmen, George B. Wesch, E[d] H. Stroeker, and George Preston, became trustees for the company's bondholders and

leased its operations to R[oy] W. Ferguson and J. E. Barrack, agents of the newly formed American Creek Operating Company.[17] The dredge operated only four days in July 1931. As of that time, the dredge had produced values totaling $102,000. Prior to dredging, operations on the creek had produced $600,000.[18]

In 1932 and 1933 the new company leased claims on American Creek.[19] The dredge did some productive work in August 1932.[20] Territorial Mining Inspector and later Commissioner of Mines B. D. Stewart confirmed that dredging had resumed in 1932 under very competent management and a crew of eighteen men.[21] The dredge did not operate in 1933 because the American Creek Operating Company, learning from the mistakes of its predecessor, prepared the ground for the 1934 season.[22] As expected, Roy Ferguson successfully managed the dredging in 1934.[23] The dredge operated again in 1935 and 1936.[24]

By 1937, Luther Hess had become a trustee of the American Creek Dredging Company. J. E. Barrack was then president of the successor American Creek Operating Company; Dawson Cooper served as secretary and later as president of the new company.[25] The dredge stood idle that summer while its crew readied ground for the 1938 season.[26] The dredge had a crew of thirty in 1938.[27] Earl Beistline, a University of Alaska Fairbanks student in 1938, worked on that crew under Ted Matthews to restore the dredge to operational status.[28] According to a territorial mining department report of September 24, 1938, prepared by H. R. Joesting, crew wages generally ranged from 70 cents to $1.00 per hour; the cost of meals at the height of the season averaged 40 cents per worker. Joesting also noted that to improve its operating capability, the company was expanding its water supply. The old ditch, three miles long, drew water from American, New York, Colorado, and California creeks, but its size proved inadequate for optimum water supply to dredge operations. Accordingly, the company built a second ditch six miles long, which was then being connected to a reservoir and dam. The positive results of the company's quality management showed in

90

its production figures. The total gold production of the dredge through 1936 had been $152,775.85. For the season of 1938 alone, production reached an estimated $80,000.[29]

The dredge operated as usual in 1939.[30] By 1940, the crew had been cut to twenty-three.[31] That summer, the American Creek Operating Company finished dredging all claims available to it.[32] The dredge never operated again, but it was never moved or fully dismantled. Today, its rotting, discarded hulk testifies mutely to its outlived usefulness, the frequent fate of obsolete equipment.

At the same time in the late 1920s as the dredge began operating on American Creek, work around Tofty and Woodchopper had slowed down, pending a decision by the Alaska Gold Dredging Company, Limited, an English

firm, to undertake operations in the region.[33] The English company optioned or purchased sixty-two claims on and around Sullivan Creek, including those formerly worked by Cleveland and Howell.[34] The Company employed at least twenty men in the survey, a crew larger than the eight to ten employed by Cleveland and Howell. At length, the company determined that the ground was not suitable for dredging because the pay streak was spotty rather than continuous, the water supply was inadequate for preparing the ground, and the value of the ground per square foot was low.[35] After drilling two hundred holes, the company rated the gold and tin content of the samples extracted from the holes as insufficient to justify further investment.[36] The company had spent $165,000—$112,000 of that to Cleveland and

Figure 20. American Creek dredge, 1938. Courtesy of the Earl Beistline Collection, University of Alaska Fairbanks. Accession Number 85-093-223.

Figure 21. *Unidentified workers at American Creek, 1938. Courtesy of the Earl Beistline Collection, University of Alaska Fairbanks. Accession Number 85-093-246.*

Howell—in obtaining claims and equipment and expended probably even more money in conducting its negative evaluation. In July 1929, company engineer G. Adeney sold all holdings to Hans Tilleson and Arthur L'Heureux for only $5,000.[37] In turn, by 1934 Tilleson and L'Heureux had transferred their Sullivan Creek claims to the Cleary Hill Mines Company, a large Fairbanks operator. Cleary Hill prepared the ground and constructed nine miles of ditches so that the company could use a dragline scraper the next year to process the gravel of the paystreak.[38] Within a short time, as a result of its use of heavy dragline and bulldozer equipment, the company became a major operator in the Hot Springs district, rivaling the output of the American Creek Operating Company. In 1938, Ben Dahl, associate manager, declined to reveal company production figures to the territorial mining department, but he did disclose that

Cleary Hill produced seven tons of stream tin per season.[39]

The American Creek dredge and the short-lived British interest in the Sullivan Creek area had focused attention on the Hot Springs district. As of 1930, the district appeared to be the busiest mining camp on the Tanana River. In a letter of August 4 to the *Fairbanks Daily News-Miner*, C. F. Spencer characterized the people there as happy workers. He reported that Al Copeland's road crew was then grading the road between Hot Springs and the settlement of Eureka. In the Eureka area, J. R. Frank was producing pay from benches near Seattle Junior Creek. Operators Farmer and Jones ran a small hydraulic plant on a bench below Eureka Creek. Spencer considered the area the best bench country in Alaska, comparable to the benches in the American Creek valley of California in 1849. Spencer also observed capterpillar tractor

Figure 22. Bull gang at American Creek, 1938. Courtesy of the Earl Beistline Collection, University of Alaska Fairbanks. Accession Number 85-093-574.

activity on the claims of Hans Tilleson and Arthur L'Heureux in Tofty and speculated that Adolph Bock and Fred Hanson on Deep Creek near Woodchopper might hold the richest ground—$3.00 to a foot.[40] The Bock and Hanson operation, which employed five to ten men, produced both gold and silver.[41]

Other claims in the Hot Springs district did not go unnoticed. Fairbanks surveyor Irving S. Reed doggedly sought clients for his surveying business. In an exchange of correspondence with J[ohn] W. Duncan, formerly of Rampart but then on Eureka Creek, Reed encouraged Duncan to patent Duncan's fifty-one claims on Eureka. Reed pointed out that patenting would be cost-effective in that the expenses of the patent process, which would include Reed's fees to survey claims, would balance out in time. In particular, a patent holder was not required to work patented claims for assessment each year,

thereby saving assessment expenses on any unworked claims. Duncan expressed interest in the proposal and notified Reed that he also held eight claims in Rampart on Little Minook Creek, among them the famous McGraw-Carr claim, No. 8 above, which was already under patent.[42]

On August 28, 1935, Reed sent Dan Wilder to make a non-patent survey of claims for Arch W. Pringle on Rhode Island Creek and its tributaries in the Eureka area. Wilder, with Pringle and Frank Miller, arrived at Pringle's claim on No. 1, Gold Run. There John Gray, holder of the adjacent claim, threatened the party with a shotgun or large-barreled rifle from a distance of 400 feet. He disputed the boundary line between the two claims. Inquiring, "What are you fellows doing here?" Gray, with his right hand over the gun's breech, ordered, "Get off this ground and stay off. I'm warning you.

Don't show up here again. Next time it will be too bad." Ominously, neighbor Gray repeated, "I'm warning you. Stay off and keep off and don't come back. That's the last warning!" At that, Wilder, Miller, and Pringle headed for Pringle's cabin while Gray stalked a parallel path, his gun aimed at them. He stopped behind a birch tree near his cabin and watched as the three moved away. Wilder immediately informed Irving Reed that he could not finish the survey without the help of law enforcement. Thereupon, District Attorney Rivers took action. Marshal Spencer flew to Hot Springs on August 20 to arrest John Gray, thus clearing the way for Wilder to survey without further confrontation.[43]

Three years later, on September 12, 1938, Irving Reed entered into a partnership with Capt. A. S. Crane, a former operator at Ruby and long-time store owner and postmaster in Rampart. The two partners formed the Big Minook Mining Corporation and leased claims on Big Minook Creek from Crane's wife, Ella. They constructed a ditch and stripped trees and moss. They also applied for and received a loan of $9,000, subsequently increased to $20,000, from the Reconstruction Finance Corporation (RFC), the federal agency that provided financial assistance to mining ventures. The project ended in bankruptcy. The partnership was dissolved in February 1941. Crane intended to continue operations although Joe Meehling held an option to prospect the claims. Reed paid creditor Ernest N. Patty of Gold Placers, Inc., $300 for his share of the $600 debt owed for shaft logs. Crane evidently failed to settle his accounts since Patty sought payment from Crane in late 1941 and in 1945 the RFC regarded the loan of $20,000 as still outstanding.[44]

Coincident with the increased developments in the area, the U.S. Geological Survey initiated an exceptionally close scrutiny of the region. In the summer of 1931, geologists A. E. Waters, Jr. and J. B. Mertie, Jr. examined the Rampart and Hot Springs districts. Waters looked at stream tin (cassiterite) and other concentrates, most especially in the Tofty area, and pointed out that the actual bedrock source for the tin in Tofty had not been uncovered. He observed, however,

a block of iron on the left side of Sullivan Creek, two miles upstream from the site of old Tofty (Sullivan City) and commented extensively on the geological mineralization and intrusions that had occurred in the two districts. He also reported on the mineral composition of forty analyzed samples of ore concentrates extracted from placers in the two districts at different times between 1918 and 1931.[45]

For his part, J. B. Mertie, Jr. relied heavily on previous U.S.G.S. bulletins as he summarized his and his predecessors' findings on the two districts in a definitive report, obviously designed as a consolidated, basic resource on the region. Mertie related, somewhat imprecisely, the history of the districts as he understood it and described the geographical features, including the drainage systems and contrasting relief structures of mountains, valleys, and flatlands. He charted climatic conditions for Rampart and for Tanana in the Fort Gibbon district—precipitation, snowfall, and temperatures in mean, monthly averages. He discussed the settlements of Rampart, which then had a population of 103, Native and non-Native, and of Hot Springs, which then had a population of forty-five, mostly white. He explained the transportation, mail, and communications systems in the area. In particular, he stressed the geological formations of bedded rocks dating from the Paleozoic, Mezozoic, or Cenozoic ages and specified characteristics, creek by creek, commenting on the type and extent of mining activity in progress during the 1931 season.[46]

At the time, the method of hydraulicking in open-cut pits during the summer predominated. Only a few miners drifted in tunnels during the winter. Mining in Rampart continued on many of the oldest claims on Little Minook Creek, Dawson Creek, Idaho Bar, and other creeks as powerful streams of water washed down auriferous gravel to depths well below those dug by the earliest miners of the pick, shovel, and windlass days. On the other hand, former gold-producing creeks in the Eureka area such as Gold Run, estimated to have produced gold valued at $200,000; and Glen Gulch, estimated to have produced $1,000,000, had been abandoned as totally worked out.[47] The abandonment turned out to be temporary as activity resumed on Gold Run and Glen Gulch a few years after Mertie's tour.

Mertie also learned a likely reason why Alder Creek, prospected heavily off and on since September 1897, had never become a regularly worked gold-producer comparable to Little Minook Creek. Prospecting in 1931 had uncovered a bedrock of coal on an upper tributary of Alder. From that discovery, Mertie theorized that a Tertiary coal-bearing formation had blanketed the old valley of Alder Creek, possibly covering gold-bearing rocks at the same geologic time as auriferous gravel was being deposited on Idaho Bar.[48]

Mertie discussed at length the Barrett lode mine on the top of Hot Springs Dome. The lode had the only cobalt then known in Alaska.[49] Although Mertie may not have realized the fact, John Barrett became a local legend in Hot Springs as he trudged up the steep climb to the summit each morning and returned down the worn but treacherous trail each evening. He patented his lode claim and single-handedly pursued its development although it apparently was never productive. Even at an advanced age, Barrett painfully continued his daily ascent whenever weather conditions permitted until he disappeared in the early 1950s, presumably as a result of a mine accident. Search parties failed to recover his body from the mine or to determine what happened to him. His heirs in Butte, Montana, visited the claim but did not resume activity there.[50]

Biennially in the 1920s, Territorial Mining Inspector B. D. Stewart reported to the governor of Alaska on the cooperation between his office and the federal government in investigating mining conditions in Alaska.[51] Strangely, the cooperative information interchange between J. B. Mertie, Jr., and the territorial mining staff apparently broke down after Mertie's 1931 study. In January 1932, surveyor Irving Reed informed Stewart that Mertie had a listing of miners in Rampart and Hot Springs. Six weeks later, Stewart directed Reed to get a list of operators in Rampart and Hot Springs since

Mertie's list was not available to Stewart's office.[52] In subsequent reports to the governor, Stewart no longer highlighted the federal-territorial cooperation.

In the late 1920s and into the Depression years of the 1930s, the records of the Fort Gibbon district indicated a high volume of newly located claims. Yet production figures for the district during the same period remained consistently negligible, a contrast suggesting that prospecting achieved so little success that prospecting companies decided not to start full mining operations. On August 14, 1928, C. Marvin Berry, agent of C[larence] J. Berry of San Francisco, located, purchased, or leased several claims on and around Lower Discovery, Indian River. Although the Berry acquisitions appeared to have been substantial, nothing developed from the intensive transactions.[53]

In 1932, E. R. Farrell absorbed claims on Mason Creek from the Coulombe family and others, thereby expanding his operations in that district.[54] Nevertheless, district production figures reflected no gain.

Similarly, in 1929 Grace and Walter Fisher secured interests in several claims on Grant Creek and Monday Gulch and over time gradually added to their holdings.[55] About seven years passed, however, before their activity impacted the district's production figures. In 1936, geologist Philip Smith reported a renewal of activity on Grant Creek in the Fort Gibbon district.[56] The next year he specified that the greatest work in the district was being done by the company of Fisher and Fisher.[57] To recover gold from their Grant Creek group, the Fishers used a diesel dragline with hydraulicking. Equipment costs totaled $32,000. The company employed a crew of six at wages between $6.00 and $12.00 a day, plus board at $2.00 per day. Fisher and Fisher's production for 1937, however, had only reached $8,312.20.[58] About the same time, L. McGee of Anchorage began to accumulate and develop claims on Indian River.[59]

Although growth in the Fort Gibbon district through the Depression years had been slow, the mining industry in the Hot Springs district showed consistent, though not always profitable, work and offered opportunities for summer employment over the same period. In the summer of 1938, the district buzzed with activity, according to territorial mining reports compiled by H. R. Joesting. Tom Dean and Company worked on Miller Gulch, a tributary of Sullivan Creek, on property held by Dean and Pete Millianick. The company met difficulties thawing and sluicing due to the amount and stickiness of the sediment.[60] Adolph Bock, with a crew of eleven, drifted on his and Fred Hanson's claims on Deep Creek.[61] Their production in 1938 reached $8,510.[62] Leo Linder also worked on Deep Creek on a claim leased from Bock. His production for 1938 was $6,300.[63] Anton D. D. Styckex, on nearby New York Gulch, produced a mere $285 in the same season. Presumably, he lost considerable gold because he had not reached bedrock and because he shoveled gravel under water without proper drainage.[64]

On the other side of the district from Deep and Sullivan creeks, the area discovered by the Boston boys in 1899, continued to be exploited. In 1938 W. N. Frank of J. R. Frank and Company operated for Mrs. Linnie F. Duncan on a bench above Pioneer Creek. Mrs. Duncan reported production beween 1911 and 1937 at $470,000, and she expected $10,000 for 1938.[65] On another bench off Pioneer, F[red] W. Whitehead of Whitehead and Company worked for Mrs. F. N. Thumm, using a bulldozer and Giant hydraulicking equiment.[66]

Over on Eureka Creek and McKaskey (McCaskie/MacCaskie) Bar, Whitehead operated for the Jones estate. Whitehead foresaw production of $6,000 for 1938, but with equipment costs of $9,000, he concluded operational expenses were too high to continue the operation the next season.[67] Arch Pringle hydraulicked his claims on Rhode Island Creek and occasionally rented a bulldozer to strip off overburden. His ground produced $7,534.80 in 1938.[68] Pete Johnson's company, Johnson and Johnson, took $14,000 in 1938 from claims owned by Robert Dinsmore, specifically claims

Nos. 1 and 2 above, originally located in 1901 by Oliver Lorencen and the Eagle Mining Company.[69]

The largest operator in the Eureka area was the Montana Mining Company of Helena, Montana, with a crew of fifteen.[70] It worked on Omega and Alpha creeks and leased claims on Rhode Island Creek. Using a bulldozer and diesel dragline as well as hydraulic methods, the company expected a return of $50,000 for 1938. According to company employee George Miscovich, the project started without prospecting the ground first, an error the company was then correcting by drilling to outline pay gravel before the 1939 mining season.[71]

In the Rampart district, mining had also progressed normally along creeks worked almost continuously since 1897, but the operations were often small. In 1935, for example, twelve mines were in operation, but they produced only a few hundred dollars each.[72] A series of territorial mining reports in 1938, filed by Irving Reed, provided information about some Rampart operations. On claim No. 16 above, Hunter Creek, E. E. Swanson used hydraulicking methods. In the twelve seasons between 1926 and 1937, Swanson had retrieved $80,000 from the claim. He employed four men at $6.00 per day plus board, estimated at $1.75 per day. He projected his operation would continue another twenty years.[73] John McKenty, on claim No. 3 above, Hunter, owned by Gertrude Clemens, thought that $10,000 had been taken from the ground between 1904 and 1937. Like Swanson, he expected production would go on for another twenty years. Unlike Swanson, McKenty worked alone, using traditional ground-sluicing and shovel-in methods.[74]

Over on the former McGraw-Carr claim, No. 8 above, Little Minook Creek, and adjacent No. 7, William J. Lynn worked for owner John W. Duncan. Lynn estimated production between 1932 and 1937 at $11,820 with another twenty years yet ahead. He employed two men and a cook at $5.00 per day with board at $3.00. Like McKenty, he used long-time splashing and shovel-in methods.[75] Lower down on Little Minook, E. R. Farrell, a Fort Gibbon district operator, and J. A. Elliott, similarly ground-sluiced and splashed to recover gold from eight claims—Nos. 5 below up through Discovery to 2 above—which they and the McCabe estate owned. The two-man operation produced $3,355 in 1937.[76]

On claim No. 2 below, Slate Creek, Frank L. Hawley also relied on old-time splashing methods to exploit ground which produced about $6,000 between 1912 and 1937. As a consequence of his methods, he lost at least one-half of his gold.[77] On Ruby Creek where William B. Ballou hydraulicked in 1904, Peter Larkin of the Novelty Milling Company prospected between 1935 and 1937 and acquired a slim $40. In his work, Larkin came upon Ballou's abandoned hydraulic plant.[78] Not too far away on Discovery, Hoosier Creek, H. C[hris] Thyman noted that production by traditional methods in 1936 and 1937 had totalled $1,100.[79]

On Florida Creek, Frank Dinan and Ernest Drexels estimated that production in 1938 was only $800, but they expected work on the claim could continue for another twenty years.[80] Finally, across the Yukon River on No. 8 below, Quail Creek, Einar and Clem Anderson, working for Capt. A. S. and Ella Crane, hydraulicked eight claims which had produced $15,000 between 1932 and 1937.[81]

By 1941, Rampart mining had been underway for forty-five years. Even small operators using old mining methods assumed mining would continue on long-producing creeks for at least twenty more years. Mining appeared to be an unshakable institution, a solid, though not universally profitable, industry. Interruption was soon to come, however, as far from Rampart, in Europe and in China, nations warred for conquest and for defense. Small countries leagued together in opposition to militant totalitarian invaders. The tragedy of World War II slowly encroached upon Alaska. Not long after Japanese forces attacked the Aleutians in 1942, War Production Board Limitation Order L-208 shut down unessential gold mining nationwide. Alaskan mine operators turned their bulldozers over to U.S. forces for use in building airfields and the Alcan, now the Alaska Highway. Mine laborers enlisted in military service. Gold mining in the Rampart, Manley Hot Springs, and Fort Gibbon districts was suspended for the duration of the war.

End Notes Chapter 4. Between the Two World Wars, 1919–1941

Short Titles

The following shortened forms referring to depositories and series are used extensively through the chapter endnotes.

Archives, UAF	Alaska Archives and Manuscripts, Alaska and Polar Regions Department, Elmer E. Rasmuson Library, University of Alaska Fairbanks.
District Recorder, Fairbanks	State of Alaska Department of Natural Resources, Office of the Commissioner, District Recorder, Fairbanks, Alaska.
Division of Mining, Fairbanks	State of Alaska Department of Natural Resources, Division of Mining, Fairbanks, Alaska.
(folder)	A copy of a creek record, dated between 1896 and 1900, at the office of the District Recorder, Fairbanks. The original is retained at the office of the State Recorder, Anchorage, Alaska.
Fort Gibbon	Fort Gibbon recording district records at the office of the District Recorder, Fairbanks, Alaska.
Manley	Manley Hot Springs recording district records at the office of the District Recorder, Fairbanks, Alaska.
Rampart	Rampart recording district records at the office of the District Recorder, Fairbanks, Alaska.
U.S.G.S.	U.S. Geological Survey.

1. J. B. Mertie, Jr., "Mineral Deposits of the Rampart and Hot Springs Districts, Alaska," in *Mineral Resources of Alaska; Report on Progress of Investigations in 1931*, ed. Philip S. Smith, U.S.G.S. Bulletin 844 (Washington: Government Printing Office, 1934), 174.

2. Manley, Leases, 1: 248–50, District Recorder, Fairbanks.

3. Ibid., 266. Manley retained a few holdings after he left the district.

4. John B. Mathews to L. D. Henderson, Superintendent of Public Schools, Juneau, AK, 30 April 1920, Lois M. Morey Collection, box 1, folder 47, Archives, UAF.

5. Ed Ness, American Creek, Department of the Interior U.S. Bureau of Mines report, 31 August 1922, Division of Mining, Fairbanks.

6. J. R. Frank & Co., Territory of Alaska Mining Department and Department of the Interior U.S. Bureau of Mines reports, 1929, 1922, and 1925, Division of Mining, Fairbanks. In late 1928, J[ames] R[obert] Frank suffered a stroke and decided to sell at the end of the 1929 season. However, he apparently changed his mind. He died in 1936, but his company operated successfully at least to 1940. Also, B. D. Stewart, *Annual Report of the Mine Inspector to the Governor of Alaska 1922* ([Juneau: Territory of Alaska, 1923]), 41.

7. Cleveland & Howell, Department of the Interior U.S. Bureau of Mines report, 1 September, 1922, Division of Mining, Fairbanks.

8. A. H. Brooks, et al., eds., *Mineral Resources of Alaska: Report on Progress of Investigations on 1922*, U.S.G.S. Bulletin 755 (Washington: Government Printing Office, 1924), 37.

9. Mertie, 177.

10. American Creek Dredging Co., Department of the Interior U. S. Bureau of Mines report, 29 June 1926, Division of Mining, Fairbanks; American Creek Dredging Co., Territory of Alaska Mining Department report, 14 August 1929. The contract price of the dredge was $73,000.

11. Manley, Mortgages, 1: 223–31, District Recorder, Fairbanks.

12. American Creek Dredging Co., 14 August 1929.

13. Philip S. Smith, *Mineral Industry of Alaska in 1928 and Administrative Report*, U.S.G.S. Bulletin 813-A (Washington: Government Printing Office, 1930), 32.

14. Philip S. Smith, *Mineral Industry of Alaska in 1929 and Administrative Report*, U.S.G.S. Bulletin 824-A (Washington: Government Printing Office, 1930), 36.

15. American Creek Dredging Co., 14 August 1929.

16. Mertie, 214.

17. Manley, Leases, 1: 305–12.

18. Mertie, 214.

19. Manley, Leases, 1: 317–21.

20. Philip S. Smith et al., eds., *Mineral Resources of Alaska: Report on Progress of Investigations in 1932*, U.S.G.S. Bulletin 857 (Washington: Government Printing Office, 1934), 33.

21. B. D. Stewart, *Mining Investigations and Mine Inspections in Alaska Including Assistance to Prospectors: Bienniun Ending March 31, 1933* (Juneau: Territory of Alaska, Division of Mining, 1933), 99.

22. Philip S. Smith, *Mineral Industry of Alaska in 1933*, U.S.G.S. Bulletin 864-A (Washington: Government Printing Office, 1934), 39.

23. Philip S. Smith, *Mineral Industry of Alaska in 1934*, U.S.G.S. Bulletin 868-A (Washington: Government Printing Office, 1936), 41.

24. Philip S. Smith, *Mineral Industry of Alaska in 1935*, U.S.G.S. Bulletin 880-A (Washington: Government Printing Office, 1937), 42; Philip S. Smith, *Mineral Industry of Alaska in 1936*, U.S.G.S. Bulletin 897-A (Washington: Government Printing Office, 1938), 51.

25. Manley, Leases, 1: 317–21.

26. Philip S. Smith, *Mineral Industry of Alaska in 1937*, U.S.G.S. Bulletin 910-A (Washington: Government Printing Office, 1939), 52.

27. B. D. Stewart, *Report of the Commissioner of Mines to the Governor for the Biennium Ended December 31, 1938* (Juneau: Territory of Alaska, 1939), 49.

28. Earl Beistline, telephone interview with author, Fairbanks, AK, 12 November 1993.

29. American Creek Operating Co., Territory of Alaska Mining Department report, 24 September 1938, Division of Mining, Fairbanks.

30. Philip S. Smith, *Mineral Industry of Alaska in 1939*, U.S.G.S. Bulletin 926-A (Washington: Government Printing Office, 1941), 47.

31. B. D. Stewart, *Report of the Commissioner of Mines to the Governor for the Biennium Ended December 31, 1940* (Juneau: Territory of Alaska, 1941), 69.

32. Philip S. Smith, *Mineral Industry of Alaska in 1940*, U.S.G.S. Bulletin 933-A (Washington: Government Printing Office, 1942), 43.

33. Philip S. Smith, U.S.G.S. Bulletin 813-A, 32.

34. Philip S. Smith, U.S.G.S. Bulletin 824-A, 37.

35. Tillison (sic) and L'Heureaux (sic), Territory of Alaska Mining Department report, 13 August 1929, Division of Mining, Fairbanks.

36. Philip S. Smith, U.S.G.S. Bulletin 824-A, 3

37. Tillison and L'Heureaux.

38. Philip S. Smith, *Mineral Industry of Alaska in 1934*, U.S.G.S. Bulletin 868-A (Washington: Government Printing Office, 1936), 41.

39. Cleary Hill Mining Co., Territory of Alaska Department of Mines report, 24 September 1938, Division of Mining, Fairbanks.

40. C. F. Spencer to the *Fairbanks Daily News-Miner*, 4 August 1930, published 16 August 1930, Irving S. Reed Collection, box 14, folder 8, Archives, UAF.

41. Buck (sic) and Hansen (sic), Territory of Alaska Mining Department report, 13 August 1929, Division of Mining, Fairbanks.

42. Reed to J. W. Duncan, 17 May 1929, Irving S. Reed Collection, box 2, folder 1929–1930; Duncan to Reed, 6 July 1929, ibid., box 1, folder "D."

43. Dan Wilder to Reed, 18 August 1935, ibid., box 8, book 53. John Gray died in early 1938.

44. Crane and Reed Co-Partnership agreement, 1 February 1939, ibid., box 5, folder 58; Reconstruction Finance Corporation loan, ibid., box 5, folder 59; Reed to John E. Norton, 19 July 1940, ibid., box 2, folder 1933-1949; agreement with Joe Meehling, 1 December 1940, ibid., box 5, folder 60; Ernest N. Patty to A. S. Crane, 16 October 1941, ibid., box 1, folder "P"; Burt M. McConnell to A. S. Crane, 12 March 1945, ibid., box 1, Miscellaneous Correspondence.

45. A. E. Waters, Jr., "Placers Concentrates of the Rampart and Hot Springs Districts," in *Mineral Resources of Alaska: Report on Progress of Investigations in 1931*, ed. Philip S. Smith, U.S.G.S. Bulletin 844 (Washington: Government Printing Office, 1934), 227–46.

46. Mertie, 163–74.

47. Ibid., 174–201, 203.

48. Ibid., 191–92.

49. Ibid., 215–16.

50. Stanley Dayo, *Stanley Dayo: Manley Hot Springs*, ed. Yvonne Yarber and Curt Madison, Yukon-Koyukuk School District of Alaska (Fairbanks: Spirit Mountain Press, 1985), 65; Stanley Dayo, personal interview with author, Manley Hot Springs, AK, 31 August 1993.

51. B. D. Stewart, *Report on the Cooperation Between the Territory of Alaska and the United States in Making Mining Investigations and in the Inspection of Mines for the Biennium Ending March 31, 1929 (Including a Report on the Operation of the Properties Aid Act)*. (Juneau: [Territory of Alaska], 1929).

52. Reed to B. D. Stewart, 4 January 1932, and Stewart to Reed, 18 February 1932, Irving S. Reed Collection, box 1, folder "S."

53. Fort Gibbon, Deeds, 1908-1954, 422–70, District Recorder, Fairbanks; Fort Gibbon, Mining Locations, vol. 1, 1908–1928, intermittant 587-639, District Recorder, Fairbanks.

54. Fort Gibbon, Deeds, 523-24.

55. Ibid., 477-80, 484–85, 552-53.

56. Philip S. Smith, U.S.G.S. Bulletin 897-A, 56.

57. Philip S. Smith, "Mineral Industry of Alaska in 1938," in *Mineral Resources of Alaska: Report on Progress of Investigations in 1938*, ed. Philip S. Smith, Fred H. Moffit, and J. B. Mertie, Jr., U.S.G.S. Bulletin 917 (Washington: Government Printing Office, 1942), 56.

58. Fisher & Fisher, Territory of Alaska Mining Department report, 15 November 1937, Division of Mining, Fairbanks.

59. Fort Gibbon, Deeds, 558, 562–69,.

60. Tom Dean & Co., Territory of Alaska Mining Department report, 24 September 1938, Division of Mining, Fairbanks.

61. B. D. Stewart, *Report of the Commissioner of Mines to the Governor for the Biennium Ended December 31, 1938* (Juneau: Territory of Alaska, 1939), 54.

62. Adolf (sic) Bock, Territory of Alaska Mining Department report, 24 September 1938, Division of Mining, Fairbanks.

63. Leo Linderer (sic) & Co., Territory of Alaska Mining Department report, 24 September 1938, Division of Mining, Fairbanks.

64. Anton D. D. Styckex, Territory of Alaska Department of Mines report, 23 September 1938, Division of Mining, Fairbanks.

65. J. R. Frank & Co., Territory of Alaska Department of Mines report, 22 September, 1938, Division of Mining, Fairbanks.

66. Whitehead and Co., Territory of Alaska Department of Mines report, 22 September 1938, Division of Mining, Fairbanks.

67. Whitehead and Bayless, Territory of Alaska Department of Mines report, 22 September 1938, Division of Mining, Fairbanks.

68. A. W. Pringle, Territory of Alaska Department of Mines report, 22 September 1938, Division of Mining, Fairbanks.

69. Johnson & Johnson, Territory of Alaska Department of Mines report, 22 September 1938, Division of Mining, Fairbanks.

70. B. D. Stewart, *Report of the Commissioner of Mines to the Governor for the Biennium Ended December 31, 1938* (Juneau: Territory of Alaska, 1939), 60.

71. Montana Mining Co., Territory of Alaska Department of Mines report, 21 September 1938, Division of Mining, Fairbanks. George Miscovich, personal conversation with author, Fairbanks, AK, 17 December 1994. Miscovich recalled working for Montana Mining on Omega Creek.

72. Philip S. Smith, U.S.G.S. Bulletin 880-A, 47.

73. E. E. Swanson, Territory of Alaska Department of Mines report, 29 July 1938, Division of Mining, Fairbanks.

74. John McKenty, Territory of Alaska Department of Mines report, 29 July 1938, Division of Mining, Fairbanks.

75. Wm. J. Lynn, Territory of Alaska Department of Mines report, 29 July 1938, Division of Mining, Fairbanks.

76. E. R. Farrell and J. A. Elliott, Territory of Alaska Department of Mines, 12 January 1938, Division of Mining, Fairbanks.

77. Frank L. Hawley, Territory of Alaska Department of Mines report, 23 July 1938, Division of Mining, Fairbanks.

78. Peter Larkin, Territory of Alaska Mining Department report, 30 July 1938,

Division of Mining, Fairbanks.

79. H. C. Thyman, Territory of Alaska Department of Mines report, 26 July 1938, Division of Mining, Fairbanks.

80. Frank Dinan and Ernest Drexels, Territory of Alaska Department of Mines report, 1 August 1938, Division of Mines, Fairbanks.

81. Anderson & Anderson, Territory of Alaska Department of Mines report, 28 July 1938, Division of Mining, Fairbanks.

Chapter 5. Into the Present Era, 1946–1994

In 1991, we completed a modest exploration program followed by aggressive programs in 1992 and 1993. Highlights of these efforts include the discovery of several areas of potentially important gold mineralization on five of the [Doyon, Limited] land blocks. The most significant discoveries have been in the Rampart and Kuskokwim blocks. In the Rampart block, where our work is ongoing, we recognize a district-scale belt of pluton-related gold mineralization.
—Jack Di Marchi, Fairbanks, Alaska, 1994.[1]

The end of World War II did not result in a rush to resume gold mining in Alaska. Operators had to replace heavy equipment and reassess their financial status. Meeting their start-up costs entailed mortgages, bank loans, silent partnerships, shares, or conditional sales with the Northern Commercial Company. Of course, prospecting and mining had always held elements of risk. The type of risks changed over time. Gold-seeking dreamers, who boarded a steamer in Seattle in the summer of 1897 heading for Alaska, needed a gold pan, pick, shovel, clothes, and supplies to last through winter. The would-be Yukoner's physical and emotional survival was at stake. By 1946, an operator carefully calculated the financial risks of long-term investment in sophisticated earth-moving machinery against projections of gold output. An operator's business survival was often at stake.

As they deliberated their course of action, the operators filed affidavits of "Intention to Hold" their claims, taking advantage of a federal wartime provision entitling operators to retain their holdings, plan their moves, and not yet initiate operations. In the Fort Gibbon district during

the first half of 1946, L. McGee, Oscar Winchell, and Joe Haley itemized in their affidavits several claims on Utopia, Indian, and Black creeks. Walter Fisher filed for his holdings on Grant Creek, Monday Gulch, and Fox Gulch. J. A. Elliott also intended to hold his claims on Illinois, Golden, and Wilson creeks.[2] Many operators continued to follow the "Intention to Hold" procedure into mid-1948.

By the end of 1946, B. D. Stewart, territorial commissioner of mines, expressed his disappointment that Alaska's gold mining industry had not returned quickly to full operational status. He cited as reasons for the slow progress a small labor force, lack of equipment, and shipping strikes which impeded the delivery of supplies to Alaska. He reported, however, that there was some activity, including dragline operations, in each of the three districts. He identified, by name, twenty operators such as the Cleary Hill Mines on Sullivan Creek and Tofty Gulch, A. W. Pringle on Rhode Island Creek, Mike Shimrock on Shirley Bar, and the Little Minook Mining Company on Little Minook Creek.[3] While placer mine operators weighed decisions about their future operations, the federal government, having entered the Atomic Age with the bombing of Hiroshima and Nagasaki, sought new resources from Alaska's gold mine sites, deposits of radioactive materials. U.S. Geological Survey teams, in association with the U.S. Atomic Energy Commission, examined potential spots throughout Alaska for uranium. In the fall of 1945, Walter Fisher notified R. M. Chapman of the Geological Survey, then in Fairbanks, of pitchblende veinlets on a hillside along a tractor trail by his Grant Creek mine in the Fort Gibbon district. Since security rules forbade discussion of the subject of pitchblende with outsiders, the Geological Survey personnel refrained from contacting Fisher directly during the ensuing winter to discuss specific details of his find. Instead, a three-man team, consisting of geologists P. L. Killeen and M. G. White and camp hand R. D. Hamilton, arrived at the Fisher mine unannounced in August 1946. To their surprise, the team learned that Walter Fisher had died a few months earlier, shortly after he had filed his "Intention to Hold" affidavit. His mine was closed, and no one in the area knew of any pitchblende veinlets. The geological team tested hillsides in the vicinity of several tractor trails and failed to uncover any evidence of pitchblende. The team concluded that Fisher had erroneously identified fragments of black hematite as pitchblende.[4]

Two years later, geologist Robert M. Moxham examined the Tofty tin belt, the Barrett lode on Hot Springs Dome, the Eureka mining area, and gold mines in Rampart. Since the 1931 trip of A. E. Waters and J. B. Mertie, Jr., the Geological Survey had known of radioactive minerals in the Tofty tin belt. Waters had mentioned the presence of monazite and eschynite in concentrates from Tofty. Moxham confirmed those materials and, in addition, identified radioactive ellsworthite, columbite, and zircon. Although he did not locate the bedrock source of the radioactive materials, he surmised some source rocks were north or northeast of the Tofty tin belt. At the same time, he presumed that the total volume of radioactive minerals in the belt was too low for commercial exploitation as a byproduct of gold and tin production.[5]

Moxham also tested other areas. He attributed minor radioactivity in granite formations on Hot Springs Dome, at Elephant Mountain, and in the Eureka area to monazite. He thought that the very limited radioactivity at Rampart mines may have been connected to zircon. As a result, he decided that none of the sites tested exhibited any possibility of having radioactive materials in commercial quantities.[6]

At the end of 1948, Commissioner of Mines B. D. Stewart again reported on the generally light activity in the three districts. He highlighted, though, the fact that the Sawtooth Mining Company had produced several tons of antimony ore from the Sawtooth Mountains near Rampart. Otherwise, only about twenty operators, including the previously named operators and Strandberg and Sons of Anchorage on Utopia Creek, had been working during the two-year period.[7]

After Stewart retired on January 1, 1950, Leo H. Saarela, a former Rampart operator in partnership with the Swanson brothers, served as commissioner for about two years and carried on the biennial practice of reviewing Alaska's mining progress. He pointed out that because of the low market price received from its antimony production in 1948, the Sawtooth company had ceased mining. According to Saarela, other activity in the three districts—twenty-one operators in all, including Tony Lanning on Thanksgiving Creek—remained comparable to the previous four years.[8]

In September 1951, [James A.] Williams of the territorial mining department reviewed on site several operations reinstated that summer in the Manley Hot Springs and Rampart districts. On Shirley Bar, first discovered in July 1901 by George R. Shirley, Mike Shimrock, along with Ed Lawler, worked a claim known as the Gold Mine in the Sky, using a bulldozer and hydraulic methods. They had produced $7,500 that season.[9] Not far away on Rhode Island and Seattle creeks, A. W. Pringle also used a bulldozer and hydraulic methods. Because of low water supply throughout the summer, Pringle had restricted sluicing to one and one-half hours per day. Perhaps because of his slow rate of gold recovery, he did not give Williams seasonal production figures.[10]

On the other side of the Manley Hot Springs district on Woodchopper Creek, Al Berg and Clyde Larson used traditional pick, shovel, and boiler methods on claims leased from Adolph Bock. Although they had uncovered much tin concentrate, they had retrieved little gold and had failed to obtain a work force to develop their operation adequately. Consequently, they were uncertain about continuing their lease.[11] Over on Sullivan Creek and Tofty Gulch, L. McGee, formerly a resident of Anchorage but by then a resident of Reno, Nevada, used a dragline and bulldozer to work claims he had purchased from the Cleary Hill Mines, reportedly for $45,000. He complained that mine laborers were inefficient and unreliable and that cyanide did not clean gold well. Nevertheless, he reported production figures of $30,000 in 1951 and his intent to mine Tofty Gulch at a deep level the following year.[12] On nearby Cache Creek, Otto Hovely had produced almost nothing, working with traditional pick, shovel, and boiler. At the end of the 1951 season, he sold his claim to Charles Proctor who planned to prospect new ground for a new shaft.[13]

Across the divide in the Rampart district, a man named Martin managed the Little Minook Mining Company for the partnership of Al Bernard, William Thorsen, Otto Arndt, and Martin. The company operated with dragline, bulldozer, and hydraulic methods on claims down from No. 4 above, Little Minook Creek. The partners considered the ground up the creek, which included the long-time producer No. 8 above, to have been worked out. Company production for 1951 had been $40,000.[14]

On Hoosier Creek, prospected by Peter Johnson, James Langford, and others in 1898, Jim Pierce and Charlie Gravy worked claims owned by Harvey [Chris] Thyman. Although Pierce and Gravy operated with a bulldozer, they panned the concentrate by hand. Further, they did not adequately mine the bedrock and most likely missed much paydirt.[15]

Finally, on Hunter Creek, named for Bill Hunter in 1896, the Swanson brothers, Emil and Albert, former partners of Commissioner Leo Saarela, took out $45,000 in 1951 through the use of hydraulic methods and bulldozers, expending $18,500 in the process. They had three workers that year but decided to operate without hired labor in 1952 since they had found labor undependable.[16]

When Leo Saarela resigned his commissioner of mines position in April 1952 to become regional mining supervisor, Conservation Division, U. S. Geological Survey, Phil R. Holdsworth replaced him. According to Holdsworth's report, L. McGee did not carry out his plans to work in Tofty Gulch in 1952, but the report did not disclose the reason for McGee's inactivity that year. Holdsworth did state that Alamco, Incorporated, of Fairbanks had a season of antimony production in the Sawtooth Mountains and that Strandberg and Sons operated simultaneously at Utopia Creek in the Fort Gibbon district and on Eureka Creek in the Manley Hot Springs district. Even though there had been twenty-two operations throughout the three districts in the two-year period, Holdsworth observed a definite trend toward a decline in mining in Rampart.[17]

By the end of 1954, Commissioner Holdsworth realized that the domestic market for antimony production had apparently lost out to the overriding competition of cheaper foreign antimony imports. Antimony production from the Sawtooth Mountains had ended. At the same time, Holdsworth viewed as a potential new resource a large asbestos deposit near Rampart. In his recapitulation of operations, Holdsworth listed only thirteen in the three districts.[18] That year, Grace Fisher, widow of Walter Fisher, had leased her holdings on Grant Creek, Monday Gulch, and Fox Gulch to Lars Indergaard, Frank C. "Tuffy" Edgington, and George Rossander.[19] Edgington's Iditarod Operating Company had long been one of the few operations, sometimes only operation, cited by the commissioners for the Melozitna/Fort Gibbon area.

Commissioner Holdsworth's report for the 1955-1956 biennium continued the prosaic listing of active operations, which by then numbered about fourteen in the three districts, including Melo Jackovitch's Hunter Creek Mining Company on Hunter Creek, Oscar Enstrom's plant on American Creek, and the outfit of Tony Lanning, working with Stanley Dayo, on Shirley Bar and Omega Creek. Holdsworth again emphasized the presence of an asbestos deposit near Rampart and noted that the Swanson brothers had sold their Hunter Creek operation to William Thomas, formerly a Kobuk miner.[20]

When the next and final report on Alaska's mining industry came out, Alaska had become a state. Holdsworth had risen to the newly created position of commissioner of Natural Resources, and James A. Williams had been appointed the director of the Division of Mines and Minerals within Holdsworth's department. In keeping with tradition, Williams listed the operations. Among the fifteen operators for the three districts were Frank C. Edgington, by then the Grant Creek Mining Company, on Grant Creek; Harry Havrilack on Ruby Creek; Tony Lanning on Thanksgiving Creek; A. W. Pringle on Rhode Island Creek; Joe Vogler on Morelock Creek; and Strandberg Mines on Eureka Creek and Indian River.[21]

Statehood brought not only administrative changes with the establishment of new departments but also a drive for the economic development of Alaska. Particular impetus was placed on the development of hydroelectric power. In 1907, after studying the water supply problem in the Rampart mining district, U.S. Geological Survey engineers C. C. Covert and C. E. Ellsworth had proposed the construction of a plant on the Troublesome River to funnel hydroelectric power to mining operations around Rampart. In their opinion, hydroelectric power would benefit Rampart miners. At the time, nothing came of their recommendation and no U.S. Geological Survey geologist repeated or reaffirmed their suggestion in later reports.

Yet the idea of hydroelectric power for the Rampart area did not die away. According to the late Edby Davis of Fairbanks, crews and passengers on steamboats passing through the whirling rapids on the Yukon River below Rampart predicted the future erection of a hydroelectric power plant at the rapids site. Davis recalled that in 1920 F. G. Noyes and Aloysious Frederick had formed a company to build a dam at the Rampart rapids, but the company suffered financial failure. Three years later, Fairbanks Exploration Company personnel studied the dam concept but soon rejected it as too large a program for their purposes. Nevertheless, Davis pointed out, the Northern Commercial Company, which then provided electric power to the Fairbanks community, postponed making improvements at its power plant for ten years in expectation of a hydroelectric plant being set up near Rampart.[22]

Again, nothing developed. During the Depression and World War II, the concept seemed to have faded out. Then, as a result of a reconnaissance study in December 1948 by the Bureau of Reclamation, the idea resurfaced and gradually gained momentum as a potential new energy source for the national electric power market.[23] With statehood, the incentive for progress in Alaska stimulated planning. By the early 1960s, the project of a dam at the Rampart rapids, also known as Rampart Canyon, had expanded to gigantic proportions, well beyond anything imagined by Covert and Ellsworth. The proposed dam was designed to be 530 feet in height and would raise water to 465 feet at the site. Its reservoir would span 280 miles in an east-northeast arc along the Yukon River toward the Canadian border and have a storage capacity of 1,265,000,000 acres at its highest point. It would flood 10,600 square miles or 6,800,000 acres. When completed, the dam would be two and one-half times the size of Grand Coulee Dam, three and one-half times the size of the Hoover Dam. According to a projected construction schedule, it would begin producing low-cost electric power in 1972 at a rate of 350,000 kilowatts. By 1989, the reservoir would be filled, and power production would have reached 3,735,000 kilowatts.[24]

The construction budget to supply the low-cost electric power totaled billions at 1964 price estimates, which can be summarized as follows:

Dam, reservoir, power plant $1, 342,000,000
Transmission system $762,900,000
Subtotal $2,104,900,000
Annual operations/maint. .... $12.440 million/year
Additional expenses for alternatives for wildlife management, navigation, and development of recreation areas—construction of fish and wildlife mitigation project $580.5 million annual maintenance of facilities $8.1 million per year.[25]

All costs were to be repaid within fifty years after the last investment. The costs were said to be justified since the project would speed Alaska's economic growth through the development of new industries and use of Alaska's natural resources.[26]

As conceived, the process of filling the massive reservoir over a 10,600 square mile area would gradually inundate the Native villages of Rampart, Stevens Village, Beaver, Birch Creek, Fort Yukon, Chalkyitsik, Circle City, the hunting and fishing grounds of Canyon Village, and parts of the Venetie reservation.[27] The village residents were to be relocated, and some would be trained for employment in the construction and operation of the dam. The progressive flooding, to be carried out over a twenty-year period, would cover everything in its path—settlements, grave sites, forests, mining claims, wildlife refuges. Gone forever would be Little Minook Creek and its tributaries; prehistoric Range Channel, probable source of the gold in the nearby creeks; and the remnants of the Pioneer coal mine. The hydroelectric plant Covert and Ellsworth espoused to aid mining in the Rampart district had been reconfigured and repositioned to eradicate the Rampart district from existence.

The proposed dam gained widespread support from political figures such as then presidential candidate, Sen. John F. Kennedy, the Alaska Congressional delegation, most Alaska business men, and the Alaskan public.[28] The Native people, about 1,200 in all, and the miners most directly affected had no voice on the appointed commitees nor invited input to the multiple official studies.

One study briefly examined the impact from an archaeological viewpoint. During the summers of 1963 and 1964, a University of Alaska team headed by Frederick Hadleigh West traveled the area to be inundated. The team concluded that some parts of the area had been inhabited as far back as 7,000 years ago. Continuous human habitation of the area had started about 5,000 to 4,000 years ago.[29] No studies recapitulated the mining history of the impoundment area, nor did any studies refer to the many relevant U.S. Geological Survey reports. Short, general statements related to the Drew (Pioneer) coal mine, patented and private land claims, and oil and gas leases appeared in one federal report.[30]

Some federal agencies hesitated to give total endorsement to the project. In May 1961, the U.S. Army Corps of Engineers advised the First Conference of the Rampart Economic Advisory Board that the board should recommend the project only if the energy cost of Rampart power was the best alternative.[31]

Opposition to the project came from wildlife conservation sources, hunters, fishermen, budget-conscious individuals, Alaska Natives, and the Canadian government, but apparently not from miners, who seemed silent on the issue. The *Alaska Sportsman* magazine editorialized against the dam, pointing to the expected loss in salmon, ducks, geese, and other natural resources, the damage to the natural beauty of Alaska, and the excessive costs of the project. The magazine called upon its readership to express opposition to their representatives in Congress.[32]

Native opposition to the Rampart Dam became one of the unifying forces for Alaska Natives, who began drawing together in common cause during the 1960s. At the meeting of Dena' Nena' Henash, or Tanana Chiefs Conference, in June 1962, conference delegates from villages throughout Alaska's Interior unanimously opposed the dam. One delegate, Percy Herbert, chief of police of Fort Yukon, informed the people in villages along the upper Yukon River about the expected effects of the dam on their lifestyle and advocated for the construction of a new elementary school in Fort Yukon. The state had declined to build a new school in Fort Yukon because the village was scheduled to be eliminated twenty years later. Meanwhile, Dena' Nena' Henash had organized a Rampart Dam committee, which demanded to be heard and actively entered into the planning and the controversy. Herbert maintained his firm position against the dam and for the school. On February 7, 1964, while in Fairbanks for meetings of the Rampart Dam committee, Herbert disappeared. His body was never recovered. Although his unexplained disappearance may have resulted from a random act of violence, in the minds of those who knew Percy

Herbert, it is still directly associated with his vocal stance against the dam.[33]

Stephen H. Spurr, project director of a University of Michigan team, studied the project's ecological and economic impact and the projected electric power demand over a twenty-year period, approximately 1965 to 1985. On the one hand, he saw an immediate need for development of an extra-high voltage power transmission system along Alaska's Railbelt that would connect the Kenai Peninsula to Fairbanks through Anchorage. On the other hand, he completely rejected the proposal for the large hydroelectric plant at Rampart as too costly, too powerful for the demand, and too destructive of wildlife resources. He also referred to a 1965 address by Arthur Laing, then Canadian minister of Northern Affairs and Natural Resources. According to Spurr, Laing had told the Alaska State Chamber of Commerce, convened in Ketchikan, that the Rampart Dam might not be attractive to Canada because of its probable negative effects on Canadian navigation and wildlife resources.[34]

After 1965, the nation, increasingly tangled in the polemics of the Vietnam War, moved away from support of the Rampart Dam. The low-cost power project lost funding. The multibillion dollar proposal collapsed, generally unregretted in its unfulfillment. The 10,600 square-mile area with its villages, cemeteries, timber, wildlife habitats, and subsurface mineral resources remained free from permanent inundation. The Yukon River, the offspring of a prehistoric channel, flowed and froze and flowed again through the whirlpool in the Rampart Canyon below Rampart as it had for centuries.

Three decades later, highly mechanized, systematic, open-pit gold mining operations continue in all three districts. They bear little resemblance to the manual operations often conducted at a hectic, stampede pace during the Gold Rush of yesteryear. Some current operators live year round in their mining community; others reside in Anchorage or Fairbanks in winter, returning to their mines each summer. Nevertheless, memories of the old days live on. Stanley Dayo, former prospector, mine laborer,

and sometimes small independent operator, chooses to stay in his long-time Manley Hot Springs home. His recollections go back to 1933 when he, only nineteen years old at the time, and his brother, Frank, arrived in the area and leased a mining claim in Rampart. His stories contain tidbits of earlier miners' lore passed on to him by the old-timers he met during his first years on the Yukon and Tanana rivers. He recalls that miners usually helped one another, providing spare parts and respecting each other's water rights. He remembers the tragic death of Bill Strandberg, killed by a bear in the mess hall at the Strandberg mine in Tofty Gulch in 1963.[35] He is familiar with the history of the Cleary Hill mine at Tofty Gulch and the moving of old buildings from one camp site to another, a common practice when operators transferred their operations from one place to another.[36]

A contemporary of Dayo, the late Harry F. Havrilack, nicknamed the Hollywood Kid by people who could not pronounce his name, floated down the Yukon River in a rowboat and arrived in the Rampart area on July 4, 1934. His father had been a coal miner, later a dairy farmer, in Pennsylvania, and son Harry quickly adapted to gold prospecting in Rampart and Eureka. He sank many holes and looked over old diggings, at first using traditional methods of pick and shovel. Since the ground he worked was shallow, with only fifteen to sixteen feet of overburden, he did not use the drift-tunnel procedure. After World War II, he started the Ruby Creek Mining Company in Rampart, operating, mostly alone, for years on Ruby Creek, where William B. Ballou had hydraulicked for gold over forty years earlier. Like Ballou, Havrilack served as magistrate and recorder in Rampart. He held the position for about thirty years until the state closed his office in 1978 and transferred to Fairbanks all the Rampart records, including those begun by Commissioner Andrew J. Balliet in December 1900 before Fairbanks existed.[37] The state action severed the final connection to the old recording ways in Rampart.

Each summer now, giant bulldozers carve out deep pits, gouging out the unwanted overburden to reach bedrock. Because of today's environmental concerns, however, federal and state regulations require that once pits are fully exploited, they must be refilled to foster quick, natural regrowth of brush cover. Consequently, dump trucks often transport overburden, stripped from a pit in progress, to a pit no longer used. The Manley Hot Springs district is dotted with unnatural looking, pyramid or cone-like formations, usually covered with brush, which are leftover tailing piles of long ago. Today's miner, using a bulldozer, flattens down and smooths over evidence of a completed operation, returning the place to nature as it was before the operation. Ed Salter of Salter and Associates, Inc., mined in 1993 on Joe Bush Creek where E. W. Bush located a claim in 1901. Salter neatly contoured the top of a pit he had filled in. His bulldozer's tracks imprinted graceful swirls in the restored ground to prepare it for inspection by government personnel charged with enforcing environmental requirements.[38]

Some past practices remain. When current developers believe a new pit is deep enough to cease digging, they revert to old ways to confirm their presumption. On the morning of September 1, 1993, three men from Shoreham Resources hunkered in a tight circle in the center of the floor of a muddy forty-foot high pit, known as the Cache Creek pit, near the old Cleary Hill mine site in the Manley Hot Springs district. A light shower splashed down on their rain gear, and heavy rain clouds cast a gloom over their surroundings. Three bulldozers sat, shut down and unoccupied, at the base of the pit walls. With the same intentness as their Gold Rush predecessors, the men carefully shook and studied a gold pan full of mud and gravel. They were evaluating its contents to determine whether their pit had been dug to its optimum depth. In this instance, Shoreham Resources decided to give up its lease on the claim and relinquish use of the property back to the claimant of record, Jack Neubauer, a former partner of L. McGee.[39]

Under current federal regulations regarding the preservation and protection of historical sites, both Shoreham Resources, and, subsequently, Neubauer had to have a three-year plan of operation near the old Cleary Hill campsite approved by the U.S. Department of the Interior Bureau of Land Management. In early 1994, BLM archeologist Howard Smith concurred in Neubauer's plan, holding that the Cleary Hill campsite did not meet the criteria for inclusion in the National Register of Historic Places. Smith cautioned, however, that if Neubauer's mining operations were to be moved closer to the site of the city of old Tofty (Sullivan City), about one and one-half miles from the Cleary Hill camp, such operations might not be permitted to begin until completion of historical mapping and possibly also salvage archaeology at Tofty.[40] The anthropology department at the University of Alaska Fairbanks has expressed some interest in attempting a dig at Tofty but has not reached a decision.[41] In former days, when there were fewer governmental regulations than there are today, mine operators never worried about disturbing historic or prehistoric sites as they dug down to bedrock and, in the process, sometimes turned up pieces of old boilers or woolly mammoth tusks.

Bruce Savage of the Savage Mining Company arrived in the Manley Hot Springs district in 1963 and, beginning about 1972, mined for over twenty-one years, much of the time on Killarney Creek where Lynn Smith shared a claim in 1910. Savage strongly regrets the increase of regulations on mining operations and the present activism of environmental organizations. He predicts that small mining operators will eventually shut down, crushed under the pressures of regulatory concerns.[42]

Don DeLima of DeLima Placers started mining in 1972 on American Creek, site of the defunct American Creek dredge. Less pessimistic about the future of small mine operations than Bruce Savage, DeLima supports the preservation of local mining history. He and other Manley Hot Springs mine owners donated seed money for the production of Curt Madison's video *Bedrock Pay*, which visually chronicles the development of mining in the Tofty valley.[43]

Thus gold mining continues in Rampart, Manley Hot Springs, and even in the Fort Gibbon district almost one hundred years after the creeks were first struck. While many of the creeks have been worked out, several still give of their non-renewable gold resources. In 1904, geologist Alfred H. Brooks explained that a broad belt of metamorphosed rock, containing gold-bearing areas, stretched from Dawson along the Yukon River to the Rampart camp.[44] Almost echoing the words of Brooks ninety years later, Jack DiMarchi, ASA, Inc., reported to a mining conference in Fairbanks in March 1994, "In the Rampart block [of Doyon, Limited, land], where our work is ongoing, we recognize a district-scale belt of pluton-related gold mineralization."[45]

End Notes Chapter 5. Into the Present Era, 1946-1994.

Short Titles

The following shortened forms referring to depositories and series are used extensively through the chapter endnotes.

Archives, UAF	Alaska Archives and Manuscripts, Alaska and Polar Regions Department, Elmer E. Rasmuson Library, University of Alaska Fairbanks.
District Recorder, Fairbanks	State of Alaska Department of Natural Resources, Office of the Commissioner, District Recorder, Fairbanks, Alaska.
Division of Mining, Fairbanks	State of Alaska Department of Natural Resources, Division of Mining, Fairbanks, Alaska.
(folder)	A copy of a creek record, dated between 1896 and 1900, at the office of the District Recorder, Fairbanks. The original is retained at the office of the State Recorder, Anchorage, Alaska.
Fort Gibbon	Fort Gibbon recording district records at the office of the District Recorder, Fairbanks, Alaska.
Manley	Manley Hot Springs recording district records at the office of the District Recorder, Fairbanks, Alaska.
Rampart	Rampart recording district records at the office of the District Recorder, Fairbanks, Alaska.
U.S.G.S.	U.S. Geological Survey.

1. Jack J. DiMarchi, ASA, Inc., "An Overview of ASA, Inc.'s Exploration Activities on Doyon, Ltd., Lands, " in *14th Biennial Interior Mining Conference "Placer and Hard Rock Too,"* 10–11 March, 1994, Fairbanks, Alaska, 17.

2. Fort Gibbon, Mining Locations, 1939–1958, 3: 105–06, 124, 131.

3. B. D. Stewart, *Report of the Commissioner of Mines for the Biennium Ended December 31, 1946* (Juneau: Territory of Alaska Department of Mines, [1947]), 10, 20, 37–47.

4. P. L. Killeen and M. G. White, "Chapter B-Grant Creek Area," in *Reconnaissance for Radioactive Deposits in Eastern Interior, Alaska, 1946,* ed. Helmuth Wedow, Jr., P. L. Killeen, et al., Geological Survey Circular 331 (Washington, D. C.: Geological Survey, 1954), 33.

5. Robert M. Moxham, *Reconnaissance for Radioactive Deposits in the Manley Hot Springs–Rampart District, East Central Alaska, 1948* (Washington, D. C.: Geological Survey, 1954), 1, 3, 5.

6. Ibid., 7.

7. B. D. Stewart, *Report of the Commissioner of Mines for the Biennium Ended December 31, 1948* (Juneau: Territory of Alaska Department of Mines, [1949]), 16, 20–21, 37–46.

8. Leo H. Saarela, *Report of the Commissioner of Mines for the Biennium Ended December 31, 1950* (Juneau: Territory of Alaska Department of Mines, [1951]), 19-21, 31, 43-54.

9. Mike Shimrock and Ed Lawler, Territory of Alaska Department of Mines report, 13 September 1951, Division of Mining, Fairbanks.

10. A. W. Pringle, Territory of Alaska Department of Mines report, 13 September 1951, Division of Mining, Fairbanks.

11. Al Berg and Clyde Larson, Territory of Alaska Mining Department report, 12 September 1951, Division of Mining, Fairbanks.

12. L. McGee, Territory of Alaska Department of Mines report, 11 September 1951, Division of Mining, Farbanks.

13. Otto Hovely, Territory of Alaska Mining Department report, 12 September 1951, Division of Mining, Fairbanks.

14. Little Minook Mining Co., Territory of Alaska Department of Mines report, 15 September 1951, Division of Mining, Fairbanks.

15. Pierce and Gravy, Territory of Alaska Department of Mines report, 15 September 1951, Division of Mining, Fairbanks.

16. Swanson Bros., Territory of Alaska, Department of Mines report, 14 September 1951, Division of Mining, Fairbanks.

17. Phil R. Holdsworth, *Report of the Commissioner of Mines for the Biennium Ended December 31, 1952*

([Juneau]: Territory of Alaska Department of Mines, [1953]), 7, 24, 26, 48–64.

18. Phil R. Holdsworth, *Report of the Commissioner of Mines for the Biennium Ended December 31, 1954* ([Juneau]: Territory of Alaska Department of Mines, 1955), 42–43, 54, 58, 83–100.

19. Fort Gibbon, [Miscellaneous], 7–8, District Recorder, Fairbanks. This record book has only a few entries, dated in the 1950s, and has no designated title.

20. Phil R. Holdsworth, *Report of the Commissioner of Mines for the Biennium Ended December 31, 1956* ([Juneau]: Territory of Alaska Department of Mines, 1957), 39-40, 51, 72–96.

21. James A. Williams, *Report of the Division of Mines and Minerals for the Year 1959* ([Juneau]: State of Alaska Department of Natural Resources, [1960]), 50–70.

22. Edby Davis, draft letter to the editor, 6 June 1964, Edby Davis Collection, box 11, folder 163, Archives, UAF.

23. Gus Norwood, Executive Secretary, Northwest Power Association, address at the Rampart Dam Conference, McKinley Park, Alaska, 7 September 1963, Fairbanks Chamber of Commerce Collection, box 33, folder 384, Archives, UAF.

24. U.S. Department of the Interior, *Rampart Project: Market for Power and Effect of Project on Natural Resources*, Field Report, vol. 1 (Juneau: U.S. Department of the Interior, 1965), 1-2, 5, 17.

25. U.S. Department of the Interior, *Rampart Project: Market for Power and Effect of Project on Natural Resources*, Field Report, vol. 2 (Juneau: U.S. Department of the Interior, 1965), 423, 492.

26. U.S. Department of the Interior, *Rampart Project, Alaska: Market for Power and Effect of Project on Natural Resources*, Field Report, vol. 3 (Juneau: U.S. Department of the Interior, 1965), 817a, 829.

27. U. S. Department of the Interior, 1: 372.

28. Various papers, commentaries, and newspaper clippings, Fairbanks Chamber of Commerce Collection, boxes 33 and 34, folders 382-400. Almost all the material favored the proposed dam. An opposing *New York Times* editorial, however, termed the dam the "world's biggest boondoggle" and "the world's biggest sinkhole for public funds."

29. Frederick Hadleigh West, H. G. Bandi, and J. V. Matthews, *Archaeological Survey and Excavations in the Proposed Rampart Dam Impoundment, 1963–1964* (N.p: [National] Park Service contract with the University of Alaska, 1965), 127.

30. U. S. Department of the Interior, 1: 123, 150.

31. U.S. Army Engineer District, Alaska, Corps of Engineers, *Rampart Canyon Dam and Reservoir: Data on Project Studies* (Anchorage: Corps of Engineers, [1961]), 2.

32. "Main Trails and Bypaths," *Alaska Sportsman*, June 1965, 7.

33. Al "Bear" Ketzler, Jr., "What Happened to Percy Herbert?" *The Council*, March 1991, 8. The Fort Yukon school, built after Herbert's death, burned on 16 February 1995.

34. Stephen H. Spurr, et al, *Rampart Dam and the Economic Development of Alaska*, vol. 1, Summary Report (Ann Arbor: University of Michigan, School of Natural Resources, 1966), 1–2, 20, 22, 28, 29, 55.

35. Dayo, *Stanley Dayo, Manley Hot Springs*, 25, 35, 78–80.

36. Dayo, personal interview, 31 August 1993.

37. Harry J. Havrilack, personal interview with author, Pioneers' Home, Fairbanks, AK, 14 June 1993. Havrilack died on 29 September 1994.

38. Ed Salter, Salter & Associates, Inc., personal interview with author, Manley Hot Springs, AK, 31 August 1993.

39. The author personally observed this scene on 1 September 1993, from a distance on the road alongside the top of the pit in the Manley Hot Springs district.

40. Howard Smith, *Cultural Resource Review Record* ([Fairbanks]: Bureau of Land Management, Kobuk District, 1994), 1, 2, 9–10.

41. Craig Gerlach, Department of Anthropology, University of Alaska Fairbanks, conversation with author, Fairbanks, AK, 18 August 1994.

42. Bruce Savage, Savage Mining Company, personal interview with author, Pioneers' Home, Fairbanks, AK, 14 June 1993.

43. Don DeLima, DeLima Placers, Manley Hot Springs, AK, phone interview with author, 19 November 1993.

44. Alfred H. Brooks, et al., *Report on Progress of Investigations of Mineral Resources of Alaska in 1904*, U.S.G.S. Bulletin 259 (Washington: Government Printing Office, 1905), 25.

45. DiMarchi, 17.

Appendix 1

Estimated Gross Production of Placer Gold in the Rampart, Manley Hot Springs, and Fort Gibbon Districts, 1896–1940

The U.S. Geological Survey's annual bulletins on the mineral resources in Alaska reported the estimated gold production year by year. The figures presented referred to estimated gross production without consideration of the owners' operational expenses. The figures were based on reports received from mine operators and were not adjusted to account for over-reporting, under-reporting, or non-reporting. The initial report extended backward to the beginning of Rampart mining in 1896 before the miners regularly reported to the U.S.G.S. and, therefore, may have been, in part, based on rumored output. In addition, the early estimated Rampart production figures included figures from the Eureka Creek area, which became a part of the Manley Hot Springs district. Between 1911 and 1921, Indian River figures were included with Gold Hill production. Later, Gold Hill production was included in Rampart figures. The chart below summarizes the reported estimates.

Year	Rampart	Manley	Fort Gibbon	Bulletin	Page
1896-1903	$616,000			520	276
1902-1903			$262,900	520	277
1904	90,000	145,500		520	276–77
1905	80,000	120,000		520	276–77
1906	120,000	180,000		520	276–77
1907	125,000	175,000		520	276–77
1908	75,000	150,000		520	276–77
1909	100,000	325,000		520	276-77
1910	43,000	325,000		520	276–77
1911	32,000	785,000	$10,000	714	83, 82, 91
1912	32,000	400,000	24,500	714	83, 82, 91
1913	32,000	400,000	32,000	714	83, 82, 91
1914	30,000	750,000	25,000	714	83, 82, 91
1915	35,000	610,000	15,000	714	83, 82, 91
1916	40,000	800,000	10,000	714	83, 82, 91
1917	33,000	450,000	5,000	714	83, 82, 91
1918	24,000	150,000	4,000	714	83, 82, 91
1919	30,000	100,000	7,000	714	83, 82, 91
1920	20,000	50,000	2,000	739	32, 31, 41
1921	20,000	35,000	2,000	739	32, 31, 41
1922	18,000	55,000	(Rampart)	773	45
1923	16,000	62,000	(Rampart)	773	45
1924	16,000	83,400	(Rampart)	783	13
1925	8,000	73,200	(Rampart)	792	17
1926	12,000	65,000	—	797	19
1927	10,000	75,000	—	810	24
1928	7,500	77,000	—	813-A	27
1929	5,000	82,000	(Rampart)	824-A	32
1930	3,500	78,500	—	836	32
1931	9,000	59,000	—	844	32
1932	9,000	72,000	—	857-A	30
1933	7,000	48,000	—	864-A	34
1934	9,000	91,000	(Rampart)	880-A	38
1935	8,000	165,000	(Rampart)	880-A	38
1936	11,200	277,000	(Rampart)	897-A	45
1937	12,000	205,000	9,500	910-A	45
1938	8,000	372,000	16,000	917	42
1939	31,000	396,000	—	926-A	39
1940	63,000	518,000	(misc)	933-A	38

| --- | --- | --- |
Production in Rampart, 1896-1904, was probably over $1,000,000.	259	106
Production in Rampart, 1896-1904, was $1,112,000.	337	65
Between 1896 and 1904, Little Minook Creek was estimated to have produced $475,000.	259	111
Between 1896 and 1904, Little Minook Creek produced $486,100.	337	75
Production of Little Minook Creek in 1903-1904 was $42,900.	337	75
Production of the [Big] Minook Creek group, including Little Minook and Hunter creeks, between 1896 and 1904, was estimated at $702,600.	337	66
Production of the [Big] Minook Creek group for 1904 was set at $86,400.	337	66
Production of Hunter Creek, 1896-1904, was estimated at $24,000.	337	73
Production of Hunter Creek for 1904 was $6,000.	337	73
Production of Ruby Creek, 1901–1904, was $13, to 14,000.	337	80
Production of Ruby Creek in 1904 was $5,000.	337	80
Glen Gulch produced approximately $150,000 between July 1901 and July 1902.	213	52
Between 1901 and 1904, Glen Gulch produced $277,500; 1904 alone, $50,500.	337	88
Production for Rampart, including Manley, for 1904 was $235,000.	259	106
Production for Rampart, including Manley, for 1904 was $232,900.	337	65
Production for Rampart, including Manley, for 1905 was $200,000.	337	98
Production for Rampart, including Manley, for 1906 was $270,000.	337	98
Production for Rampart, including Manley, 1896–1906, was $1,582,000.	337	61
Between 1910 and 1919, the Hot Springs district produced about 262 tons of stream tin valued at $155,490.	714	82
At the end of 1930, geologist Philip S. Smith ranked the total output of the forty-one gold-producing districts in Alaska. The three leaders were Fairbanks, Nome, and Iditarod. Hot Springs ranked sixth; Rampart, twentieth; Indian River, thirty-seventh; and Gold Hill, forty-first.	857-B	96
In 1938, Smith ranked Hot Springs in fifth place.	917	50

Appendix 2
U.S. Geological Survey Acknowledgements, 1906–1940

U.S. Geological Survey personnel frequently thanked individuals in the Rampart, [Manley] Hot Springs, and Fort Gibbon (Gold Hill) districts for special help given to the U.S.G.S. staff as they collected data for their reports. The contributors were miners like George W. Ledger and John Minook, district recorders like Mrs. Jessie M. Howard and Chris Thyman, or agents for the Northern Commercial Company (NC) like J. W. Farrell. The chart below identifies persons from the three districts thanked in U.S.G.S. bulletins and water supply (W/S) papers between 1906 and 1940.

Year	Individual(s) Thanked	Bulletin or W/S No.	Page
1906	H. F. Thumm, Rampart	314	37
	W. B. Ballou, Rampart	314	37
1907	H. F. Thumm, Rampart	345	6
	W. B. Ballou, Rampart	345	6
1908	W. B. Ballou, Rampart	379	6
	Frank G. Manley, Hot Springs	379	202
	A. V. Thorns, Hot Springs	379	202
	M. E. Koonce, Rampart	379	202
	F. G. Manley, Baker Hot Springs	W/S 228	9
	A. V. Thorns, Baker Hot Springs	W/S 228	9
	M. E. Koonce, Rampart	W/S 228	9
1909	Ralph Donaldson, Rampart	442	6
	V. L. Bevington, Hot Springs	442	6
1910	Ralph Donaldson, Rampart	480	6
	Benjamin F. Baker, Tofty	480	6
	Joseph H. Eglar, Tofty	480	6
[1910]	F. G. Manley, Baker Hot Springs	W/S 342	13
	A. V. Thorns, Baker Hot Springs	W/S 342	13
	M. E. Koonce, Rampart	W/S 342	13
1911	no one thanked		
1912	W. B. Ballou, Rampart	542	6
	H. F. Thumm, Hot Springs	542	6
1913	no one thanked		
1914	no one thanked		
1915	George W. Ledger, Rampart	642-A	6
	W. B. Ballou, Rampart	642-A	6
	Adolph Bock, Hot Springs	642-A	6
	S. S. Rowell, Hot Springs	642-A	6
1916	G. W. Ledger, Rampart	662	2
	S. S. Rowell, Hot Springs	662	2
	J. C. Felix, Hughes	662	2
1917	George L. Morrison, Hot Springs	692	2
	S. S. Rowell, Hot Springs	692	2
	A. Bock, Tofty	692	2

	Joseph Heller, Tofty	692	2
	George W. Ledger, Rampart	692	2
	W. H. Carney, Tanana	692	2
1918	George L. Morrison, Hot Springs	712-A	2
	George W. Ledger, Rampart	712-A	2
1919	M. T. Robinson, Tofty	714	4
	George W. Ledger, Rampart	714	4
1920	John B. Mathews, Hot Springs	722-A	6
	George W. Ledger, Rampart	722-A	6
1921	Ronald Campbell, Hot Springs	739	vi
	George W. Ledger, Rampart	739	vi
	John Minook, Tanana	739	vi
1922	George W. Ledger, Rampart	755	2
1923	testimonial to George W. Ledger[1]	773	2
1924	no one thanked through 1928		
1929	Chris Thyman, Rampart	824-A	5
	Jessie M. Howard, Tanana	824-A	5
1930	Jay Buzby, Hot Springs	836	4
	Chris Thyman, Rampart	836	4
	Jessie M. Howard, Tanana	836	4
1931	Hans Tilleson and Arthur L'Heureux Hot Springs	844	228
	Chris Thyman, Rampart	844-A	4
	Jessie M. Howard, Tanana	844-A	4
1932	Jessie M. Howard, Tanana	857	4
	Chris Thyman, Rampart	857	4
1933	Jessie M. Howard, Tanana	864-A	4
	A. B. Webster, Rampart	864-A	4
	J. W. Farrell, NC agent, Hot Springs	864-A	4
1934	Orie Shade, NC agent, Tanana	868-A	4
	J. W. Farrell, NC agent, Hot Springs	868-A	4
1935	J. W. Farrell, NC agent, Hot Springs	880-A	4
1936	J. W. Farrell, NC agent, Hot Springs	897-A	4
1937	J. W. Farrell, NC agent, Hot Springs	910-A	
1938	J. W. Farrell, NC agent, Hot Springs	917	4
1939	J. W. Farrell, NC agent, Hot Springs	926-A	5
1940	J. W. Farrell, NC agent, Hot Springs	933-A	5
	J. J. Coughlin, Rampart	933-A	5

Note 1. In Bulletin 773, geologist Alfred H. Brooks acknowledged the free service to the Geological Survey that George W. Ledger had done from 1914 until his death in 1923. Annually, Ledger had summarized mineral discoveries and mining developments in the Rampart district. Brooks considered the service of Ledger and many others of "inestimable value" to the U.S.G.S. staff as they acquired information on the mineral wealth of Alaska.

Appendix 3
Coal Lands

In the very early period, some business men and prospectors from the Rampart district located coal lands along the Yukon River. By U.S. law, coal lands were 160 acres per claim. Only the Pioneer coal mine on the Yukon River thirty miles above Rampart actually operated. Mining ceased there when the property, deeply in debt, was sold at a marshal's sale in 1902. Coal claims, such as those listed below, are filed in Rampart district record books at the District Recorder, Fairbanks.

Claimant(s)	Location	Source
Thomas Crawford	Black Diamond coal mine, 160 acres opposite Mike Hess Creek, was recorded on 28 May 1898. It became the Pioneer mine.	Rampart, Journal, 5.
	It was originally located in 1895 by O. C. Miller, Jules Prevost, and Al Mayo.	*Alaska Forum*, 17 January 1901.
Al Mayo	The Mayo claim, 160 acres, was recorded on 24 September 1898. It was located 3,000 feet above the mouth of Mike Hess Creek on the opposite side of the Yukon River.	Rampart, Journal, 106.
J. P. Bouscaren	The J. P. Bouscaren, 160 acres, was located on 2 January 1898, on the Yukon River opposite Mike Hess Creek, at the lower line of the Black Diamond mine which constituted the upper boundary of Bouscaren's mine.	Rampart, Minook Creek (townsite) (folder), 95.
	It was transferred to Thomas Drew on 18 July 1898.	Rampart, Journal, 47, 216.
Thomas D. Drew	Pioneer coal mine, 160 acres, was recorded on 1 July 1897 and again on 22 December 1898. It adjoined Bouscaren's mine thirty miles from Rampart opposite Mike Hess Creek.	Ibid., 128, 216–17.
S. R. Hudson	The Hudson claim, 160 acres, was located on 2 January 1898, on the first butte of solid rock on the east side of Big Minook Creek where Hunter Creek joins Big Minook.	Rampart, Big Minook Creek (folder), 3: 201.

	In February 1902, the Rampart Coal Company located a coal vein on Big Minook Creek below the mouth of Hunter Creek.	*Alaska Forum*, 8 February 1902.
Sidney Cohen	The Cohen claim, 160 acres, was located on 2 January 1898, northwest of S. R. Hudson's coal claim on Big Minook Creek.	Rampart, Big Minook Creek (folder), 3: 202.
John Spencer	The Spencer mine, 160 acres, was located on 20 August 1898, ten miles upstream from Rampart on the first high bluff on the left hand side of the Yukon River.	Rampart, Journal, 95.
William Walsh	The Palisade coal mine, 160 acres, was located on 13 July 1899 near the Palisade Mountains.	Ibid., 222, 227.
B. W. Kearny, Frank Schidell, J. A. Marion	The Mastodon coal mine, 160 acres, was located on 13 July 1899, adjacent to the Palisade mine, 115 miles downstream from Rampart.	Ibid., 222-23, 227.
Philip Godley	The "D" location, 160 acres, was located on 28 September 1901, twenty-five miles upstream and east of Rampart.	Rampart, Mining Locations and Declaratory Statements, 1: 136.
John Palm	The Palm claim, 160 acres, was located on 17 October 1901, twenty-five miles upstream on the north bank of the Yukon River.	Ibid., 191-92.
Jules A. Marion	The Marion claim, 160 acres, was located on 16 October 1901, on the north bank of the Yukon River, twenty-five miles from Rampart.	Ibid., 192.
Adolph Biederman	Biederman's claim, 160 acres, was located on 18 October 1901 on the north side of the Yukon River about twenty-five miles from Rampart.	Ibid., 195.

Appendix 4
Lodes

Although the three districts had many placer mines, they had very few lodes. Prospectors searched for a mother lode, generally without success. The staked lodes, mainly on Troublesome and Slate creeks in the Rampart district and on Quartz Creek in the Fort Gibbon district, apparently never produced anything of value. Like coal lands, lode claims were usually 160 acres. Claims are filed in Rampart, Manley, and Fort Gibbon record books at the District Recorder, Fairbanks. A representative sampling of lode claims follows.

Claimant(s)	Location	Source
unknown	The remains of a lode mine, believed to have been the first lode mine in the Alaska Interior started in 1890, was in the Gold Hill district on the river slope of a ridge that descends to the Yukon River, twenty miles below Tanana.	A. G. Maddren, U.S.G.S. Bulletin 379, 236.
unknown	The Red Stocking quartz mine was located on the edge of the Virginia mining district near Idaho Bar.	Rampart, Miller Creek (folder), 15 August 1898.
Noble Wallingford, James Mabee	The Little Minook quartz mine was located on 17 December 1898, two miles from the mouth of Little Minook Creek at the lower end of placer claim No. 4 above.	Rampart, Little Minook Creek (folder), 3: 83.
Frank Neumyar Chapman	The George Washington lode was located on 6 August 1899 on the left bank of Troublesome Creek about fifty miles from the Yukon River in rolling country.	Rampart, Journal, 227.
James Langford, Peter Johnson, John W. Spencer, Ernest H. Chapman	The Pioneer lode mine was located on 21 August 1899 on Troublesome Creek, south of the Bald Mountains.	Rampart, Mining Locations, Old Book, 75
James Wishard	The Blue Stone Creek quartz lode was located on 17 April 1900, twenty-two miles north of the Tozikaket River, forty miles from the Yukon River.	Ibid., 161.

Henry M. Dahler	The Dahler quartz lode was located on 17 April 1900, twenty miles from the Tozikaket River, forty-three miles from the Yukon River on the bank of Blue Stone Creek.	Ibid., 162.
S. I. Randall	The Sarah quartz claim was located on 30 August 1900, one and one-half miles from the mouth of Slate Creek.	Rampart, Slate Creek (folder), 2: 1–2.
Samuel E. Chace	The Ora Sierra lode was located on 30 August 1900 about three-fourths of a mile from the mouth of Slate Creek.	Ibid., 3–4.
William D. Hatch	The Mary P quartz claim was located on 30 August 1900 about one-half mile from the mouth of Slate Creek.	Ibid., 5–6.
H. George C. Baldry	The Ella M. D. quartz claim was located on 30 August 1900 near the mouth of Slate Creek.	Ibid., 7-8.
E. C. Austin	The Berkeley quartz claim was located on 3 September 1900 at the mouth of Slate Creek.	Ibid., 9-10.
W. H. Brenmen	The Bonanza quartz claim was located on 30 August 1900, one mile west from the mouth of Slate Creek.	Ibid., 11–12.
H. Gaeny	The Eldorado quartz claim was located on 30 August 1900, next to the Sarah claim.	Ibid., 13-14.
Ben B. Baker	The Josephine quartz claim was located on 3 September 1900, one and three-fourths miles from the mouth of Slate Creek in a westerly direction.	Ibid., 15.
M. N. Kimball, Milton P. Fleischman, Joe Anicich	The Troublesome quartz mine was located on 25 September 1900 on Troublesome Creek twenty-four miles from Rampart.	Rampart, Mining Locations, Old Book, 51.
	Kimball sold his interest to Fleischman and Anicich on 17 November 1900.	Rampart, Deeds, 1: 11-13, 19–21.

E. H. Chapman	The Morning Star quartz mine was filed on 5 January 1901. It was located on Troublesome Creek.	Rampart, Mining Locations, Old Book, 70-71.
Ben F. Baker	The Tyone quartz mine was located on 26 January 1901 near the Troublesome mine.	Ibid., 110.
M. P. Fleischman	The Ot-sie-kie quartz mine was located on 26 January 1901, presumably near the Troublesome mine.	Ibid., 112.
J. T. Roberts	The Arctic lode quartz claim was located on 20 April 1901 near the mouth of Ruby Creek on Big Minook Creek, nine miles from Rampart.	Rampart, Locations and Affidavits, 1901, 105.
W. B. Ballou	The Philadelphia quartz claim was located on 12 July 1901 near the Tyone claim.	Ibid., 107.
R. G. Ferguson	The Pittsburgh quartz claim was filed on 23 July 1901. It was near the Troublesome claim.	Ibid., 106.
Robert D. Cicero	The Wolverine quartz lode was located on 19 October 1901 on the the north fork of Quail Creek.	Rampart, Mining Locations and Declaratory Statements, 1: 265–66.
Robert D. Cicero	The Brown Bear quartz lode was located on 19 October 1901 on the north fork of Quail Creek, three miles from Mount Wolverine on the slope between the Tanana River and Quail Creek.	Ibid., 266.
J. Murray, R. Martin, Thomas Sullivan, William Cheeseman	The Cornucopia lode was located on 11 December 1901 in the Manley district (not further defined).	Ibid., 295.
Frank Stevens	The Keep Cool lode mine was located on 8 February 1902, thirty miles south of Rampart near claim No. 4 above, Glen Gulch.	Ibid., 285-86

James Dalton	The Ozark claim was filed on 11 July 1902. It was located on Troublesome Creek one-half miles from the junction with Quail Creek.	Ibid., 411-412.
G. T. Edgar	The Edgar lode was located on 21 June 1907, somewhere in the Manley district. Edgar sold one-third to A. V. Thorns on 1 November 1908 and one-third to Wally Laboski, the same day.	Fort Gibbon, Deeds, 1908-1954, 55-56, 97.
Wally Laboski	The Laboski lode was located on 21 June 1907, somewhere in the Manley District. Laboski sold one-third to A. V. Thorns and one-third to G. T. Edgar, both on 1 November 1908.	Ibid., 95-96.
Otto Anderson	The Edna lode was located on 25 March 1909, one mile up from the mouth of Quartz Creek and three miles above Schieffelin Creek and one mile below Morelock Creek on the right limit of the Yukon River.	Fort Gibbon, Miscellaneous Record, 64-65.
Dan Halford	The Bubee lode was located on 12 January 1909 on Quartz Creek	Fort Gibbon, Mining Locations, 1: 38
W. H. Davis	The Eldorado lode was located on 12 January 1909 on Quartz Creek.	Ibid., 39.
C. R. Corbusier	The Yukon lode was located on 12 January 1909 on Quartz Creek.	Ibid., 39–40.
W. H. Fairbanks	The Delta lode was located on 12 January 1909 on Quartz Creek.	Ibid., 41.
E. E. McCammon	The Moora Queene lode was located on 12 January 1909 on Quartz Creek.	Ibid., 42.
E. A. Dunlap	The Dunlap lode was located on 12 January 1909 on Quartz Creek.	Ibid., 43.
E. Sullivan	The Sullivan lode was located on 12 January 1909 on Quartz Creek	Ibid., 44.

Otto Anderson	Anderson sold the Michigan and Alaska lodes, presumably on Quartz Creek, to D. G. Hosler on 21 April 1916.	Fort Gibbon, Deeds, 1908–1954, 270.
Mattie Campbell, Lon Snepp	Campbell and Snepp sold the Wounded Ptarmigan lode on Fox Gulch and Ash Creek, a tributary of Moran Creek, to George Lindsey on 29 March 1920.	Ibid., 338-39.
I. W. Purkeypile	The Purkeypile lode was located on 29 July 1944 on the right limit of the Yukon River, 200 feet below the mouth of Lancaster Slough.	Fort Gibbon, Mining Locations, 3: 96.
Joe Vogler, Earl Hirst	The lode was located on 9 August 1957 on the right limit of Quartz Creek, one and one-half miles above the junction of the creek with the Yukon River.	Ibid., 449.
Sinclair Oil & Gas Company	The company performed assessment work on claims No. 1 through No. 11 on Quartz Creek during the year July 1962–July 1963.	Fort Gibbon, [Miscellaneous], 1: 115.
Joseph C. Manga, Azel L. Crandall	Cam No. 1 and No. 2 were located on 6 September 1970 on the right limit of Utopia Creek, a tributary of Indian River.	Fort Gibbon, [Miscellaneous]. 2: 271–72.
Joseph C. Manga, Azel C. Crandall	The Whiz Bang No. 1, located on the right limit at the head of Utopia Creek, was recorded on 30 September 1971.	Ibid., 303.
Walter H. Bullwinkle, Edgar F. Curtis	Bullwinkle and Curtis performed assessment on claims No. 1 through 12 on Quartz Creek in 1970 and 1972.	Fort Gibbon, [Miscellaneous], 2: 276; 3: 469.
Dean Vaughn	Het No. 101 through No. 200 were located on 23, 25 April 1972 between Fish Creek and the Upper Kanuti River.	Ibid., 107–206; 2: 315–16.

Robert T. Phillips	The Tintic Pot Hole claim was located on 27 May 1972, about one mile northwest of the junction of Quartz Creek and the Yukon River, twenty-three miles up the Yukon from Tanana.	Fort Gibbon, [Miscellaneous], 3: 470.
Charles B. Woodruff	The Woodruff claim was located on 9 October 1974 on an unnamed tributary of the Tozitna River about seven miles from Mt. Tozi.	Fort Gibbon, [Miscellaneous] 4: 41.

Appendix 5
Photographic Resources of the Rampart, Manley Hot Springs, and Fort Gibbon Districts

There are several photographs of town life and mining activities of the Rampart, Manley Hot Springs, and Fort Gibbon mining districts scattered through both manuscript and photo collections in the Alaska Archives and Manuscripts, Alaska and Polar Regions Department, Elmer E. Rasmuson Library, University of Alaska Fairbanks. In addition, some U.S. Geological Survey bulletins contain photographs and maps of the districts. A representative, not exhaustive, listing of photographic resources available in the Archives follows.

Agricultural Experiment Station. Photographic Collection. The collection has many pictures of fruit, vegetables, and grains as well as farming activities at the experiment station in Rampart.

Ballou, William B. Collection. There are many photographs in this manuscript collection. Several were taken by Ballou's niece, Edna Marcy. Some are of mining on Hunter Creek.

Beistline, Earl. Collection. In 1937, Beistline took several photographs of operations pertaining to the gold dredge on American Creek in the Manley Hot Springs district.

Carey, Fabian. Collection. The Carey collection features trappers, some of whom were also prospectors like Frank Reinosky and John Folger.

Cottnair, Rita. Collection. The Cottnair collection contains photos of the telegraph construction party in Hot Springs and the town of Tanana in the early 1900s.

Drane, Frederick. Collection. The Drane collection has a picture of the Boston Divide, the mountain pass between Rampart and Hot Springs, as well as views of Big Minook Creek and many photographs of Native people in Tanana and Hot Springs between 1920 and 1926.

Erskine, Wilson F. Collection. The Erskine collection has photos of the Northern Commercial Company store in Rampart, the Discovery Roadhouse on Sullivan Creek, and the first cabin on Sullivan Creek.

Farnsworth, C. S. Collection. The Farnsworth collection has photos of Fort Gibbon and Weare/Tanana in 1899, including some of Tanana miners.

Heller, Herbert. Collection. Lynn Smith had some photographs of mining activities on Glen Gulch, the senatorial party of 1903, some sketches of mining claims in Sullivan country, and a picture of his store in the city of old Tofty in 1911.

Hoeppel, John H. Photo Collection. Hoeppel was a sergeant in the U.S. Army Signal Corps, stationed at Fort Gibbon in 1904 and early 1905 and at Fort Egbert in late 1906 and 1906. As telegraph operator-in-charge, he traveled the Yukon River extensively. He photographed Army telegraph activities, Native people, and scenery. The collection has many pictures of the village of Tanana but none on mining.

Joslin, Falcon. Photo Collection. Joslin photographed mines in the Eureka area of the Hot Springs district about 1909. At the time, Frank G. Manley owned or leased most of the operations. Joslin's comments attached below some photographs are extremely informative.

Judkins, Perry. Collection. The Judkins collection has sketches of the Chapman Creek and Eureka Creek areas.

Kokrine, Effie. Collection. The Kokrine collection contains a panoramic photo of the village of Tanana about 1920.

MacGowan, George B. Collection. MacGowan took several photographs during his one year, 1897–1898, in Rampart, selling some to meet his expenses.

Mozee, Ben. Collection. The Mozee collection has photos and postcards of Tanana, mail dog teams, reindeer, the American Creek Roadhouse, and the Rampart school in 1926.

Murphy, Merritt N. Photo Collection. The members of the U.S. Mining Development and Lumber Company of Cincinnati, Ohio, spent the winter of 1898–1899 on Mike Hess Creek aboard the *Arctic Boy*, captained by Herbert Merideth. They took pictures of sluicing off the sides of the *Arctic Boy* and of the Pioneer coal mine across the Yukon River from their icy anchorage.

Peterson, Patt. Photo Collection. The Peterson collection contains pictures of a survey party, probably road survey, on Hootlanana Creek and at Elephant Gulch in the Manley Hot Springs district.

Pope, Francis. Collection. The Pope collection has pictures of early road and bridge construction in and around Rampart and Hot Springs. It includes photos of the house of Rex Beach in Rampart and the Manley Hotel.

Vertical File. The Vertical File contains pictures of Rampart, including the 1903 senatorial party inducted into the Rampart camp of the Arctic Brotherhood and a photo of John Minook with his family.

Appendix 6
Place Names in the Rampart, Manley Hot Springs, and Fort Gibbon Districts

The following place names appear in materials about the three mining districts and illustrate the vast extent of prospecting in those districts and, for many creeks, the date of the initial locations of claims. Many of the names are no longer used. The spelling of several names have been changed over the years and sometimes with the change, the intent of the original name was lost. Some names were shortened, perhaps to fit on maps. A few names outside the districts have been included because they are associated with an incident involving someone associated with one of the districts. Many names are found in Donald S. Orth's *Dictionary of Alaska Place Names*. The listing is not all-inclusive of place names within the three districts.

Alameda Creek flows 1.2 miles to Kentucky Creek, 1.1 miles north of that stream's junction with Hutlinana Creek, twenty-three miles south of Rampart. (Orth, 60) R. H. Wright had claim No. 3 as of 1 June 1901. (Manley, Locations, 1: 248-49.)

Alaska Creek runs along the southern boundary of No. 15 above, Hunter Creek. Henry Papin located the Discovery claim on 12 July 1902. (Rampart, Mining Locations and Declaratory Statements, vol. 1, 1901-1902, 413.)

Alder Creek flows north nine miles to the Yukon River, twelve miles northeast of Rampart. (Orth, 63.) George P. MacGowan participated in a stampede to Alder Creek in mid-September 1897. (MacGowan's diary, 75–81.)

Alder Gulch Creek is a tributary of Lynx Creek. J. Allen, William Cheeseman, and two others filed for the eighty-acre Discovery Association claim on 4 September 1909. (Fort Gibbon, Mining Locations, 1: 89.)

Allan Creek/Allen Creek flows southwest 7.8 miles to New York Creek, twenty-four miles south-southwest of Rampart. (Orth, 67.) Allan Creek is west of California Creek and empties into Baker Creek. Peter Allan located claim No. 3 above on 14 April 1899. (Rampart, Allan Creek (folder), 10, 12, 48-49.)

Allard Creek is a tributary of Old Man Creek, which is a tributary of the Koyukuk River. J., P. H., N. E., William, George, and E[dwin] P. Allard, together with Dave and Mike Kanaley, held the Allard Association claim as of 16 August 1911. (Fort Gibbon, Mining Locations, 1: 353, 156.)

Alloa Creek/Aloha Creek heads on Elephant Mountain and flows southwest and west three miles to [Big] Minook Creek, seventeen miles south of Rampart. (Orth, 67.) Joe Bush and William Graham prospected Alloa Creek in August 1904. (*Yukon Valley News*, 3 August 1904.)

Alpha Creek flows southwest 0.8 miles to Omega Creek, 3.5 miles west of Eureka and twenty-three miles south-southwest of Rampart. (Orth, 68.) The creek empties into Omega Creek at claim No. 8 above. O. A. Diver located claim No. 3 on 29 November 1901. (Manley, Locations, 1: 450.)

Alta Creek is a tributary of the Koyukuk River. Arland Jordan held the Alta Association claim as of 18 June 1911. (Fort Gibbon, Mining Locations, 1: 282.)

American Creek heads east of Eureka Dome, flows south-southeast 1.4 miles to Eureka Creek, twenty miles south of Rampart. (Orth, 71.) Albert Dalton did assessment work on claim No. 1 in 1908. (Manley, Annual Labor, 1: 43-45. (Orth, 71.)

American Creek heads at the west end of Serpentine Ridge, flows southwest 8.5 miles to Fish Lake, twenty-three miles east southeast of Tanana. On 29 February 1912, Thomas White sold to W. S. Riley one-half of one-sixth interest in the Fairweather Association claim. (Manley, Deeds, 2: 499-500.)

American Gulch is a tributary of Lynx Creek. Fred C. Zickwolff divided the Discovery claim with Sam Sackotich on 23 October 1910. (Fort Gibbon, Miscellaneous Record, 37-38.)

Anaconda Creek is a tributary of Hootlanana Creek on the Tanana River side of the divide. C. E. Danforth located claim No. 3 below on 6 November 1901. (Manley, Locations, 1: 451-52. 1901.)

Anvil Creek is a tributary of the Melozi. N. R. Hudson and three others were members of the eighty-acre Discovery Association, located on 14 December 1908. (Fort Gibbon, Mining Locations, 1: 28.)

Applegate Creek flows southwest twelve miles to Hootlanana Creek, sixty-two miles east of Tanana. (Orth, 84.) Joseph H. Eglar located claim No. 12 below on 29 September 1902. (Rampart, Locations and Statements, 1: 547.) At the time, a man named Applegate prospected in the vicinity of the creek.

Arctic City is the site of an Indian village on the right bank of the Koyukuk River, opposite to the mouth of the Kanuti River. (Orth, 85.) The lost, starving Folger party reached the city in late December 1898. (The *Rampart Whirlpool*, (15 January 1899.)

Arctic Creek is a tributary of Indian Creek. J. E. Nussbaum and seven others held the 160-acre Arctic Bench Association claim as of 13 December 1910. (Fort Gibbon, Mining Locations, 1: 181.)

Argo Gulch is a ravine which extends southwest 0.9 miles to the Yukon River, east of Minook Island, three miles north-northeast of Rampart. (Orth, 86.) J. F. Roberts relocated the Argo Claim on 25 April 1901. (Rampart, Mining Locations, Old Book, 276.)

Arizona Creek flows from the high mountains between California and Allen (Allan) creeks and empties into New York Creek, twenty-nine miles southwest of Rampart. A. H. Monroe located the Discovery claim on 10 August 1901. (Manley, Locations, 1: 344.)

Armstrong Bar is a bar between Eureka and Boston creeks, adjoining claim No. 2 above, Eureka Creek. W. B. Armstrong located a claim there on 26 June 1901. (Ibid., 237.)

Arroyo Grande apparently is a tributary of Bear Creek, the salted creek. H. D. Fountain served as deputy recorder. J. H. Paget held claim No. 8 as of 6 September 1898. (Rampart, Arroyo Grande folder).

Ash Creek flows southeast two miles to Tozimoran Creek, three miles east of Moran Dome and twenty-five miles northwest of Tanana. (Orth, 89.) Thomas Talbot, Oscar Lundine, and six others held the 160-acre Discovery Association claim as of 17 August 1909. (Fort Gibbon, Mining Locations, 1: 86.)

Aurum Creek/Orum Creek flows west ten miles to Stevens Creek, 3.6 miles north of Roughtop Mountain and thirty-seven miles miles east-northeast of Tanana. (Orth, 728.) Aurum Creek was described as one and one-half miles west of Wolverine Creek and thirty-eight miles from Rampart. E. W. Bush located claim No. 7 below on 2 July 1901. (Manley, Locations, 1: 311-12.) George R. Shirley held the Discovery claim as of 22 June 1901. (Rampart, Locations and Statements, 1:49,70.)

Baker Creek flows east, then southwest twenty-eight miles to Tanana River, fifty-seven miles northeast of the Bitzshtini Mountains. (Orth, 101.) James Osborn located the Discovery Claim on 19 June 1901 (Rampart, Locations and Statements, 1:5). The Indian name for Baker Creek was Suthluhchucket. *(Alaska Forum, 5 October 1901.)*

Baker Station. On 30 November 1901, the Northern Manley, Commercial Company of New Jersey located a trading post on the north bank of the Tanana River, 758 feet west of the point where Baker Creek flows into Tanana River. (Manley, Locations 1: 447-48.)

Baldry Mountain, elevation 3,846 feet, fourteen miles south-southwest of Rampart. (Orth, 102.) H. G[eorge] C. Baldry was active in mining in the area at least as early as 17 October 1898. (Rampart, Slate Creek (folder), 2: 136-40.)

Basin Creek is a tributary of Deadwood Creek. On 2 August 1902, C[harles] I. Jordan located claim No. 2 for James B. Wingate (Rampart, Locations and Statements, 1: 556.)

Basin Creek is a tributary of Lanchester/Lancaster Creek. S. E. Lanchester held a claim on the creek as of 16 November 1907. (Fort Gibbon, Mining Locations, 1907-1908, 83.)

Battles Creek is a tributary of Slew (presumably Slough) Creek, near Lancaster Creek. D. W. Fitzgerald held claim No. 1 as of 11 November 1907. (Ibid., 84.)

Beaches Gulch is on the right side of claim No. 6 above, Little Minook Creek. H. L. Beach located claim No. 1 on 29 November 1897. (Rampart, Little Minook Creek (folders) (index), and 3: 49.)

Bear Creek flows northwest 2.3 miles to Hootlanana Creek, eighteen miles southeast of Rampart. J. H. Paget held the Discovery claim as of 22 August 1898. (Rampart, Beare *(sic)* Creek (folder). According to letters in the Herbert Heller Collection, Paget salted the creek. (Smith to Folks, 10 December, 1898.)

Bell Boy Gulch empties into Seattle Creek at claim No. 6 above. H. G. C. Baldry had a claim on the gulch as of 17 August 1901. (Manley, Locations 1: 382.)

Big Bear Creek is a tributary of Hootlanana Creek. Peter Roberts located claim No. 1 above on 18 August 1902. Samuel Fox located the Discovery claim on 2 August 1902. (Rampart, Locations and Statements, 1: 454-55, 460.)

Big Boulder Creek is a tributary of the Tanana River, heading on Baker Creek Dome. William Staples located the Discovery claim on 24 August 1906. (Manley, Locations, 3: 39.)

Big Minook Creek/Manook/Mynook/ Munook/Minook Creek heads on Eureka Dome and flows north twenty-two miles to the Yukon River one mile north of Rampart (Orth, 646.). Joe Wiehl located the Discovery claim on 8 October 1897. (Rampart, Big Minook Creek (folder), 1: 10.)

Birches Creek flows south-southeast five miles to the Yukon River, one mile west of Birches. (Orth 136.) William Corby held claim No. 1 as of 13 September 1908. (Fort Gibbon, Mining Locations, 1: 50.)

Black Creek is a tributary of Felix Fork. J. C. Felix and G. F. Bemis held claim No. 1 as of 1 January 1913. (Ibid., 320.)

Blowback Creek heads on Manley Hot Springs Dome and flows north 4.5 miles to join Killarney Creek to form Baker Creek, six miles south-southeast of Roughtop Mountain and forty miles east-southeast of Tanana. (Orth, 146.) Tom Ellingson was the discoverer of the creek. (*Hot Springs Post*, 23 January 1909.)

Blue Bell Creek is a tributary of the Tozikaket. Frank Fox and three others located the eighty-acre Hobo Association claim on 3 August 1909. (Fort Gibbon, Mining Locations, 1: 67.)

Blue Cannon/Blue Canyon Creek is a tributary of Hootlanana Creek. It empties into the Hootlanana at claim No. 7 below, Upper Discovery. J[ohn] J. Belsea located the Discovery claim on 27 February 1902. (Rampart, Locations and Statements, 1: 341-42, 369.)

Blue Stone Creek is a stream twenty-two miles north of the mouth of the Tozikaket. James Wishard and Henry M. Dahler located quartz lode claims there on 17 April 1900. (Rampart, Mining Locations, Old Book, 161-62.)

Bonanza Creek flows southwest four miles to Morelock Creek, 4.3 miles northwest of that stream's junction with the Yukon River, twenty-four miles east northeast of Tanana. (Orth, 151.) George Ledger located claim No. 1 above on 14 April 1908. (Fort Gibbon, Mining Locations, 1907-1908, 202.)

Booster Creek is a tributary of Hootlanana Creek. Samuel Fox located the Discovery claim on 8 August 1902. (Rampart, Locations and Statements, 1: 461.)

Boothby Creek flows south 0.8 miles to a diversion ditch parallel to Pioneer Creek, 1.6 miles northeast of Eureka and twenty miles south of Rampart. (Orth, 152.) J. Willis Boothby located claim No. 3 on 16 July 1901. At the time, Boothby Creek was a tributary of Pioneer Creek. (Manley, Locations, 1: 283.)

Boston Creek flows southwest 2.2 miles to Eureka Creek, 2.5 miles south of Eureka Dome and twenty-one miles south of Rampart. (Orth, 153.) As of 3 April 1899, Boston boy Elliot L. Gaetz held claim No. 1; John Walsh, No. 2; J. W. Moore, No. 3; W. S. Ramsey, No. 4; H[erbert] S. Russell, No. 5; and Angus Hebb, No. 10. (Manley, Locations, 1: 57, 60.)

Boulder Creek is a tributary of Hot Springs Slough,.sixty miles south of Rampart. J[ohn] F. Karshner located claim No. 1 below on 9 August 1902. (Rampart, Locations and Statements, 1: 444-45.)

Bowman Bar is a bar between Seattle and Rhode Island creeks, thirty miles south of Rampart. Charles Bowman located claim No. 1 on 14 August 1901. (Manley, Locations, 1:431.)

Bryan City was a tiny settlement on the Tanana River about one and one-half miles from the town of Hot Springs and connected to it by a road. (*Hot Springs Post*, 8 May 1909.)

Buckingham Pup is a pup (very small creek) on the right hand fork of Little Minook Creek. Oliver Tingley located claim No. 3 on 6 May 1898. It may have been named in November 1897 for William Buckingham, partner of Harold Sturges. (Rampart, Little Minook Creek (folder) (index).)

Bull Run Creek is a tributary of Hootlanana Creek. E. D. Howe located claim No. 4 for L[atham] A. Jones on 20 June 1902. (Rampart, Locations and Statements, 1: 422, 451.)

Burke Creek is a tributary of Moran Creek. Harold Sedden, Grant Burke, and N. R. Hudson held the sixty-acre Discovery Association claim as of 31 August 1909. (Fort Gibbon, Mining, Locations, 1: 106.)

Cache Creek flows southwest eight miles and joins Sullivan Creek to form Patterson Creek, thirty-three miles east southeast of Tanana. (Orth, 173.) Pat Maloney sank two holes on the creek in the summer of 1905. (*Hot Springs Post*, 18 July 1908.) Rod McKenzie and seven others located a 160-acre claim on 13 August 1907. (Manley, Locations, 3: 90-91.)

Cairo Creek flows southwest four miles to Hutlinana Creek, twenty-two miles southeast of Rampart. (Orth, 174.) Tom Sullivan was working on the creek in February 1902. Water prevented him from reaching bedrock. (*Alaska Forum*, 8 February 1902.)

California Bar, elevation 2,800 feet, extends southeast three miles from the junction of Hoosier and Minook creeks, 4.5 miles southeast of Rampart. (Orth, 174.) E. T. Townsend held contiguous claims, namely Mother Mine, Frisco Mine, and Pharisee Mine in 1900. (Rampart, Mining Locations, Old Book, 55.)

California Creek. Headwaters are partially diverted by Thanksgiving Ditch, flows southwest 6.2 miles to New York Creek, twenty-three miles south-southwest of Rampart. (Orth, 175.) Angus Hebb, a Boston boy, had claim No. 6 below as of 23 February 1901. (Manley, Locations, 1: 195-96.)

California Creek flows northwest 1.4 miles to Minook Creek, seven miles south of Rampart. George R. Shirley relocated claim No. 2 below on 5 January 1901. (Rampart, Mining Locations, Old Book, 181.)

Cambridge Creek is a tributary of Applegate Creek. Robert Compton located claim No. 2 above on 26 September 1902. (Rampart, Locations and Statements, 1: 510.)

Camp Creek flows southwest 3.5 miles to Woodchopper Creek, 3.3 miles north of that stream's junction with Patterson Creek. (Orth, 178.) W. Mosiman located the Discovery claim on 6 September 1907. (Manley, Locations, 3: 114.)

Camp Creek is not precisely located. Moses Henry, a Native, held claim No. 2 as of 2 January 1911. (Fort Gibbon, Mining Locations, 1: 239.)

Campbell Creek is a tributary of Jackson Creek. Arthur Campbell was a member of the Cornucopia Association which had a 160-acre claim as of 22 August 1908. (Fort Gibbon, Mining Locations, 1907-1908, 214.)

Caribou Creek flows south three miles to Hootlanana Creek, eighteen miles southeast of Rampart. (Orth, 186.) E. A. Norman located No. 10 above on 30 August 1898. (Rampart, Big Minook Creek (folder), 4: 310-11.)

Carlton Pup is a pup off the left side of claim No. 23 above, Little Minook Creek. C. P. Carlton located No. 2 on 4 October 1898. (Rampart, Little Minook Creek (folder) (index).)

Carr's Pup is a pup off the right side of claim No. 23 above, Little Minook Creek. E[dward] M. Carr located claim No. 7 on 24 November 1897. (Ibid.)

Cayuse Creek is the left fork ascending (upstream) Pioneer Creek, twenty-seven miles south southeast of Rampart. E. T. Townsend and Marie Baty located the forty-acre Townsend Mine on 4 November 1901. (Manley, Locations, 1: 431-32.)

Channel Creek empties into New York Creek between claims Nos. 3 and 4 below. S. R. Hudson located a claim there on 18 August 1902. (Rampart, Locations and Statements, 1: 581-82.)

Chapman Creek flows west five miles to Minook Creek, fifty-eight miles northeast of Tanana. (Orth, 200.) John Folger and Michael Doud held the Discovery claim as of 4 November 1897. Ernest H. Chapman had claim No. 1 above as of 25 September 1897. (Rampart, Chapman Creek (folder), 2.)

Charley Creek is a tributary of Baker Creek. Fred Hoffman located the Discovery claim on 7 September 1907. (Manley, Locations, 3: 112.)

Chicago Creek flows northwest nine miles to the Yukon River, four miles north of Rampart. (Orth, 206,) [two similar entries]. The miners organized on Sunday, 3 October 1897. George MacGowan served as secretary and held claim No. 1 below. (MacGowan's diary,3,95.)

Chicago Creek flows southwest 1.3 miles to Thanksgiving Ditch, 4.1 miles west of Eureka and 2.2 miles south-south-west of Rampart. (Orth, 206). B. F. Sundstrom located claim No. 2 above on on 21 August 1901 (Manley, Locations, 1:429.)

Chicago Pup is a pup off the left side of claim No. 14, above, Little Minook Creek. Mrs. A. B. Llewellyn located claim No. 2 on 25 January 1898. (Rampart, Little Minook Creek (folder) index.)

Chickadee Creek is a tributary of the Hootalaqua, forty miles southeast of Rampart. (*Alaska Forum*, 11 December 1901.) M. E. Koonce and E. T. Townsend held the forty-acre Alpha Mine as of 14 November 1901. (Manley, Locations 1: 435.)

Chicken Creek is a tributary of Jackson Creek. Ida E. Johnstone located claim No. 2 above on 7 August 1908. (Fort Gibbon. Mining Locations, 1907-1908, 208.)

Chicken Creek flows southwest 1.3 miles to Tozimoran Creek, one mile east of its junction with Ash Creek, twenty-five miles northwest of Tanana. (Orth, 208.) Alfred, a Native, located claim No. 2 on behalf of Old Al, also a Native. (Fort Gibbon, Mining Locations, 1: 238.)

Chicken Gulch joins the left limit of claim No. 2 below French Creek, near claim No. 2 below, Willow Creek. E. B. Gilmore located claim No. 1 on 19 August 1909. (Ibid., 95.)

Clearwater Creek is a tributary of Blue Bell Creek. R. C. Conklin, C. K. Snow, and six others held the 160-acre Clearwater Association claim as of 3 August 1909. (Ibid., 97.)

Collier Pup is a pup off the left side of claims Nos. 7 and 8 above, Little Minook Creek. O. Collier located claim No. 1 on 11 May 1898. (Rampart, Little Minook Creek (folder) index.)

Colony Pup is a pup on the north side of Claim No. 1 above, Little Minook. Thirty-seven men, including Valentine Schmitt, filed for joint ownership on 14 February 1899. (Rampart, Little Minook (folder), 2:137.)

Colorado Creek flows southeast 3.6 miles to Utah Creek, five miles east southeast of Roughtop Mountain and twenty-eight miles southwest of Rampart. (Orth, 231.) The creek, which is near Echo Gulch, is also said to be a tributary of Ohio Creek, which is a tributary of Hootlanana Creek. John Murray located claim No. 2 above on 24 February 1902. (Rampart, Locations and Statements, 1: 352-53.)

Colorado Gulch is a tributary of Hootlanana Creek. Harry Buhro located the Discovery claim on 15 March 1902. (Ibid., 356.)

Cooney Creek flows south four miles to Killarney Creek, 0.8 miles north of that stream's junction with Baker Creek forty miles east southeast of Tanana. (Orth, 236.) Lynn Smith did assessment work on the Discovery claim and No. below, Cooney, in 1908. At that time, J[ohn] J. Cooney was working on the Liberty Bench claim on the left limit of Sullivan Creek. (Manley, Annual Labor, 1: 1, 4.) Cooney bought the upper 600 feet of the Discovery claim, Cooney Creek, from Smith, Dan Kanalley, and Dan Brown in May 1908. (Manley, Deeds, 2: 90-92.)

Coptic Creek is the fork of Ionic Creek at the headwaters of Baker Creek, about twenty-five miles west of Glen Gulch. Robert Meston located the Discovery claim on 25 August 1902. (Rampart, Locations and Statements, 1: 574-75.)

Cory Creek is a tributary of the Yukon River. John Cory and seven others held the Sixteen Mile Association claim as of 9 September 1909. (Fort Gibbon, Mining Locations, 1: 108.)

Cripple Creek is a tributary of Alder Creek, entering Alder at claim No. 18, ten miles east of Rampart. William Graham located the Discovery claim on 6 September 1901. (Rampart, Locations and Statements, 1: 130, 151-52.)

Cub Creek is a tributary of Hootlanana Creek on the southeast slope of Wolverine Mountain. It empties into the Hootlanana at claim No. 7 above, Upper Discovery. William Cheeseman located the Discovery claim on 22 February 1902. (Ibid., 345, 360.)

Dakota Creek is a tributary of Applegate Creek. John Donahue located claim No. 2 below on 29 August 1902. Robert Compton located the Discovery claim on 1 September 1902. (Ibid., 536-37, 586-87.)

Dalton Creek presumably is in the vicinity of Sullivan Creek. Mr. and Mrs. Al[bert] Dalton were members of the Silver Dollar Association, which located a 160-acre claim on 11 August 1907. (Manley, Locations, 3: 90.)

Davis Creek is a tributary of Gold Creek. W. Davis, Edd Grider, and six others held the 160-acre Rambler Association claim as of 17 August 1909. (Fort Gibbon, Mining Locations, 1: 86.)

Dawson Creek flows north three miles to Hunter Creek, six miles southeast of Rampart. (Orth, 259.) Capt. [Bensley] Collenette would not take $15,000 for his claim No. 25 as of 12 October 1897. (MacGowan's diary, 105.)

Deadwood Creek heads on Elephant Mountain and flows southwest 3.5 miles to Pioneer Creek, twenty miles south of Rampart. (Orth, 261.) John C. Riley located the Lewiston Mine on 28 January 1902. (Manley, Locations, 1: 496-97.)

Deakyme/DeaKyne was the site of a Belt & Hendricks store five miles from the mouth of Baker Creek in 1901. A man named Riley managed it. In 1902, it was moved to the mouth of the creek, opposite to the N. C. Co. store at Baker Station. The store was closed in 1904. (*Alaska Forum*, 28 December 1901, 1 February 1902, and 11 June 1904.) The site may have been named for a Capt. E. H. DeaKyne who was recorder for Sunnyside Creek in November 1898 and who owned claim No. 12 below, Big Minook Creek, as of 30 May 1899. (Rampart, Triple Creek (folder), 23; Rampart, Big Minook (folder), 4: 356.)

Deep Creek flows southeast one mile through Innesvale Gulch, then southwest two miles to Wood-chopper Creek, thirty-two miles east-southeast of Tanana. (Orth, 263.) Matthew Harter, C. P. Snyder, and George Kemper were members of the Fredrica Association, a 160-acre claim, located on 27 July 1907. (Manley, Locations, 3: 106.)

Denver Creek is a tributary of Hootlanana Creek. E. D. Howe located claim No. 9 on 21 June 1902. (Rampart, Locations and Statements, 1: 420, 452.)

Denver Creek is a tributary of Patterson Creek. John Morgan located claim No. 2 above, the Star claim, on 15 September 1907. (Manley, Locations, 3: 101.)

Dexter Creek is ten miles southwest of Thanksgiving Creek and 150 feet south of the Sullivan cabin on the trail between Thanksgiving and Sullivan creeks. Angus and James Hebb located the forty-acre Hebb Brothers claim on 3 September 1907. (Ibid., 119.)

Divide Creek is a tributary of Golden Creek. C. H. Hull and seven others held the 160-acre Napa Association claim as of 25 March 1909. (Fort Gibbon, Mining Locations, 1: 51.)

Dixon Creek is a tributary of Mason Creek. H. P Sheppard located the Discovery claim on 6 August 1908. (Ibid., 14.)

Dome Creek flows north two miles to Hudson Creek, north of Gold Mountain, about eight miles north northwest of Birches. (Orth, 279.) The John Minook Association held a 100-acre claim as of 27 February 1908. (Fort Gibbon, Mining Locations, 1907-1908, 80.)

Dome Creek is a tributary of Anvil Creek. Harold Sedden, N. R. Hudson, and two others held the Discovery Association claim as of 4 January 1909. (Fort Gibbon, Mining Locations, 1: 29.)

Doric Creek flows south 1.3 miles to a diversion ditch, parallel to Pioneer Creek, one mile northeast of Eureka and twenty-two miles south of Rampart. (Orth 281.) S. Spyres located claim No. 2 on 11 June 1901; Angus Hebb, claim No. 1 on 11 July 1901. (Manley, Locations, 1: 243-44, 266-67.)

Duck Creek is a tributary of Hootlanana Creek. John Donahue located the Discovery claim on 1 September 1902. (Rampart, Locations, and Statements, 1: 537.)

Eagle Gulch is a tributary of Pioneer Creek. M. E. Koonce located a claim on the left fork of Eagle Gulch on 16 September 1901. (Manley, Locations, 1: 368-69.)

Eagle Gulch is a tributary of the Yukon River. E. Sullivan and John Package located the forty-acre Tegetoff Group on 2 August 1909. (Fort Gibbon, Mining Locations, 1: 75.)

Earl[e]'s Pup is a pup off the left side of claim No. 20 above, Little Minook Creek. Edward Earle Keeley held claim No. 1 as of 26 November 1897. (Rampart, Little Minook Creek (folder), 3: 73.)

Easy Money Creek is a tributary of Sullivan Creek renamed Quartz Creek. A. S. Riley, August Pahlke, and six others located the 160-acre Moose Mountain Association claim on 23 July 1907. Herman Tofty, M. J. Sullivan, and six others located the 160-acre Moose Association Claim on 26 July 1907. (Manley, Locations, 3: 96, 110.)

Echo Gulch is a tributary of Ohio Creek. William M. Cheeseman located the Discovery claim on 24 February 1902. (Rampart, Locations and Statements, 1: 366-67.)

Egg Island is an island 0.4 miles long in Norton Sound, twelve miles northeast of St. Michael. (Orth, 304.) In June 1900, Lynn Smith witnessed the federal government's removal of Native people to make the island a quarantine station during a smallpox outbreak in Nome. (Smith to Folks, 16 June 1900, Herbert Heller Collection.)

Elephant Gulch is a ravine which trends southeast two miles to Hutlinana Creek, twenty miles southeast of Rampart. (Orth, 308.) A. Johnson located a claim on the gulch on 14 September 1901. At the time, the gulch was considered to be thirty-five miles southeast of Rampart. (Manley, Locations, 1: 359-60.)

Ellen Pup is a small pup off claim No. 3 above, Chapman Creek, where R. R. McRae had a claim as of 27 February 1899. (Rampart, Chapman Creek (folder), 49.)

Eureka Creek flows southwest twelve miles to Baker Creek at Overland Bluff, fifty-three miles east-southeast of Tanana. (Orth, 321.) Boston boy Elliot L. Gaetz located the Discovery claim on 21 March 1899. (Manley, Locations, 1: 4.)

Eureka Creek flows northwest thirteen miles to the Little Melozitna River, nineteen miles north of the Birches. (Orth, 321.) Albert Lind and seven others filed for the 160-acre Ruby Association claim on 4 January 1909. (Fort Gibbon, Mining Locations, 1: 5.)

Eva Creek is a tributary of Hootlanana Creek between Elephant and Mukluk creeks. Peter Johnson located claim No. 1 below on 19 September 1901. (Manley, Locations, 1: 461.)

Excelsior Bar is a bar between Eureka and Rhode Island creeks on the Tanana River side of the divide. J. W. Moore held a claim as of 1 May 1899. Jay E. Tibbetts was creek recorder then. (Ibid., 2.)

Farnsworth Island is an island ten miles above Fort Gibbon on the Yukon River. In the summer of 1900, troops went on a logging expedition there. The cook hunted blueberries but dropped his bucket when he was chased by a big brown bear. (J. R. Coons to Farnsworth, 24 January, circa 1906, C. S. Farnsworth Collection.)

Felix Fork is a tributary of Indian Creek. J. C. Felix held claim No. 11 as of 1 June 1912. (Fort Gibbon, Mining Locations, 1: 358.)

Flat Creek flows southeast two miles to Hootlanana Creek, eighteen miles southeast of Rampart. (Orth, 340.) Samuel Fox located the Discovery claim on 1 August 1902. (Rampart, Locations and Statements, 1: 459-60.)

Florida Creek flows northwest 1.7 miles to Minook Creek southwest of McDonald's Bar, six miles south of Rampart. (Orth, 343.) F. R. Edwards (possibly T. R. Edwards) located the Discovery claim, known as the Edwards claim, on 13 March 1899. (Manley, Locations, 1: 137.)

Forest Gulch is a gulch off of the left hand side of claim No. 5 above, Little Minook Creek. G. W. Ledger held No. 2 on 7 January 1900. (Rampart, Little Minook Creek (folder) (index).)

Fort Get There was the site of the NAT&T trading post on St. Michael Island, a short walk from the A.C. post there. (Letterhead, Herbert Heller Collection.)

Fort Gibbon was a military reservation at the junction of the Tanana and Yukon rivers. Capt. C. S. Farnsworth, USA, built the garrison, beginning in the late summer of 1899. (History of Fort Gibbon, C. S. Farnsworth Collection.)

Fort Hamlin was a trading post on the left bank of the Yukon River, north of Hamlin Creek, forty miles northeast of Rampart. (Orth, 346.) At the request of the Northern Commercial Company, William B. Ballou shut down the post in July 1902. (Ballou to Mother, 11 July 1902, William B. Ballou Collection.)

Fox Gulch flows west 3.2 miles to Grant Creek west of Gold Hill, twenty-two miles west-northwest of Tanana. William Lord held claim No. 2 above as of 19 September 1907. (Fort Gibbon, Mining Locations, 1907-1908, 150.)

Frankie C. Creek is a tributary of the right limit of Golden Creek. Frank C. Edgington held the Discovery claim as of 1 September 1966. (Fort Gibbon, 1 October 1965-19 May 1972, 38.)

French Creek is a tributary of the Tozikaket River. Lon Snepp and seven others located the 160-acre Webb Association on 19 August 1909. (Fort Gibbon, Mining Locations, 1: 85.)

Gallaher Creek is a tributary of the Yukon River. John Cory, Phil Gallaher, and six others held the 160-acre Cory Association claim as of 9 September 1909. (Ibid., 107.)

Garnet Creek flows northwest seventeen miles to the Yukon River at Garnet Island, eighteen miles west-southwest of Rampart. (Orth, 361.) It was previously known as Stephens Creek. The miners organized the creek district on 31 August 1898. B. W. Moore, Jr. held the Discovery claim. (Rampart, Garnet Creek folder, 8, 11)

Gilmore Creek is not precisely located. On 10 December 1908, E. B. Gilmore located the Discovery bench on the left limit of Gilmore Creek. H. A. Gilmore located bench No. 1 below, the same day. (Fort Gibbon, Mining Locations, 1: 2-3.)

Giroux's Bluff is on the right bank of the Tanana River, 0.5 miles southeast of Baker. (Orth, 368.) Joseph Giroux held a claim on Eureka Creek as of 18 April 1899. (Manley, Locations, 1: 93.) Philip Giroux did assessment work in 1908 on Golden Creek. (Fort Gibbon, Affidavit/Annual Labor, 1908-1952, 1.)

Glacier Creek is a tributary of the left fork of Baker Creek, twenty-two miles from Deakyme. Nels Johnson located the Discovery claim on 22 May 1902. (Rampart, Locations and Statements, 1: 373.)

Glazier Gulch Creek is a tributary of Grant Creek. M. Barry held claim No. 2 as of 26 August 1909. (Fort Gibbon, Mining Locations, 1: 84.)

Glen Gulch/Glenn Creek flows south 3.2 miles to Eureka Creek, 2.4 miles south of Eureka and twenty-five miles south of Rampart. (Orth, 371.) Oliver Lorencen (sometimes Lawrence) located claim No. 1 above on 25 June 1901. W. P. Beardsley named the gulch and located the Discovery claim on 1 July 1901. His two Eagle Mining Company partners, John Belsea and James W. Dillon, witnessed his location. (Manley, Locations, 1: 245-46, 252.)

Glenn Gulch is a tributary of Lynx Creek. William Cheeseman and seven others located the 160-acre Eclypse Association claim on 5 August 1909. (Fort Gibbon, Mining Locations, 1: 75.)

Gold Basin Creek flows southeast 2.6 miles to Killarney Creek, 0.4 miles north of that stream's junction with Baker Creek, thirty-nine miles east-southeast of Tanana. (Orth, 373.) Harry Burrus located claim No. 3 below on 24 August 1907. (Manley, Locations, 3: 118.)

Gold Pan Creek/Goldpan Creek flows southwest three miles to [Big] Minook Creek, eleven miles south of Rampart. (Orth, 375.) William Ballou visited a camp there in late October or early November 1898 when the temperature was thirty-eight below zero, a rise from an earlier forty-five below. (Ballou to Folks, 7 December 1898, William B. Ballou Collection.)

Gold Rim Creek is a tributary on the west side of Kentucky Creek, just above Alameda Creek. H. G. C. Baldry located claim No. 3 above on 25 July 1901. (Manley, Locations, 1: 396-97, 468-69.)

Gold Run/Gold Run Creek flows southwest 0.8 miles to Rhode Island Creek, 1.5 miles west of Eureka, twenty-two miles south of Rampart. (Orth, 376.) M. S. Gill located claim No. 1 on 10 July 1901. (Manley, Locations, 1: 282.)

Gold Run Creek is a tributary of Wilson Creek. J. A. and Ed Frederickson and six others held the 160-acre Ishpenning Association claim as of 18 August 1909. (Fort Gibbon, Mining Locations, 1: 99.)

Gold Run Swail/ Swale is a tributary of Rhode Island Creek, one-half mile east of claim No. 4 above, Rhode Island. It appears at times to be identical with Gold Run and at other times near to but different from Gold Run. E. D. Howe held the Spring Water claim as of 10 July 1901. (Manley, Locations, 1: 264, and Rampart, Locations and Statements, 1: 42.)

Golden Creek flows southwest eleven miles to join Wilson Creek to form Illinois Creek, seventeen miles northeast of Birches. (Orth, 374.) Peter Coulombe held the Discovery claim as of 31 October 1927. (Fort Gibbon, Mining Locations, 1: 572.)

Goldstream Creek is a tributary of Grant Creek. M. Barry located the Discovery claim on 30 November 1908. (Ibid., 18.)

Grand Gulch is on the left limit of Jackson Creek. Mikel Kanaley located claim No. 1 on 16 September 1908. (Fort Gibbon, Mining Locations, 1907-1908, 268.)

Granite Creek flows northeast 8.5 miles to Minook Creek, fourteen miles south of Rampart. (Orth, 384.) H. M. McLernan relocated the H. M. McLernan claim on 2 January 1901. At the time John Bock held the Discovery claim. (Rampart, Mining Locations, Old Book, 240-41.)

Grant Creek heads on Grant Dome and flows southwest eleven miles to the Yukon River, twenty-five miles west of Tanana. (Orth, 385.) J. J. O'Brien located the Discovery claim on 22 June 1907. (Fort Gibbon, Mining Locations, 1907-1908, 66.)

Green Gulch is a tributary of Glacier Creek which is a tributary of the left fork of Baker Creek, twenty-two miles from Deakyme. On 29 May 1902, Nels Johnson located claim No. 1 for James R. Green. (Rampart, Locations and Statements, 1: 380.)

Grimkop was the site of a U.S. telegraph station on the Yukon River, eighty miles north of Kaltag. (Heiner, *Alaska Mining History*, 250.) On 25 February 1907, the commander, Company D, 10th Infantry, Fort Gibbon, was ordered to detail one non-commissioned officer and nine privates to work on the right of way between Grimkop and Koyukuk. (Fort Gibbon Collection, 5, Archives, UAF.)

Gum Boot Gulch, also known as Easy Money Creek, later renamed Quartz Creek, is a tributary on the left limit of Sullivan Creek. George Kern located the Discovery claim on 27 July 1907. (Manley, Locations, 3: 92.)

Gundy's Pup is a pup on the left hand side of No. 2, Little Minook Creek. Charles F. Gundrum (Gundy) located claim No. 1 on 25 October 1898. (Rampart, Little Minook Creek (folders) (index), and 3: 35.)

Gunnison Creek flows northwest 6.5 miles to Troublesome Creek, fifteen miles southeast of Rampart. (Orth 398.) J. H. Kelly held the Discovery claim as of 27 August 1898. Rampart, Gunnison Creek (folder.)

Hanlon Creek empties into Blue Cannon Creek. George McQuarrie located the Discovery claim on 17 September 1902. (Rampart, Locations and Statements, 1: 490.)

Harter Creek/Harter Gulch extends south 1.9 miles to Cache Creek, 1.2 miles southeast of Tofty (Orth, 408.) Matthew Harter located the Discovery claim on 24 August 1907. (Manley, Locations, 3: 97.)

Hartford Creek is not precisely located. Louie Iverson had a claim on the creek in January 1901. (*Alaska Forum,* 17 January 1901.)

Hay Creek is the first stream entering the Tolavana River on the right hand side, going upstream. In July 1900, Sgt. Lucas cut hay in the meadow nineteen miles up the creek for the horses at Fort Gibbon. (Farnsworth to Lucas, 12 July 1900, C. S. Farnsworth Collection.)

Helena Creek is a tributary of Little Butte Creek, twenty-two miles from Rampart. John Murray located claim No. 3 above on 24 February 1902. William Cheeseman located the Discovery claim on 9 March 1902. (Rampart, Locations and Statements, 1: 354-55, 387, 390.)

Henderson Creek flows southwest 2.7 miles to Mason Creek, 6.5 miles northwest of that stream's mouth. (Orth, 415) Otto Oman held the Discovery claim and Ray R. Henderson held claim No. 1 above, both on 6 September 1907. (Fort Gibbon, Mining Locations, 1907-1908, 90.)

Hiawatha Creek is a tributary of Indian Creek. F. G. Manley, H. Himes, and six others held a 160-acre claim as of 5 May 1911. (Fort Gibbon, Mining Locations, 1: 241.)

Himes Creek is a tributary of the east fork of Indian Creek. H. Himes held interests in claims on creeks in the area as of May 1911. (Ibid., 216, 241.)

Hinckley's Pup is a pup off the right hand side of claim No. 10 above, Little Minook Creek. P. Hinckley held No. 1 as of 18 April 1898. (Rampart, Little Minook Creek (folder) (index.)

Hi'yu Creek is not precisely located, but is somewhere on the west side of the Yukon River across a large lake and eight miles inland. W. F. Pinkham interested George P. MacGowan in the creek in October-November 1897. (MacGowan's diary, 93, 119-21, George P. MacGowan Collection.) Hi'yu was an Athabascan Indian expression meaning "big."

Hogged Creek is a tributary of Hootlanana Creek, twenty-five miles southeast of Rampart on the south slope of Wolverine Mountain. It empties into Hootlanana Creek at claim No. 4 above, Upper Discovery. L[atham] A. Jones located the Discovery claim in the name of James W. Dillon on 9 March 1902. (Rampart, Locations and Statements, 1: 338-39.)

Holden's Pup is a pup on the left side, lower end, of claim No. 6 above, Little Minook Creek. D. Holden held claim No. 1 on 1 June 1898. (Rampart, Little Minook Creek (folders) (index), and 3: 47.)

Honolulu Pup is a pup on the left side of claim No. 1, Little Minook Creek. G. Hopkins had claim No. 1 as of 17 September 1897. (Ibid., (index) and 3: 61.)

Hoosier Creek flows northwest 8.5 miles to Minook Creek between California and McDonald bars, four miles southeast of Rampart. (Orth, 429.) [Pete] Johnson and James Langford held the Discovery claim in 1898. (Rampart, Miller Creek (folder), 29 January 1898, and Rampart, Gunnison Creek (folder).)

Hootalaqua Creek/Hutlitakwa Creek flows southwest thirty-two miles to Hootlanana Creek, fifty-five miles southeast of Tanana. (Orth, 440.)

Hootlanana Creek/Hutlinana Creek flows southwest twenty-eight miles to Baker Creek, fifty-five miles southeast of Tanana. (Ibid., 440.) There were two Discovery claims, Upper Discovery located by John (Jack) Murray on 25 March, 1902, and Lower Discovery located by Charles Beach on 21 July 1902. (Rampart, Locations and Statements, 1: 353-54, 518-19.)

Hot Springs/Manley Hot Springs is a settlement on Hot Springs Slough, fifty-four miles northeast of the Bitzshtini Mountains. In 1907, Frank G. Manley (Hillyard B. Knowles) built a four-story hotel there. (Orth, 619.)

Hot Springs Creek is a tributary of Hot Springs Slough. J[ohn] F. Karshner located the Discovery claim on 10 August 1902. (Rampart, Locations and Statements, 1: 442.)

Hot Springs Slough heads at Baker Lake and flows southwest fifteen miles to the Tanana River. See the Slough of Superstition (Orth, 433).

Houklee Gulch/Hoaklee Gulch/Hokeley Gulch extends south 1.3 miles to Deep Creek, four miles southwest of Tofty and thirty-three miles east-southeast of Tanana (Ibid., 424.) Samuel Houklee, along with Michael J. Sullivan, Herman Tofty, and five others, was a member of the 160-acre Houklee Association claim located on 29 July 1907. (Manley, Locations, 3: 132.)

Hoveley Gulch probably is the same as Houklee Gulch. Prospector and miner Otto Hoveley worked and operated in the Manley Hot Springs district from about 1922 to 1951. (B. D. Stewart, *Report of the Mine Inspector to the Governor of Alaska,* 1922, 42 Territory of Alaska Mining Department report, Cache Creek, 12 September 1951.)

Howard's Pup is a pup off the left side of claim No. 5 above, Little Minook Creek. F. R. Howard located claim No. 1 on 25 October 1898. (Rampart, Little Minook Creek (folder) (index.)

Hudson Creek/Dick Hudson Creek heads north of Gold Mountain and flows eight miles to the Little Melozitna River, thirteen miles north-northwest of Birches (Orth, 435.) On 5 August 1949, Warren Thompson, James Hansa, A. G. Vachon, and four others sold one-half interest to all their claims on Dick Hudson Creek to Strandberg & Sons. (Fort Gibbon, Deeds, 1908-1954, 630-31.) On 4 October 1907, S. R. Hudson deeded the lower 1,000 feet of the Alaska claim, Hudson Creek, to Joe Kaminski. (Fort Gibbon, Miscellaneous, 1908-1910, 1-2.)

Hungry Creek is a tributary of Mason Creek. Ray R. Henderson located the Discovery claim on 3 September 1907. (Fort Gibbon, Mining Locations, 1907-1908, 120.)

Hunker Creek is a tributary of Hot Springs Slough. J[ohn] F. Karshner located the Discovery claim on 27 June 1902. (Rampart, Locations and Statements, 1: 443-44.)

Hunter Creek heads at the junction of Forty-seven Gulch and Ninety-two Hunter Creek and flows west six miles to Minook Creek, two miles east-southeast of Rampart. (Orth, 438.) Bill Hunter located the Discovery claim about April 1896. *(Rampart Whirlpool,* 15 January 1899*)* Another source credits Hunter and John Minook with discovering the creek in 1894. Minook and Dan Carolan held Discovery and No. 1 above in December 1900. *(Alaska Forum,* 13 December 1900.)

Huron Creek flows north nine miles to Troublesome Creek, twenty-seven miles west of Livengood. (Orth, 439.) A stampede to Huron Creek occurred in the fall of 1904. *(Alaska Forum,* 10 December 1904.)

Idaho Bar elevation 1,900 feet, trends southeast three miles from [Big] Minook Creek, between Little Minook and Hunter creeks, six miles southeast of Rampart. (Orth, 442.) Charles I. Range, Dayton, WA, and W. S. Harmon, Burke, ID, discovered the Idaho Bar mining district, effective 2 May 1898. (Rampart, Idaho Bar (folders,) [1]: 3, and [2]: 44.)

Idaho Creek is a tributary of Hot Springs Slough. J[ohn] F. Karshner located claim No. 1 below on 13 August 1902. A. J. Hutchinson located the Discovery claim the same day. (Rampart, Locations and Statements, 1: 445-46, 564-65.)

Illinois Creek is formed by the confluence of Wilson and Golden creeks. It flows 7.5 miles to the Yukon River at Kallands. (Orth, 450.) The 160-acre Berry Association claim, of which H. F. Berry was a member, was located on the creek on 15 October 1908. (Fort Gibbon, Mining Locations, 1: 11.)

Indian Creek/Indian River heads on Indian Mountain and flows fifty-three miles to Mathews Slough, east of Huggins Island, sixty miles northwest of Gold Mountain. (Orth, 454.) Alfred, a Native, sold the Discovery claim to Edward Marsan on 25-26 March 1911. On November 1912, the partnership of Marsan and Lessing sold the claim to the Northern Commercial Company. (Fort Gibbon, Miscellaneous Record, 48-49, 70.)

Innisfail Creek is a tributary of Sullivan Creek on the right limit below the Discovery claim on Sullivan Creek. Michael J. Sullivan located the Innisfail Discovery claim on 22 November 1906. (Manley, Locations, 3: 33, 130.)

Ionic Creek is a tributary and at the headwaters of Baker Creek, twenty-five miles west of Glen Gulch. Robert Meston located the Discovery claim on 25 August 1902. (Rampart, Locations and Statements, 1: 577.)

Irish Creek/Irish Gulch extends southeast 1.7 miles to Killarney Creek, five miles south of Roughtop Mountain and thirty-eight miles east-southeast of Tanana. (Orth, 460.) John Foster located claim No. 1 on 28 July 1907. (Manley, Locations, 3: 100.)

Isabella Creek is not precisely located. J[osh] L. Ray recorded claim No. 1 above on 8 January 1901. (Rampart, Mining Locations, Old Book, 76.)

Jack Creek is a tributary of Golden Creek. Frank J. Miller and Dan C. Beyer held a forty-acre claim as of 19 December 1927. (Fort Gibbon, Mining Locations, 1: 568-69.)

Jackson Creek flows south eleven miles to the Yukon River, eight miles east-northeast of Tanana. (Orth, 468.) Ida E. Johnstone located claim No. 10 above on 4 July 1908. (Fort Gibbon, Mining Locations, 1907-1908, 200.)

Joe Bush Creek/Gulch flows south 1.1 mile to Pioneer Creek, 0.5 miles west of that stream's head, twenty-one miles south of Rampart. (Orth, 473.) E. W. Bush located claim No. 3 above, on 15 September 1901. (Manley, Locations, 1, 353-54.)

Joe Bush, Jr., Creek is a tributary of Joe Bush Gulch/Creek. George W. Sundborg held the Discovery claim as of 20 April 1902. (Rampart, Locations and Statements, 1: 399.) Sundborg, Charles Nelson, P. M. Olson, and E. W. Bush held claim No. 1 as of 9 May 1906. (Manley, Locations, 3: 5.)

Joseph Creek flows east two miles to Minook Creek, seventeen miles south of Rampart. (Orth, 478.) A Mr. Joseph chaired a meeting of Little Minook claim holders on 27 May 1898. (Rampart, Bylaws of Rampart Mining District (folder), 31.)

Judson Gulch joins Grant Creek at claim No. 13 above on the right limit. Sam J. Callahan, M. P. Fleischman, and Nellie E. Heeter were members of the Judson Gulch Association claim, located on 15 October 1908. (Fort Gibbon, Mining Locations, 1: 60.)

Julia Creek flows west-southwest two miles to Minook Creek, east of that stream's junction with the Yukon River, 1.3 miles northeast of Rampart. (Orth, 479.) G[arnet] W. Coen and C. Sallinger held the Discovery claim as of 5 October 1897. (Rampart, Julia Creek (folder.)

Kemperville was a small settlement on the Tanana River at the mouth of Hot Springs Slough. It was named for George Kemper. Mail for Tofty and Hot Springs had to pass through Kemperville in the summertime. *(Hot Springs Post,* 16 January 1909.)

Kentucky Creek flows southwest 4.8 miles to Hootlanana Creek, five miles south of Eureka Dome, fifty-six miles east of Tanana. (Orth, 510.) C. H. Olsen relocated the Discovery claim on 28 May 1901. (Manley, Locations, 1: 230-31.)

Killarney Creek flows south 4.7 miles, joins Blowback Creek to form Baker Creek, forty miles east-southeast of Tanana. (Orth, 519.) Michael J. Sullivan located the Discovery claim on 14 December 1906. (Manley, Locations, 3: 63.) Locations, Sullivan and Ed Taggert sank a hole to bedrock in the spring of 1904. *Hot Springs Echo,* 18 July 1908.)

Lake Creek is a tributary of Old Man Creek. Ed Huppenstall, Tom Hocker, and six others held the 160-acre First Chance Association claim as of 2 January 1911. William Schutt held the Discovery claim as of 16 November 1910. (Fort Gibbon, Mining Locations, 1: 156, 183.)

Lanchester/Lancaster Creek flows southeast two miles to the Yukon River, twenty miles west of Tanana. (Orth, 563.) D. W. Fitzgerald held claim No. 7 above as of 13 November 1907. S. E. Lanchester also held a claim as of 12 November 1907. (Fort Gibbon, Mining Locations, 1907-1908, 83, 85.)

Langford Creek is a tributary of Melozi Creek. On 29 September 1908, J. S. Langford located eighty acres for the Minook Group, which included himself, John Minook, and others. (Fort Gibbon, Mining Locations, 1: 2.)

Last Chance Gulch lies between Eureka Creek and Glen Gulch. H. G. C. Baldry located a claim on the gulch on 2 September 1901. (Manley, Locations, 1: 381-82.)

Leadville Gulch is a tributary of Hootlanana Creek. E. D. Howe located claim No. 3 on 25 June 1902. (Rampart, Locations and Statements, 1: 420, 451.)

Lenora Creek is two and one-half miles above the mouth of Big Minook Creek and is the second creek running into Big Minook from the north side. Its mouth is about one mile from the Yukon River. Frank J. Franken held the Discovery claim as of 28 April 1898. (Rampart, Lenora Gulch (folder).)

Little Ax Creek is a tributary of Moran Creek. Grant Burke, Harold Sedden, and N. R. Hudson held the sixty-acre No. 2 Association Above as of 1 September 1909. (Fort Gibbon, Mining Locations, 1: 105).

Little Bear Creek is a tributary of Hootlanana Creek near claim No. 10 above, Upper Discovery. J[ohn] J. Belsea located the Discovery claim on 22 February 1902. (Rampart, Locations and Statements, 1: 337-38.)

Little Bonanza Pup is a pup off the left side of Little Minook Creek. W. E. Stringal held claim No. 1 as of 25 November 1897. (Rampart, Little Minook Creek (folder), 2: 172.)

Little Boulder Creek is a tributary of Big Boulder Creek. William Staples located the Discovery claim on 3 September 1906. (Manley, Locations, 3: 39.)

Little Butte Creek is a tributary of Hootlanana Creek. William Cheeseman located claim No. 2 above on 22 February 1902. (Rampart, Locations and Statements, 1: 361.)

Little Mascott is a tributary of Mascott Creek. William Staples held claim No. 1 on 5 November 1906. (Manley, Locations, 3: 59.)

Little Minook Creek flows northwest five miles to Minook Creek between Idaho and California bars, 3.5 miles southeast of Rampart. (Orth, 585.) James S. Langford held the Discovery claim as of 29 April 1896. John Minook, for whom the creek was named, held No. 19 above. (Rampart, Little Minook Creek (folder) index.)

Little Minook, Jr. Creek heads on California Bar, and flows northwest 2.1 miles to Minook Creek, four miles south-southeast of Rampart. (Orth, 585.) In November 1899, Valeria Myers and John Bock amended the location of claim No. 23, originally staked by Ben Stickney on 24 January 1898. (Rampart, Little Minook Creek Junior (folder), 73-74.)

Lucky Pup is a pup off the left side of claim No. 13 above, Little Minook Creek. John Thompson located claim No. 1 on 2 July 1898. (Rampart, Little Minook Creek (folder) (index.)

Lynx Creek flows south five miles to Grant Creek, two miles north of that stream's junction with the Yukon River, twenty-five miles west of Tanana. (Orth, 605.) William Lord held Upper Discovery as of 26 September 1907. (Fort Gibbon, Locations, 1907-1908, 140.)

Macaroni Creek is a tributary of the Indian River, twenty miles east of Hughes. Helen McGee held the Discovery claim as of 4 September 1936. (Fort Gibbon, Mining Locations, 2: 302.)

McCaskie/MacCaskie Bar is one and one-half miles south of the confluence of Eureka and Pioneer creeks, thirty miles south of Rampart. S. T. Houklee located the Houklee claim on 20 October 1901. Peter MacA. MacCaskie located No. 3 above, Martin Creek, on 1 November 1901. (Manley, Locations, 1: 392, 442-43, 481.)

Magic/Majestic Creek is located eight miles from the trail between Thanksgiving and Sullivan creeks. John D. Kaulbach located claim No. 1 on 5 September 1907. (Manley, Locations 3: 112, 118-20.)

Magnet Gulch is a tributary of Hootlanana Creek. Red Rogers was prospecting the gulch in February 1902. (*Alaska Forum*, 8 February 1902.)

Magnet Gulch is a tributary of Grant Creek. C. H. Hull, J. Cavanaugh, and J. M. Gallaher together held the Discovery claim on 6 January 1909. (Fort Gibbon, Mining Locations, 1: 15.)

Mariposa Bar is near the fork of Garnet and Rock creeks at claim No. 10 below, Garnet. E[d] C. Allen held the Discovery claim as of 8 September 1898. It was named for Mariposa County, California, home of the sweetheart of Perry Judkins. (Rampart, Mariposa Bar and Omega Creek (folder.)

Marshall Creek, not precisely located, is near Stevens Creek. In September 1898, while mining on Stevens Creek, Perry Judkins found a caved-in boat on Marshall Creek. (Judkins's journal, entries of 1-10 September 1898, Perry Judkins Collection.)

Martin/Marten Creek is a tributary of Silver Bow Creek. H. W. Walbridge located claim No, 2 above on 31 October 1902. (Manley, Locations 1: 476-77.)

Martin Gulch Creek is a tributary of Lynx Creek. Sam, J. S., and David Sokotich and Julius Martin held the eighty-acre Bedrock Association claim as of 21 September 1909. (Fort Gibbon, Mining Locations, 1: 113.)

Mascott Creek is a tributary of Little Boulder Creek. E. H. Herbert held claim No. 1 as of 5 November 1906. (Manley, Locations, 3: 59.)

Mash Creek is a tributary of Chitanana Creek. Albert Hoserud performed assessment work for the year ending June 1922 on his claims, Discovery, Nos. 1 and 2 below and 1 above. (Fort Gibbon, Original Entry Index, 1908-1951, loose paper dated 26 May 1922.)

McDonald Bar, elevation 2,600 feet, ridge extends south three miles from the junction of Hoosier and Minook creeks, 5.5 miles south-southeast of Rampart. (Orth, 608.) The bar is on the north side between Hoosier and Florida creeks. John R. McDonald, Owen P. Thomson, and Mrs. T. R. Edwards located the Discovery claim, known as the Zetta claim, on 10 June 1900. (Rampart, McDonald Bar (folder.)

McKinley Creek is a tributary of Baker Creek. Max Neville located the Discovery claim on 20 September 1906. (Manley, Locations, 3: 56.)

McKinley Gulch/McKinley Creek flows 3.5 miles to Rhode Island Creek, 0.3 miles north of that stream's junction with Omega Creek, twenty-six miles south of Rampart. (Orth, 611.) Alfred Lavigne located the Discovery claim on 10 June 1901. (Manley, Locations, 1: 258-59.)

McManus Gulch is a tributary of Sullivan Creek. W. P. McManus located the 160-acre Peg Leg Association claim for himself, Herman Tofty, and six others on 23 July 1907. (Manley, Locations, 3: 108-09.)

McMullen Creek is a tributary of the Melozi. E. Sullivan, J. Cowie, and two others located the eighty-acre Discovery Association claim on 30 January 1909. (Fort Gibbon, Mining Locations, 1: 31).

Miller Creek flows southwest three miles to Hunter Creek, 0.5 miles east of that stream's junction with Minook Creek and three miles southeast of Rampart. (Orth, 643.) B. W. Moore, Jr., probably held claim No. 6 above in late 1897. (Rampart, Miller Creek (folder).)

Miller Gulch is a ravine extending three miles southeast to Sullivan Creek, thirty-four miles east-southeast of Tanana. (Orth, 643.) H. Miller sank a hole in the gulch in the winter of 1904-1905, and M. W. Sinclair staked a claim the same winter. (*Hot Springs Echo*, 18 July 1908.) Oscar Bergman staked the 160-acre Troy Association for himself and seven others on 7 September 1907. (Manley, Locations, 3: 99.)

Miners Creek is a tributary of Wilson Creek. W. B. Dunkel and seven others located a 160-acre claim on 20 August 1909. (Fort Gibbon, Mining Locations, 1: 78.)

Minnehaha Creek is a tributary of Hiawatha Creek. P. A. Rettig was working on Minnehaha Creek in September 1908. (Ibid., 242. *Hot Springs Post*, 1 October 1908.)

Mission Creek flows southwest eight miles to the Yukon River, east of Mission Hill, four miles northeast of Tanana. (Orth, 648.) Clarence Berry and seven others held the 160-acre Idaho Association claim as of 23 July 1908. (Fort Gibbon, Mining Locations, 1907-1908, 128.)

Monday Creek/Gulch flows south 1.8 miles to Grant Creek, 4.5 miles northeast of that stream's junction with the Yukon River, twenty-three miles west-northwest of Tanana. (Orth, 651.) Sam J. Callahan acted as agent for the 160-acre Monday Association claim, located on 30 September 1907. (Fort Gibbon, Mining Locations, 1907-1908, 160.)

Montana Bar is a bar in the vicinity of Alameda and Kentucky creeks in the Eureka (Hot Springs) mining district. Recorder Jay Whipple held the Florence claim as of 12 May 1899. (Rampart, Montana Bar (folder.)

Montana Creek/Montana Gulch extends east 1.9 miles to Minook Creek, three miles south-southeast of Rampart. (Orth, 652.) The claim holders considered the creek to be a continuation of Little Minook Gulch, although separated by Big Minook Creek. They estimated it to be seven miles east of Rampart. Frank M. Canton held the Discovery claim as of 5 February 1898. (Rampart, Montana Creek folder.)

Montana Creek is a tribuary of Hootlanana Creek. H. B. Knowles (birth name for F. G. Manley) was a member of the Palace Association, which held a 160-acre claim as of 25 May 1907. (Manley, Locations, 3: 73-74.)

Montana Creek is a tributary of the Yukon River. Charles Coulombe located the Discovery claim on 26 August 1908. (Fort Gibbon, Mining Locations, 1: 1.)

Moose Creek is a tributary of the left fork of Baker Creek about twenty-two miles from Deakyme. On 22 May 1902, Nels Johnson located claims for himself, John Bock, and A[ndrew] J. Balliet. (Rampart, Locations and Statements, 1: 373-75.)

Moose Mountain Gulch is a gulch on Baker Flats. Michael J. Sullivan, Samuel Houklee, and six others located a 160-acre claim on 5 September 1906. (Manley, Locations, 3: 18.)

Moraine Creek is a tributary of the Tozi River. Fred C. Zickwolff held the Discovery claim as of 23 July 1924. (Fort Gibbon, Mining Locations, 1: 506.)

Moran Creek flows northwest nineteen miles to the Little Melozitna River, twenty-two miles north of Birches. (Orth, 657.) William Moran located the Discovery claim on 4 September 1907. (Fort Gibbon, Mining Locations, 1907-1908, 46.)

Morelock Creek flows southwest fourteen miles to the Yukon River, twenty-three miles east-northeast of Tanana. (Orth, 657.) A. B. Culp located Upper Discovery on 1 June 1908. (Fort Gibbon, Mining Locations, 1907-1908, 180.)

Muck Creek is a tributary of the Tanana River about seven miles northwest from the village of Tanana and about thirty-six miles from the mouth of Baker Creek. William Barnett located the Discovery claim on 29 August 1902. (Rampart, Locations and Statements, 1: 573-74.)

Mukaluk Creek is a tributary of Hootlanana Creek. It heads into the same dome as does Kentucky Creek and is forty miles south of Rampart. John Mackenzie (or McKenzie) located claim No. 1 on 21 July 1901. (Manley, Locations, 1: 328-29.)

Muskegon Creek is a tributary of Mason Creek. Alfred and Aneline Roy, Phil Giroux, and two others located the 100-acre Roy Association claim on 8 August 1908. (Fort Gibbon, Mining Locations, 1: 40.)

Nevada Creek is a tributary of New York Creek between Allen (Allan) and California creeks. James Halley located claim No. 2 above on 10 August 1901. (Ibid., 288, 397.)

New Haven Creek empties into Big Minook Creek almost opposite Ruby Creek. It had been fully staked by late October 1898. (Ballou to Folks, 7 December 1898, William B. Ballou Collection.)

New Haven Creek, not precisely located, is probably a tributary of Rhode Island Creek. J. T. Roberts held claim No. 1 above as of 8 January 1901. (Manley, Locations, 1: 166-67.)

New York Creek flows southwest ten miles to the north fork of Baker Creek, forty-five miles east of Tanana. (Orth, 685.) Boston boy Herbert A. Russell held the Discovery claim as of 6 April 1899. (Manley, Locations, 1: 79-80.)

Nugget Creek is a tributary of Wilson Creek. Paul Solka, Frank, Otto, Charles, Oscar, and August Lundine, and two others held the 160-acre Calumet Association claim as of 20 August 1909. (Fort Gibbon, Mining Locations, 1: 98.)

Nunabislogarth in 1897 was the first Yup'ik Eskimo village on the Kwichpak, or northern branch of the Yukon River delta, a few miles above Moore's Place. (Francis Barnum, S.J., "The Yukon Delta Region," Alaska-*Yukon Magazine,* January 1908, 422.) Thomas Wiedemann wintered in 1897-1898 on the steamer *W. K. Merwin* about twenty-five miles upstream of the village. (Thomas Wiedemann, *Cheechako into Sourdough,* 71-72.)

Nunivak Slough/Creek/Bar/Nanvaranak Slough heads on Nanvaranak Lake and flows northwest seven miles to Kwikpak Pass, eighteen miles west of Kwiguk. (Orth, 673.) Perry Judkins and other passengers on the ice-locked steamer *Thomas Dwyer* wintered there, beginning on 17 October 1897. (Perry Judkins Collection, folders 6, 11, 12, 19.)

O'Brien Creek is a tributary of Grant Creek. S. F. McDill and seven others located the 160-acre Bessie Association claim on 14 October 1908. (Fort Gibbon, Mining Locations, 1: 68-69.)

Ohio Creek flows southeast 1.7 miles to Hootlanana Creek, eighteen miles southeast of Rampart. (Orth, 716.) On 24 February 1902, Thomas Sullivan located claim No. 2 below, considered to be twenty-five miles from Rampart. (Rampart, Locations and Statements 1: 364.)

Oliver Creek is a tributary of Baker Creek midway between Glen Gulch and claim No. 6 above, Eureka Creek. On 21 October 1901, F. E. Diver located claim No. 1. (Manley, Locations, 464, 478-79.)

Olson's Landing was a steamboat landing on the Tanana River one-half mile below Kemperville. It was probably named for G. A. Olson of Hot Springs. (*Hot Springs Post,* 10 April 1909.)

Omega Creek flows south nine miles to Baker Creek, twenty-eight miles south-southwest of Rampart. (Orth, 723.) J. E. Jones held claim No. 1 above as of 14 April 1899. (Rampart, Mariposa Bar and Omega Creek (folder.)

Oransic Creek is a tributary of the Yukon River. John Welsh located the Discovery claim on 1 July 1902. (Rampart, Locations and Statements, 1: 432.)

Orofino Creek is a tributary of Spicer Creek. O. W. Browman held the Discovery claim as of 6 March 1909. (Fort Gibbon, Mining Locations, 1: 57.)

Owl Creek is a tributary of the east fork of Indian Creek, near Himes Creek. J. S. Huntington held the Discovery claim as of 1 July 1911. (Ibid., 269, 276.)

Patterson Creek formed by the junction of Sullivan and Cache creeks, flows west twenty-six miles to the Tanana River. (Orth, 742.) George Kemper located the Discovery claim on 20 July 1907. (Manley, Locations, 3: 103.)

Peters Gulch is a tributary of Big Minook Creek. Clarence Peters held claim No. 2 as of 29 October 1898. (Rampart, Big Minook Creek (folder), 2: 184.)

Peterson's Pup is a pup off of claim No. 3 above, Little Minook, originally held by Pete Peterson. W. A. Trinkle located a fraction claim on 18 September 1897. (Rampart, Little Minook (folder) (index).)

Pigeon Creek is a tributary of Hootlanana Creek near Upper Discovery. J[ames] W. Dillon held the Discovery claim as of 17 February 1902. (Rampart, Locations and Statements, 1: 336-37.)

Pioneer Creek is formed by the junction of its north fork and Deadwood Creek, flows southwest 3.8 miles to Eureka Creek, twenty-three miles south of Rampart. (Orth, 759.) M[iddleton] S. Gill held the Discovery claim as of 3 April 1899 and abandoned it on 14 September 1900. (Manley, Locations, 1: 53.)

Plumenden Gulch joins Arroyo Grande at claim No. 13, Arroyo. A. J. Plumenden held claim No. 1 as of 12 October 1898. (Rampart, Arroyo Grande (folder.)

Pocahontas Creek is a tributary of Indian Creek. H. E. Gardner, Tom Lloyd, and six others held the Big Mountain Association claim as of 4 December 1910. (Fort Gibbon, Mining Locations, 1: 166.)

Poker Gulch is a tributary of Omega Creek, twenty miles south of Rampart. H. L. Myers located claim No. 2 on 21 October 1901. (Manley, Locations, 1: 460.)

Poverty Pup is a pup off the left side of claim No. 11 above, Little Minook Creek. Carrie Plough located claim No. 1, possibly about 10 May 1898. (Rampart, Little Minook Creek (folder) (index).)

Prospect Creek is a tributary of Fish Creek/Fish Lake. S. G. Sutherland was a member of the Lost Rocker Association which located a 160-acre claim on 26 August 1907. (Fort Gibbon, Mining Locations, 1907-1908, 250.)

Quail Creek flows southeast 5.6 miles to Troublesome Creek, sixteen miles southeast of Rampart. (Orth, 785). The creek received its name because the original stakers could not spell ptarmigan. Clint DuMire, Charles Olsen, and Cal Richardson left Quail in February 1903 for Chena. (*Alaska Forum*, 7 March 1903). (Ibid., 21 February 1903.)

Quartz Creek heads on Serpentine Ridge and flows southwest 4.6 miles to Sullivan Creek, 1.2 miles northwest of Tofty. (Orth, 786.) See also Easy Money Creek.

Queeny Gulch is a tributary of Golden Creek. A. B. Culp, B[elle] Daneke, and H. A. Rockefellow located the sixty-acre Queenie Association on 2 January 1909. (Fort Gibbon, Mining Locations, 1: 15.)

Rampart is a settlement on the south bank of the Yukon River, sixty-one miles east-northeast of Tanana.

(Orth 791.) At a meeting on 6 June 1897, James S. Langford proposed the name Rampart for the townsite. The miners agreed. (Rampart, Minook Creek (townsite) (folder), 1.)

Rampart Canyon/Rampart Gorge (also Lower Ramparts, the Ramparts) on the Yukon River, extends southwest twenty miles from Garnet Island, twenty-seven miles northwest of Tanana. (Orth, 792). The canyon's rapid whirlpool waters inspired the name for the 1899 monthly newspaper *The Rampart Whirlpool*. In the 1960s, the canyon became the site for a proposed hydroelectric dam.

Rampart Creek flows northwest two miles to the Yukon River just south of Rampart. (Orth 792.) William Frizelle relocated claim No. on 1 January 1899. (Rampart, Rampart Creek (folder), 1.)

Range Channel is the channel bed of an ancient stream, forerunner of the present Yukon River, located above Idaho Bar. It was discovered by Charles I. Range in early 1898 and was considered to be the source for the gold in nearby creeks. (*The Rampart Whirlpool*, [15 January 1899].)

Range's Pup is a pup off the left hand fork of the left hand fork of Peterson's Pup. Charles I. Range and W. S. Harmon located the Eliza Anderson claim on 7 May 1898. (Rampart, Little Minook Creek (folder), 3: 13.)

Raven Creek is a tributary of the Koyukuk River. C. M. Hoagland held the Discovery claim as of 10 April 1923. (Fort Gibbon, Mining Locations, 1: 502.)

Red Mountain Creek heads on Red Mountain and flows south six miles to the Koyukuk River, twenty miles northeast of Hughes. (Orth, 798.) Frank E. Howard and seven others held the 160-acre Howard Association claim as of 10 January 1911. (Fort Gibbon, Mining Locations, 1: 181.)

Rhode Island Creek flows southwest seven miles to Omega Creek, fifty miles east of Tanana. (Orth, 804.) A. L. Kepner located the Discovery claim on 11 April 1899. (Manley, Locations, 1: 72.)

Rock Creek flows north seven miles to Garnet Creek, thirteen miles southwest of Rampart. (Orth, 809.) P. W. Judkins held the Discovery claim as of 7 September 1899. (Rampart, Rock Creek (folder), 6.)

Rock Creek is a tributary of Sullivan Creek. George Kern and A. D. Williams located the forty-acre Kern Association claim on 29 August 1907. (Manley, Locations, 3: 95.)

Roovers Gulch, not precisely located, is apparently off Pioneer Creek. A[lfred] W. Roovers located claim No. 2 on 9 April 1899. (Manley, Locations, 1: 48.)

Rossi's Pup is a pup on the left hand side, off claims Nos. 3 and 4, of Little Minook Creek. O. Rossi located claim No. 1 on 2 August 1898. (Rampart, Little Minook Creek (folders) (index) and 3: 33.)

Rouse Pup is a tributary of Mason Creek. W. B Rodman, George Rouse, and J. C. Thornson located the Discovery claim on 25 February 1909. (Fort Gibbon, Mining Locations, 1: 47.)

Ruby Creek flows northeast seven miles to Minook Creek, seven miles south of Rampart. (Orth, 819.) William Ballou participated in a stampede to Ruby Creek in October 1898 but was too late to stake a claim. In 1904, he had a hydraulicking operation on the creek. (Ballou to Folks, 7 December 1898, William B. Ballou Collection.)

Ruby Pup is a pup off the left hand side of claim No. 5 above, Little Minook Creek. M. C. Egan had a claim on the creek as of 31 October 1898. (Rampart, Little Minook Creek (folder) index.)

Rudiland Bar is not precisely located. F. E. Drake relocated the Gold King bench claim on 18 November 1901. (Manley, Locations, 1: 437.)

Russian Creek flows north 8.5 miles to the Yukon River, three miles southwest of Rampart. (Orth, 821.) The organizing meeting for the creek district was held on 30 September 1897. Fred B. Gleason served as secretary. (Rampart, Russian Creek folder.)

Sailor Creek empties into Baker Creek, thirty miles south of Rampart. Oliver Lorencen located the Discovery claim on 16 October 1901. (Manley, Locations, 1: 436.)

Sally's Pup is a pup off of the left side of claim No. 8 above, Little Minook, originally owned by John Sally. R. E. Beach sold claim No. 2, Sally's Pup, one-half to W. H. Hubbard of Chicago in June 1898, and one-half to James D. MacDonald in September 1898. (Rampart, Little Minook Creek folder, 2: 162-63, 166.)

Sandusky Creek flows northwest 3.7 miles to Stevens Creek, 3.4 miles north of Roughtop Mountain and thirty-seven miles east-northeast of Tanana. (Orth, 835.) Is considered a tributary of Aurum Creek. G[eorge] R. Shirley located the Discovery claim on 5 July 1902. (Rampart, Locations and Statements, 1: 429.)

Scholefield's Pup is a pup off the left side of claim No. 6 above, Little Minook Creek. John Scholefield had claim No. 2 as of 15 May 1898. (Rampart, Little Minook Creek (folders) (index) and 3: 43.)

Seattle Creek flows south-southeast 1.5 miles to Rhode Island Creek, three miles south-southwest of Eureka Dome and twenty-two miles south of Rampart. (Orth, 849.) Elliot L. Gaetz held claim No. 2 as of 1 January 1901. (Manley, Locations, 1: 163-64.)

Seattle Gulch Pup is a pup off of claim No. 12 above, Little Minook Creek. George Thisby relocated claim No. 1 on 23 July 1898 and sold it to Mary F. Llewellyn on 31 July 1898. (Rampart, Little Minook Creek (folder), 2: 178-79.)

Seattle, Jr., Creek flows south one mile to Pioneer Creek, two miles northeast of that stream's junction with Eureka Creek, twenty-one miles south of Rampart. (Orth, 849.) J. W. Young held a claim on the creek as of 4 September 1901. (Manley, Locations, 1: 315-16.)

Shale Creek is a tributary of Golden Creek. S. F. McDill, Belle Daneke, Joe Anicich, and five others located the 160-acre Nugget Association claim on 2 January 1909. (Fort Gibbon, Mining Locations, 1: 12.)

Shirley Bar is a bar between Glen Gulch at claim No. 4 above and Gold Run. George R. Shirley located the Discovery claim on 19 July 1901. (Manley, Locations, 1: 286-87.)

Sidney Gulch is on the right side of claim No. 13, Little Minook Creek. J. J. McKinnon held claim No. 2 as of 13 May 1898. (Rampart, Little Minook Creek (folders) (index) and 3: 57.)

Silver Bow Creek is forty-five miles south of Rampart. S. T. Houklee located claim No. 13 above on 31 October 1901. (Manley, Locations, 1: 447.)

Siwash Pup is a tributary of Hunter Creek near to Yukon Bar. Perry Judkins held claim No. 1 in 1898. (Judkins's journal, entry of 16 April 1898, Perry Judkins Collection.)

Sixteen Mile Creek is a tributary of the Yukon River, sixteen miles above Tanana on the left limit of the Yukon. Ed McKay and seven others held the McKay Association claim as of 9 September 1909. (Fort Gibbon, Mining Locations, 1: 107.)

Skookum Creek is a tributary of Rosy Creek. Pete Pemberton held claim No. 2 above as of 17 February 1909. (Fort Gibbon, Mining Locations, 1: 34.)

Skookum Gulch/Skookum Creek flows south 1.3 miles to Pioneer Creek, 2.4 miles northeast of Eureka and twenty-one miles south of Rampart. (Orth, 885.) Sam Roddie had claim No. 4 as of 17 April 1899. (Manley, Locations, 1: 41.)

Slate Creek heads on Baldry Mountain, flows northeast seven miles to Minook Creek, ten miles south of Rampart. (Orth, 887.) William G. Atwood relocated the Discovery claim on 21 July 1900. The original claim had been recorded around 17 October 1898. (Rampart, Slate Creek (folder), 2: 125, 131-35, 143.)

Slate Creek flows northeast five miles to Tozimoran Creek, two miles west of the mouth of Wells Creek, twenty-three miles west-northwest of Tanana. (Orth, 887.) Miners considered the creek a tributary of Moran Creek. The Parchment Association had a 160-acre claim on Slate as of 12 September 1907. (Fort Gibbon, Mining Locations, 1907-1908, 75.)

Slough of Superstition/Renamed Hot Springs Slough, is fifteen miles below Baker Station on the Tanana River. It runs into the divide toward Rampart. Mike Laboski, Jim Dalton, and J. F. Karshner staked claims in the area in the summer of 1902. (*Rampart Miner,* 19 August 1902.)

Smoke Creek is a tributary of Grant Creek. Johnnie Smoke located the Discovery claim on 15 October 1907. (Fort Gibbon, Mining Locations, 1907-1908, 170.)

Snyder/Snider Creek is a tributary of Pigeon Creek. W[illiam] M. Cheeseman located the Discovery claim on 31 July 1902. (Rampart, Locations and Statements, 1:565, 514.)

Sourdough Creek is a tributary of Squaw Creek. In October 1904, Louis Iverson had a cabin on the Discovery claim. Bob Roberts had a cabin on claim No. 1 below. (*Alaska Forum,* 15 October 1904.)

Spencer Creek is the first left tributary of Fish Creek going upstream. Spencer Cain located the Discovery claim on 11 June 1901. (Rampart, Locations and Statements, 1: 32-33, 187-88.)

Spicer Creek heads in the Rampart Mountains and flows south eleven miles to the Yukon River, eleven miles east-northeast of Tanana. (Orth, 907.) George Ledger prospected there in the of 1904-1905 (*Alaska Forum,*15 October 1904. In 1905, Dick Hudson renamed Spicer Creek, Fortune Creek, and then renamed it Misfortune Creek. Ibid., 29 April 1905.) J. C. Spicer was a passenger to Alaska on the *Humboldt* in August 1897 (*Seattle Post-Intelligencer,*) 15 August 1907. In October 1904, Spicer had a roadhouse at the fork of Eureka and Boston creeks. (*Alaska Forum,*) 22 October 1904.

Spring Creek is a tributary of Hot Springs Slough. J[ohn] F. Karshner located the Discovery claim on 10 August 1902. (Rampart, Locations and Statements, 1: 440-41.)

Spring Gulch is on the left side off a fraction claim on Little Minook Creek. Otis Beverstock had claim No. 1 as of 4 January 1898. (Rampart, Little Minook Creek (folder) (index).)

Spruce Creek flows southwest 1.5 miles to [Big] Minook Creek, nine miles south of Rampart. (Orth, 909.) May Presko relocated claim No. 1 above on 8 January 1901. Viola Presko held the Discovery claim. (Rampart, Locations, Old Book, 247, 249.)

Spruce Gulch is a tributary of Cache Creek. George A. Salisbury, Harry Ferree, and six others located the 160-acre Myrtle Association claim on 15 August 1907. (Manley, Locations, 3: 108.)

Squirrel Gulch is on the north limit of Grand Gulch on Jackson Creek. M. Cooper located claim No. 1 on 18 September 1908. (Fort Gibbon, Mining Locations, 1907 1908, 260.)

Stevens Pup is a pup off the left side of claims Nos. 3 and 4 above, Little Minook Creek. Frank Stevens located claim No. 1 on 9 October 1898. (Rampart, Little Minook Creek (folders) (index) and 3: 3.)

Sullivan City was the settlement started in 1907 on Michael J. Sullivan's Discovery claim on Sullivan Creek. It was renamed Tofty. (Manley, multiple sources, 1908.)

Sullivan Creek heads on Serpentine Ridge, flows south 7.5 miles, and joins Cache Creek to form Patterson Creek, thirty-four miles east-southeast of Tanana. (Orth, 926.) The Indian name is said to be Zach tich da la na. (*Hot Springs Echo,* 18 July 1908). Michael J. Sullivan located the Discovery claim on 21 November 1906. (Manley, Locations, 3: 63.) Clint DuMire named the creek for Sullivan in 1905. (*Hot Springs Echo,* 18 July 1908.)

Sunnyside Creek is not precisely located. F. A. Sennet located claim No. 4 on 2 November 1898. (Rampart, Triple Creek (folder).)

Surry Gulch is a pup off of claim No. 2 below, Gunnison Creek. Herman Tofty held claim No. 3 as of 11 October 1898. (Rampart, Gunnison Creek and Tributaries (folder).)

Sydney Gulch runs into Little Minook Creek at claim No. 10 above. R. E. Beach sold one-fourth of claim No. 2 to W. H. Hubbard on 4 June 1898. (Rampart, Little Minook Creek (folder), 2: 165.)

Tamrack Gulch/Tamarack Creek flows east two miles to Sullivan Creek, six miles southwest of Roughtop Mountain. (Orth, 945.) George Kern located the Discovery claim on 27 July 1907. (Manley, Locations, 3: 93.)

Tanana is a settlement near the junction of the Tanana and Yukon rivers. (Orth, 947.)

Terra Haute Pup/Creek is a tributary of Washington Creek. Allen Chisholm located claim No. 2 on 12 August 1902. J[ohn] F. Karshner located the Discovery claim on 24 June 1902. (Rampart, Locations and Statements, 1: 433, 435, 444.)

Teton Gulch/Teton Creek flows south 1.7 miles to Hootlanana Creek, twenty miles southeast of Rampart. (Orth, 958.) Teton Gulch was one mile above Elephant Gulch. John C. Fluga located the Discovery claim on 30 July 1901. (Manley, Locations, 1: 365-66, 386.)

Texas Creek flows northwest three miles to Troublesome Creek, sixteen miles southeast of Rampart. (Orth, 958.) The creek was said to be twenty-seven miles from Rampart in Mike Hess Creek country. Charles B. Allen relocated claim No. 13 on 29 July 1901. (Rampart, Locations and Statements, 1: 159.)

Thanksgiving Creek flows southeast 5.5 miles to Omega Creek, 1.2 miles north of that stream's junction with Baker Creek, twenty-seven miles south-southwest of Rampart. (Orth, 958.) Tom Antonson located claim No. 1 above on 28 November 1901. (Manley, Locations, 1: 485.)

Tiffany Creek is a tributary of the Little Melozi River near Gold Mountain below Langford and Hudson creeks. It was presumably named for George Tiffany, store manager and postmaster in Tanana from about 1903 to 1913. (A. G. Maddren, "The Innoko Gold Placer District, Alaska," U.S.G.S. Bulletin 410, map plate v.)

Tofty is a settlement on the east bank of Sullivan Creek, seven miles southwest of Roughtop Mountain, thirty-five miles east-southeast of Tanana. (Orth, 972.) It was originally named Sullivan City.

Tofty Gulch flows southeast 1.1 mile to Sullivan Creek 0.9 miles southwest of Tofty and thirty-five miles east-southeast of Tanana. (Ibid., 972.) W. P. McManus and Clint DuMire sank a hole in the gulch in the spring of 1905 (*Hot Springs Echo*, 18 July 1908). Herman Tofty, M. J. Sullivan, and six others held the 160-acre Independence Association as of 23 July 1907. (Manley, Locations, 3, 110-11.)

Tolavanna/Toolavana/Tolovana was a settlement on the right bank of the Tanana River near the mouth of the Tolovana River, sixty-four miles west of Fairbanks. (Orth, 974.) The Toolavanna district, halfway between Rampart and Fairbanks, had opened by October 1904 (*Alaska Forum* 15 October 1904.)

Tonawanda Creek flows south three miles to Baker Creek, seven miles southeast of Roughtop Mountain. (Orth, 975.) Roy Moseley located claim No. 3 above on 10 September 1907. (Manley, Locations, 3: 116-117.)

Tozikaket/Tozi/Tozitna River heads in the Ray Mountains and flows west and south between the Ray and Rampart Mountains, eighty-three miles to the Yukon River, ten miles west-southwest of Tanana. (Orth, 980.) In December 1897, George Walter Sundborg walked 150 miles to Rampart from the mouth of the Tozikaket where the steamer *Mae West* was ice-bound. (Sundborg, *Our Family*, 99.)

Tozimoran Creek flows east thirteen miles to the Tozitna River, seventeen miles northwest of Tanana. (Orth, 980.) David M. Purkey held the Discovery claim in 1973. (Fort Gibbon, 22 October 1973-28 May 1975, 4: 3.)

Triangle Bar is five miles below the mouth of Schieffelin Creek. In September 1901, Herman Tofty was in charge of a raft owned by Ben Baker. The raft, with a load of wood, was being towed by the steamer *Rebecca* when it stuck on the bar. The steamer *Monarch* broke a hawser in an unsuccessful attempt to free the raft. The wood was off-loaded, and the raft was released. (*Rampart Miner*, 17 September 1901, and *Alaska Forum*, 19 September 1901.)

Triple Creek flows east 1.7 miles to Minook Creek, twelve miles south of Rampart. (Orth, 984.) Frank Stevens located the Discovery claim on 15 October 1898. (Rampart, Triple Creek (folder), 6.)

Troublesome Creek flows north forty miles to (Mike) Hess Creek, eighty miles northwest of Fairbanks. (Orth, 986.) J[ames] R. Austin held the Discovery claim as of 14 December 1897. (Rampart, Troublesome Creek folder.) The creek, an integral part of early Rampart area activity, was later absorbed into the Tolovana district. By order of Judge Harry E. Pratt, U.S. District Court, on 28 September 1938, Troublesome Creek and its tributaries, including Quail Creek, were restored to the Rampart district. (*Fairbanks Daily News-Miner*, 29 September 1938.)

Trout Creek flows east three miles to Granite Creek, fourteen miles south of Rampart. (Orth, 986.) Bernard Vogt located the Berlin claim on 29 January 1901. (Rampart, Mining Locations, Old Book, 142.)

Utah Creek heads on Roughtop Mountain and flows southeast 9.5 miles to Baker Creek, forty-five miles east-southeast of Tanana. (Orth, 1015.) Nicklos Nelson located claim No. 2 above on 21 February 1902. (Rampart, Locations and Statements, 1: 346.)

Utopia Creek flows east 4.5 miles south of the mining community of Utopia to the Indian River, sixty miles north of Birches. (Orth, 1015.) As of 13 April 1914, Harry Colter and George Light held the Discovery claim, which was eight miles below Discovery, Indian River. (Fort Gibbon, Mining Locations, 1: 419.)

Vaughn Gulch is a tributary of Grant Creek. Dennis Healy located claim No. 1 below on 25 September 1907. (Fort Gibbon, Mining Locations, 1907-1908, 130.)

Wake Up Creek is a tributary of Fish Creek. It empties into the Yukon River twenty-five miles west of Rampart. D. F. O'Brien located the Wake Up claim on 19 June 1901. (Rampart, Locations and Statements, 1: 6.)

Washington Creek heads on Bean Ridge and flows southeast five miles to Hot Springs Slough, three miles east of the village of Manley Hot Springs and forty-six miles east-southeast of Tanana. (Orth, 1029.) The creek is sixty miles south of Rampart. J[ohn] F. Karshner located claim No. 1 above on 24 June 1902. (Rampart, Locations and Statements, 1: 441.)

Weare was an early name for the village of Tanana.

Wells Creek flows southeast 5.5 miles to Tozimoran Creek, six miles northwest of that stream's junction with the Tozitna River, twenty-three miles northwest of Tanana. (Orth, 1033.) Is also considered to be a tributary of Moran Creek. W. H. Davis held the Discovery claim as of 24 October 1918. (Fort Gibbon, Mining Locations, 1: 476.)

What Cheer Bar is a bar between Pioneer and Eureka creeks, about twenty-eight miles from Rampart. G[eorge] R. Shirley located the G. R. Shirley claim on 29 August 1901. (Manley, Locations, 1: 332-33.) Later, Dan Rarick claimed to have discovered the bar in the late spring of 1899. (*Alaska Forum*, 18 March 1905.)

Wickersham was a townsite on the right limit of the Yukon River 200 yards east of Grant Creek. Recorder Frank Fox and trustees Mickey Barry, William Carney, and Joe Springer were elected on 2 August 1909. (Fort Gibbon, Miscellaneous Record, 17.)

Wildcat Creek is a tributary of Golden Creek. S. F. McDill located the 160-acre Eldorado Association claim for himself, Joe Anicich, and six others on 2 January 1909. (Fort Gibbon, Mining Locations, 1: 12.)

William Creek is a tributary of the Tozikaket River. William Brown, M. Gilmore, George Tiffany, and five others held the 160-acre What Cheer Association claim as of 17 August 1909. (Ibid., 91.)

Williams Gulch is a tributary of Pioneer Creek, about five or six miles from the mouth of Pioneer Creek on the left side going upstream. L. M. Williams located claim No. 3 above on 19 September 1901. (Rampart, Locations and Statements, 1: 91.)

Willow Creek is a tributary of the Yukon River near Gold Mountain. J. P. Tramper located the 160-acre Independent Association on 3 December 1907. (Fort Gibbon, Mining Locations, 1907- 1908, 112.)

Willow Creek is a tributary of the Tozikaket River. E. B. Gilmore and Lon Snepp located a forty-acre claim on 18 August 1909. (Fort Gibbons, Mining Locations 1:94)

Willow Creek is a tributary of Blue Bell Creek. J. R. Macdonald, William J. Stoneman, E. Sullivan and N. R. Hudson located the eighty-acre Willow Association claim on 23 July 1909. (Ibid.79.)

Wilson Creek flows northeast seven miles and joins Golden Creek to form Illinois Creek, seventeen miles northeast of Birches. (Orth, 1051.) John Carey held claim No. 1 above as of 17 July 1907. (Fort Gibbon Mining Locations 1907-1908, 35.)

Windy Creek is a tributary of Mason Creek. H. P. Sheppard located the Discovery claim on 8 August 1908. (Fort Gibbon, Mining Locations, 1:8.)

Wolverine Mountain, elevation 4,580 feet, is fourteen miles southeast of Rampart. (Orth, 1057.) In the summer of 1900, Hunter Fitzhugh described the mountain, which he estimated to be 9,000 feet high, as having black volcanic rocks like druid temples. From the summit, he could see Mt. McKinley, but the mosquitoes tormented him, preventing him from enjoying the view. (Fitzhugh to Father, 5 July 1900, Robert Hunter Fitzhugh Collection.)

Woodchopper Creek heads on Serpentine Ridge, and flows south-southeast 8.5 miles to Patterson Creek, thirty-three miles southeast of Tanana. (Orth, 1058.) Rod McKenzie and seven others located the 160-acre Illinois Association on 16 August 1907. (Manley, Locations, 3: 91.)

Yellow Mystery Gulch is a tributary of Baker Creek, forty miles south of Rampart. E.T. Townsend located claim No. 7 above on 6 November 1901. (Manley, Locations, 1:434.)

Yukon Bar, elevation 2,600 feet, is a ridge that extends east two miles from the junction of Hunter and Miller creeks, four miles southeast of Rampart. (Orth, 1069.) Perry Judkins held claim No. 7 in 1898. (Judkins to Alice, 3 November 1898, Perry Judkins Collection.)

Annotated Bibliography

Rampart, Manley Hot Springs, and Fort Gibbon Mining Districts

The following resources were consulted in the preparation of the thesis, but not all are actually cited in the thesis text. They are listed below to aid others who may wish to research specific subjects associated with the three mining districts and to provide a basic working bibliography for those districts. The listing is not exhaustive. Some resources that were examined were omitted from the listing because they did not contribute substantially to the body of information on the districts. Almost all sources listed are available in Fairbanks, Alaska, most in the Alaska-Polar Regions Department, Elmer E. Rasmuson Library, University of Alaska Fairbanks, or at the office of the District Recorder.

Alaska Forum, Rampart, Alaska. Weekly newspaper, published Thursdays, 28 September 1900–19 September 1901; Saturdays, 28 September 1901–4 August 1906. M/F 36. Not all copies are extant. The *Forum* reported regularly on mining activities and other events around Rampart and on mining news from elsewhere in Alaska and from the Klondike. On 21 February 1903, the *Forum* reported that Fanny Minook had died of consumption the previous Saturday (14 February 1903), and on 24 October 1903, the paper wrote that John Stanley had succeeded in forming a dredging company for work on Big Minook. A large suction dredge was to be shipped the next spring. In several issues of late 1904 and early 1905, the *Forum* editor, James B. Wingate, accused Judge James W. Wickersham, Deputy Marshal George Dreibelbis, and Commissioner J. Lindley Green of improprieties in office. The editor openly opposed Wickersham's reappointment as district judge.

Alger, R. A. Letter from the Secretary of War: Alaska Gold Fields. 13 December 1897. 55th Cong., 2d sess., 1898. S. Doc. 14. Wickersham Collection 7769A. Alaska Archives, Alaska and Polar Regions Department, Elmer E. Rasmuson Library, University of Alaska Fairbanks. Secretary Alger submitted the report of Captain P. H. Ray and Lt. W. P. Richardson on their trip to the gold fields in 1897. Ray had reported that there would be starvation if supplies did not reach the miners in Dawson. He had also reported that Rampart's population as of 7 September 1897 was 350.

Ballou, William B. Collection. Alaska Archives, Alaska and Polar Regions Department, Elmer E. Rasmuson Library, University of Alaska Fairbanks. Ballou lived in Rampart from 1898 to 1917. He carried on an extensive correspondence with relatives in Vermont, detailing his fortunes or misfortunes in mining and providing glimpses into the life of the community.

Barnum, Fr. [Francis], S.J. "The Yukon Delta Region." 14 November 1897. *Alaska-Yukon Magazine,* January 1908, 422–23. Fr. Barnum explained the Yukon Delta and the short-cut passage to St. Michael. Thomas Wiedemann, Perry Judkins, and others were icebound in the area during the winter of 1897-1898.

Beach, Rex. *The Barrier*. New York: Harper & Brothers, 1908. In his romantic novel, Beach described people in the mining camp of Flambeau, a fictive Rampart. He interspersed real events and real characters, including Fr. Barnum, from his Rampart experience throughout his imaginary account.

————. *Personal Exposures*. New York: Harper & Bros., Publishers, 1940. In his autobiography, Rex Beach recounted several episodes about his time in Rampart.

Brainerd, Erastus. Alaska and the Klondyke. Alaska Archives, Alaska and Polar Regions Department, Elmer E. Rasmuson Library, University of Alaska Fairbanks. Microform. Brainerd served as secretary for the Bureau of Information of the Seattle Chamber of Commerce from the fall of 1897 through the spring of 1898. In that position, as shown by his letters in the microform, he publicized Seattle as the departure point for Alaska and the Klondike and promoted the need to develop gold mining in Alaska.

Brooks, Alfred H. *The Alaskan Mining Industry in 1915*. U.S. Geological Survey Bulletin   642-A. Washington: Government Printing Office, 1916. Brooks visited the Hot Springs district in the summer of 1915. At the time there were thirty placer mines. Eight operators had recovered stream tin in the production of gold. Rampart had only fifteen mines.

———. *The Alaska Mining Industry in 1920*. U.S. Geological Survey Bulletin 722-A. Washington: Government Printing Office, 1921. Brooks reported that production in the Hot Springs district was only one-half as large as it had been in 1919. Eleven mines operated in the district in the summer. Ten mines operated in Rampart that summer. Mining had practically ceased on Indian River and Gold Hill.

Brooks, Alfred H., et al. *Report on Progress of Investigations of Mineral Resources of Alaska in 1904*. U.S. Geological Survey Bulletin 259. Washington: Government Printing Office, 1905. Brooks referred to a broad belt of metamorphosed rock which stretched westward from Dawson along the Yukon to the Ramparts. Many areas in the belt were known to be gold-bearing.

———. *Report on Progress of Investigations of Mineral Resources of Alaska in 1905*. U. S. Geological Survey Bulletin 284. Washington: Government Printing Office, 1906. Brooks stated that mining costs had been reduced since the early mining days in Alaska. Pioneer miners could not afford to work gravel that averaged less than $10 to $15 a cubic yard. By 1905, though, miners could work gravel averaging less than $5.00 a yard. Brooks strongly advocated for a railroad, including a line from Fairbanks to Rampart, to improve transportation for the miners.

———. *Report on Progress of Investigations of Mineral Resources of Alaska in 1906*. U.S. Geological Survey Bulletin 314. Washington: Government Printing Office, 1907. Brooks went with the Alaska Road Commission survey party to Rampart in 1906. He found out that thirty-three claims were worked that summer and that three hydraulic plants operated. He noted F. G. Manley's new Hot Springs to Eureka (Glen) road. The total gold output of the Rampart region for 1906 was estimated to be $270,000.

———. *Mineral Resources of Alaska: Report on Progress of Investigations in 1907*. U.S. Geological Survey Bulletin 345. Washington: Government Printing Office, 1908. Brooks summarized activity in Rampart in 1907, including the area that became the (Manley) Hot Springs district. He also mentioned the 1907 discovery in the Gold Hill (Fort Gibbon) region.

———. *Mineral Resources of Alaska: Report on Progress of Investigations in 1908*. U.S. Geological Survey Bulletin 379. Washington: Government Printing Office, 1909. Brooks reported that insufficient water in the summer of 1908 resulted in the closure of most mining in the Rampart district. Although low water limited operations in the Hot Springs district, miners continued to work along the gold belt between Sullivan Creek and Elephant Gulch.

————. *Mineral Resources of Alaska: Report on Progress of Investigations in 1909*. U.S. Geological Survey Bulletin 442. Washington: Government Printing Office, 1910. Brooks commented that there were instances of stream tin on Sullivan Creek and that there was mining on Mason and Grant creeks in the Gold Hill district.

————. *Mineral Resources of Alaska: Report on Progress of Investigations in 1910*. U.S. Geological Survey Bulletin 480. Washington: Government Printing Office, 1911. Brooks noted that some unimportant mining was going on in the Gold Hill district.

————. *Mineral Resources of Alaska: Report on Progress of Investigations in 1912*. U.S. Geological Survey Bulletin 542. Washington: Government Printing Office, 1913. Brooks noted that mining was continuing in the Indian River region. (Parts of that region were sometimes considered to be in the Koyukuk district, sometimes in the Fort Gibbon district.)

————. *Mineral Resources of Alaska: Report on Progress of Investigations in 1913*. U.S. Geological Survey Bulletin 592. Washington: Government Printing Office, 1914. Brooks wrote that the largest producers in the Hot Springs district were Sullivan, Patterson, and American creeks.

————. *Mineral Resources of Alaska: Report on Progress of Investigations in 1916*. U.S. Geological Survey Bulletin 662. Washington: Government Printing Office, 1918. Brooks reported that there was much stream tin in the Hot Springs district which had an output of $800,000 in gold in 1916. There had been new discoveries in Big and Little Boulder creeks.

————. *Mineral Resources of Alaska: Report on Progress of Investigations in 1921*. U.S. Geological Survey Bulletin 739. Washington: Government Printing Office, 1923. Brooks reported that mining in the Hot Springs district was on a small scale due to the high cost of operation.

————. *Mineral Resources of Alaska: Report on Progress of Investigations in 1922*. U.S. Geological Survey Bulletin 755. Washington: Government Printing Office, 1924. Brooks reported that production in the Hot Springs district, which had been declining since 1916, had increased, a fact he attributed somewhat to the construction of the Alaska Railroad which was expected to reduce costs of transporting mining supplies.

————. *Mineral Resources of Alaska: Report on Progress of Investigations in 1923*. U.S. Geological Survey Bulletin 773. Washington: Government Printing Office, 1925. Brooks acknowledged the service of the late George W. Ledger of Rampart and others who annually gave information to the geologists. Brooks also reported that the summer of 1923 had been an abnormally dry season.

Brooks, Alfred H., and George C. Martin. "The Alaskan Mining Industry in 1919." In *Mineral Resources of Alaska: Report on Progress of Investigations in 1919*, edited by Alfred H. Brooks, et al., 59-95. U.S. Geological Survey Bulletin 714. Washington: Government Printing Office, 1921. Brooks and Martin defined a placer as a gold deposit capable of being exploited at a profit. They reported that only twelve mines operated in the summer of 1919 in the Hot Springs district; seven in Rampart; and only five in Gold Hill/Indian River.

Buske, Frank E. "Rex Beach: A Frustrated Gold Seeker Lobbies to 'Win the Wilderness over to Order.'" *The Alaska Journal* 10.4 (Autumn 1980): 37–42. Buske synthesized Beach's pro-development, pro-mining position on Alaska. After Beach left Alaska, he retained a life-long interest in mining in Alaska.

Carey, Michael. "History Uncovered: Putting a Face to a Place on the Map." *Anchorage Daily News*, 9 May 1993. Carey reports on the search that John Graham of Baltimore is making to learn more about the activities of his grandfather, Herman Tofty, in Alaska from 1897 to 1908. The settlement of Tofty (originally Sullivan City) on Sullivan Creek was named for Herman Tofty.

Charlton, Cora Chase. "Was He Justified?" *Alaska-Yukon Magazine,* April 1909, 47–51. Charlton wrote a very short story about two characters named Hillyard and Bascom, which may have been a gibe at Frank G. Manley's real name. Charlton probably knew Manley, who, in 1909, was incarcerated in Texas.

Chapin, Theodore. "Mining in the Hot Springs District." In *Mineral Resources of Alaska: Report on Progress of Investigations* in 1917, edited by G[eorge] C. Martin, 331–35. U.S. Geological Survey Bulletin 692. Washington: Government Printing Office, 1919. Chapin reported that the gold production in the Hot Springs district dropped in 1917 because the firm of Cleveland & Howell stopped its operations on Woodchopper Creek. He discussed, in some detail, the presence of tin ore on Sullivan Creek.

Cobb, Edward. *Summary of References to Mineral Occurrences (other than Mineral Fuels and Construction Materials) in the Tanana Quadrangle, Alaska.* Open-File Report 77-432. Menlo Park, CA: U.S. Department of the Interior, Geological Survey, 1977. Cobb summarized information on each creek in the Tanana quadrangle, which encompasses the Rampart, Manley Hot Springs, and Melotzitna districts, from U.S. Geological Survey reports, 1898–1973.

———. *Summaries of Data on and Lists of References to Metállic and Selected Nonmetallic Mineral Occurrences in the Tanana Quadrangle, Alaska: Supplement to Open-File Report 77-432. Part A— Summaries of Data to June 1, 1981.* Open-File Report 81-1313A. U.S. Department of the Interior, Geological Survey, 1981. This report is similar to, but shorter than, Cobb's 1977 report. In it he summarized information on the creeks from past U.S. Geological Survey reports.

———. *Summaries of Data on and Lists of References to Metallic and Selected Nonmetallic Mineral Occurrences in the Tanana Quadrangle, Alaska: Supplement to Open-File Report 77-432. Part B— Lists of References to June 1, 1981.* Open-File Report 81-1313B. U.S. Department of the Interior, Geological Survey, 1981. Cobb itemizes references to the creeks in various U.S. Geological Survey reports.

Cochrane, Marjorie, ed. *Alaska's Past: Regional Perspectives.* Pilot test edition. The Alaska Historical Commission. Anchorage: The Alaska Historical Society, 1982. The book refers to the inspection trip along the Yukon River by Capt. Patrick Ray and Lt. Wilds P. Richardson, U.S Army, in 1897.

Cole, Terrence. *Crooked Past: The History of a Frontier Mining Camp: Fairbanks, Alaska.* Fairbanks: University of Alaska Press, 1991. Cole tells how E. T. Barnette formed the Yukon Miners Cooperative Association and purchased the Jesuit river steamer St. Michael to go up the Yukon in 1897. The steamer temporarily lost power at Rampart. The listing of association members is in the George P. MacGowan Collection.

Coleman, Jane. "Gamblin' Man." *Alaska Magazine,* May 1990, 43+. Coleman discusses Wyatt Earp in Alaska, from information derived from Josie Earp's book.

Collier, Arthur J. *Coal Resources of the Yukon.* U. S. Geological Survey Bulletin 218. Washington: Government Printing Office, 1903. In 1902, geologist Collier investigated coal resources on the Yukon. The oldest coal mine was the Drew (Pioneer) mine. There, only one coal seam out of seven seams had been exploited. The coal sold to steamers was not satisfactory. Collier's initial report on coal resources appears in Bulletin 213, 276–83.

———. "The Glenn Creek Gold Mining District, Alaska." In *Contributions to Economic Geology, 1902,* edited by S. F. Emmons and C. W. Hayes, 49–56. U.S. Geological Survey Bulletin 213. Washington: Government Printing Office, 1903. Collier reported on the Glen Gulch discovery on the northern edge of Baker Flats. He hypothesized that the lowland of Baker Flats was the bed of an extinct lake and the benches of Glen Gulch were once the beach of that lake. The gold was derived from a zone of mineralization.

Couch, Jim. "Tomorrow is for Hot Springs." *The Alaska Sportsman,* October 1956, 20+. Couch writes about early miners in the Hot Springs district, including John F. Karshner, Jim Dalton, Mike Laboski, and Frank Manley. He also discusses the history of Karshner's hot spring vegetable farm and Tom Woolard's fox farm.

Covert, C. C., and C. E. Ellsworth. "Water Supply of the Yukon-Tanana Region." In *Mineral Resources of Alaska: Report on Progress of Investigations* in 1908, edited by Alfred H. Brooks, et al., 201-28. U.S. Geological Survey Bulletin 379. Washington: Government Printing Office, 1909. Engineers Covert and Ellsworth reported on the construction of ditches in the Rampart and Hot Springs districts and discussed the potential for the development of hydroelectric power to solve the water-supply problem.

———. *Water-Supply Investigations in the Yukon-Tanana Region, Alaska, 1907 and 1908: Fairbanks, Circle, and Rampart Districts.* U.S. Geological Survey Water-Supply Paper 228. Washington: Government Printing Office, 1909. Covert and Ellsworth summarized data on water supply gathered during their work in the Yukon-Tanana region in 1907 and 1908. In particular, they stressed the issue of the development of water power for electric transmission.

Dart, Charles. Manley Collection. Alaska Archives, Alaska and Polar Regions Department, Elmer E. Rasmuson Library, University of Alaska Fairbanks. The collection mainly contains registration records for the Manley Hotel in Hot Springs, 1907–1911. There is a short record that seems to be an itemization of long overdue accounts, unpaid as of 31 May 1901, associated with a Rampart store.

Dart, Chuck, and Gladys Dart. *Chuck and Gladys Dart: Manley Hot Springs.* Edited by Yvonne Yarber and Curt Madison. Yukon-Koyukuk School District of Alaska series. Fairbanks: Spirit Mountain Press, 1983. In 1983, the Darts owned the hot springs homestead originally staked by John F. Karshner and subsequently leased to Manley. The Darts related the history of Manley Hot Springs as they knew it, including the death of Bill Strandberg, killed at his Tofty mine by a bear.

Davis, Edby. Collection. Alaska Archives, Alaska and Polar Regions Department, Elmer E. Rasmuson Library, University of Alaska Fairbanks. Davis wrote a letter to the editor, supporting the construction of the proposed Rampart Dam.

Dayo, Stanley. *Stanley Dayo: Manley Hot Springs.* Edited by Yvonne Yarber and Curt Madison. Yukon-

Koyukuk School District of Alaska series. Fairbanks: Spirit Mountain Press, 1985. Miner Dayo related his personal story, including his mining first in Rampart and later at Hot Springs. He also told what he knew about the history of mining in the Manley Hot Springs district.

District Recorder, Fairbanks. (Short, preferred title for State of Alaska Department of Natural Resources, Office of the Commissioner, District Recorder, Fairbanks.) The creek records in a "(folder)" are copies of documents held in the office of the State Recorder, Anchorage. Not all record books available for the three districts (sometimes termed "precincts") are inventoried in the following listing.

Dixon, Mim. "History—Rampart, Alaska." *In The Baan O Yeel Kon Corporation Shareholders Handbook*, 1–18. [Fairbanks]: Baan O Yeel Kon Corporation, 1980. (Cited with permission.) The history points out that Athabascan people moved through the Rampart area in the early days. John Minook discovered gold and lived in Minook Village. Early Native businesses included commercial fishing, woodchopping, and mail delivery. The history contains several pictures of Rampart people between the 1900s and 1920s.

Eakin, Henry M. "The Rampart and Hot Springs Regions." *In Mineral Resources of Alaska: Report on Progress of Investigations in 1911*, edited by Alfred H. Brooks, et al., 271–86. U.S. Geological Bulletin 520. Washington: Government Printing Office, 1912. Geologist Eakin reported on his geologic reconnaissance of the Rampart, Hot Springs, and Gold Hill (Gold Mountain) districts in 1911. He discussed the geology of the region, its water supply, the mining then in progress, and the existence of stream tin (cassiterite) in Sullivan Creek.

———. *A Geologic Reconnaissance of a Part of the Rampart Quadrangle, Alaska.* U.S. Geological Survey Bulletin 535. Washington: Government Printing Office, 1913. Eakin expanded upon his report of his 1911 trip included in Bulletin 520. He summarized previous investigations of the region which encompassed 12,000 square miles, and he included photographs, charts, and maps.

Earp, Josephine Sarah Marcus. *I Married Wyatt Earp: The Recollections of Josephine Sarah Marcus Earp.* Edited by Glenn G. Boyer. Tucson: The University of Arizona Press, 1976. Wyatt Earp's wife, Josie, related events of 1898–1899 in Rampart. The Earps rented Rex Beach's cabin which Beach may have purchased from Frank Canton.

Ellsworth, C. E. "Placer Mining in the Yukon-Tanana Region." *In Mineral Resources of Alaska: Report on Progress of Investigations in 1909,* edited by Alfred H. Brooks, et al., 230-50. U.S. Geological Survey Bulletin 442. Washington: Government Printing Office, 1910. Ellsworth stated that cheaper and more systematic methods than then used had to be developed in the Rampart district to reach ground too deep for open cut work and too susceptible to flooding if drifted.

———. "Water Supply of the Yukon-Tanana Region, 1909." *In Mineral Resources of Alaska: Report of Investigations in 1909,* edited by Alfred H. Brooks, et al., 251-82. U.S. Geological Survey Bulletin 442. Washington: Government Printing Office, 1910. Ellsworth examined the drainage systems in the Rampart area and reported on the measurements from gauging stations on various creeks. He recommended that Troublesome Creek might be the only creek in the area suitable for development as a source of hydroelectric power to Rampart mines.

Ellsworth, C. E., and R. W. Davenport. "Placer Mining in the Yukon-Tanana Region." *In Mineral Resources of Alaska: Report on Progress of Investigations in 1912*, edited by Alfred H. Brooks, et al., 203-22. U.S. Geological Survey Bulletin 542. Washington: Government Printing Office, 1913. Ellsworth and Davenport reported that mining in the Hot Springs district in 1912 took place mainly in the Patterson Creek and American Creek basins. Mining in Rampart continued as it was in 1911.

Ellsworth, C. E., and G. L. Parker. "Placer Mining in the Yukon-Tanana Region." *In Mineral Resources of Alaska: Report on Progress of Investigations in 1910*, edited by Alfred H. Brooks, et al., 153-72. U. S. Geological Survey Bulletin 480. Washington: Government Printing Office, 1911. Ellsworth and Parker reported that increased gold production from Sullivan country was offset by a decrease in production from the Baker Creek area. As a result, production in the Hot Springs district for 1910 matched that of 1911. In contrast, Rampart's 1910 production was less than one-half of its 1909 production.

————. "Water Supply of the Yukon-Tanana Region." *In Mineral Resources of Alaska: Report on Progress of Investigations in 1910*, edited by Alfred H. Brooks, et al., 173-217. U.S. Geological Survey Bulletin 480. Washington: Government Printing Office, 1911. Ellsworth and Parker commented that rainfall was very low in 1910. Precipitation at Rampart was one-half of the average since 1905.

Fairbanks Chamber of Commerce. Collection. Alaska Archives, Alaska and Polar Regions Department, Elmer E. Rasmuson Library, University of Alaska Fairbanks. Boxes 33 and 34 of the collection contain information on the proposed Rampart Dam, projected to be one of the largest dams for electric power in the world.

Fairbanks Daily News-Miner (and predecessors such as the *Fairbanks Evening News*), Fairbanks, Alaska. Microform. The News-Miner occasionally had items about the three districts. On 8 March 1933, it reported the death of Frank Stevens at his cabin in Manley Hot Springs. On 29 September 1938, it reported that Judge Harry E. Pratt, U.S. District Court, had transferred Troublesome and Quail creeks out of the Tolovana district and into the Rampart district.

Fairbanks Daily Times, Fairbanks, Alaska. M/F 88. The Daily Times had some items related to the activities in the three districts. For example, on 30 July 1906, the Times reported that Frank Manley had made a big investment at Baker Creek. Also, in various issues between 12 July and 6 September 1906, the Times reported extensively on the theft of Washington-Alaska Bank gold bricks from the steamers *Ida May* and *Tanana* as well as on the arrest and conviction of those involved. Feature writer Clara Wright had been editor of the *Rampart Whirlpool* in 1899.

Farnsworth, C[harles] S. Collection. Alaska Archives, Alaska and Polar Regions Department, Elmer E. Rasmuson Library, University of Alaska Fairbanks. Farnsworth, a career U.S. Army officer who rose to the rank of major general, served two tours at Fort Gibbon, specifically 1898–1899 and 1910–1911. Correspondence by and to him reveals the status of the Tanana and Rampart areas, not only during his stay at the post but also at other times.

Fitzhugh, Robert Hunter. Collection. Alaska Archives, Alaska and Polar Regions Department, Elmer E. Rasmuson Library, University of Alaska Fairbanks. Engineer Hunter Fitzhugh mined in Southeast Alaska and then moved to Rampart in 1898. His letters to his family in Kentucky disclose his activities in the Rampart area, including his survey of a trail from Rampart to Eureka in the spring of 1899. He died in a snowslide accident in November 1900.

Fort Gibbon District. Affidavit/Annual Labor. 1908–1952. The record book contains affidavits that claim owners had performed the necessary annual assessment work. Affidavits are from John Minook, Marvin Berry, Frank X Edgington, the Strandbergs, and others.

Fort Gibbon District. Deeds. 1908–1954. The book includes the transfer to other ownership of interests in early claims in the district as well as transactions involving the Berry claims on the Indian River in 1928.

Fort Gibbon District. Index to Mortgages of Real Estate. 1909–1916. There are relatively few entries in this index. Most refer to buildings in Tanana.

Fort Gibbon District. Leases/Liens. 1908–1952. The record has relatively few entries. There are lease agreements for claims on Grant, Indian, Mason, Golden, and other creeks.

Fort Gibbon District. Mining Locations. 1907–1908. The record contains locations of claims, many for 160 acres, on Moran, Golden, Hudson, Dome, Lancaster, Lynx, Grant, Mission, and other creeks.

Fort Gibbon District. Mining Locations. Vol. 1. 1908–1928. The volume contains several early (1908–1912) claims of 160 acres, claims of John Minook and associates, lode claims on Quartz Creek, F. G. Manley claims in the Red Mountain area in 1911 and 1927, the 1928 Berry claims on Indian Creek, and some early 1911 claims on Long Creek, south of Ruby.

Fort Gibbon District. [Mining] Locations. Vol. 2. 1928–1939. The record contains placer claims on Moraine, Grant, Lynx, Tozi, and other creeks and lode claims on Quartz Creek.

Fort Gibbon District. Mining Locations. Vol. 3. 1939-1958. The record contains claims on Black, Indian, Dick Hudson, and other creeks and post-war intention-to-hold notices.

Fort Gibbon District. Miscellaneous. 1908–1910. The book contains deeds, affidavits of assessment work, power of attorney agreements, mortgages, leases, location of homesteads, and grubstake agreements.

Fort Gibbon District. Miscellaneous Records. 1908–1952. The book contains a marshal's attachment, sales of town lots, marriage certificates, townsite of Wickersham vote, quit claims, grubstake agreements, homesteads, mining leases, disincorporation of Tanana, and missing person reports.

Fort Gibbon District. [Miscellaneous]. c. 1950–1954. This undesignated book has only a few entries, including the lease by Grace Fisher of her holdings on Grant Creek to Lars Indergaard, Frank C. Edgington, and George Rosander.

Fort Gibbon District. [Miscellaneous]. [Vol. 1]. 1 November 1960–30 September 1965. The book contains several affidavits of annual labor for the Indian River area as well as some deeds and records of placer and lode claims.

Fort Gibbon District. [Miscellaneous]. Vol. 2. 1 October 1965–19 May 1972. The book records locations, quit claims, and powers of attorney.

Fort Gibbon District. [Miscellaneous]. Vol. 3. 19 May 1972–22 October 1973. The record contains lode claims on Quartz Creek, relocations, and affidavits of assessment work performed.

Fort Gibbon District. [Miscellaneous]. Vol. 4. 22 October 1973–28 May 1975. The record contains affidavits of labor and certificates of locations.

Fort Gibbon District. Power of Attorney. 1908-1939. The book records powers of attorney, including several for Berry claims.

Godbey, W. G. "A Visit to Manley Hot Springs." *Alaska Sportsman,* May 1965, 11–14. Godbey described his visit to Manley Hot Springs and to the deserted Woodchopper settlement. He mentioned talking with miner and postmaster Gus Benson who had arrived in Hot Spings in 1926. He related some of the personal history of Adolph Bock, "the Flying Dutchman," who hit rich pay on the Bock Fraction in Tofty.

Hanson, Douglas. *Forest Resources: Rampart Village/Yukon River Watershed, Alaska, 1984.* Fairbanks: Tanana Chiefs Conference, Inc., 1984. Hanson headed a team that inventoried forest resources on certain Native lands selected by the Baan O Yeel Kon Corporation, Rampart.

————. *Forest Resources: Manley Hot Springs Village/Tanana River Watershed, Alaska,* 1985. Fairbanks: Tanana Chiefs Conference, Inc. 1985. The Forestry Department, Tanana Chiefs Conference, conducted a forest inventory for the village council and village corporation of Manley Hot Springs.

Hanson, Douglas, William E. Putnam, and Roselynn Resa Smith. *Forest Resources of Doyon, Ltd., Lands: Rampart/Tanana Units, Alaska, 1988.* Fairbanks: Tanana Chiefs Conference, Inc., 1988. The Forestry Department, Tanana Chiefs Conference, collected forest resource data on the regional corporation lands of Doyon, Limited, near Rampart and Tanana.

Heiner, Virginia Doyle. *Alaska Mining History: A Source Document.* University of Alaska Museum History and Archaeology Series No. 17. Anchorage: Office of History and Archaeology, 1977. Heiner identifies sources for place names associated with mining history, including settlements in the Rampart, Manley Hot Springs, and Fort Gibbon districts.

Heller, Herbert. Collection. Alaska Archives, Alaska and Polar Regions Department, Elmer E. Rasmuson Library, University of Alaska Fairbanks. Heller's uncle, R. Lynn Smith—miner, jeweler, fur-trader, and, finally, marshal—arrived in Rampart in 1898. He later lived in Chena, Hot Springs, and Ruby, before settling in Fairbanks. His correspondence to relatives provides an in-depth insight into mining and other activities in Interior Alaska for over a quarter century.

Hess, Frank L[ee]. "Placers of the Rampart Region." *In The Fairbanks and Rampart Quadrangle, Yukon-Tanana Region,* Alaska, edited by L. M. Pringle, 64–98. U.S. Geological Survey Bulletin 337. Washington: Government Printing Office, 1908. Hess studied placers in Rampart for ten days in September 1904 and initially reported his findings in Bulletin 280. His party visited every working claim except claims on Gunnison Creek. By 1904, claims were in three general groups, specifically Minook Creek, Baker Creek, and Troublesome Creek. The revised report discusses the region, creek by creek, and adds some 1907 information.

————. "Tin Resources of Alaska." *In Mineral Resources of Alaska: Report on Progress of Investigations in 1911,* edited by Alfred H. Brooks, et al., 89-92. U.S. Geological Survey Bulletin 520. Washington: Government Printing Office, 1912. Hess discussed the cassiterite ore in Sullivan Creek and noted that the miners threw away most stream tin. Joseph Eglar, however, had netted $209 from tin ore he shipped out in 1911.

Hook, Joanne. "He Never Returned: Robert Hunter Fitzhugh in Alaska." *The Alaska Journal 15*, no. 2 (Spring 1985): 33–38. Hook summarizes information from the Robert Hunter Fitzhugh Collection. Fitzhugh reached Rampart in 1898 and mined on Hoosier and Slate creeks. He died in a snowslide on 4 November 1900.

Holdsworth, Phil R. *Report of the Commisioner of Mines for the Biennium Ended December 31, 1952.* [Juneau]: Territory of Alaska, Department of Mines, [1953]. Mining operations were limited in the three districts. Holdsworth listed nineteen operators; not all operated in both 1951 and 1952.

———. *Report of the Commissioner of Mines for the Biennium Ended December 31, 1954.* [Juneau]: Territory of Alaska, Department of Mines, 1955. Holdsworth commented that there was no more antimony production because there were no buyers. He noted a large asbestos deposit near Rampart. He listed thirteen placer mine operators active within the three districts.

———. *Report of the Commissioner of Mines for the Biennium Ended December 31, 1956.* [Juneau]: Territory of Alaska, Department of Mines, 1957. Holdsworth again reported the presence of an asbestos deposit above Rampart and listed a total of about fifteen placer operators in the three districts.

Hot Springs Echo, [Manley] Hot Springs, Alaska. Weekly newspaper, published mostly on Saturdays but sometimes on Sundays, Mondays, Tuesdays, or Thursdays, 31 August 1907–8 June 1913. M/F 677. Not all copies are extant. *The Echo,* edited by George Hinton Henry, concentrated more on world and national issues than on local news. Much of the local information consisted of one sentence, reporting an individual visiting or leaving Hot Springs. Some editorials severely criticized commissioners Bathurst, Gallaher, Bevington, and Olsen.

Hot Springs Echo and *Tanana Citizen,* [Manley] Hot Springs, Alaska. Weekly newspaper, published Saturdays, 20 July 1907–17 August 1907. M/F 677. It became the *Hot Springs Echo* on 31 August 1907. In the 3 August 1907 issue, the editor praised William B. Ballou for his work as commissioner for the Rampart district.

Hot Springs Post, [Manley] Hot Springs, Alaska. Weekly newspaper, published briefly on Thursdays and then on Saturdays, 1 October 1908–15 May 1909. M/F 964. Not all copies are extant. The Post, published by Arbuckle A. Ward, commented extensively on the activities in the town of Hot Springs and on the creeks in the district. On 1 October 1908, the *Post* reported that Herman Tofty, a popular sourdough of 1897, had left to visit his eighty-two-year-old father in Watertown, SD. It was Tofty's first visit to the states in eleven years. The issue of 29 October 1908 stated that Commissioner V. L. Bevington had almost completed transferring records for old books to a creek index.

Hunt, William R. "Deadly Frank Canton." *The Alaska Journal. 1986.* History and Arts of the North 16. Edited by Terrence Cole, 244–49. Hunt discusses Frank M. Canton, whose real name was Joe Horner. Canton was the first officially appointed law officer to serve in Interior Alaska. He spent time at Rampart in 1897 and 1898 before taking up his deputy marshal position in Circle City. Because of suspicion about some of his activities as a peace officer in Oklahoma, he soon lost his Alaska job.

———. *Distant Justice: Policing the Alaskan Frontier.* Norman: University of Oklahoma Press, 1987. Hunt recounts episodes of lawlessness in Alaska's early days. He notes the appointment of Frank

M. Canton as the first U.S. deputy marshal on the Yukon. He also relates the murder case of Dan Carolan from court records of Carolan's trial.

———. "Judge Ballou of Rampart." *The Alaska Journal 2*, no. 1 (Winter 1972): 41–47. Hunt details information from the William B. Ballou Collection.

Johnson, James Albert. Carmack of the Klondike. Fairbanks: Epicenter Press, 1990. Johnson recounts the biography of George Washington Carmack who discovered gold in the Klondike on 17 August 1896. His discovery precipitated the stampede to the Klondike.

Judkins, Perry. Collection. Alaska Archives, Alaska and Polar Regions Department, Elmer E. Rasmuson Library, University of Alaska Fairbanks. From 1897 to mid-1901, Judkins wrote to his sweetheart, Alice Weston, in Mariposa County, California, about his travels and his life as a miner around Rampart and at the Pioneer coal mine. The collection includes a copy of the January 1899 issue of The Rampart Whirlpool.

Kerr, Sara. "Mrs. Katherine Boucher Recalls Alaskan Gold Rush Days in 1900s." *Fallon County Times,* Baker, MT, 8 December 1966. A reporter interviewed Mrs. (Catherine/Katie Wiehl) Boucher who, with her sister (Elizabeth), their brother (John), and an uncle (S. F. Wiehl) joined another uncle (Joe Wiehl) in Rampart in the early 1900s. She and her sister operated a restaurant there. She left Alaska in 1908, the spring after she married Horace Boucher.

Ketzler, Al "Bear," Jr. "What Happened to Percy Herbert?" *The Council,* March 1991, 8. Percy Herbert of Fort Yukon, an outspoken opponent of the proposed Rampart Dam, disappeared in February 1964 in Fairbanks where he was attending meetings on the dam project. The mystery was never solved, and Herbert's permanent disappearance remains linked to his stand against the dam.

Killeen, P. L., and M. G. White. "Chapter B–Grant Creek Area." *In Reconnaisance for Radioactive Deposits in Eastern Interior Alaska, 1946,* edited by Helmuth Wedow, Jr., P. L. Killeen, et al., 33–36. Geological Survey Circular 331. Washington, D.C.: Geological Survey, 1954. In August 1946, geologists Killeen and White investigated on-site a report of pitchblende near the placer mining property of the late Walter Fisher on Grant Creek. The geologists hypothesized that the report was incorrect and that the presumed pitchblende material had been fragments of black hematite. The chapter contains a good map of the Fisher holdings on Grant Creek.

Kitchener, L. D. *Flag over the North: The Story of the Northern Commercial Company.* Seattle: Superior Publishing Company, 1954. The book chronicles the story of the Alaska Commercial/Northern Commercial Company, which considered itself a direct descendant of the Russian fur trading stations in Alaska in the 1760s. Volney Richmond, who was with the company for over fifty-four years and its president for about thirty-two of those years, arrived in Rampart in 1898. He brought six friends with him, including Frank Stevens who spent the rest of his life in the area. The book also reports on the prospecting expedition above Tanana by Edward Schieffelin of Tombstone, Arizona.

L'Ecuyer, Rosalie E. *Ruby-Poorman Mining District, Ruby Quadrangle, Alaska.* BLM-Alaska Open File Report 49. Anchorage: Bureau of Land Management, U.S. Department of the Interior, 1993. The public history surveys developments in the Ruby-Poorman mining district from 1907 to the present. Some of the miners who originally prospected in Rampart and Hot Springs later prospected in the Ruby district.

MacGowan, George P. Collection. Alaska Archives, Alaska and Polar Regions Department, Elmer E. Rasmuson Library, University of Alaska Fairbanks. MacGowan served as purser for E. T. Barnette aboard the river steamer St. Michael in August 1897. He and several of the other passengers got off at Rampart where he prospected for a year and kept a detailed diary of events.

Maddren, A[lfred]. G[eddes]. "Placers of the Gold Hill District." *In Mineral Resources of Alasks: Report on Progress of Investigations in 1908,* edited by Alfred H. Brooks, et al., 234-37. U.S. Geological Survey Bulletin 379. Washington: Government Printing Office, 1909. Geologist Maddren examined the new Gold Hill district. He noted a mountain divide that naturally separated the district into two sections. In one section, the creeks ran southward into the Yukon; in the other, creeks ran northward into the Melozitna. He also saw the ruins of an old lode mine, dating from 1890.

———. "Placers of the Gold Hill District." *In The Innoko Gold-Placer District, Alaska, with Accounts of the Central Kuskokwim Valley and the Ruby Creek and Gold Hill Placers,* edited by A. G. Maddren, 80-83. U.S. Geological Survey Bulletin 410. Washington: Government Printing Office, 1910. Maddren's report on the Gold Hill placers stemmed from his 1908 trip there. The report reiterated the information reported in Bulletin 379. It added maps of the region and comments on the nugget gold in Grant Creek and the birdshot pellets of gold in Mason Creek.

Madison, Curt. *Bedrock Pay* (video in production). The video, sponsored by current miners of the Manley Hot Springs district, portrays some of the district's history and contains interviews of long-time miners of the district.

Main Trails and Bypaths." *Alaska Sportsman,* June 1965, 7. The editorial encouraged readers of the Alaska Sportsman to write their congressmen in opposition to the proposed Rampart Dam. The magazine held that the dam would destroy too many natural resources, particularly fish and game

Maloney, William. *Report of the Territorial Mine Inspector to the Governor of Alaska for the Year 1915.* Juneau: [Territory of Alaska], 1916. Inspector Maloney visited Hot Springs in January 1915 when little mining was underway. He reported a small production of stream tin as a byproduct of gold production.

———. *Report of William Maloney, Territorial Mine Inspector, to the Governor of Alaska for the Year 1917.* Juneau: [Territory of Alaska], 1918. Maloney noted a decrease in gold production in the Hot Springs district in 1917 as compared with production in 1916. He listed the operators in the district.

Manley Hot Springs District. Annual Labor. Vol. 1. 21 August 1908–28 December 1918. The book contains affidavits of assessment work by J. J.Cooney, Lynn Smith, Henry Papin, Manley & Chute, Curry & Aitken, Cleveland & Howell, and others.

Manley Hot Springs District. Deeds. Vol. 1. 25 April 1901–6 May 1908. The book records several transactions connected with Glen Gulch, including the controversial Ella R. Garratt claim, No. 4 above, and the Eagle Mining Company partnership.

Manley Hot Springs District. Deeds. Vol. 2. 8 May 1908–29 February 1912. The book contains several transfers of part interests in claims, particularly in the Sullivan Creek country.

Manley Hot Springs District. Leases. Vol. 1. 7 October 1907–6 May 1958. The book contains the leases of early claims on Sullivan Creek, Frank G. Manley's lease of J. F. Karshner's homestead, and several Cleveland and Howell leases.

Manley Hot Springs District. Locations. Vol. 1. 1 May 1899–10 November 1909 (actually 18 February 1902). The volume contains extracts of creek records, copied in 1909, including the records of Eureka, Pioneer, Boston, Florida, Rhode Island and New York creeks, Excelsior Bar, and parts of Rampart records pertaining to the Hot Springs district. The records date between May 1899 and 18 February 1902.

Manley Hot Springs District. Locations. Vol. 3. 28 August 1904–7 September 1912. The record book contains several 160-acre claims in which either F. G. Manley or H. B. Knowles was a member of the association. It also includes Michael J. Sullivan's Discovery claim on Sullivan Creek.

Manley Hot Springs District. Mortgages. Vol. 1. 27 July 1903–18 May 1965. The book contains mortgages wherein miners put up their claims on Glen Gulch, What Cheer Bar, and on Thanksgiving and other creeks as security for loans. It includes the transaction by the American Creek Dredging Company with the First National Bank of Fairbanks in November 1926.

Martin, G[eorge] C., et al. *Mineral Resources of Alaska: Report on Progress of Investigations in 1917.* U.S. Geological Survey Bulletin 692. Washington: Government Printing Office, 1919. Martin reported on tin in old tailings and unworked ground in Sullivan Creek. Additionally, he pointed out that there were thirty mines operating in the Hot Springs district in the summer of 1917; ten, in Rampart; and there was no production in the Gold Mountain district.

————. *The Alaskan Mining Industry in 1918.* U.S. Geological Survey Bulletin 712-A. Washington: Government Printing Office, 1919. According to Martin, an estimated forty-four tons of tin concentrate had been recovered from old tailings and dumps in the Hot Springs district. Most mining in 1918 had been suspended because of the wartime shortage of labor and high operational costs.

Mertie, J. B., Jr. *"Mineral Deposits of the Rampart and Hot Springs Districts." In Mineral Resources of Alaska: Report on Progress of Investigations in 1931,* edited by Philip S. Smith, et al., 163-226. U.S. Geological Survey Bulletin 844. Washington: Government Printing Office, 1934. Mertie provides a very comprehensive geological review of the Rampart and Hot Springs districts, based on earlier U.S.G.S. reports and on his own trip to the districts in 1931.

Moffit, F. H., et al. *Mineral Resources of Alaska: Report on Progress of Investigations in 1925.* U.S. Geological Survey Bulletin 792. Washington: Government Printing Office, 1927. Moffit noted that a shortage of water reduced mining activity in the Hot Springs and Rampart districts in 1925.

Morey, Lois M. Collection. Alaska Archives, Alaska and Polar Regions Department, Elmer E. Rasmuson Library, University of Alaska Fairbanks. The collection contains letters regarding the Tofty school district in the 1920s. At the time, a teacher earned $175 per month.

Moxham, Robert M. *Reconnaisance for Radioactive Deposits in the Manley Hot Springs–Rampart District, East-Central Alaska, 1948.* Geological Survey Circular 317. Washington, D.C.: Geological Survey, 1954. Moxham reported the results of his 1948 survey for radioactive material in the Tofty tin belt, the Hot Springs Dome, the Eureka area, and in Rampart. He uncovered nothing which would suggest there was any radioactive material sufficient for commercial production.

Orth, Donald J. *Dictionary of Alaska Place Names.* U.S. Geological Survey Professional Paper 567. Washington: U.S. Government Printing Office, 1967. Orth listed most, but not all, of the creeks and settlements associated with the Rampart, Manley Hot Springs, and Fort Gibbon districts.

Polk's Alaska-Yukon Gazetteer. 1901–1935. The annual gazetteer series lists residents of Rampart, Hot Springs, and Tanana. Although the names are often misspelled and not all residents are included, the listings are still somewhat useful as a general guide to the people and businesses in the mining communities.

Prindle, L[ouis]. M[arcus]. "Yukon Placer Fields." *In Report on Progress of Investigations of Mineral Resources in Alaska in 1905*, edited by Alfred H. Brooks, et al., 109–27. U.S. Geological Survey Bulletin 284. Washington: Government Printing Office, 1906. Prindle reported on the extension of ditches to the benches of Eureka Creek and the installation of hydraulic plants on Minook, Ruby, and Hoosier creeks. He thought little was accomplished in hydraulicking because of a lack of experienced management.

———. *The Fairbanks and Rampart Quadrangles, Yukon-Tanana Region, Alaska. U.S. Geological Survey Bulletin 337. Washington: Government Printing Office, 1908.* Prindle summarized the results of geologic surveys between 1904 and 1907. He was aware of the loss of timber in the valley of the [Big] Minook Creek as a result of mining operations but estimated that sufficient birch and alder for fuel remained around Hot Springs. He showed interest in the deposits of the high bench of Minook Creek (Idaho Bar).

———. "Occurrences of Gold in the Yukon-Tanana Region." *In Mineral Resources of Alaska: Report on Progress of Investigations in 1907*, edited by Alfred H. Brooks, et al., 179-86. U.S. Geological Survey Bulletin 345. Washington: Government Printing Office, 1908. Prindle reported on the remnants of old valley deposits in the bench gravels 500 feet high in the Rampart district. He also discussed the existence of several hot springs, which he considered a factor in the mineralization of the region.

Prindle, L. M., and Frank L. Hess. "Rampart Placer Region." *In Report on Progress of Investigations of Mineral Resources of Alaska in 1904*, edited by Alfred H. Brooks, et al., 104–19. U.S. Geological Survey Bulletin 259. Washington: Government Printing Office, 1905. Prindle and Hess gave a comprehensive report of the Rampart region, including the Glenn Creek (Glen Gulch) area. They commented on each creek, indicating the creeks mined for years were largely worked out. They noted that the cost of production was often 50 percent of output and that installation of hydraulic equipment in Rampart required much more funding than similar operations in the states. Other reports on the same trip are in Bulletins 280 and 337.

———. *The Rampart Gold Placer Region, Alaska.* U.S. Geological Survey Bulletin 280. Washington: Government Printing Office, 1906. This report, based on the Prindle and Hess trip to Rampart in 1904, discussed the route from Cleary Creek across the White Mountains and the drainage systems of the Tolovana River and Beaver, Hess, Minook, and Baker creeks. It noted that the area had closely folded sedimentary rocks, mostly from the Devonian age.

Purington, Chester Wells. "Methods and Costs of Gravel and Placer Mining in Alaska." *In Report on Progress of Investigations of Mineral Resources of Alaska in 1904,* edited by Alfred H. Brooks et al., 32-46. U.S. Geological Survey Bulletin 259. Washington: Government Printing Office, 1905. Purington cited geologic evidence that bench deposits probably occurred in the region between Fairbanks and Rampart. Gravel could be moved on natural grading. Small amounts of gold could be produced by hydraulic methods.

The Rampart Miner, Rampart, Alaska. Weekly newspaper, published Tuesdays, 17 September 1901–19 August 1902. M/F 142. Not all copies are extant. *The Miner,* edited by W. R. Edwards, reported on the events in Rampart and on the creeks. For example, the issue of 11 February 1902, reported that John Minook and son, Sinook, were working a lay on 13 above, Hoosier Creek, and that John had found a $50 nugget the previous week. The issue of 19 August 1902 related that Walbridge, Tofty, Foley, and Carlo were expected down on a scow loaded with lumber from Eagle for a new jail and courthouse.

The Rampart Whirlpool (two copies available). Rampart, Alaska. A monthly newspaper published in 1899 by Mrs. C[lara] E. Wright. The first issue, presumably 15 January 1899, is filed in the Perry Judkins Collection. The issue of [15] April 1899 is filed in the William B. Ballou Collection. Both collections are in the Alaska Archives, Alaska and Polar Regions Department, Elmer E. Rasmuson Library, University of Alaska Fairbanks. The January issue reported on the early strike on Little Minook Creek and the return of the lost Folger party. It alluded to the Bear Creek scam. The April issue referred to the Boston boys who struck Eureka, Pioneer, and Boston creeks in what is now the Manley Hot Springs district. Editor Wright later wrote for the *Fairbanks Times.*

Reed, Irving McK. Collection. Alaska Archives, Elmer E. Rasmuson Library, University of Alaska Fairbanks. Surveyor Reed surveyed claims for patent applications and did some mining inspections in the Alaska Interior in the 1930s. He also co-owned with Capt. A. S. Crane the Big Minook Mining Corporation in Rampart in 1939–1940. Their operation failed.

Rex Beach, Author, Ends his Life at 72." *New York Times,* 8 December 1949. Microform. The article reported the suicide of Rex Beach in Sebring, Florida, on 7 December 1949. Beach had suffered from incurable cancer of the throat for three years.

Ricks, Mel. "Rex Ellingwood Beach: The Man With the Golden Pen." *Northern Lights 1,* no. 1 (November 1966): 23+. Ricks detailed the life and works of Rex Beach, including information on Beach's time in Rampart. He did not indentify his sources.

Saarela, Leo H. *Report of the Commissioner of Mines for the Biennium Ended December 31, 1950.* Juneau: Territory of Alaska, Department of Mines, [1951]. Saarela listed twenty-two operators within the three districts.

Satterfield, Archie. He Sold the Klondike: Seattle's First Huckster." *Seattle Times Magazine,* 2 January 1972. Satterfield suggests that Erastus Brainerd invented the gold rush. As the energetic secretary of Seattle's Bureau of Information, Brainerd encouraged people to outfit for Alaska in Seattle. Seattle business profitted, and Seattle's population increased. Seattle became the chief gold rush port. Brainerd died insane in a mental institution.

Seattle Post-Intelligencer, Seattle, Washington. Microform. In the summer of 1897, the newspaper listed the names of ship passengers, departing from Seattle for Alaska and the Klondike. Many passengers entering Alaska from St. Michael by way of river steamer up the Yukon River eventually stopped at Rampart. For example, the issue of 5 August 1897 reported on passengers who would sail on the Cleveland at noon that day. The long list included J. L. Muldowney, E. T. Barnett (sic), Adolph Bock, George B. MacGowan, F. M. Canton, and about twenty others associated with Rampart.

Sims, Virginia Crowe. "But His Name Wasn't Manley." *Alaska Sportsman,* May 1965, 14+. Sims recounts the personal story of Frank G. Manley or Hilliard B. Knowles (Hillyard Bascom Knowles) and describes the hotel he built in [Manley] Hot Springs in 1907.

Smith, Howard. *Cultural Resource Review Record.* [Fairbanks]: Bureau of Land Management, Kobuk District, 1994. The review assesses plans to conduct gold placer mining in 1994 near the site of the old Cleary Hill camp in the Tofty area of the Manley Hot Springs district. It looks at recent and historical past mining activities in and around the historic city of Tofty and concludes that the Cleary Hill camp site does not meet criteria for inclusion in the National Register of Historic Places, although the original historic Tofty site might.

Smith, Philip S. *Fineness of Gold from Alaska's Placers.* U.S. Geological Survey Bulletin 910-C. Washington: Government Printing Office, 1941. Smith reported on the fineness of gold in the Gold Hill (Fort Gibbon), Hot Springs, and Rampart districts.

——. *Mineral Industry of Alaska in 1928 and Administrative Report.* U.S. Geological Survey Bulletin 813-A. Washington: Government Printing Office, 1930. Smith wrote that the dredge of the American Creek Dredging Company on American Creek in the Hot Springs district began operations too late in the season of 1928 to be effective.

——. *Mineral Industry of Alaska in 1929 and Administrative Report.* U.S. Geological Survey Bulletin 824-A. Washington: Government Printing Office, 1930. Smith reported that a management controversy over the dredge on American Creek hampered operations there. He added that an English company had drilled extensively on Sullivan Creek. At the time, Rampart operations were small, and there was some prospecting in the Gold Hill district.

——. *Mineral Industry of Alaska in 1931 and Administrative Report.* U.S. Geological Survey Bulletin 844-A. Washington: Government Printing Office, 1933. Smith wrote that two-thirds of the gold production in the Hot Springs district was from hydraulic and open-cut mining. The dredge on American Creek had only operated a few hours. Only eight to ten small camps operated in Rampart. Some prospecting was going on in the Gold Hill district.

——. *Mineral Industry of Alaska in 1932.* U.S. Geological Survey Bulletin 857-A. Washington: Government Printing Office, 1934. Smith stated that more than two-thirds of the gold recovered in the Hot Springs district was from dredging, hydraulicking, and open-cut methods. The Rampart district had eight camps. There was only a little prospecting going on in 1932 on Mason Creek in the Gold Hill district.

——. *Past Placer-Gold Production from Alaska.* U.S. Geological Survey Bulletin 857-B. Washington: Government Printing Office, 1933. Smith listed estimated production figures from the districts in Alaska from 1880 to 1930. Out of forty-one districts, Hot Springs ranked sixth in total production; Rampart, twentieth; and Gold Hill, last.

————. *Mineral Industry of Alaska in 1933.* U.S. Geological Survey Bulletin 864-A. Washington: Government Printing Office, 1934. Smith indicated that the Hot Springs district had its lowest production total in years, but he anticipated an increase of prospecting since gold prices had risen. Production in Rampart was low; in Gold Hill, negligible.

————. *Mineral Industry of Alaska in 1935.* U. S. Geological Survey Bulletin 880-A. Washington: Government Printing Office, 1937. Smith saw a noticeable increase in production in the Hot Springs district attributable to the operation of the dredge of the American Creek Operating Company. At the same time, Rampart production was low, only a few hundred dollars per mine.

————. *Mineral Industry of Alaska in 1936.* U.S. Geological Survey Bulletin 897-A. Washington: Government Printing Office, 1938. Smith reported on the activities of the dredge of the American Creek Operating Company and the Cleary Hill Mines Company in the Hot Springs district and on the revival of mining activity on Grant Creek in the Fort Gibbon district.

————. *Mineral Industry of Alaska in 1937.* U.S. Geological Survey Bulletin 910-A. Washington: Government Printing Office, 1939. Smith reported that production in 1937 in the Hot Springs district decreased while it increased in Rampart, Fort Gibbon, and other districts in the Yukon region.

————. "Mineral Industry of Alaska in 1938." *In Mineral Resources of Alaska: Report on Progress of Investigations in 1938,* edited by Philip S. Smith, Fred H. Moffit, and J. B. Mertie, Jr., 1-106. U.S. Geological Survey Bulletin 917. Washington: Government Printing Office, 1942. Smith stated that the federal government's policy of making loans to mining operations through the Reconstruction Finance Corporation had resulted in improved production, making the repayment of the loans likely.

————. Mineral Industry of Alaska in 1939. U.S. Geological Survey Bulletin 926-A. Washington: Government Printing Office, 1941. Smith noted a contrast in water supply in the Interior. Fairbanks reported a water shortage; Rampart, too much water. In the Hot Springs district, the dredge on American Creek and the Cleary Hill Mines Company were the largest producers.

————. *Mineral Industry of Alaska in 1940.* U.S. Geological Survey Bulletin 933-A. Washington: Government Printing Office, 1942. Smith noted that the dredge had completed mining of all land owned or leased by the American Creek Operating Company. Further, the summer of 1940 had little rainfall so some mining operations ceased.

Smith, Philip S., et al. *Mineral Resources of Alaska: Report on Progress of Investigations in 1924.* U.S. Geological Survey Bulletin 783. Washington: Government Printing Office, 1926. Smith reported an increase in production in the Hot Springs district in 1924 over that of 1923.

————. *Mineral Resources of Alaska: Report on Progress of Investigations in 1926.* U.S. Geological Survey Bulletin 797. Washington: Government Printing Office, 1929. Smith reported on activities on Woodchopper Creek and in the Eureka Creek area of the Hot Springs district.

————. *Mineral Resources of Alaska: Report on Progress of Investigations in 1927.* U.S. Geological Survey Bulletin 810. Washington: Government Printing Office, 1930. Smith reported that the American Creek Dredging Company had begun to operate its dredge on American Creek in the Hot Springs district. The mines in Rampart produced very little, the value of the output being no more than a few hundred or a few thousand dollars. There was no activity in the Gold Hill district.

————. *Mineral Resources of Alaska: Report on Progress of Investigations in 1930.* U.S. Geological Survey Bulletin 836. Washington: Government Printing Office, 1933. Smith reported that fiscal problems had resulted in the suspension of dredge operations on American Creek. There was activity in the Tofty and Eureka areas of the Hot Springs district. Operations in Rampart were small. Some prospecting was going on in the Gold Hill district.

Rampart District. Allan Creek (folder). 14 April 1899–27 November 1899. The folder contains the minutes of the miners' meeting of 15 April 1899. Peter Allan located No. 3 above on 14 April 1899. The creek was considered to be in the Tanana district (now Manley Hot Springs).

Rampart District. Arroyo Grande (folder). 4 October–5 November 1898. The folder contains the rules of 4 October 1898 and a listing of claimholders, few of whom are readily identifiable. Arroyo Grande is associated with Bear Creek.

Rampart District. Record of Beare Creek (folder). 28 August 1898–4 November 1898. The record contains the Bear Creek bylaws and listing of claimholders, only a few of whom are readily identifiable. J. H. Paget held the Discovery claim. Letters from Lynn Smith in the Herbert Heller Collection disclose that Paget salted the creek.

Rampart District. Big Minook Creek (four folders). 16 November 1897–23 October 1899. The record contains the locations and sales of claims on Big Minook. The claims numbered at least to No. 130 above. The creek miners organized on 16 November 1897. On 20 December 1897, the Klondyke Gold Mining and Transportation Company offered the earliest claimholders 800,000 shares of stock for their claims.

Rampart District. Big Minook Creek (folder). Vol. 2. 9 August 1899–26 December 1900. The record continues the series on Big Minook claims. It includes transfers, sales, and relocations.

Rampart District. Bylaws of Rampart Mining District: Little Minook and Hunter Creek Bylaws (folder). The bylaws, originally passed on 20 April 1896, specify that no claim should exceed 1,000 feet and that no Indian except John Minook should hold a claim. The record also contains minutes of several miners meetings between 24 May 1898 and 20 November 1900.

Rampart District. Chapman Creek (folder). 25 September 1897–26 May 1900. The folder records the creek bylaws, bylaw revisions, and early claimholders. John Folger and Michael Doud shared the Discovery claim; Ernest Chapman held No. 1 above. B. S. Goodhue served as recorder.

Rampart District. Deeds and Power of Attorney. Vol. 1. 1900–1901. The records detail deeds, lays (leases), and powers of attorney between September 1900 and 27 June 1901.

Rampart District. Deeds. Vol. 2. 1901. The records continue deeds, lays, quit claims, and powers of attorney in 1901. Indentures include Erastus Brainerd's purchase of claims on Idaho Bar.

Rampart District. Fee Book 2. December 1900–July 1902 and 28 March through 24 May 1905. The book itemizes fees paid to the recorder during the period. It can be used to crosscheck recording actions. An example is E. M. Carr's payment for a certified abstract title to No. 8 above, Little Minook, on 23 November 1901.

Rampart District. Fee Book 3. 1 July 1902–3 January 1908. The book continues the listing of fees paid. It includes fees for records apparently no longer available, as for instance, for Judge Wickersham's Discovery claim, Chitsiak, filed on 14 July 1903.

Rampart District. Garnet Creek (folder). 31 August 1898–11 September 1900. The name of the creek, which had been Stephens Creek, was changed to Garnet on 31 August 1898. B. W. Moore, Jr. located Discovery on 1 September 1898. The record includes a few relocations for Rock Creek on 2 January 1900.

Rampart District. General Index. 1913–1929. This index has entries and loose papers for dates outside the dates associated with its title as entries to 4 April 1939, and February 1942–15 July 1942, 18 September 1946, and a few city treasurer accounts for 1898. It lists filing fees, mining locations, assessments, trappers' licenses, marriages, births, and deaths.

Rampart District. General Index. 1915–1918. This index is an alphabetical grouping of the names of persons who paid recorder's fees. The names appear under the first letter of the last name, listed as they paid.

Rampart District. Gunnison Creek and Tributaries (folder). No pagination. The record simply indexes claims beginning with Discovery, filed by J. H. Kelly on 27 August 1898. It also has undated by-laws for Hoosier Creek.

Rampart District. Idaho Bar (folder). [Vol. 1]. 4 May 1898–28 August 1898. This book is a copy of the original record (now unavailable), prepared at the request of Erastus Brainerd. It includes the minutes of the miners' meeting of 4 May 1898, the bylaws of the district, and locations by the original claimholders and by relocators. Claims had to be named, not numbered.

Rampart District. Idaho Bar (folder). [Vol. 2]. 1 August 1898–27 June 1900. The folder contains claim locations and minutes of miners' meetings of 17 November 1898, 3 January 1899, and 9 May 1899, and an amendment to the bylaws. It includes the transfer of Charles Range's Discovery claim to Erastus Brainerd on 16 February 1899.

Rampart District. Journal. 1898–1901. The book records sales of town lots and locations of some creek claims and coal mines.

Rampart District. Julia Creek (folder). 18 September 1897–26 May 1898. The folder contains the minutes of the miners' meeting of 18 September 1897, the record of stock of the Minook Quartz Mining and Milling Company of Alaska, and the record of claims on Julia Creek in the Coen mining district. A preliminary listing of claimholders identifies Sally Manook (sic) as holder of No. 6 above, and Susan, an Indian girl, as holder of No. 7 above; the official registration omits both.

Rampart District. Lenora Gulch (folder). 28 April 1898–1 May 1900. No pagination. The folder contains the bylaws of 28 April 1898. Frank J. Franken held the Discovery claim.

Rampart District. Little Minook Creek (folder). Vol. 2 (possibly vol. 1). 29 April 1896–23 October 1900. The record contains the sale of the early claims on Little Minook, the minutes of several miners' meetings, the location of the thirty-seven-member Colony Pup claim on Valentine's Day, 1899, and the sale of R. E. Beach's claim on Sally's Pup.

Rampart District. Little Minook Creek (folder). Also Vol. 2. 29 April 1896–26 December 1899. This record appears to be a modified index for Volume 1 (possibly the other vol. 2) and volume 3 (Book 3). It briefly lists claims on the creek and its tributaries.

Rampart District. Little Minook Creek (tributaries) (folder). Book 3. 3 October 1898–7 June 1900. This record applies mostly to claims on tributaries of the creek. It includes the transfers of those claims, summaries of miners' meetings in January and February 1899, and the sale of Range's Eliza Anderson claim on Range's Pup to Erastus Brainerd.

Rampart District. Little Minook Junior (folder). Vol. 2. 1899–1900. The book records transfers of claims or parts of claims on the creek. It includes reference to the much disputed claim, No. 24 above, involving Valeria Myers.

Rampart District. Locations and Affidavits of Labor. [Vol. 2]. 4 May 1901–23 June 1901. This book follows the Old Book and contains claims and affidavits of assessment work. It includes claims owned by Erastus Brainerd on Idaho Bar, a lode claim near Ruby Creek, and Discovery, Glen Gulch.

Rampart District. Mariposa Bar and Omega Creek. 11 October 1898–22 April 1899. The record contains the minutes of the miners' meeting of 11 October 1898 to form the Mariposa Bar mining district at the forks of Garnet and Rock creeks and the meeting of 14 April 1899 to form the Omega Creek district.

Rampart District. McDonald Bar (folder). 10 June 1900–3 August 1900. John R. McDonald held the Discovery claim; T. R. Edwards was the creek recorder.

Rampart District. Miller Creek (folder). 13 December 1897–30 August 1898. This record is a diary by an unidentified miner who had been on the St. Michael. The philosophic author might be B. W. Moore, Jr. He spent time at Miller Creek and Little Minook Creek. He was a friend of C. A. Packard, Frank Canton, W. G. Pinecoffin, and Philip Godley. The diary includes minutes of the meetings of the Virginia mining district miners on 15 August and 30 August 1898.

Rampart District. Mining Locations. Vol. 1. Old Book. 24 December 1900–23 June 1901. The book records claims, powers of attorney, and affidavits of assessment work primarily in the area of Rhode Island and New York creeks, now in the Manley Hot Springs district. It does, however, contain lode claims on Troublesome Creek and a location by Daniel A. Sutherland on Slate Creek; both creeks are in the Rampart district.

Rampart District. Mining Locations and Declaratory Statements. Vol. 1. 1901–1902. The book records claims, a few for more than twenty acres, from 26 July 1901 through 15 November 1902. Most of the claims are in the Glen Gulch–Hootlanana area. A few are town lots. Andrew J. Balliet was commissioner and recorder; J. Lindley Green replaced him.

Rampart District. Minook Creek (townsite) (folder). Vol. 1. 1897–1898. The record begins with the minutes of the miners' meeting of 6 June 1897, which changed the name of the town of Minook Creek to Rampart and began the official layout of the town. Because of the large influx of people during the summer of 1897, the town plat was redesigned several times.

Rampart District. Montana Bar (folder). 12 May 1899. No pagination. The very brief book records the first nine claims on Montana Bar in the Eureka (now Manley Hot Springs) mining district, all recorded on 12 May 1899. Jay Whipple was recorder.

Rampart District. Montana Creek (folder). 5 February 1898–14 April 1900. No pagination. The folder contains the minutes of the miners' meetings of 5 February 1898 and 24 March 1900. F. M. Canton held the Discovery claim. The first claims were relocated by other miners in 1900.

Rampart District. Rampart Creek (folder). 12 January 1899–2 February 1899 and 28 November 1900. The folder records twelve claims on the creek, twelve on the left hand fork, and eleven on the right fork. It also summarizes a miners' meeting on 10 January 1899 at which the bylaws were rewritten.

Rampart District. Rock Creek (folder). 11 October 1898–3 January 1900. The folder contains the by-laws of 1 October 1898 and the early claims. P. W. Judkins located Discovery on 7 September 1898.

Rampart District. Russian Creek (folder). 30 September 1897–28 April 1899. The folder contains the minutes of the miners' meeting of 30 September 1897, which established the creek rules, and the meetings of 11 May and 18 May 1898, which replaced the recorder. In a meeting of 7 February 1899, R. E. Beach lost a dispute over two claims. The folder does not record locations.

Rampart District. Slate Creek. Vol. 2. (two folders). 3 April 1899–24 December 1900. The first folder begins with claim No. 35 above as of 3 April 1899. Charles B. Allen acted as attorney in fact for several claimholders. The second folder records quartz claims near the mouth of Slate Creek.

Rampart District. Triple Creek (folder). 5 November 1898–20 January 1900. The folder records the miners' organizing meeting on 5 November 1898, the early claims, and the transfer or relocation of those claims.

Rampart District. Troublesome Creek (folder). 14 December 1897–22 April 1899. According to the record, creek recorder James R. Austin held the Discovery claim. H. C. Wallick was deputy recorder.

Spurr, Stephen H., et al. *Rampart Dam and the Economic Development of Alaska.* Vol. 1. Summary Report. Ann Arbor: University of Michigan, School of Natural Resources, 1966. The study discussed the ecological and economic consequences of the proposed Rampart Dam and noted that Canada was concerned about the negative effect of the dam on wildlife. It recommended against the construction of the dam and recommended for the development of extra-high voltage transmission in the Railbelt area.

State of Alaska, Department of Natural Resources, Division of Mining, Fairbanks. The Division of Mining has maintained a KARDEX file of active and inactive claims since 1954. Fort Gibbon claims are in the Melozitna quadrangle file (47); Manley Hot Springs and most Rampart claims are in the Tanana quadrangle file (48); a few Rampart claims, particularly those on Hess, Gunnison, and Troublesome creeks are in the Livengood quadrangle file (49). The division also has thirty-six mining inspection reports, dated 1922–1925, 1938, and 1951, on individual claims in the Tanana quadrangle, including some pertaining to the dredging operation on American Creek.

Stewart, B.D. *Annual Report of the Territorial Mine Inspector to the Governor of Alaska: 1920.* Juneau: Alaska Daily Empire Print, 1921. According to the report, an excessively dry season in 1920 hampered sluicing operations in the Hot Springs district. There was some hydraulicking on Eureka Creek and Tofty Gulch and some prospecting on quartz lodes four miles from the town of Hot Springs.

———. *Annual Report of the Mine Inspector to the Governor of Alaska.* [Juneau]: [Territory of Alaska, Department of Mines], [1923]. Stewart stated that the summer of 1922 in Alaska was one of the coldest and wettest in history. Consequently, mining by dredging and scraping was hurt; hydraulic operations benefitted. Stewart also detailed conditions on creeks in the Hot Springs district.

———. *Mining Investigations and Mine Inspection in Alaska Including Assistance to Prospectors: Biennium Ending March 31, 1933.* Juneau: [Territory of Alaska, Department of Mines], 1933. Stewart reported on the resumption of operations of the dredge on American Creek in 1932 and on other activities in the Hot Springs district. In contrast, only five men were working in the Fort Gibbon district.

———. *Report on Cooperation Between the Territory of Alaska and the United States in Making Mining Investigations and in the Inspection of Mines for the Biennium Ending March 31, 1929.* Juneau: [Territory of Alaska, Department of Mines], 1929. Stewart listed the seven mine operators in the Hot Springs district who employed five or more more men in 1927 and 1928.

———. *Report on Cooperation Between the Territory of Alaska and the United States in Making Mining Inspections and in the Inspection of Mines for the Biennium Ending March 31, 1931.* Juneau: [Territory of Alaska, Department of Mines], 1931. Stewart listed the six mine operators in the Hot Springs district who employed five or more men in 1929 and 1930.

———. *Report of the Commissioner of Mines to the Governor for the Biennium Ended December 31, 1938.* Juneau: Territory of Alaska, 1939. Stewart identified the operators in the Hot Springs, Fort Gibbon, and Rampart districts, their types of operations, and the total of their crew.

———. *Report of the Commissioner of Mines to the Governor for the Biennium Ended December 31, 1940.* Juneau: Territory of Alaska, 1941. Stewart listed the operators in the three districts, their types of operations, and the total of their crew.

———. *Report of the Commission of Mines for the Biennium Ended December 31, 1946.* Juneau: Territory of Alaska, Department of Mines, [1947]. The pace of recovery of the mining industry after World War II was disappointing. Operators lacked manpower and equipment. Two draglines operated in the Fort Gibbon district in 1946; one dragline operated in Hot Springs, and one in Rampart. Additionally, there were bulldozers, hydraulics, and drifts in all three districts. Altogether, there were twenty operators.

———. *Report of the Commissioner of Mines for the Biennium Ended December 31, 1948.* Juneau: Territory of Alaska, Department of Mines, [1949]. Stewart reported that the Sawtooth Mining Company had an antimony lode mine near Rampart in 1948. He listed twenty-one gold placer operators in all, active within the three districts.

Stuck, Hudson, D.D., F.R.G.S. *Voyages on the Yukon and its Tributaries: A Narrative of Summer Travel in the Interior of Alaska. New York:* Charles Scribner's Sons, 1917. Capsulizing episodes of his summer travel on the Yukon between about 1910 and 1915, Archdeacon Stuck commented on some of the history of the Yukon River, the deserted appearance of Fort Hamlin and the (Pioneer) coal mine, and the melancholy look of Rampart, which had few residents and several boarded up buildings.

Sundborg, George. *Our Family: Described From What I Have Been Able To Find Out About It.* Washington, D.C.: privately published, 1970. (Cited with permission.) Sundborg's family genealogy includes his uncle, George Walter Sundborg, who arrived in Rampart from San Francisco in December 1897 and remained in Interior Alaska until mid-1913.

Tanana Chiefs Conference, Inc. *Forest Resources of Doyon, Ltd., Lands: Tanana Region, Alaska, 1992.* Fairbanks: Tanana Chiefs Conference, Inc., 1992. The Forestry Department, Tanana Chiefs Conference, followed up the 1988 report by Douglas Hanson and others for Doyon with a more extensive forest inventory.

Tanana News, Tanana, Alaska. Weekly newspaper, published Saturdays, 14 June 1913–25 October 1913. M/F 677. *The News* succeeded the *Hot Springs Echo.* The issue of 12 July 1913 reported the sudden death of miner Jim Langford as he was walking past the gate at Fort Gibbon on Sunday, 6 July 1913.

Tanana Valley Gold Dredging Company. Collection. Alaska Archives, Alaska and Polar Regions Department, Elmer E. Rasmuson Library, University of Alaska Fairbanks. Box 9 of the collection contains Frank G. Manley's will of 17 December 1909, made at San Angelo, Tom Green County, Texas. The will gave Manley's true name as Hillyard Bascom Knowles.

Tower, Elizabeth A. "Rex Beach's Alaska: Novels and Autobiography." *Alaska History News 20,* no. 4 (October 1989): 7. Tower briefly reviews the works of Beach. She considers *Personal Exposures* his best book.

U.S. Army Corps of Engineers. *Proceedings, First Conference, Rampart Economic Advisory Board.* [Anchorage]: U.S. Army Corps of Engineers, 1961. The report gives the minutes of the first meeting of the board discussing the pros and cons of the economic usefulness of the proposed Rampart Dam.

U.S. Army Engineer District, Alaska. *Rampart Canyon Dam and Reservoir: Data on Project Studies.* Anchorage: Corps of Engineers, [1961]. The Corps of Engineers prepared its report for the First Conference of the Rampart Economic Advisory Board which met in May 1961. The report contains aerial photographs of the proposed dam site and diagrams of the layout. The Corps would only recommend the project if it could be demonstrated that the project would be cost effective.

U.S. Department of the Interior. *Rampart Project, Alaska: Market for Power and Effect of Project on National Resources. Field Report.* Vol. 1. Juneau: U.S. Department of the Interior, 1965. The report provides the specifications of the proposed Rampart Dam. The impoundment area was to flood a major fish habitat and the villages of Rampart, Stevens Village, Beaver, Fort Yukon, Chalkyitsik, Birch Creek, Circle, part of the Venetie reservation, and the hunting ground of Canyon Village.

———. *Rampart Project, Alaska: Market for Power and Effect of Project on National Resources. Field Report.* Vol. 2. Juneau: U.S. Department of the Interior, 1965. The report gave the plan of development of the Rampart Dam, its capacity, and estimated annual operational costs. The dam was expected to be completed by 1975 and its reservoir filled by 1995.

———. *Rampart Project, Alaska: Market for Power and Effect of Project on National Resources. Field Report.* Vol. 3. Juneau: U.S. Department of the Interior, 1965. The report estimated that all costs for the dam would be repaid within fifty years after investment ended. An area of 10,600 square miles would be inundated, causing a loss of all timber, land, mineral resources, and fish and wildlife in the area. The Native residents of villages to be destroyed would be moved, and a new economy would be created for them.

U.S. Senate. *Conditions in Alaska: Report of Subcommittee of Committee on Territories Appointed to Investigate Conditions in Alaska.* 58th Cong., 2d sess., 1904. S. Rept. 282, pt. 1. Washington: Government Printing Office, 1904. This report presents the results of the senatorial subcommittee's 1903 investigation of conditions in Alaska and the subcommittee's findings and recommendations to the full Senate.

———. *Conditions in Alaska: Hearings before Subcommittee of Committee on Territories Appointed to Investigate Conditions in Alaska.* 58th Cong., 2d sess., 1904. S. Rept. 282, pt. 2. Washington: Government Printing Office, 1904. The report provides the texts of testimony before the Senate subcommittee which held hearings in Alaska, including at Rampart, in July 1903.

Waring, Gerald A. *Mineral Springs of Alaska.* U.S. Geological Survey Water-Supply Paper 418. Washington: Government Printing Office, 1917. Waring discussed the various hot springs within the Yukon River basin.

Waters, A. E., Jr. "Placer Concentrates of the Rampart and Hot Springs District." In *Mineral Resources of Alaska: Report on Progress of Investigations in 1931,* edited by Philip S. Smith, et al., 227–46. U.S. Geological Survey Bulletin 844, Washington: Government Printing Office, 1934. In 1931, Waters accompanied J. B. Mertie, Jr. in a tour of the Tofty area of the Hot Springs district. He discussed the cassiterite in Tofty and noted a block of iron ore in Sullivan Creek two miles upstream of old Tofty.

West, Frederick Hadleigh, H. G. Bandi, and J. V. Matthews. *Archaeological Survey and Excavations in the Proposed Rampart Dam Impoundment, 1963–1964.* N.p.: [National Park Service] in association with the University of Alaska, 1965. The archaelogical survey team concluded that part of the Rampart region proposed to be flooded had been inhabited as early as 7,000 years ago. It had been occupied continuously for 4,000 or more years.

Wickersham, Hon. James. *Old Yukon: Tales—Trails—and Trials.* Washington; D. C.: Washington Law Book Co., 1938. Judge Wickersham conducted court Rampart in 1900 and 1901. In July 1903, he testified before the senatorial subcommittee then in Rampart and filed his Kantishna claims with the commissioner at Rampart.

Wiedemann, Thomas (The Klondike Kid). *Cheechako into Sourdough.* Portland, OR: Binfords & Mort, 1942. Wiedemann related the story of his journey to Alaska in 1897 aboard the *Eliza Anderson,* his winter quarters on the lower Yukon, and his stop at Rampart in the spring of 1898.

Williams. James A. *Report of the Division of Mines and Minerals for the Year 1959.* [Juneau]: State of Alaska, Department of Natural Resources, [1960]. Williams listed about fourteen placer operators in the three districts.

Yukon Press, Tanana and Fort Gibbon, Alaska. Weekly newspaper, published on Saturdays, 4 November 1905–24 March 1906. M/F 1008. *The Yukon Press,* edited by Commissioner John Bathurst, reported very briefly on local mining news. In the 24 March 1906 issue, Bathurst reported his own resignation and disdained the commissioner's position.

Yukon Valley News, Rampart, later Tanana, Alaska. Weekly newspaper, published Wednesdays, 3 August 1904–11 January 1913. M/F 1002. Many issues missing. The *Yukon Valley News,* published, initially, by Sam Heeter, reported on the mining activities in the Interior. An example is a news item of 3 August 1904, reporting that Joe Wiehl returned from three weeks unsuccessfully prospecting on Morelock and Grant creeks.

The Bureau of Land Management is responsible for the stewardship of our public lands. It is committed to manage, protect, and improve these lands in a manner to serve the needs of the American people for all times. Management is based on the principles of multiple use and sustained yield of our nation's resources within a framework of environmental responsibility and scientific technology. These resources include recreation, range, timber, minerals, watershed, fish and wildlife, wilderness, air, scenic, scientific and cultural values.